Comfortable Everyday Life at the Swec
Eighteenth-Century Näs Manor

Comfortable Everyday Life at the Swedish Eighteenth-Century Näs Manor

Carolina Brown

Translated by
Wendy Davies

Routledge
Taylor & Francis Group
LONDON AND NEW YORK

The publication of this book is made possible by a grant from the Carl-Göran Adelswärd Foundation and the Vilhelm Ekman University Foundation in Uppsala.

First published in 2024 by Amsterdam University Press Ltd.

Published 2025 by Routledge
4 Park Square, Milton Park, Abingdon, Oxon OX14 4RN
605 Third Avenue, New York, NY 10158

Routledge is an imprint of the Taylor & Francis Group, an informa business

ISBN: 9789048562374 (hbk)
ISBN: 9781041177265 (pbk)
ISBN: 9781003692867 (ebk)
NUR 685

Cover illustration: Niclas Lafrensen the Younger, *Lady Drinking Tea*, around 1780. Gouache on paper, 28 × 21.9 cm. Harvard Art Museums/Fogg Museum, Gift of Charles E. Dunlap, (1956.248).

Cover design: Coördesign, Leiden

DOI 10.5117/9789048562374

For Product Safety Concerns and Information please contact our EU representative:
GPSR@taylorandfrancis.com
Taylor & Francis Verlag GmbH, Kaufingerstraße 24, 80331 München, Germany

Table of Contents

Acknowledgements

When this book was published in Swedish in 2020, it was unavailable to the large and active eighteenth-century community outside of Scandinavia. It was one of its leading scholars, Professor Michael Yonan, who proposed an English-language translation. I want to thank him for his initiative and encouragement, which led on to editor Erika Gaffney, who excellently guided the project forward at AUP.

Generous financial support from the Carl-Göran Adelswärd Foundation enabled Wendy Davies to translate the Swedish book into English, and the Vilhelm Ekman University Foundation in Uppsala assisted with the necessary funds for printing the book. To all I offer my warmest and most heartfelt thanks.

List of illustrations

Colour plates

med 2ne flickor (detail), *c.* 1774. Oil on canvas, 33.5 × 49.5 cm. Private ownership. Photo: Bukowskis.

Plate 12. Johan Niclas Eckstein, Wadenstierna's secretaire, signed 1773. Veneered with jacaranda, plumwood, citron wood, maple, dark poplar and amaranth (purpleheart wood). W 94.5 cm, H 106 cm, D 49.5 cm. Private ownership. Photo: Christie's.

Plate 13. Georg Haupt, secretaire completed for Wadenstierna, signed 1775. Veneered with coloured birch, maple, walnut and possibly mulberry wood. W 82 cm, H 106 cm, D 55 cm. Private ownership. Photo: Åmells.

Plate 14. François Boucher, *La marchande de modes*, 1746. Oil on canvas, 64 × 53 cm. Nationalmuseum, Stockholm (NM 772). Photo: Cecilia Heisser.

Plate 15. Pehr Hilleström, *Ett Fruent: som snör en flicka* (A woman lacing a girl's corset). Oil on canvas, 32 × 41 cm. Private ownership. The painting was part of Wadenstierna's commission of Hilleström's works in the 1770s.

Plate 16. In the eighteenth century, Näs was home to Pehr Hilleström's painting *Interiör med ung dam och gumma som spår i kaffesump* (Interior with young lady and old woman reading coffee grounds), from *c.* 1775. Oil on canvas, 38.5 × 30 cm. Private ownership. Photo: Bukowskis.

Plate 17. Pehr Hilleström, *Ett fruentimmer sitter och läser, kammarjungfrun kommer med Thé* (A woman sits reading, the lady's maid brings tea), 1775. Oil on canvas, 53 × 62 cm. Nordiska museet, Stockholm (NM.0177655*1).

Plate 18. Niclas Lafrensen the Younger, *Lady Drinking Tea*, *c.* 1780. Gouache on paper, 28 × 21.9 cm. Harvard Art Museums/Fogg Museum, Gift of Charles E. Dunlap (1956.248).

Plate 19. Cup from Wadenstierna's armorial tableware. Polychrome decoration with the cross of the Royal Order of the Polar Star hanging around the coat of arms after Wadenstierna was awarded the distinction in 1767. Private ownership.

Plate 20. Georg Haupt, Wadenstierna's tea table, 1775. L 80 cm, W 57.5 cm, H 75 cm. Private ownership. Photo: Bukowskis.

Images

Introduction

Abstract
During the eighteenth century, comfortable everyday life became a new ideal. The privileged life of the elite was no longer about grand representation or manifestation of material excess. Instead, the new luxury was a domestic ideal: life set at home, with rooms arranged for relaxed living in comfortable furniture. Research has highlighted the development of a new culture of comfort within French and British elite circles and examined how it reflected a notable change in upper-class identity. The purpose of this study is to examine the development of similar changes in the north of Europe and to investigate how various attitudes towards comfort were formed and expressed in the material and social culture of a Swedish country estate environment.

Keywords: eighteenth century, material culture, visual culture, consumption, comfort, *commodité*

Free of the noise of the wider world,
among books and among good friends,
to be loved more, rather than become famous,
enables you to feel the force and right sweetness of life.

These words can be read on one of the overdoor decorations that embellish the entrance hall of Näs Manor in Uppland.[1] Splendour, magnificence or grand mannerisms are not what impart strength and sweetness to life; life's little pleasures do that instead. Good, comfortable everyday life was the new luxury of the eighteenth century. Carl Eric Wadenstierna, who commissioned the new manor house on the Näs country estate in 1775, felt the winds of change blowing in Sweden and elsewhere in the wider world. Social, political and economic changes in Sweden, together with impressions from sources such as the French Enlightenment and

1 The author of the overdoor text is unknown, although Carl Eric Wadenstierna himself has been singled out as the possible writer ; Karl Asplund, 'Näs i Rö', *Fataburen*, Nordiska Museet, Stockholm 1960, pp. 14–5.

Brown, C., *Comfortable Everyday Life at the Swedish Eighteenth-Century Näs Manor.*
Taylor & Francis Group, 2024
DOI 10.5117/9789048562374_INTRO

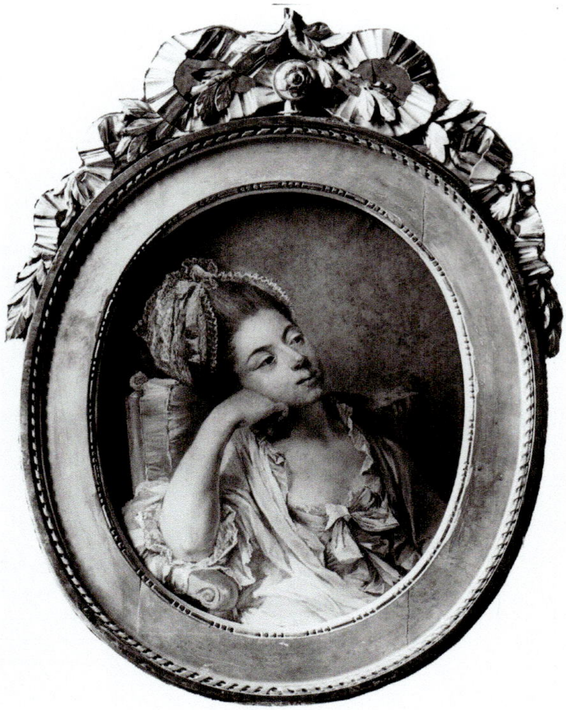

1. Gustaf Lundberg (attrib.), *Unknown Woman*. Pastel, 53 × 43 cm. Nationalmuseum, Stockholm (NMGrh 2306).

the British bourgeoisie, contributed to creating conditions for new lifestyle ideals within the upper strata of society at that time. These ideals are the subject of this study of the eighteenth-century culture of comfort, focusing on the Gustavian estate Näs. From here, we view a changing European upper-class culture, and this study continually returns to this small manor house in the coastal Roslagen area of Uppland Province – to the furniture, paintings and rooms that surrounded the Wadenstierna family.

At some point in the 1770s, a woman relaxes in a comfortable armchair. She sinks into the soft cushion and rests her head tranquilly on her hand. Perhaps daydreams will soon drift into dozing. The relaxed atmosphere conveyed by the small painting is accentuated by the woman's soft clothes (Image 1). Unbuttoned and creased, they do not appear to have been arranged to be seen in public. The scene feels intimate, and it is easy to imagine the room in which the woman is sitting, where the light and warmth are reflected from the fireplace, if it is a cold time of year, and the shadows are cast onto the warm wooden floor. The painting, attributed to the artist Gustaf Lundberg, depicts a now unknown woman. Yet, she – or what she represents – seems familiar. However, the familiarity is not with her role as a decorative eye-catcher, the sleeping beauty, *la belle dormeuse*, but with the moment when there is no friction, neither figuratively nor literally, and where the context requires no formalities. Why were depictions of comfortable everyday life created in the eighteenth century that viewers still feel affinity with today?

In a sense, the emergence of a new culture of comfort, sometimes described as a 'comfort revolution', that developed within the upper strata of society in the eighteenth century shaped modern people.[2] Its significance is confirmed by the recognition evoked by a scene such as this. However, only contemporary sources can bear witness to how radical this was once perceived to be. By shining a light on the people who implemented, developed and experienced it, we can understand the change that it entailed. The changes may not seem particularly drastic to us, but the transformation of people's lives was shown in everyday details, in how they designed and used their clothes, furniture and possessions, and in how they described themselves and their day-to-day life in words and pictures. This study aims to investigate what the new comfortable everyday life could mean for a few individuals who emerge from the eighteenth century's rich source material. Here, 'comfort' refers to both idea and practice in an eighteenth century where a new material culture and a new lifestyle with new ideals developed in constant interplay. Comfort was both an individual, physical experience and a social standpoint and attitude.[3]

The feeling of comfort expressed in the introductory painting is likely to have been even more striking to a contemporary viewer. A woman who wore the formal attire of that era must have experienced the contrast in thin, soft garments in a particularly tangible and concrete way. Rigid corsets and stiff petticoats, heavy, lined layers of fabric and parts of the outfit that were sewn or pinned into place, resulted in complicated conventional garb that was difficult to wear and restricted movement, and meant that the wearer required assistance when dressing and undressing. In such clothing, a woman would hardly be able to sit in the same way as the woman in the painting. In formal fashion, women instead had to stand up straight and subordinate themselves to the rules of social etiquette which accompanied the demands of presenting a distinguished appearance. The revolutionary aspect of the woman in the painting being portrayed *déshabillé* was perhaps not that she showed herself 'undressed' (the French word referred rather to the fact that she had abandoned wearing formal attire) but the new freedom that her body was thereby given. Here, the clothes did not shape and control her body; instead, her

2 It was not a revolution in the true sense of the word, but the word is used here as a rhetorical device to emphasise the radical changes that this meant. For information on the present-day consequences of this early modern comfort revolution, *Bekvämlighetsrevolutionen. Stockholmshushållen och miljön under 150 år och i framtiden*, Ronny Pettersson (ed.), Stockholm 2008.

3 Cristina Prytz and Jon Stobart, 'Comfort in English and Swedish country houses, c. 1760–1820', *Social History*, Vol. 43, No. 2, 2018, pp. 239–40.

body gained freedom to shape itself – and feel.[4] This sensuous freedom sparked criticism in contemporary debate, but in parallel, criticism also grew of the formal, artificial and affected conventional garb and the lifestyle that accompanied it.[5]

The French philosopher and author Denis Diderot formulated his view of comfort in a similar way at around the same time. This was expressed in his metaphorical reflection on a beloved old dressing gown. *Regrets sur ma vieille robe de chambre ou avis à ceux qui ont plus de goût que de fortune* was written in 1768 and published the following year in *Correspondance littéraire.* The old dressing gown had shaped itself to Diderot's body, and every fold and stain conveyed something about his personality and way of life. This was a garment that he effortlessly mastered and that did not control or hinder him in the slightest. In comparison, Diderot's new dressing gown was rigid, formal and demanding in its expensive and delicate fabric, which required him to be careful and constantly aware of how he moved and behaved. It represented a luxury that was enslaving and costly, and it offered no relaxation for body or soul. It was for public display, not for personal comfort.

Xavier de Maistre presents a corresponding experience of his furniture in the 'travelogue' from his room – *Voyage autour de ma chambre* – in which he was placed under house arrest for six weeks following an unsuccessful duel in Turin in 1790.[6] He praises his armchair, so important and useful for a contemplative man, in which he could recline on long winter evenings, shielded from the noise and din of the surrounding world. He describes the perfect sitting position: how he slides forwards on the seat so that his feet rest on the adjacent mantelpiece. He emphasises his warm bed in which to meditate, while his footman discreetly busies himself with his morning duties around him.[7] It is the lived-in, informally relaxed home that provides comfort, like being in the undemanding company of an old friend. In one of his drawings from the mid-eighteenth century, Louis Carrogis (Carmontelle), artist and *lecteur* in the service of Louis Philippe I, Duke of Orléans, has depicted a friend of the duke, Louis de Mornay, in a similar position (Image 2). Clothes and furniture clearly enabled a new form of comfort, and the sources confirm how it was valued, but also normalised. These different experiences and depictions of physical comfort, from both the early and late eighteenth century, and the fact that they were documented in words and pictures, were all manifestations of a change process that shaped new approaches and values. In turn, they had consequences for how people chose to shape their lives.

4 Joan DeJean, 'Dressing for comfort', *The Age of Comfort. When Paris Discovered Casual – And the Modern Home Began*, New York 2009, pp. 186–204.

5 For an example, see the critical statement 'De l'usage des paniers' about the absurdity of the fashion's stiff petticoats in Antoine-Angelique Chomel, *Aménités Littéraires, et Recueil D'Anecdotes*, II, Amsterdam 1773, pp 247–9.

6 Xavier de Maistre, *Voyage autour de ma chambre*, Lausanne 1794. Translated into Swedish in 1798.

7 Xavier de Maistre, New York 1994, p. 8 and p. 25.

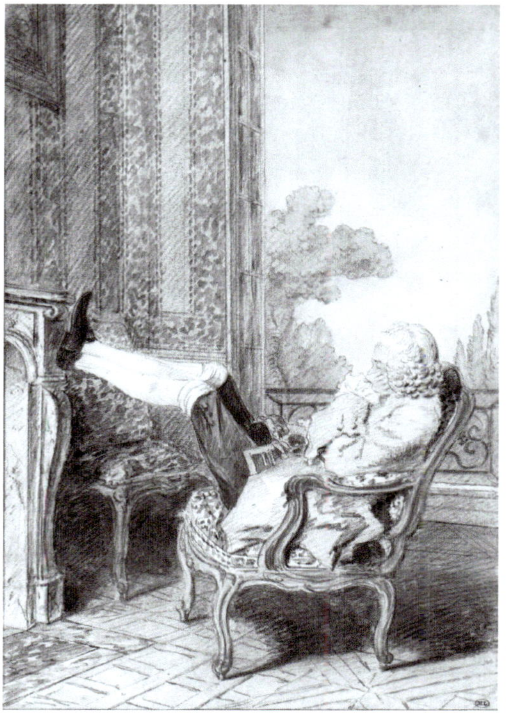

2. Louis Carrogis (Carmontelle), *Mr de Mornay, Gouverneur de St Cloud, dessiné d'après nature dans la posture habituelle de sa siesta.* Watercolour and gouache, 27.1 × 19 cm. Private ownership. Photo: Sotheby's.

A portrait miniature, contemporary with the introductory painting, also shows a woman in soft *déshabillé*, but her comfort is expressed in a different way (Plate 1). Admittedly, her pose is at ease, but it is rather her surroundings that are presented as comfortably furnished. The elegant and dainty sewing table on which she is resting her arm is perfectly adapted to her needs. It is just the right height, equipped with practical storage boxes so that she does not need to stand up and fetch various accoutrements of her work, and the edging of the table top is softly rounded to avoid abrasion of a delicate forearm or fragile piece of embroidery. Her garments and furniture make her everyday tasks easier and her life pleasant. In eighteenth-century Swedish, the word *kommoditet* (commodity) from the French *commodité*, was sometimes used as the apt term for this modern form of comfort and amenity.[8] Originating from the Latin *commodus*, it meant something of just the right dimensions, something suitable, practical and comfortably appointed. French culture applied *commodité* in descriptions of most things that made life easier, from *fauteuils de commodité* with adjustable backrests (though a *siège de commodité* referred to a toilet chair/commode chair), to hair pomades and modes

8 Peter Thornton, *Authentic Decor. The Domestic Interior 1620–1920*, London 1985, p. 17, and Stobart and Prytz 2018, p. 239.

of transport.[9] The suitability of giving the new storage unit with drawers the name *commode* was self-evident. The difference between a compact, modern chest of drawers and the older storage solution in the form of a heavy, bulky chest, was like comparing a negligee with a rigid corsetted court dress.

The fact that the Swedish word *kommoditet* was associated with the new range of products and services was also clear. By portraying herself in *déshabillé* next to a modern, practical sewing table, the woman showed her physical comfort but also her informed taste as a consumer *à la mode*. The dividing line between private and social comfort was not always clear or discernible. An eighteenth-century woman who viewed the introductory painting may have observed the expressions of physical freedom, but probably paid equally close attention to the portrayed woman's fashionable lace bonnet *à la dormeuse* – in keeping with the latest French trend. This lace bonnet symbolised the depicted woman's social, cultural and economic status, and whoever she was, it must have afforded her a special sense of well-being in the context. The experience of comfort was therefore strongly linked to the social self and to social norms and conventions, as well as a sensibility to changes in them. *Kommoditeter* could be for personal benefit and enjoyment but could also serve as socially coded signs, as expressions of conspicuous consumption.[10] They were thereby part of incessant social aspirations for novelties, which constantly generated a new range of products and new demand in the growing market.

Comfort as an idea and practice

> Comfort, my good Sir, is unknown in Savoy. – What we English call comfort, is not understood I believe in any other country, nor to be exprest in any other language. It is rest of the body, it is repose of the mind, without business, without bustle, and with every thing convenient and pleasant about you: – it is often lost in a palace, and found in a cottage, – it is in itself a trifle: – a trifle gives it – a trifle takes it away: – it is a cheerful room – a good fire – a dish of tea – but – not as I am now drinking it, with a chimney that smokes, a door I can't shut, and a window that is broken.[11]

9 In D'Alembert and Diderot's *Encyclopédie*, the word *commodité* above all referred to the concealed spaces in which the toilet chair/commode chair could be stowed, Paris 1751, III, p. 714.

10 Thorstein Veblen's often referenced term 'conspicuous consumption' was presented in his socio-economic study *The Theory of the Leisure Class. An Economic Study of Institutions*, London 1899. For a more recent discussion, see economic historian Jan De Vries *The Industrious Revolution. Consumer Behavior and the Household Economy, 1650 to the Present,* Cambridge 2008.

11 Beckford 1805, pp. 53–54.

In his letters from his sojourn in Italy in the 1780s, the English country gentleman Peter Beckford summarised his view of comfort. In all simplicity, it was the relaxation that came from an everyday life that ran smoothly. In the book *Home: A Short History of an Idea* from 1986, Witold Rybczynski discusses how the concept of comfort is relative. In his investigation he found how a view, a conversation by letter, a piece of embroidery, a card game or just a cup of tea could be called 'comfortable' in the eighteenth century – as readily as a soft armchair.[12] But one common denominator was the satisfaction felt via emotions and sensations. When Johan Gabriel Oxenstierna in his diary in 1771 tries to describe the most pleasurable form of 'comfort' he can imagine, it is an experience that involves all the senses:

> In the moment of being happily in love, in the moment of visual and sensual delight, one should rest on a bed of lilies and lavender, hear exquisite music and hold a piece of pineapple in one's mouth. This thought is somewhat giddy and slightly too sensual, but as pleasure occurs so rarely, could it not be permissible to savour it for once in all its glory?[13]

Oxenstierna's words perhaps exceeded the experience of normal everyday comforts but were nonetheless characteristic of the Age of Enlightenment's confidence in the ability of the senses to discover and experience what made life good and comfortable – and ultimately their ability to further civilisation.[14] Philosopher Étienne Bonnot de Condillac summarised his thoughts on sensations and their fundamental significance for how our surroundings are perceived and how knowledge is built in his *Traité des sensations* published in 1754. He shared his ideas with the Encyclopaedists such as Diderot and D'Alembert, who, in words and pictures, described the conditions for comfort in their work on the *Encyclopédie* (1751–72). Advances in science and technology resulted in everything from new furniture to new textiles adapted to the human body's sensory needs. According to the *Encyclopédie*, the new luxury was not ostentatious; it instead comprised what could make daily life more comfortable and pleasant: a flushable toilet, a table specially adapted for certain functions, an armchair that offered the body support and repose.[15] And for Diderot, naturally a dressing gown adapted to the body's needs.

This positivism based on sensory experiences entailed a new attitude to the human body and by extension to its health and hygiene – aspects that were also

12 Witold Rybczynski, *Home. A Short History of an Idea*, New York 1986, pp. 230ff.

13 Johan Gabriel Oxenstierna, *Dagboksanteckningar. Åren 1769–1771*, II, Uppsala 1881, pp. 145f.

14 Here, compare the discussion of luxury in relation to the view on desire, the body and pleasure in Sonya Petersson, *Konst i omlopp. Mening, medier och marknad i Stockholm under 1700-talets senare hälft*, Stockholm 2014 [diss.], pp. 109–24.

15 DeJean 2009, pp. 15, 67–79, 80–92.

linked to personal and social comfort. In *De la santé. Ouvrage utile à tout le monde* by Armand-Pierre Jacquin from 1771, we are reminded of the importance of regularly changing shirts and shifts, bathing, ventilating one's home and avoiding sleeping next to an unemptied chamber pot.[16] It was deemed particularly important to guard the distinction between private and public spheres and in all social contexts to comply with *propreté*, cleanliness and tidiness – a crucial condition for sociality.[17] Here, reference was made to a sensibility that could easily be offended by both strong odours and clumsy body language. People who were deficient in *propreté*, were deficient in social judgement and revealed this in each context by appearing *uncomfortable*, in the sense of appearing to be awkward or an embarrassment to themselves and to those around them. A person who was socially comfortable was instead someone who had honed this sensibility through their upbringing, taste and cultivation. *Propreté* and *politesse* were the conditions for casual comfort – the essential skill in all social relations. In 1774, the Earl of Chesterfield, Philip Stanhope, wrote instructions for fashionable comfort and corresponding body language. Straight and rigid were wrong at that time and were associated with social insecurity. The view of comfort had instead brought new ideals:

> You may also know a well bred person by his manner of sitting. Ashamed and confused, the awkward man sits in his chair stiff and bolt upright; whereas the man of fashion is easy in every position; instead of lolling or lounging as he sits, he leans with elegance, and by varying his attitudes, shews that he has been used to good company.[18]

The significance of emotions to comfort became a cherished theme at the time. In Jean-François Bastide's strange tale *La petite maison* from 1758, sensuous comfort is used as a means of power and manipulation in the romantic drama between the wooing suitor Trémicour and the resistant Mélite. Trémicour is convinced that he can make Mélite fall for him by showing her his house, designed and furnished with exquisite and refined taste. The material luxury offers an orgy of sensations that are heightened with each new room that Mélite enters. Everything seems to be furnished to offer comfort and pleasure. Sofas and armchairs swell with soft down cushions,

16 Armand Pierre (Abbé) Jacquin, *De la santé. Ouvrage utile à tout le monde*, Paris 1771, (http://gallica.bnf.fr/ark:/12148/bpt6k9763540b/f23.item.r=propreté), pp. 329–30, 355–7.

17 Armand Pierre (Abbé) Jacquin 1771, p. 351.

18 Christopher Daniel Bunth, *An Essay on English Lecture, Selected for the most part from late authors*, Lund 1792, p. 189. Bunth was an associate professor in English and French at Lund University. In his book, Swedish readers can peruse extracts from English literature. The Earl of Chesterfield's advice on 'cleanliness of person' and 'genteel carriage' dating from 1774 shows how a gentleman should conduct himself, and it also includes specific instructions for fashionable comfort.

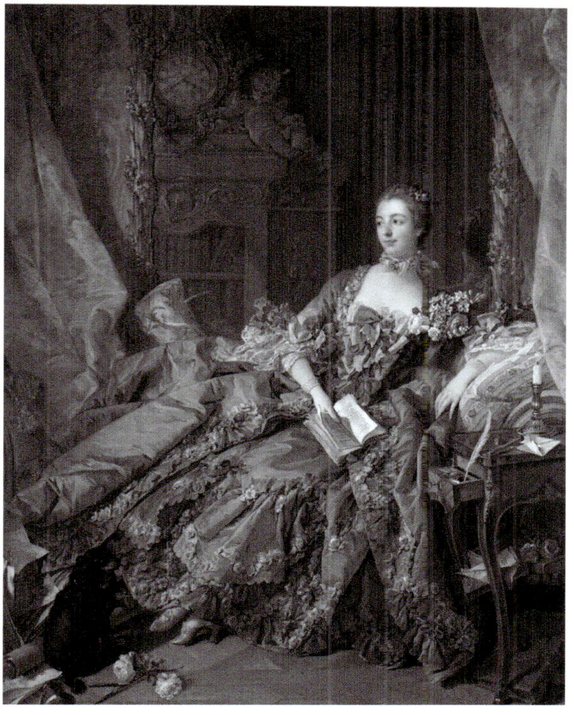

3. François Boucher, *Madame de Pompadour, Jeanne-Antoinette Poisson*, 1756. Oil on canvas, 201 × 157 cm. Alte Pinakothek, Munich (HUW 18). Wikimedia Commons.

and expensive sulphur-yellow and purple silk fabrics frame illuminated mirrors, sliding doors and all sorts of mechanical furniture. A hidden orchestra fills the rooms with music and the paint on the walls has been mixed with perfume scented with violets and roses. Oxenstierna's pineapple would have been a fitting addition here. It all becomes an overwhelming physical experience for Mélite. She sighs, trembles, pants and, finally, overpowered with emotions, sinks into one of the boudoir's armchairs. Mélite's sensibility is what makes her so receptive to the impact of the environment, but also her informed taste. She is experienced in the ways of the world, a connoisseur of fashion, luxury and *commodité* and immediately identifies works painted by Bachelier and carved by Dandrillon or the various imported artworks. Her receptive gaze also notices how the joints between the panes of mirror glass have been concealed with realistically created 'tree trunks' adorned with flowers. This was a fashionable eye-catching detail. Two years earlier, François Boucher's portrait of the Marquise de Pompadour had taken Paris by storm, in which she rested on a soft daybed in front of a mirror framed by sulphur-yellow silk drapes – and where the joints of the mirror glass were hidden by gilded 'tree trunks' (Image 3).[19]

19 Critics, such as Friedrich Melchior von Grimm in *Correspondance littéraire* in February 1761, claimed that the true aim of Bastide's tale was to advertise the fashion and art merchants in Paris, *marchandes de*

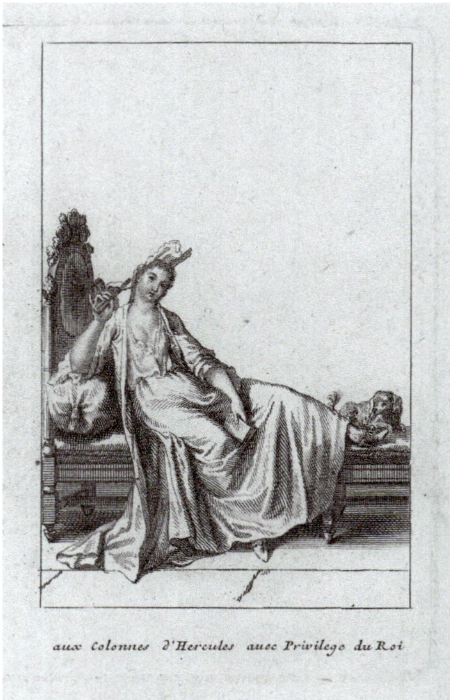

4. Bernard Picart, *Mode: aux colonnes d'Hercules avec Priv. du Roy*. Engraving, 10.3 × 6.5 cm. Rijksmuseum, Amsterdam.

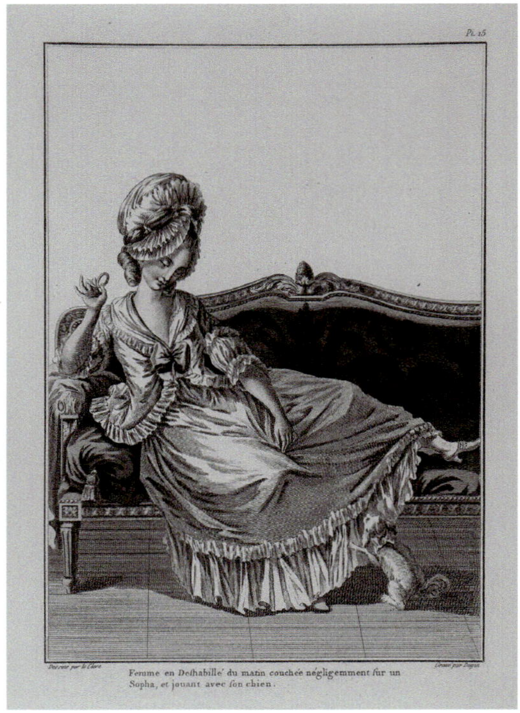

5. Nicolas Dupin after Pierre-Thomas Le Clerc, *Femme en deshabillé du matin couchée négligemment sur un Sopha, et jouant avec son chien*. From *Galerie des modes et costumes français*, Paris, 1778.

The desire evoked by Trémicour's comfortably furnished rooms echoes the eighteenth century's expanding commercial culture in general and the market for luxury items and *commodité* products that enhanced everyday comfort in particular.[20] Having the knowledge to be able to buy the 'right' thing – knowledge that the sensorily informed consumer Mélite possessed – was necessary in a market that tended to focus on specific groups of consumers within an increasingly heterogeneous

modes; Paul J Young, *Seducing the Eighteenth-Century French Reader. Reading, Writing, and the Question of Pleasure*, Farnham 2008, p. 56. The title of Bastide's book also alludes to the '*petites maisons*' that Louis XV had commissioned for his rendezvous with his mistress Madame du Barry and that subsequently developed into the name for brothels; Jean-François de Bastide, *The Little House. An Architectural Seduction (La Petite Maison)*, (1763) New York 1996, pp. 13–4. The descriptions of the surroundings, which make Boucher's portrait topical, were apt in the context, both through the roles of the Marquise de Pompadour and Mélite as mistresses and through their informed feeling and taste for the era's fashion and trends.

20 *The Social Life of Things. Commodities in Cultural Perspective*, Arjun Appadurai (ed.), Cambridge 1986, p. 37.

upper stratum of society, where producers, sellers and consumers were all very familiar with the complicated social and cultural codes of the era.[21] The value of the products as status symbols also became ever more rapidly characterised by their novelty value rather than more lasting qualities.[22] The regularly published and increasingly distributed fashion plates in the latter half of the eighteenth century were an expression of the value of the products as novelties. The fashion images were also mainly aimed at women, who now emerged as a new target group with considerable spending power.

The fact that this market and the forces that drove it were certainly not new for the eighteenth century is obvious by the fashion plates shown here (Images 4 and 5). They also clarify that comfort as a type of luxury was not only a feature of the eighteenth century.[23] The woman in the figure-enhancing thin negligee, nonchalantly reclining on the chaise longue in Bernard Picart's engraving from Paris in the 1690s, could still be regarded as modern just under a century later in Leclerc's version from 1778.[24] Comfort, formulated as *négligemment* or nonchalance in the eighteenth-century plate, was already well established in the late seventeenth century.[25] The fashion plate conveys which products were necessary to attain it – a *deshabillé du matin* and *un sopha* – and how the woman should position herself and what she should occupy herself with to demonstrate an air of *négligemment*. The woman resting at the start of this chapter was obviously not only sitting comfortably; she was also deceptively similar to the ideal woman portrayed in the contemporary fashion image: a consumer well-versed in fashion and trends of that time. Comfort was thus also fashion and an inexhaustible stream of 'lifestyle goods' associated with the fashionable comfort that filled the market.

The market grew in the eighteenth century, even though the phenomenon itself was not new. The fashion image from the 1690s, engraved *avec privilège du roi*, was part of Louis XIV's extensive campaign to launch France's leading position in Europe. The multifaceted images spread the idea of the superiority of French taste, an idea

21 This was important in pre-industrial production when artisan knowledge and artisan qualities were met with connoisseurship among merchants and consumers, but this changed with the advent of industrially manufactured goods and the spotlight shifting to the production technique itself. See 'Introduction. Commodities and the politics of value' in Appadurai 1986, pp. 41–5.

22 Erin Mackie, *Market à la Mode. Fashion, Commodity and Gender in The Tatler and The Spectator*, London 1997, p. 13.

23 Thornton 1985, p. 17.

24 The word 'nonchalant' spread as a loanword from French in the 1670s in Swedish. According to Elise Urbain Ruano, 'The Négligé in Eighteenth-Century French Portraiture', *The Journal of Dress History*, I, issue 1, Spring 2017, p. 92, the word *négligemment*, in the late seventeenth century, was applied to an attitude of affected indifference or elegant casualness (source: *Dictionnaire de l'Académie Française*, 1694).

25 *Kommoditet* in the sense of comfort, comfortable furnishings, was used in Swedish from the mid seventeenth century and for the first time at the start of the seventeenth century.

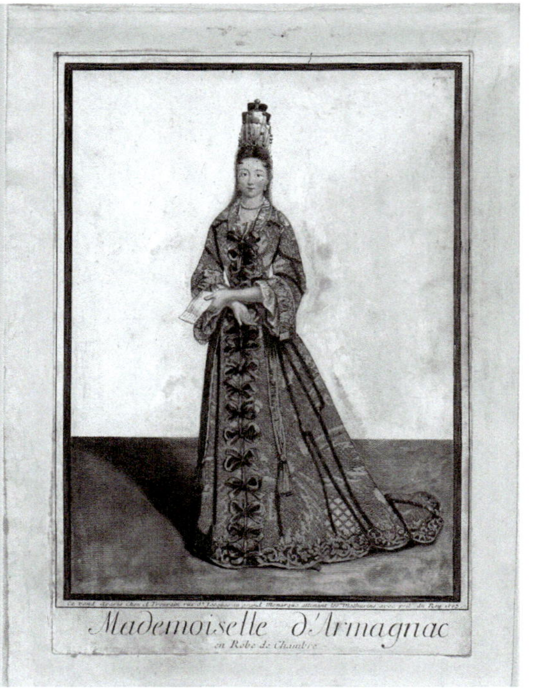

6. Antoine Trouvain, *Mademoiselle d'Armagnac en robe de chambre*, 1695. *Découpure*, engraving and textile, 27.31 × 20.32 cm. Minneapolis Museum of Art, the Minnich Collection, Ethel Morrison Van Derlip Fund, 1966 (66.25.5).

that continued to be conveyed in the eighteenth century and did not encounter competition until the end of the century from English ideals as well as ideals with more bourgeois influence. The development surrounding Louis XIV's Versailles had launched luxury as an asset that, at least theoretically, could be accessible to ever more people. The fashion plates reflected a growing production and market but also hinted at new lifestyles. Louis XIV, and later also Louis XV, often preferred to conduct their unofficial everyday lives in their smaller rooms and preferably in the company of a mistress rather than an official queen.[26] The significance of the royal mistresses for the development of the informal lifestyle as an ideal and their impact on fashion and consumption culminated with the Marquise de Pompadour in the mid-eighteenth century.

The engraving *Mademoiselle d'Armagnac en robe de chambre* by Antoine Trouvain from 1695 is a reminder of how relaxed everyday life was portrayed as an ideal (Image 6). The picture is both a society portrait of Princess Charlotte de Lorraine-Armagnac at the royal court of Louis XIV and a fashion plate in its own right. The princess posing in a dressing gown was a confirmation of the new culture of comfort

26 Nicole Castan, 'The Public and the Private', *A History of Private Life*, III, Roger Chartier (ed.), Massachusetts and London 1989, pp. 422–5.

and the eye-catching fabric was proof of the significance of trade and the market for this fashion. In this *découpure*, parts of the engraving have been cut away and replaced by sections of fabric that were pasted in, which emphasises the effect of the fabric here – a *robe de chambre* could also be known as *une indienne* to specify the influences.[27] The efforts to achieve comfort can partly be explained by the impressions and impulses from the increased accessibility of the surrounding wider world. With trading contacts and diplomatic connections came insight into foreign cultures, and the introduction of new, high-status products that extensively came to be linked to *kommoditet* (comfort, amenity). Dressing gowns and negligees were inspired by Indian or Persian garments and sofas, divans and drinking coffee by Turkish customs, for example. The radically loose garments, the relaxing furniture and spicy beverages were accompanied by perceptions of a freer lifestyle in which sensuous experiences were given preference.

The homes of the elite also gradually gained the imprint of changed lifestyles. A typical Baroque floor plan contained the *appartement de parade* with rooms for morning entertaining and the *appartement de société* for afternoon entertaining, but also an *appartement de commodité* for secluded or private life.[28] One of the new rooms, the boudoir in the lady's apartment, could also be used for informal socialising.[29] Differentiating between the functions of rooms was deemed to contribute to comfort in several ways. The possibility of retiring to 'private' rooms such as a study or dressing room was an expression of a privileged lifestyle and clarified the distance between the gentry and servants, but also unwanted socialising. Passages and hidden staircases – *dégagements* – separated the public and private spheres of the home but additionally constituted effective connecting links behind the scenes.[30] The planning often resulted in more but smaller rooms, which also contributed to comfort in terms of heating and proximity to various functions.[31] Architects also acted as interior decorators and designed furniture that was suitable for the home layouts and lifestyles of the new era.[32] Specific rooms required specific furniture, which became increasingly specialised and focused on function.

27 DeJean 2009, p. 207.

28 Thornton 1985, pp. 93–7.

29 Diana Cheng, *The History of the Boudoir in the Eighteenth Century*, Montreal, Quebec 2011, [diss.], pp. 35f.

30 Carl Wijnblad, *Ritningar på Fyratio Wåningshus Af Sten, och Trettio af Träd, Samt åtskilliga Lusthus, m.m.*, Stockholm 1755, p. A3 and Gösta Selling, *Svenska herrgårdshem under 1700-talet*, (1937) Stockholm 1991, p. 41.

31 Gunhild Eriksdotter, 'När slottet blev beboeligt. Inneklimatets betydelse på Skoklosters slott under Wrangels tid', *Bebyggelsehistorisk tidskrift* No. 66, 2013, pp. 8–29.

32 DeJean 2009, p. 128. There were clearly similar aims between the images that launched the new fashion and the images that showed the new furniture. For example, Jean-Charles Delafosse's engravings of new types of furniture were in the style of 'fashion images'.

The role played by France in these changes is noticeable in the many words that were incorporated into the Swedish language in the eighteenth century and that were associated with room layouts, interior design and types of furniture, including *korridor, garderob, fåtölj, schäslong* and *sekretär*.[33] The architect Nicodemus Tessin the Younger brought the new ideals to Sweden following trips to France, but also to Italy, the Netherlands, Austria and Germany.[34] He was ably assisted by the young diplomat Daniel Cronström, specially dispatched to purchase drawings and engravings that illustrated the new ideals. This pictorial treasure trove became a key source of reference for artists and architects throughout the eighteenth century in Sweden. Tessin summarised his impressions in an initial tract about interior design in 1717: 'Traictè de la Decoration Interieure, pour toutes sortes de Maisons Roÿales, et autres de distinction tant â la Ville, qu'â la Campagne.'[35] The aim was above all to provide guidelines for the construction of the new Royal Palace in Stockholm, which came to serve as a channel for new French impulses in much of the eighteenth century. Its innovative significance is also seen in the Swedish environments that arose in its wake, designed by architects such as Carl Hårleman, Jean Eric Rehn or Carl Wijnblad.[36]

After the death of Louis XIV in 1715, the lifestyle from Versailles moved to the elite's smaller private residences, known as *hôtels particuliers*, in Paris. Jean-François de Troy's painting from 1728, sometimes called *Lecture de Molière*, portrays comfortably appointed city life (Image 7). The wide armchairs with comfortably angled backrests and armrests were designed to accommodate the women's wide dresses. The fashion's mantua or *manteau* was partly related to the dressing gown, and it was worn with high-heeled mules. The armchairs have been moved in front of the fire, where coffee awaits and a folding screen creates spatial intimacy and warmth around the group of people. All the interior decoration details display an ideal that prevailed throughout the eighteenth century. Parquet flooring and silk-clad walls provided sound insulation and warmth, and the candle arms were positioned to create the most light and least shadow when you looked into the mirror.[37] The positioning of the chairs and the generously proportioned styles of dresses demonstrate how

33 Corridor, garderobe, fauteuil, chaise longue, écritoire.

34 Bo Vahlne, 'Inredningskonst i teori och praktik', *Tessin. Nicodemus Tessin d.y. Kunglig arkitekt och visionär* (Nationalmuseum) Stockholm 2002.

35 *Nicodemus Tessin the Younger. Sources, Works, Collections: Traictè de la decoration interieure 1717*, ed. Patricia Waddy, (Nationalmuseum & the Swedish Museum of Architecture), Stockholm 2002.

36 Queen Lovisa Ulrika made a notable statement about the Royal Palace of Stockholm in a letter to her brother August Wilhelm in 1749: 'Everything is very beautiful and completely magnificent, but without the slightest comforts. The decorations are extremely tasteful and very splendid, yet I believe that comfort in an apartment is preferable above all else' (Vahlne 2012, p. 112).

37 DeJean 2009, p. 155.

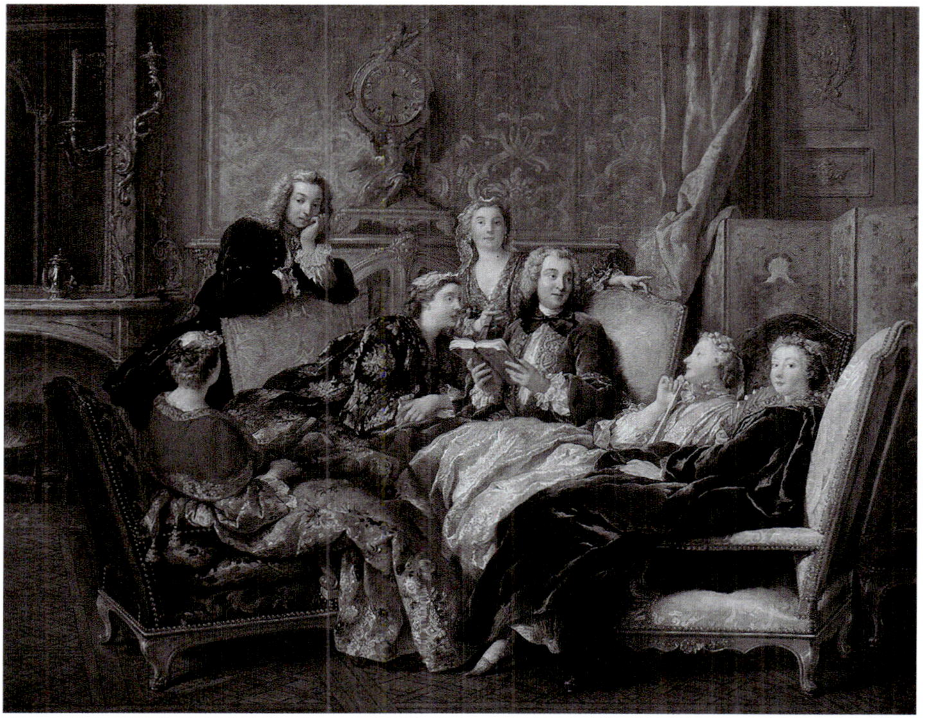

7. Jean-François de Troy, *Lecture de Molière*, *c*. 1728. Oil on canvas, 74 × 93 cm. Private ownership.

furniture had become movable and clothes now gave the wearer greater ease of movement. The clock on the bookcase shows us that the time is half past three, and the pastime during the afternoon is reading aloud. The book in the centre of the painting indicates that the people wearing the clothes and using the furniture also have freedom to spend their time in the way they choose.[38]

The choice of Molière, if the title of the painting is contemporary with the time of its creation, may well have been the group's own free choice of book to read aloud. Molière's social criticism remained topical in 1728 and could also convey something of the elite's attitude to themselves and the world around them. Perhaps the man with the book had gathered the women to entertain them by reading aloud from *Les précieuses ridicules* from 1659, which was about a group of society ladies who distinguished themselves through exaggerated refinement and complicated ceremony in society. In the satire, the affectatious figures represent everything artificial and affected that characterised the official and strictly regulated life

38 See Thorstein Veblen's study (1899) and to those who own production but engage in consumption, both 'conspicuous consumption' and 'conspicuous leisure'.

at the royal court and in aristocratic drawing rooms. Molière's play now became a reverse mirror for the new modern people who could be entertained by the old mannerisms that they had now distanced themselves from. In the painting, the members of the group embody the criticism through their relaxed, comfortable postures.

Comfort for all?

Jean-François de Troy's painting depicts urbane and aristocratic social life in Paris in the 1720s. The new comfort is the privilege of a limited elite. During the rest of the eighteenth century, concurrently with social, economic and political changes, the issue of this lifestyle democratisation became a recurring topic of debate. However, products that enhanced everyday comfort and new consumption behaviours had already started spreading outside the top social elite, and the celebrities in high society and the performing arts influenced new trends in fashion and socialising.[39] The desired ideals were no longer exclusively taken from the aristocracy and royal courts, which were instead associated with conservative norms, strict etiquette and formal ceremony. During the embourgeoisement processes in the late eighteenth century, old social structures were further dissolved. The royal court gossip that young Malla Silfverstolpe reflects on in her memoirs echoes these changes. The rigid formality personified by the queen dowager Sofia Magdalena in the late eighteenth century clearly shows that she was part of a bygone era:

> She described how, during the more than twenty years that she had visited the queen almost daily, she had never ever seen the queen leaning; she constantly sat up straight and rigidly, and her closest friends Mrs Manderström and Mrs Ehrengranat had to do likewise.[40]

Even without capital, creditors or contact networks, a broader echelon of society was now able to utilise copies and versions of the market's more exclusive range of products. What had been the luxuries of the elite at the end of the seventeenth century, had become more everyday elements for broader levels of society in the mid-eighteenth century. The gradual levelling of social classes gave increasing numbers of people the opportunity to experience comfort. 'The furniture of the large houses is now filling ordinary people's drawing rooms, and one sees women

39 DeJean 2009, p. 35.

40 *Malla Montgomery-Silfverstolpes memoarer*, published by Malla Grandinson, I (1799), Stockholm 1908–20, p. 213.

without rank, mixed with the most distinguished of people, with the same ornaments,' Pierre-Joseph Boudier de Villemert complains in his educative *L'ami des femmes* from 1758, which was translated into Swedish in 1763.[41] Many regarded the changes as threatening. Instead of being a democratic opportunity, the critics saw a demoralising danger in offering comfort to the masses.[42] This could only result in a weakened, unproductive society, in which everyone wishes to live as 'gentlemen' – where conspicuous consumption leads to conspicuous indolence.[43] Fittingly, *Sedolärande Mercurius* raised the subject of moral degeneracy back in 1731:

> Nature and reason advise us to work and move the body. Fashion says it is base conduct. Sit still and receive guests, enjoy yourself with them, learn to play cards, so that you will always have something to occupy your hands with. If you finally wish to go out, use your carriage for your comfort, do not let the wind blow on you, it disfigures the complexion and dishevels your coiffure; we do this until the blood rots in our bodies, and many illnesses afflict our health. … But what do the people care about nature and reason?[44]

However, the increasingly widespread desire for comfort was also a driving force, of which the energy could be harnessed as an asset. Handled correctly, this energy could increase employment and occupation and spur the competition that developed society financially – for the welfare of all citizens. The idea had already taken shape in the wake of the emerging comfort reforms of the late seventeenth century. In *The Fable of the Bees* (1714) by philosopher Bernard Mandeville, the bee colony thrives as long as the bees are driven by a desire, and this metaphor drove the debate onwards during the Age of Enlightenment, and also in Sweden during the Age of Liberty (1719–72).[45] Anders von Höpken from the political party called the Hats, gave an inflammatory speech about the utility of luxury at the Royal Swedish Academy of Sciences in 1740. The speech was praised by many who claimed that the production of luxury goods sustained the entire social pyramid.[46] But the attitude that each layer in the pyramid shared the same driving force that had previously been the privilege of the elite was new for the eighteenth century.

41 Pierre Joseph Boudier de Villemert, *Qvinno-könets wän. Öfwersatt ifrån fransyskan*, Västerås 1763, p. 45.

42 Leif Runefelt, *Att hasta mot undergången: anspråk, flyktighet, förställning i debatten om konsumtion i Sverige 1730–1830*, Lund 2015, p. 199.

43 See note 38.

44 *Sedolärande Mercurius*, Second part, No. 15, Stockholm 9 March 1731.

45 Bernard Mandeville, *The Fable of the Bees: or, Private Vices, Publick Benefits*, London 1714.

46 Anders von Höpken, *Tal, om yppighets nytta. Hållit för kongl. swenska wetenskaps academien, år 1740*, Stockholm 1741.

The architect Carl Fredric Adelcrantz, trained at and later responsible for the construction of the Royal Palace in Stockholm, saw the power in art to develop and civilise society for all. In his speech about the value and utility of the fine arts in 1757, he explains that wealthy and healthy people 'are those who in addition to the sustenance of life, own several comforts and pleasures'.[47] A country where the arts are driven to the highest heights also has the greatest opportunity to contribute to its citizens' comfort.[48] The explanation is found in Mandevillian 'desire':

> The bourgeoisie are by nature entitled to the same pleasures and comforts as the nobility: they pursue their trade and craft with unusual drive and cheerfulness: they get up early in the morning and go to bed late, in order to, as the former, have a comfortable house, decorated rooms, modern furniture. ... If the farmers cannot extend their desires as far as the bourgeoisie, they at least strive for fine-looking clothes, elegant and beautiful household utensils. This desire encourages them, with doubled diligence, to cultivate their soil, of which the produce must not solely suffice as the farmers' necessary food, but also for their comforts and pleasures.[49]

Comfort for all developed into a key political ideology in the eighteenth century, but also into a concrete manifestation of a process of social change.[50] In an article written during the Age of Liberty in Stockholm, the politician Carl Eric Wadenstierna writes about 'the natural right to utilise and harness one's wealth for comfort and for one's own benefit'.[51]

In similarity with several others in the field of eighteenth-century consumption and manifestation research, in the anthology *A Taste for Luxury in Early Modern Europe* (2017) the historians Johanna Ilmakunnas and Jon Stobart describe how changed attitudes led to a new form of luxury in the eighteenth century. In contrast to the older, ostentatious consumption, it was more about different aspects of comfort and about new expressions of cultivated social life within the urban upper middle class – a social group that was also less inclined to follow the older consumption patterns and lifestyle of the elite.[52] The 'new luxury' admittedly still

47 Carl Fredric Adelcrantz, *Tal om de fria konsters värde och nytta*, Stockholm 1757, p. 17.

48 Adelcrantz 1757, p. 19.

49 Adelcrantz 1757, pp. 19–20.

50 Petersson 2014, pp. 109–33 and Charles Saumarez Smith, *Eighteenth Century Decoration. Design and the Domestic Interior in England*, London 1993, pp. 50–3.

51 Carl Eric Wadenstierna, *Fria Tankar*, Stockholm 1769, p. 16.

52 *A Taste for Luxury in Early Modern Europe*, Jon Stobart and Johanna Ilmakunnas (ed.), London 2017; see the chapter 'Display, Acquisition and Boundaries of Luxury and Taste', pp. 1–17. Stobart and Ilmakunnas here refer to the historians Woodruff Smith (*Consumption and the Making of Respectability, 1600–1800*,

remained an expression of distinction, but was shaped more by taste, sensibility and cultivation.

The development of comfort was therefore linked to the eighteenth century's dynamic changes in social hierarchies, where an upper-class culture based on birth and descent had to make way for the emergence of an urban culture characterised by the bourgeoisie. Luxury now became above all tantamount to a functioning everyday life with comfortable, practical clothes and beautiful, functional furniture and household utensils.[53] The aspirations of the bourgeoisie to a good and comfortable life were also formulated on the basis of Christian virtues such as industriousness, diligence and order. The literature, drama, music and art of the era highlighted bourgeois values and ideals of happiness as an alternative to aristocratic decadence and wastefulness. The changes brought new attitudes to home and family as well as a different relationship to nature.[54] The idea of every individual's responsibility to seek their natural context, fostered by the Enlightenment's philosophers, gained renewed topicality during the structural transformations that imbued the latter half of the eighteenth century. Comfort was associated with unaffected, simple and informal family life, preferably in a country home, and it was linked to moral values and sentimental, nature-romantic and patriotic ideas. According to this ideological 'natural order', the woman's place was in the home, and it was her task to endeavour to keep it tidy and pleasant. Moralising texts presented an antithesis and warning examples in the form of the self-absorbed woman who devoted her time to fashion, social calls and balls and made her home a 'public space' where people came and went.[55] The idealisation of the family and the home and their significance in shaping character and morals developed into one of the strongest expressions of a bourgeois-tinted culture in the late eighteenth century. For example, the aim of Pierre Jean-Baptiste Legrand d'Aussy's work *Histoire de la vie privée des français depuis l'origine de la nation jusqu'à nos jours* (1783) was to explain, from a historical perspective, the character of a nation based on how its people designed their homes and their habits – how they furnished their rooms, dressed and ate.[56]

New York 2002); John Crowley (*The Invention of Comfort. Sensibilities and Design in Early-Modern Britain and Early America*, Baltimore 2003) and the economic historian Jan De Vries (*The Industrious Revolution. Consumer Behavior and the Household Economy, 1650 to the Present*, Cambridge 2008), whose differentiation between 'old and new luxury' they use as a basis.

53 'When luxury became bourgeois, its illegitimate margins needed to be neutralised by other social signs,' Petersson 2014, pp. 128ff.

54 Martin Lamm, *Upplysningstidens romantik. Den mystiskt sentimentala strömningen i svensk litteratur*, II, Lund (1920) 1963, pp. 459–66.

55 Boudier de Villemert 1763, p. 55.

56 Pierre Jean-Baptiste Legrand d'Aussy, *Histoire de la vie privée des Français depuis l'origine de la nation jusqu'à nos jours*, Paris 1783, 3 Vol. d'Aussy's work discusses all the furniture, utensils, textiles, lighting, manners and customs required for a meal.

In the eighteenth century, the home thereby gained a new and central position in the upper-class culture of the era.[57] And the homely feeling and feeling of comfort went hand in hand. When Jean-François Marmontel's opéra-comique *Lucile* from 1769 was performed in Stockholm in 1776, translated into Swedish by Anna Maria Lenngren, this was the launch of the genre in Swedish, but also for the staging of everyday life in a home environment.[58] The protagonists who had gathered for breakfast in the dressing room, wearing dressing gowns and *déshabillé*, sigh contentedly: 'Believe me, one cannot become blissful and happy if one does not seek happiness within one's own home.'[59] The theme of the plot, which criticised descent and ancestry, was about the triumph of love over inherited titles, and it added bourgeois contours to the morals and innocent virtues of the characters. The intimate room and the informal, unaffected attire, without pretensions and mannerisms, not only expressed their comfort but also signalled the sincerity of their emotions and actions. The sensibility represented by the aristocratic Mélite in *La petite maison*, her ability to identify and experience comfort, had now become a possibility in wider social contexts. One's own house and home were symbolically charged expressions in the cultural and political debate of the time. The home became the place where the private individual could find fulfilment. Witold Rybczynski regards the rise of the new luxury – comfort in the home – as being linked to a new, crucial view of humankind, the individual and the family during the eighteenth century.[60] In 1767, Alexander Roslin portrayed Marmontel holding a manuscript in his hand – and wearing a dressing gown.[61]

Aim, materials and method

In recent years, research has above all highlighted the development of a new culture of comfort within eighteenth-century French and British upper-class circles and has investigated how it reflects a revolutionary change in the elite's self-image

57 Hanna Greig's article 'Eighteenth-Century English Interiors in Image and Text' centres on English source material but is also applicable to the phenomenon from a larger perspective, *Imagined Interiors. Representing the Domestic Interior Since the Renaissance*, Jeremy Aynsley and Charlotte Grant (ed.), V&A, London 2006, pp. 102–27.

58 Jean François Marmontel, *Lucile, opera-comique i en act, öfversatt från fransyskan och upförd på kongl. svenska theatren, i deras majestäters och det kongl. husets närvaro, första gången den 19 junii 1776.* Stockholm 1776. Gustaf Johan Ehrensvärd, *Dagboksanteckningar förda vid Gustaf III:s hof, utgifna af D:r E. V. Montan*, I, Stockholm 1877, p. 40: 'never has any play been received in such a way; it seems as though seeing the adventures of people is preferred over those of the gods'.

59 Marmontel 1776, p. 12.

60 Rybczynski 1986, p. 35.

61 Alexander Roslin, *Jean-François Marmontel*, 1767, oil on canvas, 64 × 54 cm, the Louvre, Paris.

and identity. The aim of this study is to assess Swedish conditions from a similar perspective. By utilising images and objects as historical sources and by analysing them in the light of source material comprising estate inventories, biographies, letters, diaries, pamphlets and newspaper articles, this is a search for the pieces of the puzzle that make up the profound change in civilisation that the culture of comfort and consumption entailed in eighteenth-century Swedish everyday life. The recurring references to the term *culture* – as in *culture* of comfort or coffee *culture* – indicate that both material and social patterns and practices are central to the study.

The overall aim is, from an art-history perspective, to examine the attitude to this change in comfort in the eighteenth century and how it was manifested in the material and social cultures of a Swedish country house environment. The relevant questions are: In what way was this international, urban elite culture translated into a wider upper-class stratum in rural Sweden? and How was a French-influenced lifestyle managed or reshaped in the shadow of the critical debate on consumption and excess in the Age of Liberty? With a focus on Swedish upper-class culture in the period from 1750 to 1800, the goal is thereby to examine how the European culture of comfort was expressed in Sweden. The study centres on an illuminating example: the Wadenstierna family on the Näs country estate in Uppland Province.

The introductory painting with the woman resting in her armchair seeks to draw attention to eighteenth-century pictorial art in general, and portraiture and genre works in particular, as a key starting point for the study. The pictures convey how 'comfort' was perceived, what was required for comfortable living and how it was expressed in accordance with various social roles and situations. The study presents a number of people from the eighteenth century, from different social groups and of different nationalities, ages and genders. Some of the individuals are familiar, whereas others remain unknown. Some of them gradually appear more prominently – such as politician Carl Eric Wadenstierna (1723–1787) and both of his wives, Jacobina Sophia Psilanderhielm von Seulenberg (1733–1768) and, subsequently, Fredrica Carleson (1743–1794). They are the protagonists in this study. Here, Wadenstierna's two daughters, Sophia (1758–1830) and Carolina (1762–1848), also play key roles. Their portraits, personal effects and homes create a picture of the eighteenth-century culture of comfort. It is specific to their family but includes elements that are representative of the social group and era to which they belonged. The story of the Wadenstierna family must also be viewed in a wider context and related to the world around them. In the following chapters, the perspective alternates between their country estate in Uppland Province and the wider world. But they are the focus of this study.

The Wadenstierna family's Stockholm residence was on the corner of Klara Västra Kyrkogata and Stora Vattugränden in the district of Norrmalm. However, in 1775 the conditions of the family's life changed through the creation of an additional home, when the new manor house Näs was built. In the years that followed, this is where a more rural home took shape, located 50 km north-east of the capital. The manor at Näs was an exemplary construction in the spirit of the architect Carl Wijnblad, and through the design of the interiors and the commissions and orders of furniture, artworks and household utensils, the Wadenstierna family created a home characterised by their own preferences, but also by the aesthetic ideals and political debates of the period. Preserved drawings, estate inventories and receipts convey a picture of a Gustavian country house environment shaped by the era's ideas of comfort, but also of social, cultural and national identity.[62] The family did not belong to the uppermost elite, but represented a flourishing and urban echelon of the upper class in late-eighteenth-century Sweden. Carl Eric Wadenstierna's roots in the enlightened and occasionally radical and young nobility who served the state in a bureaucratic capacity also gave him a degree of freedom in relation to conventions linked to the hereditary aristocracy which was steeped in tradition. This freedom may have also been significant for the design of the family's country home at Näs. Compared to many older and grand upper-class environments in the countryside, Näs was much more modest. Here, design and function were coupled with new values and with a more pronounced desire to create a comfortable and well-functioning home for a more informal day-to-day life. It is in this type of environment that the modern culture of comfort becomes most clearly visible in Sweden in the eighteenth century – the new form of luxury that research has highlighted in various international contexts.

The choice of the Wadenstierna family as the case study here also involves examining the entire family and not only the father in his role as patriarch and as an individual with status and influence in the Gustavian society. He certainly stands out as the formal commissioner of the construction of Näs and the person who ordered furniture and paintings, but in this study the manor at Näs is perceived as an environment shaped by the entire Wadenstierna family. Fredrica Carleson and Wadenstierna's daughters Sophia and Carolina probably participated in the creation of this milieu that comprises the family's private sphere and their public sphere for entertaining. They are depicted in the paintings performing various tasks, and some of the rooms and furniture around them were especially for the women in the family. The lack of sources prevents detailed scrutiny of the family relations and decision-making paths in the creation of Näs, and in the patriarchal system of the era Carl Eric Wadenstierna would have unquestionably had extensive influence on the construction, orders and commissions, and furnishings. In this study, the environment that emerged at Näs will therefore also be interpreted in the light of

62 The link between national identity and norms associated with taste and consumption has been pointed out by, among others, Stobart and Ilmakunnas 2017.

his social roles and political standpoints. Nonetheless, it was also an environment in which the women had decisive significance, and this study will largely centre on their activities at various types of tables. The following chapters are therefore based on the assumption that the women also played a key part in the creation of the home at Näs. Their roles, tasks and comfort constitute the main core of the environment.

The ambition here is also to include source material that has previously been relatively unused. Alongside archival documents, the collections of paintings and objects that can be linked to Näs when it was owned by the Wadenstierna family offer a rich source of knowledge about eighteenth-century Swedish upper-class culture. Today, the source material is in both public collections and private ownership. Archival materials in the form of legal documents such as insurance policies, estate inventories and wills are stored in Stockholm's city archive and the Swedish National Archives, while inventory lists and reports and a small collection of photographic documentation from Näs in the 1960s is stored in the museum archive at Nordiska museet. The large collection of objects has now been dispersed and is largely in private ownership. The art collection has partly been found in various public collections, including those of Nationalmuseum, while the photographic documentation of the Swedish Portrait Archive (SPA) can provide some information about the privately owned items. An important purpose of the study has been to compile the data about this now dispersed source material in order to recreate a picture of life at Näs and thereby provide new insights into Gustavian country house culture.

From an international perspective, Sweden has an extensive and largely unexplored holding of portraits, not least in private collections. Swedish portraiture also constitutes one of the primary sources for this project. The portraits of Wadenstierna and his wives, by Johan Henric Scheffel and Niclas Lafrensen, recur during this study. Regarded as important artefacts permeated by a specific culture and social practice, they are also studied in dialogue with the rest of the eighteenth-century pictorial world. The art collection at Näs also included eleven paintings by Pehr Hilleström. Wadenstierna commissioned the suite in the run-up to the completion of Näs in the 1770s, and the thematic motifs interplayed with the environment for which they were intended as well as the family and social circle who inhabited it. Hilleström's paintings, dated to around 1774 and 1775, were early works in the artist's oeuvre. They were commissioned shortly after Gustaf III repealed the obligation to belong to a guild in 1773 for artists associated with the reformed Royal Swedish Academy of Fine Arts; they were thereby given the opportunity to work in an open market.[63] The paintings for Näs were one of the most extensive private commissions

63 Mikael Ahlund, 'Konsten att försörja sig som konstnär. Pehr Hilleström och konstmarknaden i 1700-talets Stockholm.', *Ekonomisk kulturhistoria. Bildkonst, konsthantverk och scenkonst 1720–1850*, Klas Nyberg (ed.), Stockholm 2017, pp. 55–71.

of Hilleström's works and were preserved in their original environment at Näs in the Roslagen area of Uppland Province right up to the second half of the twentieth century.

Equally notable is Wadenstierna's commission of around twenty paintings from the landscape painter Johan Philip Korn, who was newly established at that time. Other categories of pictorial art were also represented at Näs and serve as pieces that make up a larger comprehensive picture. A collection of cut-out silhouette portraits documented the family's circle of friends and their social life, and the library's collections of books, engraved plates and maps provide additional references to the Wadenstierna family's way of life and preferences. Furthermore, five painted overdoor decorations remain in their original location in the entrance hall of Näs Manor, and their inscriptions convey ideas about placid life in the countryside. This pictorial source material at Näs is studied here in the light of the eighteenth century's wider visual culture, represented in both international and Swedish collections.

The estate inventory of Carl Eric Wadenstierna dated 1787 goes through the disposition of the rooms at Näs and offers readers a fascinating tour of the family's home. This document reveals an environment full of life, furniture and objects.[64] The inventory shows which items of furniture belonged to the part of the home used for entertaining and which belonged to the more private or personal rooms in the gentleman's and lady's respective areas. The economic valuation of the objects also hints at how the era rated Swedish veneer furniture by makers such as Georg Haupt or examples of faience from the Marieberg factory in Stockholm. Viewed individually, the different parts of the source material are fragments, but together they create coherence. Other sources may also contribute to the overall picture – the lack of personal letters or diaries associated with the family can be complemented by other contemporary memoirs and written correspondence that sheds light on the ways of life and patterns of socialising that characterised the Wadenstiernas' era and circle. The preserved portraits and collections of art, furniture and literature that can be connected with Näs are also key statements on self-image and identity. Studying the preserved fragments in the light of a wider context also clarifies the connections. Although the Wadenstierna family chose to create a comfortable everyday life for themselves in the Uppland countryside, the reasons for their choices and their taste can be found in the wider world around them. The French fashion

64 Estate inventories have their limitations. They can never provide a comprehensive view of what a person owned throughout their life; instead they give us an insight from a specific point in time. Additionally, these types of inventories cannot tell us what the person acquired themselves and what they received as gifts or inheritances, nor do they indicate which items were personally valued or not; Gudrun Andersson, *Stadens dignitärer. Den lokala elitens status- & maktmanifestation i Arboga 1650–1770*, Stockholm 2009, pp. 133ff.

that disseminated the knowledge of the eighteenth century's new ideals regarding comfort can be traced in the source material's variety of expressions – from the '*commodes*' (chests of drawers and cabinets) listed in the estate inventory to the indoor scenes depicted in Hilleström's paintings.

The fragments' relationship to a complex and multifaceted whole also involves the methodological approaches used in this study. To find paths to the choices made by the family – such as selecting Lafrensen to create the portraits, commissioning furniture from Haupt or paintings by Hilleström, or having their home designed in the style of Carl Wijnblad's models – requires examination of a series of different types of textual and pictorial sources. A portrait can be studied in detail using iconographic methods and analysed comparatively in relation to the visual culture of that time, but it must also be studied in a broader context. Choices, preferences and taste could be shaped by fashion images and opinion pieces in newspapers and magazines, as well as by supply and demand or decrees and ordinances. A wide variety of written source materials, from estate inventories to novels, have been used in this study to obtain greater understanding of how ideas regarding concepts such as comfort were disseminated and took root.[65]

There is also interplay between texts of that time and the era's pictorial world, objects and environments, and this constantly interactive process that shaped eighteenth-century culture requires different readings of both contemporary and older sources. For example, engraved pictures from Paris in the 1670s can serve as reminders of how the eighteenth century's culture of comfort was a consequence of earlier changes and ideals. Witold Rybczynski uses 'the Onion Theory of Comfort' when he asks himself how changed attitudes to comfort came about:

> Like an onion, the notion of comfort has many layers, which were added historically. The image of the onion also conveys the elusive nature of comfort: if you take it apart and look at the layers one by one, you lose the overall shape, and yet the layers are still visible one beneath the other. These layers consist of ideas such as privacy or intimacy, convenience, physical ease. Each generation has added something to the definition, has added a layer without necessarily contradicting what came before.[66]

It is not sufficient to analyse one of the outermost layers because they have in turn been shaped by previous layers and, ultimately, by their core.

65 Source material from various databases has proved useful: Litteraturbanken.se; Project Runeberg (runeberg.org); Digitaltmuseum.se; Nationell ArkivDatabas (NAD) and the database tidningar.kb.se.
66 Witold Rybczynski in an interview with Barbara Spronk 1990, http://aurora.icaap.org/index.php/aurora/article/view/65/77, accessed: 10 January 2020.

Theoretical starting points

This study connects with international art-history research that in recent years has deepened the inclusion of the subject in new and interdisciplinary research contexts, where, for example, pictorial art is perceived as an integrated part of a wider material culture and of wider social and economic contexts. The theoretical starting points are mainly taken from interdisciplinary research that focuses on consumption and manifestation, from gender research and from perspectives that have been developed within the research fields of material and visual culture studies. With these starting points, the aim of the study is to deepen understanding of the material culture and cultural identity that shaped the elite's self-image in the eighteenth century and thereby also their attitude to comfort.

The fact that the pictures and objects can tell us about the identity-building processes that shaped individuals and groups in Swedish eighteenth-century upper-class culture is thereby a fundamental starting point for the study. The Wadenstierna family's Näs, along with their portraits and furniture, or the clothes and books described in the estate inventory, were filled with meanings in the social context in which the family lived and worked. The objects convey their taste, cultivation, contact networks and lifestyle – perhaps also some of their thoughts and feelings. Their possessions represented the family in their contact with the world around them. Material culture studies is one of the theoretical gateways into analysing this relationship between people and their possessions and what this relationship can tell us. To define a concept that is as elusive and relative as 'comfort', the approach here has been to examine a selection of the tangible objects that the family owned, how they were used, by whom and in what context. The selection has been made on the basis of the thematic starting points of the study, each of which are significant for the era's attitudes to comfort for body and soul: at writing and sewing tables, and at dressing tables, coffee tables and games tables. These themes are presented in more detail in the section on the disposition of the study.

The material culture's economic, aesthetic and emotional value is therefore the focus of the study, and a selection of furniture, clothes, pictures and texts – in combination with their original contexts for which they were intended – thereby constitute some of the study's primary sources. Interpreting objects as meaningful social and cultural signs, *incarnated signs*, that convey messages about their owners and users, is the point of departure for social-cultural anthropologist Arjun Appadurai's work *The Social Life of Things: Commodities in Cultural Perspective* from 1986.[67] His examination of how goods (and services), commodities, are charged with values and associations that have been projected onto them and that make

67 Appadurai 1986, p. 38.

them desirable within a social group, has been a key theoretical starting point for this study. With similar points of departure, Maureen Daly Goggin and Beth Fowkes Tobin have compiled three anthologies that analyse women's relationship with material culture from various perspectives. In *Material Women, 1750–1950: Consuming Desires and Collecting Practices* (2009), *Women and Things, 1750–1950: Gendered Material Strategies* (2009) and *Women and the Material Culture of Needlework and Textiles, 1750–1950* (2009) the authors give examples of how production and consumption of objects shaped women's day-to-day life and identity over the course of 200 years.[68] The attitude to activities that were defined as particularly female, such as letter writing or embroidery, and the items related to these activities and how they can be linked to aspects of everyday life and comfort, have been of considerable interest to this study.

The field of research grouped under the term *visual culture studies* is especially significant here. As shown, pictorial art can also be studied as actively coded signs or traces in a specific culture and social practice.[69] The pictures' function as meaningful objects also comprises the identity-building relationship between people and pictures – essential in a generally visually oriented culture such as that of the eighteenth century. Through the portraits, and the cultural and social values with which they were associated, Wadenstierna and his family wanted to define their role and their position as people of rank. But people were also shaped by their belongings. Based on both eighteenth-century literary fiction and the century's different material cultures, art historian Mimi Hellman uses trains of thought from visual culture studies when she examines the relationship between French people in the eighteenth century and their furnished rooms.[70] In the interplay between people and furniture, Hellman regards the objects as social actors, designed to meet the requirements of and even actively govern people's social role-play and movement patterns: 'objects were not simply owned, but indeed *performed*'.[71] Joan DeJean, in her study *The Age of Comfort: When Paris Discovered Casual – and the Modern Home Began* (2009), claims that the new armchairs encouraged and taught – or

68 *Material Women, 1750–1950. Consuming Desires and Collecting Practices*, Maureen Daly Goggin and Beth Fowkes Tobin (ed.), New York (2009), 2016; *Women and Things, 1750–1950. Gendered Material Strategies*, Maureen Daly Goggin and Beth Fowkes Tobin (ed.), New York 2009; *Women and the Material Culture of Needlework and Textiles, 1750–1950*, Maureen Daly Goggin and Beth Fowkes Tobin (ed.), New York 2009.
69 Lena Johannesson, 'Att studera konsthistoria och visuell kultur. Begrepp, metod och historiografi', *Konst och visuell kultur i Sverige. Före 1809*, Lena Johannesson (ed.), Stockholm 2007, pp. 12–21. To place eighteenth-century portraiture in the field of visual culture studies, works by Marcia Pointon and Mary D. Sheriff have been of crucial significance.
70 Mimi Hellman, 'Furniture, Sociability, and the Work of Leisure in Eighteenth-Century France', *Eighteenth Century Studies*, Vol. 32, No. 4 (1999), pp. 415–45.
71 Hellman 1999, p. 417.

even forced – people to relax.[72] Correspondingly, this study aims to show how the possessions that surrounded the Wadenstierna family were not only expressions of identity-building consumption but also normative co-creators of their social roles.

Many researchers of eighteenth-century cultural history paraphrase the relationship between people's material and social culture as a piece of theatre. This device is often applied in consumption research. In *Consumption and the World of Goods* (1993), John Brewer and Roy Porter examined a culture of consumption during the seventeenth and eighteenth centuries which had the social game or performance as its motives: 'material life formed a stage with its sets, props and actors engaged in the drama of being'.[73] Defining oneself as an informed consumer (the actor) was an active identity-building action (the role on the stage) that conveyed who you were in relation to your surroundings (the audience). Sociologist and anthropologist Erving Goffman used the stage as a metaphor in his study *The Presentation of Self in Everyday Life* (1959), where he showed that people, based on social and cultural norms and attitudes, endeavoured in different ways to control themselves and the impressions they wished to make on the people around them. Goffman called this social control mechanism 'impression management'. To take to the stage and act convincingly as an 'actor' in front of an 'audience', the correct mask, costume and decor were required for the role in question.[74] The country house that Wadenstierna commissioned for himself and his family served as such a social stage, on which furniture and people took part in the performance. In the same way, his portraits can be regarded as the most refined and lasting from of 'impression management'. Through the portraits, he was able to control the image of himself that he left for posterity, in a similar way to controlling the image of his deceased wife by commissioning a posthumous portrait of her.

The metaphor is far from a recent construction. In 1730, Wadenstierna's father-in-law, Edvard Carleson, describes in *Sedolärande Mercurius* how people strive in various ways to gain prestige and accolades in their attempts to distinguish themselves in life. But how should people handle their aspirations? He refers to the rules of life of the Greek Stoic philosopher Epictetus:

> Epictetus utilises a different allusion, which is quite agreeable, and relatively serviceable to convince us to be careful with the class in which divine providence has placed us. Here we are, he says, as if in a theatre, where each individual has his assigned role. A person's greatest obligation is to play their role to perfection. We could very well say that our role does not suit us and that we could play another

72 DeJean 2009. p. 103.
73 John Brewer and Roy Porter, *Consumption and the World of Goods*, New York (1993) 2003, p. 6.
74 Erving Goffman, *Jaget och maskerna. En studie i vardagslivets dramatik*, (1959) Stockholm 2004.

> better. But he says that is not our business. All we should care about is to excel in the part given to us. But if the part is unserviceable, that is not our fault, but that of he who allocates all the roles and who is the director of the entire drama.[75]

In an age when consumption enabled unprecedented social climbing and where increasing numbers of people seemed to be able to adopt whatever role their finances permitted, or rather the appearance of credibility permitted, it was tempting to take matters into one's own hands. However, the key was to navigate, and do so elegantly, in the expanding, material world that the eighteenth century became. The sources are permeated by a sense of wonder at living in an era when everything appeared to be possible, and where everything was available for purchase that could make life beautiful, pleasant and comfortable. The newspapers enthusiastically report on the new inventions: a comfortable and elastic hooped petticoat; paper that is not destroyed by water or fire; English fans that imitate Chinese ones; a new type of blinds used in *voitures anglaises*; a harpsichord that imitates a number of different instruments; various kinds of dentures; artificial fruit to wear in hairstyles; a new fabric made of grass – more lustrous than silk – from which coats, waistcoats and trousers can be made; a washing machine from London that can wash up to twenty-four shirts at the same time, and new, comfortable furniture to meet all needs.[76]

The constant supply of new consumables had consequences that challenged older conventions and in the longer term also the foundations of the hierarchical class society. The assignment of roles between groups in society was affected by the distribution of resources, for example, between men and women, as women were identified as the eighteenth century's new major consumers.[77] As claimed by Brewer and Porter, women therefore feature more prominently in consumption research in contrast with production research.[78] The restless changeableness that was deemed to characterise the market for new fashions and luxury objects was also ascribed to women, who, according to attitudes at the time, were vain, sensual, capricious, impressionable, coquettish and envious, which made them

75 *Sedolärande Mercurius*, 8 September 1730.

76 *Almanac de Gotha contenant Diverses Connoissances Curieuses et Utiles*, pp. 102, 104; 1787, pp. 80, 132; 1789, p. 75; 1791, pp. 67, 169; in the 1791 issue 1776, pp. 99, 100; 1792, p. 75. Detailed descriptions of new fashions were also distributed through the fashion images of the era, for example, in *Cabinet des modes* (1785–6) and *Magasin des modes nouvelles, françaises et anglaises* (1786–9).

77 See the articles in the section on 'Shopping' in *Gender, Taste and Material Culture in Britain and North America, 1700–1830*, John Styles and Amanda Vickery (ed.), *Studies in British Art* 17, New Haven and London 2006, pp. 125–225. Here, the male consumer is also highlighted, as well as the fact that the sources are often silent about whether the woman's or the man's decisions are behind the household accounts and purchases, pp. 5–8.

78 Brewer and Porter 2003, pp. 1–7.

especially susceptible to the temptations of consumption and constant stream of new products.[79] In a satire in the newspaper *Stockholms Posten* in 1782, a young wife rebuking her husband for taking an interest in the purchases exclaims, 'But my God! Is it suitable for a man to meddle in such trifles? No, frankly, *mon cher*, you don't understand such things.'[80]

This distinction between the genders, with their specific rules and spheres, was reinforced during the eighteenth century. The woman's role in the home in contrast to that of the man in society was rooted in the changed perceptions and attitudes that developed during the century.[81] As mentioned, the woman was assigned a large part of the responsibility for the design of the home and the housekeeping.[82] The woman's aesthetic and social abilities and her feeling for taste and refinement made her the new, strong target group for fashion and consumables, associated with the comfort and representativeness of the home. The market was quickly adapted to these gender-specific norms and ideals, which were confirmed and reinforced in the various pictures and texts of the time.[83] In France, the women-dominated influential salon culture was also important in shaping 'female' taste and consumption.[84] Women within the elite took on the role of promoters of art and culture and therefore also became shapers of taste – such as the Marquise de Pompadour.[85] In contrast with Louis XIV, who had extensive control over the royal court's aesthetic expression as a key manifestation of autocracy and the sovereignty of French taste, Louis XV and Louis XVI transferred much of this responsibility to their queens or mistresses. The eighteenth-century market for specific 'women's furniture' such as various types of dressing tables, writing tables and sewing tables was one result of this development. New, lightweight, moveable items of furniture

79 Throughout the eighteenth century, the female consumer is also portrayed as immoral, indolent and to blame for the country's social and economic imbalance. Malicious portraits and caricatures were thought to be educational and corrective (*Sedolärande Mercurius*, 31 August 1731).

80 'Om rika Flickors upfostran', *Stockholms Posten*, 21 December 1782.

81 Here, the distinction between ideal and reality should be highlighted: although the norm advocated these two separate spheres, in reality the relationships between men and women and their responsibilities and tasks were more differentiated and complicated; *Everyday Revolutions. Eighteenth-Century Women Transforming Public and Private*, Diane E. Boyd and Marta Kvande (ed.), University of Delaware Press, Newark 2008, pp. 17–29.

82 See the description of the woman's areas of responsibility in *En fullkomlig Ägta Hustrus Bild, Teckrad Efter den målning, som finnes i Ord-språks-Bokens sidsta Capitel*. Translation from German by Eric Forssén, Gothenburg 1787.

83 Dutch seventeenth-century painting, which was coveted in the eighteenth century, also affected the attitude to marriage, family and homes. The paintings and engraved pictures conveyed bourgeois ideals to eighteenth-century upper-class consumers. Eighteenth-century artists, such as Chardin and Greuze, dressed the ideal in modern attire, and their pictures had a major impact on a wide audience.

84 Leora Auslander, *Taste and Power: Furnishing Modern France*, London 1996, p. 64.

85 DeJean 2009, p. 163.

were designed on the basis of a specific female decorum, with everything from drawer mechanisms that meant women did not need to pull drawers out towards them – a gesture regarded as unseemly for a woman – to armchairs and sofas with female names such as '*bergère*' or '*duchesse*'.[86] So when Trémicour tries to seduce Mélite in *La petite maison*, he knows exactly how to do it: the perfect home with the latest in interior decoration will make the connoisseur fall for him. The luxury that Mélite sees and experiences makes her constantly want more.

On the basis of the gender theory perspective described here, the female Swedish eighteenth-century consumer accordingly gains a prominent role in this study. Both of Wadenstierna's wives and his two daughters come to the fore in the various chapters. Their portraits and possessions constitute the main examples in the study.

Previous research

It is clear that there are many and extensive paths of discovery leading into the eighteenth-century culture of comfort. The recent decades' interest in eighteenth-century material culture and how it related to concepts such as comfort or consumption is one of these broad paths that encompasses a wealth of research initiatives within a series of different disciplines. A few examples that have been of particular interest to this study are highlighted here in the following condensed research review.

The study *The Age of Comfort: When Paris Discovered Casual – and the Modern Home Began* (2009) by literary historian Joan DeJean became a crucial starting point for the project and sparked curiosity about what the consequences of the comfort revolution were in a corresponding Swedish context.[87] DeJean starts from the changes in late-seventeenth-century France that led to the comfortable eighteenth century. She emphasises the concrete conditions for eighteenth-century home environments and the consequences of changed attitudes to the human body, clothes and furniture for the growth of a new lifestyle. In 2011, the exhibition 'Paris: Life & Luxury in the Eighteenth Century' was shown at the J. Paul Getty Museum in Los Angeles, which developed a few of the issues that DeJean had raised in her book. In the extensive annotated exhibition catalogue, DeJean presents the themes of the exhibition in more detail, followed by a series of more in-depth studies of the relationship between the material and social culture of the eighteenth century by Charissa Bremer-David, Kimberly Chrisman-Campbell, Mimi Hellman and

86 Auslander 1996, p. 67.

87 Joan DeJean, *The Age of Comfort. When Paris Discovered Casual – And the Modern Home Begun*, New York 2009.

Björn Kerber.[88] The physical objects are here not only regarded as expressions of shape and function during the eighteenth century but also as sources of the relationship between people and environment and pertinent norms and values. Here, art historian Katie Scott's studies of eighteenth-century art and interiors in relation to physical and social contexts should also be highlighted, for instance, in *The Rococo Interior* (1996) and in the anthology *Between Luxury and the Everyday: Decorative Arts in Eighteenth-Century France* (2006).[89]

The significance of the eighteenth century's considerable visual culture for the era's identity-building processes is further discussed in many new art-history and interdisciplinary publications. The influential artists of the eighteenth century such as François Boucher or Jean Siméon Chardin consciously endeavoured to meet the needs of an audience shaped by new lifestyle ideals, in which fashion, comfort and sociality were important expressions. In turn, their works generated new ideals. Both Paula Radisich's *Pastiche, Fashion and Galanterie in Chardin's Genre Subjects: Looking Smart* (2014) and Melissa Hyde's *Making up the Rococo: François Boucher and His Critics* (2006) provide new angles on known oeuvres, where aspects such as gender, consumption and manifestation are highly significant.[90]

Within consumption research, the anthology *Consumption and the World of Goods* (1993) by John Brewer and Roy Porter is a standard work, as is Maxine Berg's *Luxury and Pleasure in Eighteenth-Century Britain* (2005), which shows how the growth of the wider commercial market had socially and culturally far-reaching consequences.[91] There is also a focus on the eighteenth-century culture of comfort in the work of historian Jon Stobart, where he and fellow researchers have recurrently examined the environments of the elite. His latest, *Comfort in the Eighteenth-Century Country House* (2022), was published after the Swedish edition of this book but has several interesting points in common. In an anthology co-edited with Andrew Hann, *The Country House: Material Culture and Consumption* (2015), and in *Consumption and the Country House* (2016), co-written with Mark Rothery, Jon Stobart examines consumption as a performative action and aspects such as the upper-class environment's male and female spheres.[92]

88 *Paris: Life and Luxury in the Eighteenth Century*, Bremer-David, Charissa (ed.), Los Angeles 2011.

89 Katie Scott, *The Rococo Interior. Decoration and Social Spaces in Early Eighteenth-Century Paris*, New Haven and London 1996; *Between Luxury and the Everyday: Decorative Arts in Eighteenth-Century France*, Katie Scott and Deborah Cherry (ed.), New Jersey, 2006.

90 Paula Radisich, *Pastiche, Fashion and Galanterie in Chardin's Genre Subjects: Looking Smart*, Plymouth 2014; Melissa Hyde, *Making Up the Rococo. François Boucher and His Critics*, Los Angeles 2006.

91 John Brewer, and Roy Porter, *Consumption and the World of Goods*, New York (1993) 2003; Maxine Berg, *Luxury and Pleasure in Eighteenth-Century Britain*, Oxford 2005.

92 Jon Stobart, *Comfort in the Eighteenth-Century Country House*, Routledge, New York 2022; *The Country House. Material Culture and Consumption*, Jon Stobart and Andrew Hann (ed.), Swindon 2015; *Consumption*

In this context, his predecessor John Crowley's *The Invention of Comfort: Sensibilities and Design in Early Modern Britain and Early America* (2003) should also be mentioned.[93] Together with historian Johanna Ilmakunnas, Stobart has also compiled the anthology *A Taste for Luxury in Early Modern Europe* (2017), which examines the identity-building significance of luxury consumption in early modern Europe.[94] Ilmakunnas has also delved deeper into studying consumption and manifestation behaviours, especially in Swedish country house culture, for example, in her book *Ett ståndsmässigt liv. Familjen von Fersens livsstil på 1700-talet* (2012).[95] Christer Ahlberger's work *Konsumtionsrevolutionen 1. Om det moderna konsumtionssamhällets framväxt 1750–1900* (1996) is another key contribution to consumption research in Sweden.[96]

Christine Adams' *A Taste for Comfort and Status: A Bourgeois Family in Eighteenth-Century France* (2000) is interesting as a comparative study as its point of departure is a high-bourgeois family from the heterogeneous upper-class stratum that characterised the eighteenth-century French countryside. Here the subject of study is not people from the uppermost echelon of the urbane French elite, which brings nuance to the picture of class-based consumption and manifestation that is otherwise often represented by the exceptional conditions that characterised royal families and the nobility. The Lamothe family in the case study were part of a privileged social stratum who, well-educated and locally influential, were critical of the aristocratic elite and royal court culture, yet also strived for a certain degree of concordance with the modern, urbane upper-class ideals. In a similar way to the Lamothe family, the status and identity of the Wadenstierna family were not based on old historical roots or an ostentatious lifestyle. Adams' description of the Lamothe family's identity-building activities can therefore, in certain aspects, also

and the Country House, Jon Stobart and Mark Rothery (ed.), Oxford 2016; 'Comfort in English and Swedish country houses, c. 1760–1820', *Social History*, Vol. 43, No. 2, 2018, pp. 234–58.

93 John Crowley, *The Invention of Comfort. Sensibilities and Design in Early-Modern Britain and Early America*, Baltimore 2003.

94 *A Taste for Luxury in Early Modern Europe: Display, Acquisition and Boundaries*, Johanna Ilmakunnas and Jon Stobart (ed.), London and New York 2017.

95 Johanna Ilmakunnas, *Ett ståndsmässigt liv. Familjen von Fersens livsstil på 1700-talet* Stockholm 2012, and Johanna Ilmakunnas, 'The Luxury Shopping Experience of the Swedish Aristocracy in Eighteenth-Century Paris', in *Luxury and Gender in European Towns, 1700–1914*, Deborah Simonton, Marjo Kaartinen & Anne Montenach (ed.), New York 2015, pp. 115–31; Johanna Ilmakunnas, 'Adelns arbete och vardag på 1700-talets svenska herrgårdar. Johan Gabriel Oxenstiernas och Jacobina Charlotta Munsterhjelms dagböcker', *Historisk Tidskrift för Finland*, the 98 2013:2 issue and Johanna Ilmakunnas, 'Konsten att avbilda arbete. Kvinnors sysselsättningar och vardag på Pehr Hilleströms genremålningar från 1770-talet till 1810-talet', *Historisk Tidskrift för Finland*, 103, 2018:1.

96 Ahlberger studies the consumption of tea and coffee during the mid-eighteenth century with the help of estate inventories. Christer Ahlberger, *Konsumtionsrevolutionen 1. Om det moderna konsumtionssamhällets framväxt 1750–1900*, the Faculty of Humanities, the University of Gothenburg 1996.

apply to the Wadenstierna family's position: 'Rather, it was dependent on family ties, professional expertise, and satisfaction, cultural contribution and personal cultivation, and a sense of local status based on their respected achievement and position in the community.'[97]

Amanda Vickery's *The Gentleman's Daughter: Women's Lives in Georgian England* (1998) and *Behind Closed Doors: At Home in Georgian England* (2009) are examples of adjacent research with strong points in common with comfort and consumption.[98] Alongside historian John Styles, Vickery is also the editor of the anthology *Gender, Taste and Material Culture in Britain and North America, 1700–1830* (2006).[99] The female consumer in the comfort revolution is also highlighted in Erin Mackie's *Market à la Mode: Fashion, Commodity and Gender in* The Tatler *and* The Spectator (1997), which discusses the significance of the press for the gender-specific dimension of consumption and the rise of 'female spheres'.[100] Jennifer Jones' *Sexing la Mode: Gender, Fashion and Commercial Culture in Old Regime France* (2004) examines how fashion was increasingly clearly defined as a female, urbane and superficial matter during the latter half of the eighteenth century.[101] *Att hasta mot undergången: anspråk, flyktighet, förställning i debatten om konsumtion i Sverige 1730–1830* (2015) by historian of ideas Leif Runefelt is a study of corresponding Swedish conditions and examines the attitudes of the press, literature and public debate in Sweden to luxury and consumption as well as their female preponderance.[102] In the anthology *Det svenska begäret. Sekler av lyxkonsumtion* (2015), edited by Paula von Wachenfeldt and Klas Nyberg, a number of researchers from various disciplines address the impact of luxury on Swedish culture in various periods; the subjects of discussion include various aspects of eighteenth-century luxury consumption.[103] Research projects focusing on eighteenth-century gender practices include the interdisciplinary project 'Early Modern Cultural History' at Uppsala University, which has, for example, resulted

97 Christine Adams, *A Taste for Comfort and Status. A Bourgeois Family in Eighteenth-Century France*, Pennsylvania 2000, p. 2.

98 Amanda Vickery, *The Gentleman's Daughter. Women's Lives in Georgian England*, New Haven (1998), 2003; Amanda Vickery, *Behind Closed Doors. At Home in Georgian England*, New Haven 2009.

99 *Gender, Taste and Material Culture in Britain and North America, 1700–1830*, John Styles and Amanda Vickery (ed.), *Studies in British Art* 17, New Haven and London 2006.

100 Erin Mackie, *Market à la Mode. Fashion, Commodity and Gender in The Tatler and The Spectator*, Baltimore 1997.

101 Jennifer Jones, *Sexing La Mode. Gender, Fashion and Commercial Culture in Old Regime France*, Oxford 2004.

102 Runefelt 2015.

103 *Det svenska begäret. Sekler av lyxkonsumtion*, Paula von Wachenfeldt and Klas Nyberg (ed.), Stockholm 2015.

in *Performing Herself: Everyday Practices and the Making of Gender in Early Modern Sweden* (2017), edited by Mikael Alm.[104]

One of the project's aims is to study how the culture of comfort is manifested in the Swedish country house environment in the light of this new and international research. In order to maintain the Swedish perspective, the active research into Swedish palaces and country houses has been of essential assistance – from Gösta Selling's *Svenska herrgårdshem under 1700-talet* (1937) to Bo Vahlne's *Frihetstidens inredningar på Stockholms slott. Om bekvämlighetens och skönhetens nivåer* (2012).[105] Another highly significant source has been Göran Ulväng's country manor research, not least his extensive works *Herrgårdarnas historia. Arbete, liv och bebyggelse på uppländska herrgårdar* (2008) and *Hus och gård i förändring. Uppländska herrgårdar, boställen och bondgårdar under 1700- och 1800-talens agrara revolution* (2004).[106] International manor house research that has also inspired this study includes Rainer Knapas' *Monrepos, Ludwig Heinrich Nicolay och hans värld i 1700-talets ryska Finland* (2003).[107]

There is, however, scant previous research into Näs Manor and the Wadenstierna family. The cultural-historical value of Näs is briefly addressed by Lars Sjöberg in his book *Svenska trähus* (2002) and in a few articles from the middle of the twentieth century: Bengt G. Söderberg, in *Slott och herresäten i Sverige* (1967); Karl Asplund, in *Fataburen* (1960) and Gunnar Mascoll Silfverstolpe, in *Svenska hem i ord och bilder* (1940).[108] Gustaf Näsström also draws attention to a few details from Näs in the cultural-historical review *Forna dagars Sverige* (1962).[109] The government official Carl Eric Wadenstierna is presented in Erik Fahlbeck's biography of Wadenstierna's

104 *Performing Herself. Everyday Practices and the Making of Gender in Early Modern Sweden*, Mikael Alm (ed.), Opuscula Historica Upsaliensia 53, Uppsala 2017.

105 Gösta Selling, *Svenska herrgårdshem under 1700-talet*, Stockholm (1937) 1991; Bo Vahlne, *Frihetstidens inredningar på Stockholms slott. Om bekvämlighetens och skönhetens nivåer*, Stockholm 2012. Selling claims that the representativeness was equally strong in eighteenth-century homes as in the seventeenth century, but that a type of integration of the functions of the reception rooms and the residential rooms (or *appartement de commodité*) occurred during the eighteenth century, p. 341.

106 Göran Ulväng, *Herrgårdarnas historia. Arbete, liv och bebyggelse på uppländska herrgårdar*, Uppsala 2008; Göran Ulväng, *Hus och gård i förändring. Uppländska herrgårdar, boställen och bondgårdar under 1700- och 1800-talens agrara revolution*, Hedemora 2004 [diss.].

107 Rainer Knapas, *Monrepos, Ludwig Heinrich Nicolay och hans värld i 1700-talets ryska Finland*, Stockholm 2003. Similar perspectives concerning Russian country house culture have also been discussed in Priscilla Roosevelt, *Life on the Russian Country Estate. A Social and Cultural History*, New Haven and London 1995.

108 Lars Sjöberg, *Svenska trähus*, Stockholm 2002; Bengt G. Söderberg, 'Näs', *Slott och herresäten i Sverige*, Malmö 1967; Karl Asplund, 'Näs i Rö', *Fataburen*, Nordiska museet, Stockholm 1960; Gunnar Mascoll Silfverstolpe, 'Näs i Roslagen. En gustaviansk herrgård' in *Svenska hem i ord och bilder*, issue 28, Stockholm 1940, pp. 1–8.

109 Gustaf Näsström, *Forna dagars Sverige* III, *Kulturhistorisk bilderbok om frihetstid och gustaviansk tid*, Stockholm 1962.

son-in-law *Lars August Mannerheim* (1969) and is also glimpsed in Hallesvik's article 'Partimotsättningarna vid 1771–72 års riksdag som bakgrund till Gustav III:s statskupp', in *Statsvetenskaplig tidskrift för politik – statistik – ekonomi* (1962).[110] Older sources that mention Wadenstierna include Anders Fryxell's *Berättelser ur svenska historien. Fyrationdeandra delen. Frihets-tidens sista år och revolutionen 1772* (1873) and Carl Gustaf Nordin's *Dagboksanteckningar för åren 1786–1792* (1868).[111]

To the table! Disposition of the study

A few cut-out silhouette pictures from the early 1780s show women at the court in Weimar, busily doing various activities at tables (Images 8–10). They are serving tea, writing letters or making lace. The pictures belonged to Johann Wolfgang von Goethe, an enthusiastic collector of silhouettes, and they provide insight into everyday life and social life at the cultural court. The silhouette as a genre of pictures was also an expression of a form of socialising at that time. As part of social life, silhouette cutting was an appreciated pastime undertaken by both amateurs and professionals. The women in the silhouette collection have been above all portrayed at tables, and the choice of table also conveys something about the depicted women. The detailed types of tables, dainty and slender in shape, were all adapted to the activities and working positions of the women – the height and width of the tea table differed from the measurements of the needlework table, and the lightweight writing table could easily be moved to the window for better light. At the tables, and via them, the women were able to express important skills and characteristics strongly associated with social and cultural status. For example, the woman brewing the tea elegantly handles the expensive utensils without tipping the tea cups over the table edge and without a quivering of the plumes in her hat. The serving of tea was additionally a social act accompanied by conversation and socialising. The interplay between objects, gestures and displays of behaviour presents a picture of a knowledgeable and cultivated person. The table plays a key part in this overall picture. The person who created the silhouettes must also have been seated at a table. The significance of the tables in various social, cultural and identity-building processes therefore occupies a central role in this study.

110 Erik Fahlbeck, *Lars August Mannerheim. Politiker. Justitieombudsman. Bruksägare. Jordbrukare*, Lund 1969; Stig Hallesvik, 'Partimotsättningarna vid 1771–72 års riksdag som bakgrund till Gustav III:s statskupp', *Statsvetenskaplig tidskrift för politik – statistik – ekonomi*, Lund 1962, pp. 383–405.

111 Anders Fryxell, *Berättelser ur svenska historien. Fyrationdeandra delen. Frihets-tidens sista år och revolutionen 1772*, Stockholm 1873, pp. 226–31; Carl Gustaf Nordin, *Dagboksanteckningar för åren 1786–1792*, Stockholm 1868.

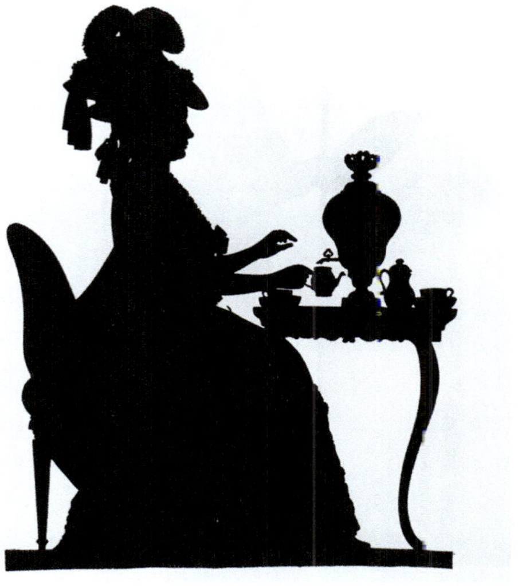

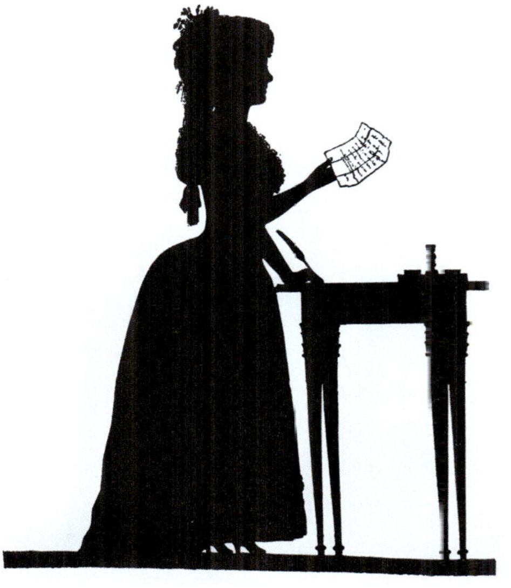

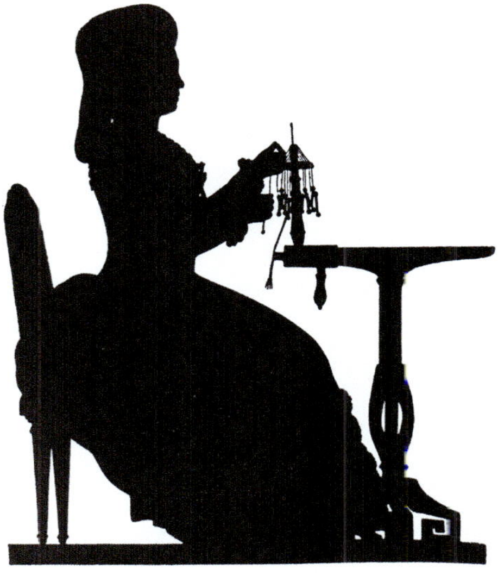

8–10. *At the Tea Table*, 30.5 × 23 cm; *Henriette von Knebel*, 24.6 × 17 cm; *Friederike Louise, princesse of Hessen-Darmstadt*, c. 1783, 25.6 × 17.8 cm. Ink on paper. From Anne Gabrisch, *Schattenbilder der Goethezeit*, Leipzig, 1966.

The comfort revolution of the eighteenth century became clearly linked to new types of furniture and new ways of furnishing rooms. Furniture became movable – mobile – as indicated in the Swedish word for furniture: *möbler*, from *mobilis* in Latin. An important aspect of the development of comfort was this new movability and flexibility in form and function that the home and its interiors now displayed. Seat furniture had already started to be developed in the late seventeenth century, while many new types of tables were launched in above all the eighteenth century. In contrast with the heavy sofas and armchairs, these small, lightweight tables, designed to be easily lifted or rolled on castors, characterised the new comfort. There were *table courante* and *table volante* – tables that 'ran' or 'flew' – that could rapidly meet all the conceivable needs of the era.[112] In Pehr Nordquist's painting *Caffe-Beslaget* from 1799 (Image 89), the women are saved from being caught drinking the forbidden coffee thanks to the lightweight and easily moveable small table that a woman hastily moves away from the scene when the law enforcers come knocking.

The new, dainty tables were associated with the modern woman for whom they had been designed and symbolised a new lifestyle, so comfortable that the woman virtually never had to leave her various tables. In 1731, *Sedolärande Mercurius* portrays the fashionable woman's day as entirely connected to the tables, from the morning's dressing table – 'where they had sufficient work until midday' – to the guests at the laid dinner table. 'After they had eaten, the coffee table appears, the visits commence, then the games table, the discourses are droll.'[113]

Dressing tables, coffee tables and games tables could be associated with pastimes and indolence, whereas other types of tables confirmed more duty-bound and normative ideals expected of women. Above all, tables for sewing and other needlework were associated with diligence and domestic virtues. Small, decorative writing tables for women were suitable for the widespread letter-writing culture but perhaps also reflect the era's uncertain attitude to women's education. The wealth of different tables that were designed in the eighteenth century for the female consumer met needs but also contributed to shape a changed role for women and in turn created new needs. Many specialised accoutrements were offered to go with the tables. They were not only marketed as '*kommoditeter*' (*commodités*, for comfort) but as necessities and ranged from specially designed candleholders to powder compacts and artistic ink pots.

The book follows the women at some of these tables. Carl Eric Wadenstierna is likely to have spent a large part of his professional and private life at various tables,

112 Compare the modern, wide dresses, a style called a *robe volante*, of the 1730s, which refer to the same comfortable and easy lifestyle, even though the convention was to wear a rigid corset under the loose garment.

113 *Sedolärande Mercurius*, II, No. 23, 4 May 1731.

but when he commissioned the portraits of himself and his wives, he arranged for the women to be depicted at these items of furniture. In the suite of paintings that Pehr Hilleström created in conjunction with the Wadenstierna family's relocation to the Näs estate, the women are also the figures positioned at sewing tables, ironing tables and coffee tables. The decision to focus this study on the women at the tables, as examples of the eighteenth-century culture of comfort, has been a conscious way to limit the extensive material.

Although the first chapter, 'Carl Eric Wadenstierna and Näs Manor', places Wadenstierna himself centre stage, the chapter also has the key aim of providing a more general background to the home and life at Näs. Here, matters concerning the floor plan, functions and logistics of the building are discussed – which are of considerable significance for the aspects of comfort that the subsequent sections focus on. This introductory presentation of the manor and its surroundings also paints a general picture of family life, social life and guests at Näs, as well as of its interiors and collections of pictures and books, with the aim of providing the reader with a more cohesive background in preparation for the subsequent chapters' more specific and detailed themes, in which the interest is also directed at Wadenstierna's wives and daughters.

The second chapter, 'At the sewing table', uses Niclas Lafrensen's portrait of Wadenstierna's first wife, Jacobina Sophia Psilanderhielm, as a starting point. Based on the portrait, the discussion examines how the eighteenth-century female ideal was associated with conceptions of fashionable taste and consumption. Additionally, Pehr Hilleström's paintings at Näs, in which the motifs primarily centre on the production and care of textiles, become the subject of Wadenstierna's own positioning in the era's debate on luxury and comfort. Wadenstierna's second wife, Fredrica Carleson, was portrayed at a different type of table and is the point of departure for the third chapter, 'At the writing table'. The diminutive desk was an example of the era's desirable 'female furniture', which both encouraged and limited women's writing activities. The disposition of the rooms at Näs and the positioning of the family's various pieces of furniture for writing reflect the view on male and female roles and spheres in the home.

The fourth chapter, 'At the dressing table', highlights the table that perhaps most clearly connects the eighteenth-century image of women to the attitude to luxury, consumption and comfort. The art of portraiture repeatedly depicted women at dressing tables – yet, Wadenstierna's Näs lacked these portraits and what were normally classed as dressing tables. What did this absence signal and how was it compensated for? Does the lack of dressing tables in Swedish portraiture in general and at Wadenstierna's country house in particular tell us something about Swedish identity in the eighteenth century?

The fifth chapter, 'At the games tables', is based on one of the paintings by Pehr Hilleström that hung on the walls at Näs. A women is dealing cards on the pull-out leaf of a chest of drawers. This temporary arrangement shows how various games became a constantly recurring activity in everyday life and society in the eighteenth century. Upper-class homes were adapted, in terms of their floor plans and furniture, to the growing culture of playing games. There were several games tables at Näs, but the tables specially designated for different games were also associated with various forms of status, which also assigned men and women separate roles and spheres. Here, the chapter examines how the eighteenth century's visual culture expresses these shifting norms and values in general and how they relate to pictures and household items at Näs in particular.

The final chapter, 'At the coffee table', discusses the significance of coffee and tableware as established symbols of the elite's luxury consumption in relation to the aspects of comfort of the new luxury. The issue of how, where, when and by whom coffee (or tea) was drunk, was circumscribed by a series of social and cultural codes, especially important at a time when both the beverages and their vessels became increasingly widespread '*commodités*'.

Social life therefore largely took place at various types of tables. The residential rooms at Näs contained at least thirty-six different tables during the Gustavian era. In addition, there were various work tables in the kitchen wing, which are not mentioned in Wadenstierna's estate inventory.[114] There is only scope to include a few of all these tables in this study. The dining room's three dining tables with double leaves and the sideboards fixed to the wall are not discussed here.[115]

The next chapter will now open the door to Carl Eric Wadenstierna's Näs – to the environment where he envisaged that his family and friends would gather. And in the subsequent chapters we make our way, together with the women in the family, between some of the manor's tables that symbolised and enabled the new age of comfort.

114 Riksarkivet, Näs Silverstolpeska arkivet, Personarkiven, vol. 60, Carl Eric Wadenstierna (1723–1787).

115 To mitigate this omission, readers can for example read about the dining table that author Mary Wollstonecraft sighs heavily about during her visit to Sweden in 1796; Mary Wollstonecraft, *Letters Written during a Short Residence in Sweden, Norway and Denmark*, 1796, Oxford 2009, 'Letter II'.

1. Carl Eric Wadenstierna and Näs Manor

Abstract
The first chapter places the owner of Näs Manor in the foreground, the Gustavian politician Carl Eric Wadenstierna. The chapter also provides a more general background to the home and life at Näs. Here, questions are raised about the building's planning, functions and logistics – of great importance for the aspects that the continued study revolves around. This introductory presentation of the manor and its surroundings also draws a general picture of family life at Näs, as well as of its interiors, pictures and book collections – in order to give the reader a coherent background for the more specific and detailed themes of the following chapters. In these the interest is also directed to Wadenstierna's wives and two daughters.

Keywords: manor house, home and garden, consumption, domestic life, furnishing

In the early 1770s, Niclas Lafrensen painted three portraits of Carl Eric Wadenstierna and his two wives, Jacobina Sophia Psilanderhielm and Fredrica Carleson. Wadenstierna is seated in the middle and is looking up from a book that he has just been reading. His signet ring with its red gemstone is visible on his splayed little finger, and the diamonds of the Royal Order of the Polar Star sparkle next to his open book.[1] The three objects at the centre of the picture summarise Wadenstierna's social position – the book as a symbol of cultivation, the royal order as proof of a meritorious career and the signet ring to denote that he was a member of the nobility. Dressed in velvet, decorated with lace and well-powdered, he appears successful with an esteemed position in society. But the pictures of the women also play a key part in the context. All three portraits were commissioned at the same time, and together they convey that domestic happiness and affectionate family

1 The ring bearing Wadenstierna's shield was intended for signing letters and documents and conveyed power and position. The estate inventory drawn up after Wadenstierna's death in 1787 includes 'One Royal Order of the Polar Star with diamonds'. Riksarkivet, Näs Silverstolpeska arkivet, Personarkiven, vol. 60, Carl Eric Wadenstierna (1723–1787). The order with precious stones occupies a special position and was awarded to a person who had performed an important personal service for the king or the royal family.

Brown, C., *Comfortable Everyday Life at the Swedish Eighteenth-Century Näs Manor*.
Taylor & Francis Group, 2024
DOI 10.5117/9789048562374_CH01

connections were also important components in the identity that is manifested here. Both the posthumous portrait of Wadenstierna's first wife, Jacobina, and the picture of his wife at the time, Fredrica, depict pleasant everyday home life. At that time, this side of life had become a self-evident part of social identity. We will follow various paths into this world. Carl Eric Wadenstierna dominates this first chapter, while Jacobina Sophia Psilanderhielm and Fredrica Carleson emerge more clearly in the subsequent ones. Niclas Lafrensen's three portraits will thereby constitute a recurring theme throughout the book.

Wadenstierna came from a family of clergymen in Uppland Province north of Stockholm. His paternal grandfather, Lars Wadensteen, was a deputy judge at the Svea Court of Appeal and was knighted by Karl XII in 1702.[2] During the Age of Liberty, Carl Eric Wadenstierna demonstrated pronounced skill in navigating the era's political disputes and was acknowledged as both a quick-thinking and argumentative politician and a thoughtful advocate of reform. But his path to becoming a *krigsråd*, senior government official for military matters, and state secretary for defence and war matters in the 1760s and 1770s had been preceded by long years of study and a short childhood. He was orphaned at the age of five and sent as a student to the university of Uppsala three years later. His mother Charlotta Strömner died in conjunction with the birth of her youngest son Per in 1725, and his father, Thomas Wadenstierna, a clerk at the Svea Court of Appeal, died three years later. They left five sons aged from three to twelve for relatives to look after, and studies at an early age became a solution to many practical problems. Carl Eric Wadenstierna's studies in Uppsala and Lund occupied him for thirteen years before the position of temporary clerk at the war office in Stockholm became available to him in 1743.

In the capital, Wadenstierna soon got involved in politics. As a young secretary at the office of the court of law, he found himself in the shadow of the royal couple's attempted coup in 1756, but he emerged through his participation in the endeavours to find a solution that was tolerably favourable for the royal family, and in doing so he navigated between the contending parties.[3] In one of his publications, he later described his situation as 'standing between two party fires, afraid of burning oneself on either'.[4] When Wadenstierna was awarded the Royal Order of the Polar Star in 1767, this was a confirmation of his dutifulness in this and other political

2 *Matrikel öfwer Swea Rikes Ridderskap och Adel, Uppå Des begäran wid 1751. års Riks=Dag, Utgifwen med Historiska och Genealogiska Anmärkningar af Anders Ant, von Stiernman*, II. Stockholm 1755, p. 1017.

3 Through an unsuccessful coup, King Adolf Fredrik and Queen Lovisa Ulrika tried to reinstate the absolute monarchy, which only resulted in continued discord between the two parliamentary parties: Hattarna (the Hats) and Mössorna (the Caps). Wadenstierna summarised his thoughts on the divided party conflicts in his publication *Swar uppå et Betydeligt Bref ifrån En Wän i Stockholm*, Gothenburg 1769.

4 Carl Eric Wadenstierna, *Bref Ifrån En Opartisk Swensk*, Stockholm 1769, p. 1.

storms. Of significance in this context was Wadenstierna's role in the Hat party (Hattarna) in parliament (the Riksdag), which had promised King Adolf Fredrik support to reinstate the monarchy in connection with the coming session of the Riksdag. The royal bribe that Wadenstierna received in 1768 was to guarantee that he and his fellow party members would not stand in the way of the plans. But the king's strategic 'inactivity', to refuse to reign until the party conflicts had been resolved, did not change the situation.[5]

Wadenstierna's position as an increasingly prominent government official was, however, clarified at the following parliamentary sessions of the Riksdag in 1769 and 1771, where as a member of *sekreta utskottet* (literally, the secret committee) he gained additional political influence. At the time of Gustaf III's coup in 1772, Wadenstierna gave the king his support and was generally regarded as knowledgeable and skilled, but also useful in the government as he understood how to perceptively decipher the king's political dealings.[6] In the regime change that followed, Wadenstierna stood out in the House of Nobility as one of the more liberal ministers who was willing to compromise but who also appeared as both resourceful and persistent. When the freedom of the press was threatened, Wadenstierna stated: 'Shouting about freedom of the press while drawing up statutes that restrict it, or on fiscal grounds charging an outspoken citizen, who tells the truth, that is to neglect the right of the people, which among other things consists of obtaining information.'[7] He personally ensured that all minutes from the House of Nobility's negotiations were printed. In 1781, Wadenstierna resigned from his position, which was partly a result of an increasingly critical attitude towards the king and the influence of former fellow party members who gradually adopted strong positions in the opposition, not least the former party leader, Count Axel von Fersen the Elder.[8] The turbulent session of the Riksdag in 1786 further strengthened the opposition. In 1787, shortly after New Year, Wadenstierna died at the age of 64, 'suddenly of a stroke'.[9] City commissioner Rutger Fredrik Hochschild described him in his memoirs as knowledgeable and experienced – and wealthy. The information about the monetary sum of 60,000 riksdaler in Wadenstierna's estate after his death was probably another knowing reference to the royal bribe that Wadenstierna had received twenty years earlier.[10]

5 *Historiska handlingar. Till trycket befordrade av Kong. Samfundet för utgifvande af handskrifter rörande Skandinafviens historia*, Vol. 6, *Dagboksanteckningar för åren 1786–1792, af Carl Gustaf Nordin*, Stockholm 1868, p. 255.

6 *Hemliga handlingar* 1822, vol. 2, p. 175.

7 *Strödda handlingar* 1822, p. 75.

8 *Dagligt Allehanda*, 21 September 1781.

9 Hochschild 1908, vol. 1, p. 105.

10 Ibid.

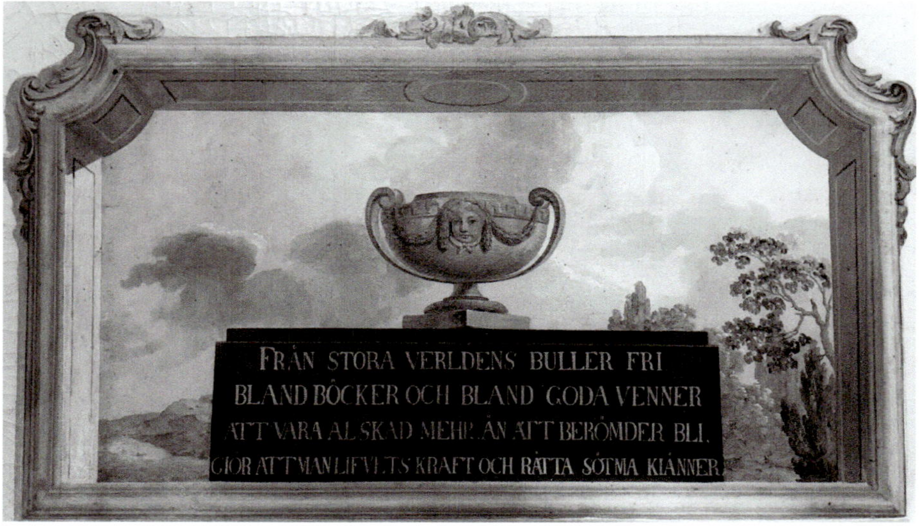

11. One of five overdoor decorations in the entrance hall at Näs, from about 1775. Unknown artist, oil on canvas. Private ownership.

Even though the sources tell us about Wadenstierna in his role as a government official, the details about his life outside of politics are markedly more limited. But in the choices he made, such as acquiring the country estate of Näs in Uppland Province north of Stockholm, or his purchases of paintings by the artist Hilleström and furniture by the cabinetmaker Haupt, we glimpse his interests and the contours of the everyday life that he created for himself and his family. It is likely that the era's political ideas, as well as Wadenstierna's opinions on consumption, luxury and comfort, also played a key part in his private life. In the light of these ideas and the environment that took shape at Näs, the portraits of him and his family also gain their meaning. How the family allowed themselves to be presented through the portraits clearly relates to their social role and material and cultural ambitions. The portraits, in constant interplay with the environment for which they were intended, thereby constitute a recurring point of reference in the following chapters.

The five painted overdoor decorations that adorned – and still adorn – the entrance hall at Näs can also be regarded as a complement to the family pictures (Image 11). The paintings' inscriptions tell us about the ideal existence in their shared country home. On archaic landscape backgrounds, urns are depicted in the style of the artists Johan Pasch or Lars Bolander, at the base of which we find the following verses (in translation):

> You then possess the pinnacle of earthly happiness
> when favourable wind steers your ship to the right harbour,

when innocence settles in your soul,
and sows pleasures, flowers and tranquillity in your path.

Do not take on too much but above all do good,
with some friends live contentedly in your little cabin,
a happy life will then be humanity's fate,
divine providence will protect you from regret every day.

Do not let envy, grudges touch your mind,
nor hate, nor favour take away your calm,
let the well-being of your fellow humans guide your soul
to joy, that good may come to them.

Free of the noise of the wider world,
among books and among good friends,
to be loved more, rather than become famous,
enables you to feel the force of life and right sweetness.

With your wife, children and king go contented to the grave,
a sure depiction of a happy life,
being respectful of divine providence and living virtuously,
makes the burden of life light and is humankind's greatest pleasure.

It is not known who painted the illusorily carved words on the heavy stone foundations, nor who originally wrote the text. But it does not seem unreasonable to imagine that it was Carl Eric Wadenstierna himself.[11] Phrases about a wife and children hint that this is a father's voice being heard – Wadenstierna's own or through a borrowed quote. Family, guests and servants would have encountered these words that praised the unassuming virtues and love for one's fellow humans. Christian, Rousseauian and physiocratic thinking echoes in the phrases about family life and the little cabin in nature's enclosure. Far from the city's noise and vain endeavours, nature imparts strength and repose, but also cultivated socialising in the company of good friends. Life at Näs is portrayed as a pastoral idyll in accordance with ancient ideals, a place for recreation and contemplation. This is where the government official was to withdraw from the duties of public life and seek rest and the simple pleasures of country life.

The verses at Näs seem to confirm what Lafrensen's portraits express, which were commissioned at the time when the inscriptions were created. The man is

11 Asplund, Karl, 'Näs i Rö', *Fataburen*, Nordiska Museet, Stockholm 1960, pp. 14–5.

enjoying his *otium* with his book, the women with their domestic crafts and friendly letters.[12] The moss-covered bases of the entrance hall's overdoor decorations seem to vouch for these eternal values and ideals, which were to be managed and last through the generations of owners who stepped over the thresholds of Näs and whose portraits were hung on its walls over time.

Näs and country life as ideal

The lines of life wisdom on the overdoor decorations had unquestionably been preceded by years of hard work and deep sorrows for Wadenstierna. He had lost both a daughter and a wife, and his working life had been permeated by political controversies in the ongoing party conflicts. After the death of his wife Jacobina Psilanderhielm in 1768, he writes a letter with rules of life to his two remaining daughters, Sophia and Carolina, as guidance for the uncertain future. As a foretaste of the words in the entrance hall at Näs, he concludes by urging them to harness the time they are given and warmly manage it well: 'Let virtue, honour and humanity adorn your life as people's worth does not consist of living for a long time but is measured by the way in which their lifetime is used.'[13] The early 1770s brought turning points, both privately and professionally. In the spring of 1770, Wadenstierna entered into a new marriage, with Fredrica Carleson, the daughter of the former president of the board of trade Edvard Carleson. And King Gustaf III's coup in 1772 temporarily halted the arduous party politics. The acquisition of Näs in 1773 became the start of a new chapter for the Wadenstierna family.

Näs is conveniently located 50 km from the capital city and is particularly beautifully nestled in the rolling countryside of the Roslagen area on a small peninsula in Lake Sparren. The opportunity of leaving city life in the summer half of the year was an upper-class privilege associated with the nobility's inherited manors and country houses and appurtenant estates. The responsibility for these estates was counterbalanced by the temporary freedom from the professional and social responsibilities of city life. Government and official duties, royal court services, mandatory meetings or duty-bound visits were all contrasted by the months in the countryside that also included a certain degree of freedom from ever-present social control and an associated incessant manifestation and maintenance of hierarchies. Country life was admittedly not the same as a secluded private life in the modern

12 The Latin *otium* was the antique word that summarised freedom from duties and an opportunity for relaxation and pleasure, but also cultivated interests.

13 Riksarkivet, Näs Silverstolpeska arkivet, Personarkiven, vol. 60, Carl Eric Wadenstierna (1723–1787).

sense.[14] The social scene also existed here, although the audience could be smaller, more sporadic and temporarily varied. The hierarchical attitude also governed life at the manor. Yet, life outside of the city, as it is today, was enveloped by notions of freedom and tranquillity. It was thought to be imbued with simplicity as a contrast to the city's multifaceted nature and associated complications.

In the eighteenth century, this idealised 'freedom' was already linked to relaxation and comfort, and by extension also to salubrity and health. The opposite perception of the city as dirty and unhealthy was perhaps more rooted in a concrete reality, especially during the warm summer months when water supplies and alleys were malodorous and diseases spread easily.[15] Newspapers of the era depicted life in the country as clean and genuine. 'Now that we are in the countryside, we finally own ourselves: Now we live anew, and equate ourselves with kings, as we have abandoned the tiring, the worrying things that one values in the city.'[16] However, country living as a way of self-fulfilment was also connected with materialistic financial status. Those who had not inherited their country property and estate had to buy themselves this position. In 1773, Wadenstierna was a wealthy man, but lacked a family manor. Although the overdoor decorations spoke of unassuming virtues, the acquisition of Näs was nevertheless a conspicuous manifestation of his ability to invest and to express taste, cultivation and contacts through the choices he made, probably in consultation with his family.

Näs appeared to be a symbol of idyllic country life. The author Jonas Carl Linnerhielm, acquainted with Wadenstierna since his years as a clerk at the war office in the 1770s, provides a lyrical description of the place during one of his trips in the early nineteenth century:

> When a minor road turned off from the main road and the Näs estate commenced, an avenue of Swedish whitebeams also began; this, if I may say so, [is a] domestic tree that thrives around farmers' unaffected dwellings, rarely however as forest trees, and with its pale greenery it contrasts the stronger colours of other trees. Over alternating hills and valleys, this avenue ran between leafy lands with views of well-cultivated fields, until it turned off by a relatively extensive garden, of which the entrance, matching the working methods used there, was composed of spades. The main building and the wings, not large, and one storey, possess

14 Runefelt, Leif, *Att hasta mot undergången: anspråk, flyktighet, förställning i debatten om konsumtion i Sverige 1730–1830*, Lund 2015, pp. 287–288 and Brown, Carolina, 'Bilder, sällskapsliv och herrgårdskultur. Maskeradporträtt, silhuetter och andra bilder från 1700-talets Tista', *Historisk Tidskrift för Finland*, årg. 98, 2013:2, Helsinki 2013, p. 190.

15 Per Anders Fogelström, 'Stockholms oordentligheter', *Yppighet och armod i 1700-talets Stockholm, Sankt Eriks årsbok*, Stockholm 1994, pp. 139–56.

16 [C.C. Gjörwell], *Fruntimmers Tidningar*, II, Stockholm 1772, p. 7.

> in their high location a view that is as tranquil as it is beautiful over meadows and groves as well as Lake Sparren, which curves in narrow bays. One of the wings contains a billiard room and a book collection. Adjacent to this building, down steps to a lower level on the slope of the hill or mound, one comes to a living folly made of aspen. The tranquillity within their trembling leaves was an easy reminder that this property is a retreat from the noise of the world for its former owner, the deceased state secretary Wadenstierna, whom my memory gratefully honoured, while we now enjoy the favour of the former's enlightened son-in-law.[17]

Linnerhielm's emphasis on the landscape and the manor's interplay with its natural surroundings was undeniably typical for that era, but it additionally highlights the motives that were also important in Wadenstierna's time in the early 1770s. The cultivated natural landscape extends from the well-kept fields to the avenue's 'domestic' Swedish whitebeams. The garden's folly made of aspen serves as a companion to the unassuming small manor house. The mention of the cultivated pleasures of the enlightened country nobleman – the library and billiards – contributed to the picture of privileged country life. Näs was the ideal, pre-Romantic summer residence but also equally reflected the era's interest in estate management, farming and forestry.

The Näs estate did not constitute a grand country house environment but was nonetheless a considerable investment encompassing several nearby farms and a large number of crofts pertaining to it. With roots in the sixteenth century and donated by King Gustaf II Adolf to the mayor of Stockholm, Näs had changed hands many times. During the eighteenth century, the estate had eight owners before Wadenstierna purchased it in 1773 from Lieutenant Colonel Carl Örnsköld for the sum of 169,000 daler copper coins.[18] Additional investments expanded the estate in the following years. At the end of the 1780s, the estate comprised ten *mantal* (units for measuring the size and productivity of farming land), of which seven were located in Rö Parish, where the Ticksta Manor farm and the Risby and Melby farms were among the largest. The estate inventory drawn up after Wadenstierna's death in 1787 conveys the extent and assets of the estate's activities. As part of the Swedish allotment system that served to keep Sweden supplied with a trained army at all times, *rusthåll* were farms that were able to support a horseman, horse and equipment in exchange for exemption from tax. The *rusthåll* on the Näs estate included six horses, eleven draught oxen, twenty cows, five bulls, nine 'swine',

17 Jonas Carl Linnerhielm, *Bref under senare resor i Sverige*, Stockholm 1816, p. 148.

18 Norrtälje Municipality's *Kulturmiljöutredning* No. 18, Norrtälje 2016; Yngve Berzén, *Sveriges bebyggelse, Stockholms län*, part III, Uddevalla 1952.

turkeys, geese, duck and hens. At Ticksta, in addition to horses, oxen, pigs and geese, they also kept 115 Spanish sheep. Alongside the animal husbandry, crop farming constituted the basis of the estate's finances, and the granaries contained barrels of wheat, rye, barley, oats, peas and 'Egyptian barley'. The store of what was known as *'ränte korn'* (literally, interest barley), as a form of payment by the estate's tenant farmers, was particularly significant. There was plenty of farming equipment, but there were also tools for fishing, smithwork and gardening. Furthermore, the estate had the use of its own mill. Wadenstierna's interest in agriculture is also revealed by his library. Books about animal husbandry and farming were purchased in the same year that the property was acquired.[19]

When Wadenstierna took over Näs, the estate had a manager, four farmhands, three maids and a group of farm workers who were registered as living at the location. Additions over the years comprised farm foremen for both Näs and Ticksta Manor farm, a gardener and two garden hands, a female head housekeeper and a number of farm and stable hands; at the end of the eighteenth century there were also six house and kitchen maids and nine barn maids.[20] In addition, the family had its own personal servants in the house, including a maid of higher status called a *jungfru* and a footman who moved together with the family between their seasonal homes. The loyalty of the servants was highly valued and was a key measure of the standard and status of the household as well as the benevolence of their masters and mistresses.[21] Wadenstierna's will particularly emphasises the farm foremen at Näs and Ticksta and 'Manservant Wel', who had all served loyally for several years and therefore had to be remembered and compensated after the death of their master.

The materialistic figures that delimited life at Näs – the number of kilometres from the capital; the number of units of farming land; the number of tenant farmers; the number of horses, oxen, pigs and sheep; the number of carts and carriages; the number of employees and the number of years they had served – were also measures of the comfort of good country life. The yield of the lands and farms could only be enjoyed through the loyal daily work of employees and subordinates. And the servant bell system that was installed in the newly built manor house was to guarantee the comfort that depended on the constant readiness of this staff.

19 Wadenstierna's estate inventory: Riksarkivet, Näs Silverstolpeska arkivet, Personarkiven, vol. 60, Carl Eric Wadenstierna (1723–1787).

20 According to the list of employees in 1795, when Wadenstierna's daughter Sophia had taken over Näs, six of the maids were house and kitchen maids and nine were barn maids (Riksarkivet, Näs Silverstolpeska arkivet, Gårdsarkivet, Äldre kassaböcker [Old cash books]).

21 Complaints about disobedient and bad servants were a recurring theme in letters, diaries and newspapers; 'Bref ifrån en Landsort om Tjenstefolk', *Hushållnings Journal*, Stockholm September 1777, pp. 476–77.

Comfortable everyday life

Comfort also involved the floor plans of manor houses. Fewer and smaller rooms, often in single-storey buildings, created intimacy and accessibility. The large number of small manor houses that were built between 1750 and the 1780s were also to a greater degree intended to be used as more or less permanent homes.[22] Fortification officer and architect Carl Wijnblad's published exemplary drawings for manor houses in 1755–6 played a key part as models for many of these new builds. Wijnblad further developed architect Carl Hårleman's French-inspired construction ideals, but he introduced a clearer emphasis on function and small-scale comfort in the various floor plans that he proposed.[23] Wijnblad died in 1768, but his exemplary drawings continued to characterise central-Swedish manor house construction for a long time and remained highly topical when Carl Eric Wadenstierna was planning to construct a new main building on the Näs estate in the early 1770s.

A map of Näs from 1748 shows the lack of a main building, although two wing buildings clearly mark its location (Image 13). Nonetheless, there was probably some kind of main building on the site when Wadenstierna purchased the estate because an insurance application from 1817 states that the main building was *rebuilt* between 1773 and 1774.[24] Wadenstierna's role as the commissioner of the construction of Näs has been pointed out in the sources and indicates that whatever had been on the site was fundamentally reworked. This possibly explains why no architect's name was linked to the new Näs. However, Wijnblad emphasises that the purpose of his drawings is to facilitate the construction of country properties: 'Architects are now rarely deployed for the construction of buildings in the countryside, and instead most of such work is assigned to craftsmen and their journeymen.'[25] Approximate adaptations according to Wijnblad's models also seem to have formed the basis of what was actually constructed. The exterior of the new main building has several similarities with Wijnblad's manor houses. The rectangular single-storey timber building – just over 20 metres long and 10 metres wide – with wooden cladding and oil-painted in a pale colour, rested on a stone cellar foundation and was shaded by a wood-shingle mansard roof with a sheet-metal ridge cap. The entrance with hewn sandstone steps was accentuated with a simple fronton that was framed by

22 Ulväng, Göran, *Herrgårdarnas historia. Arbete, liv och bebyggelse på uppländska herrgårdar*, Uppsala 2008, p. 186.

23 Carl Wijnblad, *Ritningar på fyratio wåningshus af sten och trettio af träd samt åtskilliga lusthus etc.* Stockholm 1755 and *Ytterligare tillökning af Ritningar på wåningshus sextio af sten och tjugu af träd etc.* Stockholm 1756.

24 Extract from insurance application No. 10992, 1817. Uppland, Sjuhundra hd, Rö sn, Näs, Nordiska museet.

25 Wijnblad 1755, p. B3.

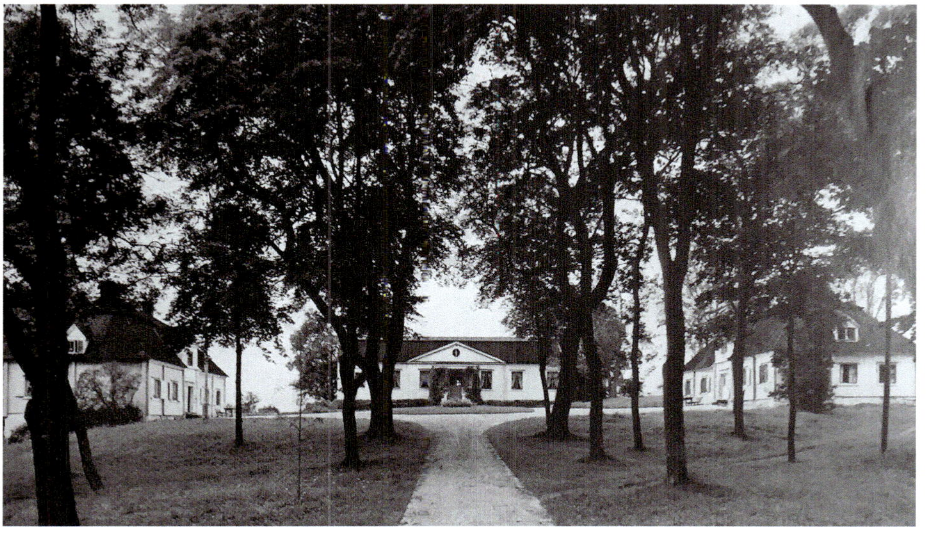

12. View of Näs Manor, from Gunnar Mascoll Silfverstolpe, 'Näs i Roslagen. En gustaviansk herrgård', *Svenska hem i ord och bilder*, no. 28, 1940, pp. 1–8.

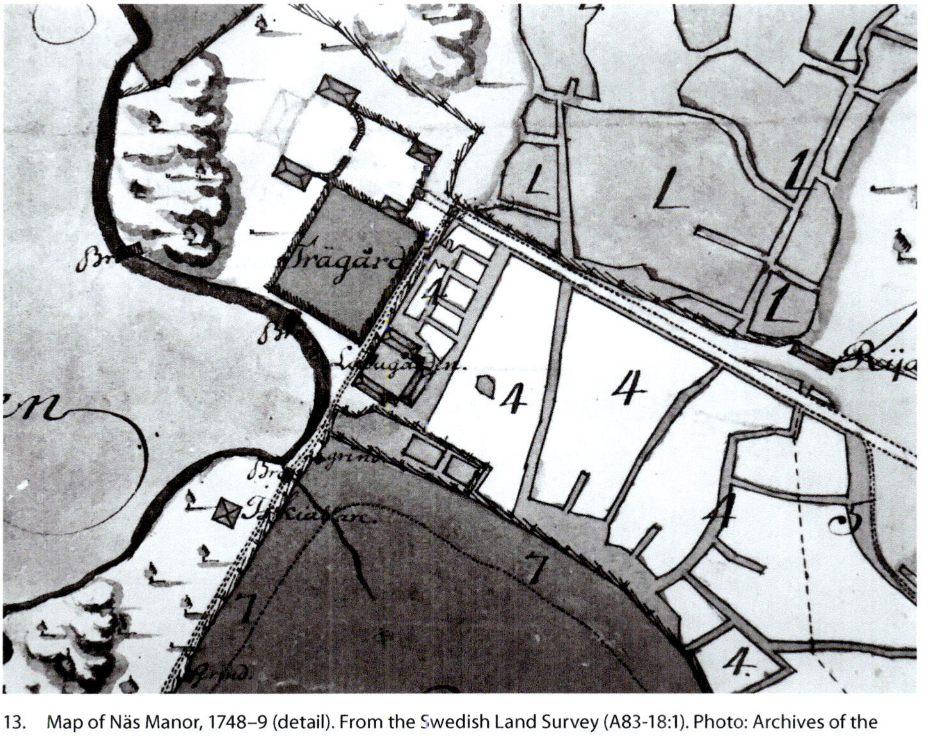

13. Map of Näs Manor, 1748–9 (detail). From the Swedish Land Survey (A83-18:1). Photo: Archives of the Nordic Museum, Stockholm.

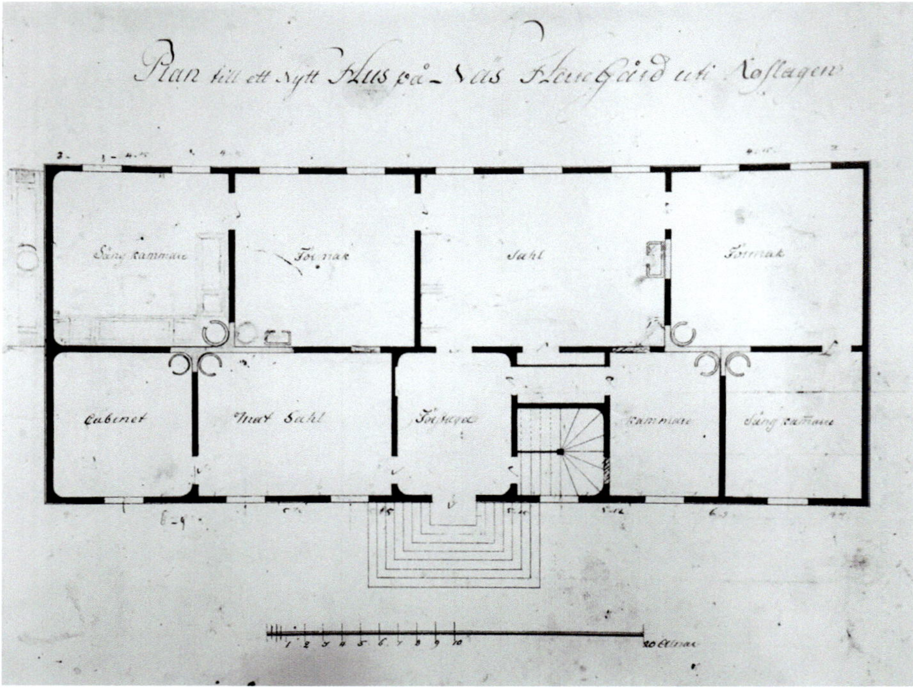

14. *Floor Plan for a New House at Näs Manor in Roslagen*, early 1770s. Photo: Archives of the Nordic Museum, Stockholm.

three symmetrically positioned windows in a row on each side. The long façade facing the lake with its row of nine windows, characterised the enfilade of reception rooms concealed within. The exterior also harmonised with the two remaining free-standing wings, which maintained their older style with their high hip roofs and marked avant-corps. The northern kitchen wing was probably built in the late seventeenth century, along with the farmhand's cottage behind it, while the southern wing is likely to have been built somewhat later, during the first few decades of the eighteenth century.[26]

The preserved floor plan for 'a new house at Näs Manor in Roslagen' largely follows Wijnblad's proposals based on modified French models. The plan only comprises eight rooms and follows the prevalent tradition with a centrally positioned entrance hall that opens out into a large dining room ('Sahl') in the heart of the enfilade of reception rooms and from which a gentleman's suite and a lady's suite are accessed, one on each side. These rooms are positioned in an enfilade towards the western garden side with a view of the lake, while the more everyday rooms face

26 Norrtälje Municipality's *Kulturmiljöutredning* No. 18, Norrtälje 2016.

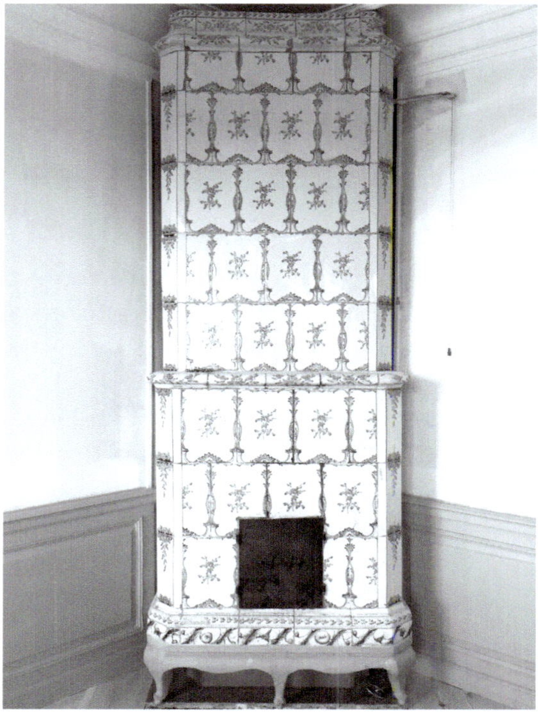

15. Tiled stove in the dining room at Näs, *c.* 1775.

the eastern side, where the proximity to the kitchen wing and servants' quarters was a practical aspect. The 'cabinet' of the lady of the house was a room positioned in the south-east of the building, which was also for convenience as her activities at writing tables, sewing tables and dressing tables required plenty of daylight.[27] In Hårleman's and many of Wijnblad's buildings, the utility rooms were often on the ground floor, but in the single-storey building at Näs, the residential rooms were on this floor, directly above the low cellar, and many domestic functions were therefore located in the free-standing kitchen wing. The floor plan also shows an additional dining room positioned west of the entrance hall, which was typical of Wijnblad's designs. This was also a pragmatic solution as the food could be quickly transferred from the kitchen wing building and served hot at the same time as giving the diners peace and quiet to eat at a distance from the activity of the servants and any cooking odours from the kitchen. A doorway between the dining room and the drawing room also shows its connection with the reception rooms. To the

27 The fact that this position of convenience was an established convention is seen in Gunhild Eriksdotter's description of the floor plan for Skokloster Castle, where the room of the countess had been purposely placed in the south-east section to offer the best possible lighting conditions, *Bebyggelsehistorisk tidskrift*, No. 66, 2013, p. 13.

right of the entrance hall, a staircase leads up to the attic, where two guest rooms had been created by the gables on each side of the large unfurnished attic space.

All the rooms had painted floors, plastered ceilings and walls clad with dado panelling and woven fabric wallpapers, painted using oil paint and embellished with painted borders and ornamentation. Single doors, featuring a raised and fielded panel with a bolection mould surround, connected the rooms, and all the rooms were equipped with elegant, patterned tiled stoves.[28] In 1775, the choice of the new efficient tiled stoves showed that comfort was prioritised, but they were also an expression of progressive modernity. In many upper-class homes, the open fireplace was preserved in the dining room ('Sahl') to emphasise the importance of the room, but at Näs it was replaced with a large tiled stove (Image 15).[29] Similarly, expressions of class such as double doors, parquet flooring or more lavish wall coverings were not chosen for the enfilade of reception rooms. It is likely that Näs was built using local materials and by local craftsmen, which was often also the case among the wealthier estate owners.[30] Simplicity and thrift were virtues, and ostentatious luxury was not strived for, especially not in country homes.[31] The reception rooms were certainly larger, although their fixed fittings did not make them particularly distinctive. Instead, the furnishings of these reception rooms are what demonstrated their rank, in the same way that art and valuable personal belongings also had their place in these rooms.

It was natural that furniture for socialising and gatherings mainly dominated the reception rooms. The gentleman's and lady's respective drawing rooms above all contained comfortable sofas and other seat furniture. 'The gentleman's drawing room' against the north gable end wall included a sofa and fifteen chairs but also a mahogany chest of drawers for clothing and two writing tables – one made of mahogany and the other of walnut. The largest sofa, with eight complementing chairs, stood in 'the lady's drawing room'.[32] Both drawing rooms were characterised by expensive mirrors, as well as curtains and upholstery in the same fabric. The lady's drawing room also contained two chandeliers and a large potpourri urn made by the Marieberg factory in Stockholm. The suite of rooms concluded with the large bedchamber, richly furnished to fulfil many functions and equipped in upper-class style with chandeliers, potpourri urns, curtains and carpet. The bedchamber and the adjacent large drawing room were specially designed for

28 Extract from insurance application No. 10992, 1817.

29 Prytz, Cristina and Stobart, Jon, 'Comfort in English and Swedish country houses, c. 1760–1820', *Social History*, 43, nr 2, London, p. 241.

30 Ulväng 2008, p. 177.

31 Runefelt 2015, p. 216.

32 The lady's drawing room' included the largest sofa in the house. Riksarkivet, Näs Silverstolpeska arkivet, Personarkiven, vol. 60, Carl Eric Wadenstierna (1723–1787).

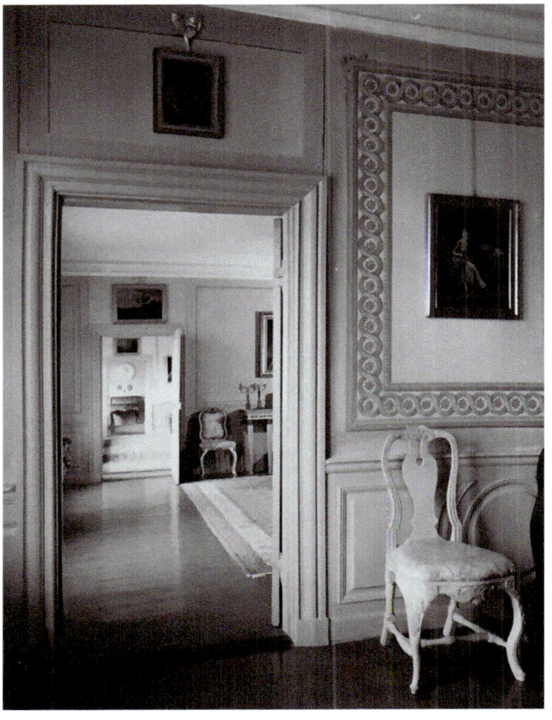

16. Enfilade with the reception rooms at Näs with the bedchamber in the foreground. Photo: Åke Grundström, 1959, Archives of the Nordic Museum, Stockholm.

comfortable socialing, and their position against the southern gable end wall also made the rooms warm and light.

Carl Eric Wadenstierna's estate inventory from 1787 provides information about how the rooms were furnished and thereby also hints at how they were used. Furthermore, the document reveals that certain deviations were made from the planned allocation of rooms. The careful crossings out and sketched additions on the floor plan also show some of these changes. The smaller and more everyday rooms were located on the side that faced the front of the house. The extension of the lady's suite of reception rooms ended with a small cabinet, a room furnished for the lady of the house and her daily activities, with a secretaire desk, and a sewing table, sofa and chairs. On the floor plan, the room is not connected with the adjacent bedchamber, as a clear boundary between official and more secluded or 'private' spheres in the home. Nevertheless, a door was fitted and thereby integrated the home's entertainment and everyday functions with each other.

As was often the case, the following intended dining room seems to have been used for other purposes. According to the estate inventory, the room appears to have served as a simply furnished dressing room, which was above all used for the storage and handling of clothes and household linen. It was unquestionably also an advantage to have these functions close to both the cabinet of the lady of the house

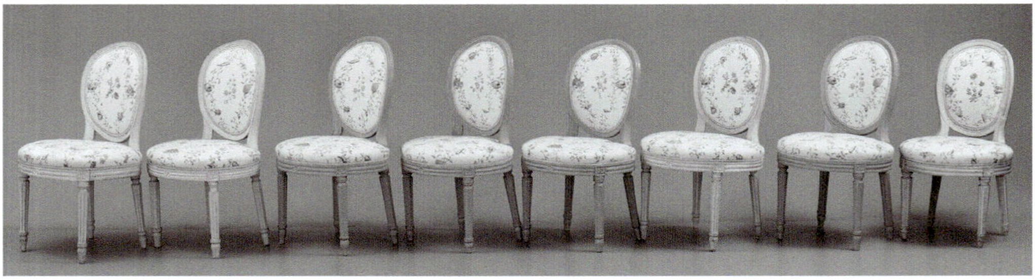

17. Drawing room chairs from Näs, about 1780. Photo: Bukowskis.

as well as the entrance with its access to the kitchen wing and the servants. The dressing room also included bedspace for two maids. In his *Observationer* in 1714, Count Nicodemus Tessin the Younger, architect of the Royal Palace in Stockholm, had already advocated this order of rooms as being '*commod*' (convenient): 'Entrance hall if possible, reception room ('sahl'), drawing room, bedchamber, cabinet and dressing room'.[33] The chamber to the right of the entrance hall appears to have been the daughters' room, where they shared a bed, upholstered in blue and white linen.[34] A small passage tucked away between the staircase and tableware pantry connected the chamber with the entrance hall and the adjacent room where the maids slept, which may have been practical when the girls were young. The house lacked other such passages or *dégagements*, which Wijnblad found less necessary in country homes that were often characterised by smallness of scale and proximity.[35] Wadenstierna and his wife also shared a bed, in the large bedchamber of the lady's suite, as Wadenstierna's own chamber – the equivalent of his wife's cabinet – lacked this item of furniture. The room that according the floor plan was the bedchamber of the gentleman's suite therefore in practice served as Wadenstierna's study, furnished with writing furniture, a sofa and chairs.

It was hardly remarkable that family members shared beds, although a shared marital bed was partly a sign of a new attitude to marriage.[36] The traditional

33 Nicodemus Tessin the Younger. *Observationer Angående så wähl Publiqve som Priuate huus byggnaders Starkheet, beqwämligheet och skiönheet, in rättade, effter wår Swänska Climat och oeconomie*, [1714], transcription and with introduction by Bo Vahlne, Stockholm 2002, p. 46.

34 Wijnblad often included a children's nursery in the published drawings, preferably next to the entrance hall or staircase to be easily accessible for the attending maids. In the cases where the kitchen was located in the main building, the nursery could be placed adjacent to it (Wijnblad 1755).

35 Wijnblad 1755, p. A3.

36 DeJean, Joan, *The Age of Comfort. When Paris Discovered Casual – And the Modern Home Began*, New York 2009, p. 173. The author Malla Silfverstolpe (1782–1861), whose family became close to Wadenstierna's daughters, describes in her memoirs how she always shared a bed with her maternal grandmother Magdalena Rudbeck during the winter months in Stockholm, *Malla Montgomery-Silfverstolpes memoarer*, I, 1908, p. 151.

disposition of rooms with a gentleman's suite and a lady's suite with separate bedchambers had been traditional for a long time. The fact that the floor plans upheld this tradition, which evidently did not always reflect solutions applied in practice, illustrates how the latter half of the eighteenth century constituted a transitional phase between older norms and new attitudes. However, the estate inventory clearly shows that, even in reality, the bedchamber of the lady's suite remained the most lavish of the reception rooms. Here, an expensive mirror and gilt pendulum clock hung next to a large 'Imperial' bed, which had a high headboard and lower footboard, with its showpiece bed cover, and the room also contained a sofa and chairs positioned around tea tables made by Georg Haupt. In the room where you slept, you also received guests for tea parties. The integration of the different functions and needs – both those for entertaining and those for 'private' life – can also be regarded as distinctive of the era and its view of the home, which during these decades seemed to oscillate between tradition and renewal.[37]

The large dining room ('Sahl') could also be used for both everyday tasks and entertaining. It contained three dining tables with double leaves, which when pushed together could seat nearly twenty people, while one of the tables gave enough space for a family dinner. Four sideboards (with folding leaves) fixed to the wall, next to the passage used as a serving room and along the windowed wall could be used for serving, and the leaves could be folded down onto the wall panelling after a meal. Eighteen armchairs with blue striped linen upholstery stood along the walls, and two games tables were also available to be used at gatherings. The handle used to operate the servant bell system was next to the dining room door. The system was connected to a bell outside the entrance, which alerted the maids in the separate kitchen wing building.

The distance between the Wadenstierna family and their employees was a clear expression of the hierarchical structure that permeated the whole estate. The manor house, symmetrically flanked by its free-standing wings, at the end of a completely straight avenue through the landscape, was situated on a hill, while other utility and farm buildings and crofts crouched on slopes and outskirts of the area without blocking the view of the garden and the surrounding lake. The barns, although an important part of the estate, were situated to form their own closed square of buildings at a fitting distance from the manor house.[38] The barns should not block the 'pleasant view' that would be seen from the manor, but on the other hand it was good if 'the country householder had the advantage of, from

37 Selling, Gösta, *Svenska herrgårdshem under 1700-talet*, Stockholm (1937) 1991, p. 341.

38 It was important that the barn buildings would not 'take away the view from the big house', Wijnblad 1756; Ulrich Lange, *Ladugården. Om lantbrukets bebyggelse och arkitektur 1600–2000*, Nordiska museet, Stockholm 2011.

the residential buildings, being able … to watch over the household's proceedings that take place daily on the farm'.[39] This hierarchy was also maintained within the walls of the household, as shown by the floor plan of the main building and the separate kitchen wing. The latter wing included space for the majority of the maids, who had to share rooms and beds, while the footman, the maid of higher status (*jungfru*), the farm foreman, the female head housekeeper, and the gardener had a room each. There was also a special room available for the footman of visiting guests. It was not the risk of fire but the need for both distance and comfort that kept cooking, kitchen chores, heavy or rough work and servants in a separate building, albeit within sight.[40] Conceptions about the sensitivity of the social elite also contributed to maintaining the distance. It was the bothersome nuisances of everyday work but also the servants' use of language and behaviour that could seem objectionable.[41] The bell that summoned the servants was governed by the needs of the ladies and gentlemen, which had also been shaped by the conventions and traditions of the hierarchical social system.

The estate inventory shows that Näs was densely furnished and followed many established norms regarding how a home should be designed, but it also indicates a degree of flexibility and innovative thinking. Many new items of furniture were designed to fulfil several functions and were easy to move between the rooms. Meals could be eaten at sofas, served on the convertible leaves of the games tables. Bedside cabinets could hide chamber pots in their cupboards but also be used as side tables at tea parties. Näs was clearly designed for convenient and comfortable everyday life. The unassuming nature that appears to imbue the verses in the entrance hall's

39 Wijnblad 1756 (tab. XLVIII); Tomas Anfält, 'Offentlighet och privatliv. Om livet på Leufsta herrgård på 1700-talet', in *Herrgårdskultur och salongsmiljö. Rapport från en nordisk konferens på Leufsta bruk 12–14 maj 1995*, Erik Kjellberg (ed.), Uppsala 1997.

40 Alain Corbin, 'Domestic Atmospheres', *The Domestic Space Reader*, Chiara Briganti and Kathy Mezei, (ed.), Toronto 2012, p. 105. L'Abbé Jacquin, *De la Santé, ouvrage utile à toute le monde*, http://gallica.bnf.fr/ark:/12148/bpt6k97635406/f23.item.r=propreté. The distance to the kitchen sometimes adversely affected the serving of food. Count Johan Gabriel Oxenstierna admonishes his wife that the food she is served must be properly covered when carried between the kitchen and the main building so that it 'may not be inspected by eyes or mixed with insects on the way'. Oxenstierna, Johan Gabriel, *Journal*, Stockholm (1805) 1964, p. 40.

41 It was deemed particularly important that children were not excessively shaped by the servants and influenced by their culture. 'Instead of them having tender care for your children, they only corrupt them through coarse and careless conduct.' *En fullkomlig Ägta Hustrus Bild, Tecknad Efter den målning, som finnes i Ord-språks-Bokens sidsta Capitel*, Gothenburg 1787, pp. 47–8. In his letters to his wife, Johan Gabriel Oxenstierna repeats how he watches over their son during the summer months at Skenäs Manor), so that he would not spend too much time in the unsuitable company of any '*Domestik*', Oxenstierna (1805) 1964, p. 70. Märta Helena Reenstierna notes the following about her son in her diary on 19 January 1794: 'Hans Abraham worried his parents immensely with the time he spent among the servants, where nothing respectable is learnt.' Märta Helena Reenstierna, *Årstadagboken 1793–1812*, I, Stockholm 1993, p. 58.

overdoor decorations was in this respect less about 'simplicity' and more about a desire to make this a pleasant home for family and friends.[42]

Pleasantness was linked to comfort. Robust wooden floors, modern tiled stoves, double-glazed windows and cosy curtains, carpets and rugs kept unpleasant chills and draughts at bay. The royal court froze at Drottningholm Palace – so much so that the women had to warm their hands on brandy-burning lamps – whereas on the comfortable estate, the country gentleman could relax.[43] The large number of chairs and sofas with horsehair-upholstered soft seats and backrests encouraged relaxed socialising or contemplative repose with a book. Sofas were not only associated with comfort but were also an expression of upper-class fashion, established in late-seventeenth-century France, where each perfect fashionable home required a sofa in every room.[44] The main building at Näs had seven of these high-status pieces of furniture, the most lavish of which stood in the drawing room of the suite of reception rooms. More sedentary time necessitated more tables for several types of activities. Näs was furnished with games tables, writing tables, sewing tables, tea tables, dining tables and side tables. The furniture indicated the intended uses of the rooms and the pretensions, habits and values of the people who used them.

Luxury and comfort

Everyday life was not therefore free of social awareness or the hierarchies that circumscribed family life at Näs. The furniture and collections that Wadenstierna filled his home with were a concrete expression of this fact. And it is clear that luxury and *kommoditet* (*commodité*, comfort, amenity) were closely related qualities within upper-class life. The heading 'NOUVELLES INVENTIONS DE Luxe & de Commodité' was the title of a supplement to the contemporary issues of *Almanac de Gotha* which showed how the European elite were linked to the newest products. It was for the elite's comfort that innovative everyday luxury, with everything from effective dentures to multifunctional tables and washing machines, was launched.[45] Although Wadenstierna's library did not include *Almanac de Gotha*, it did contain nine whole years of *Mercure de France* (totalling eighty-three magazines between 1772 and 1780), with reports on the latest products and offerings. The magazine

42 The social aspect of comfort – the home's possibilities of providing 'emotional well-being' – are highlighted by Prytz and Stobart 2018, pp. 234–58 and Stobart, Jon, *Comfort in the Eighteenth-Century Country House*, Routledge, New York 2022.

43 Hochschild 1908, vol. 1, pp. 79–80.

44 DeJean 2009, pp. 125, 127.

45 *Almanac de Gotha contenant Diverses Connoissances Curieuses et Utiles*. See references in note 76 of the introductory chapter.

also included advertisements for *Almanach général des marchands, négocians & commerçans de la France & de l'Europe*, where readers could find out which cities stocked which goods, names of trading houses and traders, buyers, bankers, artists, studios, manufactories, shops and boutiques. In addressing its readership, *Mercure de France* specified the significance of consumption for the self-image of the elite. A subscription was deemed necessary to stay informed of news concerning art, culture and literature, as well as the growing range of products in the commercial market.[46] But the increasingly dominant issue that readers of *Mercure de France* in eighteenth-century Sweden were confronted with was nevertheless that of the raison d'être of French luxury. As difficult to obtain as it was desirable, it seemed to be the constant point of reference for every class-conscious consumer, to such a degree that it developed into a growing political problem. For Wadenstierna, this became a concrete issue when he acquired Näs in 1773. Was it possible to furnish a comfortable home without falling into a French 'luxury trap'? This issue was, however, more patriotic than pecuniary in nature for a government official and nobleman in the Age of Liberty.

It was evident that the construction and furnishing of a new manor was the ultimate expression of upper-class consumption. This signalled Wadenstierna's status within his family, his social class circle and society as a whole. When the construction of Näs was complete, he commissioned furniture and mirrors from Stockholm's leading craftsmen and cabinetmakers (*ébénistes*) – Johan Niclas Eckstein, Georg Haupt, Christian Linning and Niclas Meunier. The rooms were embellished with faience wares from the Marieberg factory in Stockholm, which were linked to the floral decoration on the tiled stoves, as well as paintings by Pehr Hilleström and Johan Philip Korn – twelve by each artist. Carl Carlsson Enhörning, a pupil of the well-known Swedish sculptor Johan Tobias Sergel, had completed classicising medallion portraits in relief, reflecting the tastes of the era, of the Wadenstierna couple as a complement to the older family portraits. The significance of the furniture and objects as social markers is clearly revealed by their position in the home, where the most expensive and eye-catching pieces were placed in the reception rooms. At elegant and newly made sofas, armchairs and tea tables, Wadenstierna was able to use the tableware decorated with his family coat of arms interwoven with the Cross of the Royal Order of the Polar Star to manifest that he received the order in 1767. Alongside the cups that bore his initials, the items of furniture were bearers of his informed taste.[47] The number of cups – thirteen

46 Wadenstierna's library also housed *L'esprit des journaux, françois et étrangers. Par une société de gens-lettres*.

47 The chest of drawers and secretaire that Wadenstierna commissioned from Georg Haupt featured a 'W' crowned with a laurel festoon and the Wadenstierna family's star inlaid in the wood veneer.

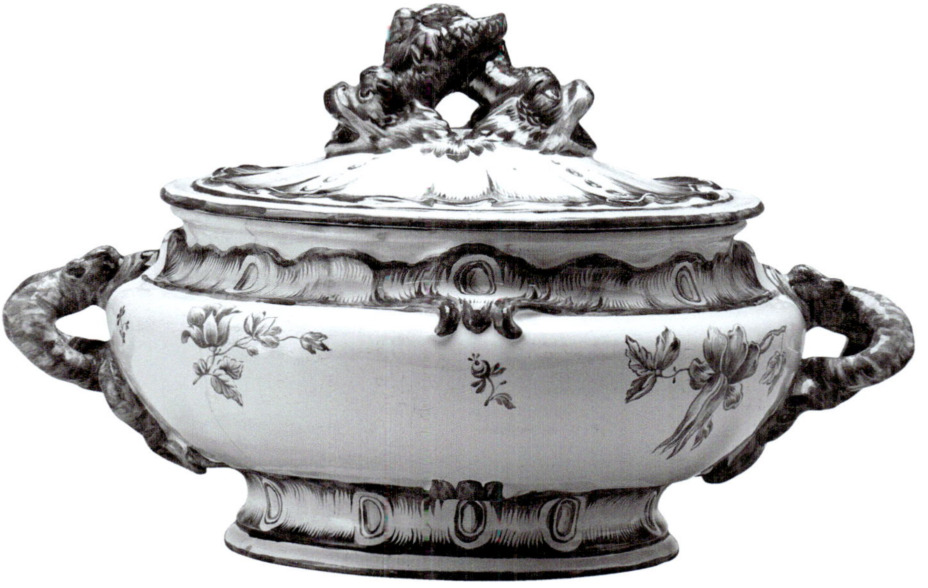

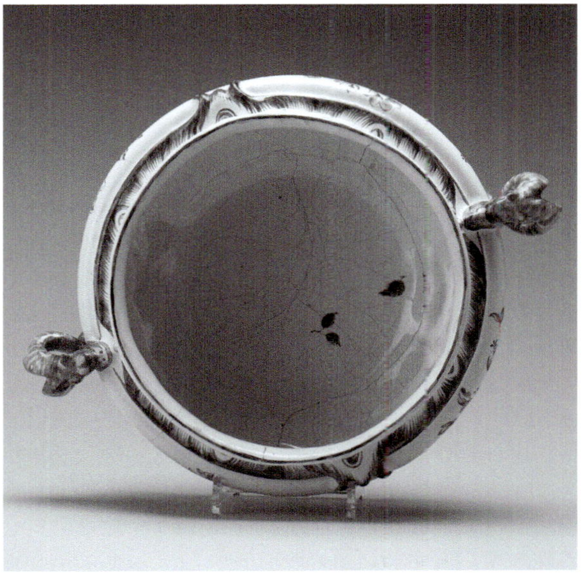

18–19. Wadenstierna's tureen from the Marieberg factory in Stockholm, marked 27/10 (17)63 and with the painter's signature of Erik Aspegren. The three small leaves inside the bottom of the bowl hide a few imperfections in the glaze. The leaves are a reminder of the value of luxury items, which were far too valuable to be sold off at a loss due to a few small irregularities. Photo: Bukowskis.

coffee cups and ten tea cups – confirm that the tableware service was intended for social gatherings. This was also the case regarding the very expensive billiard table, placed in the southern wing building with its well-stocked library and the row of guest rooms – a remarkable luxury for the 'little cabin' into which the entrance hall's overdoor decorations invited visitors.

All this naturally constituted conscious manifestations of status in the upper-class home. But the sole focus on Swedish-made objects – furniture, art and items of applied and decorative art – can also be seen as contributions by Wadenstierna to the ongoing debate on luxury and excess and thereby an expression of his political standpoint and identity. Consumption was an obligation of the upper class, but consuming Swedish products was the responsibility of every honest and upright citizen. The long-lasting criticism of Swedes' weakness for foreign fashion had both economic and moral motives since the first half of the eighteenth century:

> [T]he for our kingdom both damaging and shameful imagined notion that no Swede is capable of doing a competent job, so that many people are almost embarrassed that a Swedish cobbler has made the shoes that he wears; nor could they presumably be buckled up unless one had purchased shoe buckles from a French boutique, where one had been assured that they were the latest French fashion, and the Frenchman swears that he himself uses the same type. As English bureaus were brought in from abroad, for which six hundred daler and more were willingly paid, and yet they rarely lasted for more than half a year before they broke; but now when they are made stronger and better by our own craftsmen and for nearly half the price, one receives hundreds of criticisms for it.[48]

The 1766 sumptuary law against 'luxury and excess' was the strictest of its kind. All foreign imports, from wines to lace, were now to be strictly regulated to create balance in Sweden's economy. In its wake, a debate stirred up the party political disagreements. Overt or covert discussions took place about moral misgivings associated with luxury and comfort. But the nobility's threatened privileges were also debated at a time when society's upper-class stratum that was ever broader and more difficult to define acquainted themselves with luxury. Wadenstierna's contribution to the debate was in line with the Hat party's mercantile politics and support of Swedish luxury production, where luxury was emphasised as an economic virtue rather than a moral threat. The luxury was justified as it kept the nation in work and breathed life into healthy competition that generated income. Made in Sweden, this was 'the legitimate luxury' that every 'patriot with the best heart and passionate feelings for the fatherland' should choose, as emphasised by furniture trader Diedrich Tellerstedt.[49] Wadenstierna was one of the advocates of the virtuous middle road that rested on the for him prevailing fundamental truth that 'a kingdom should, with its own *Industrie*, gain all possible profit from foreign

48 *Sedolärande Mercurius*, II, No. 20, 13 April 1731.

49 Diedrich Tellerstedt, *Berättelse, om swenska meuble-handelens första inrättning, och de öden, meuble-handlaren Diedrich Tellerstedt uti 23 års tid, undergådt*, Stockholm 1771, p. 4.

purses'.[50] It was not an issue of rolling in imported luxury, but he despised how honourable, hard-working citizens were not allowed to enjoy their well-earned comfort without evoking indignation and envy in people, irrespective of social position, who lacked their assiduity and diligence.[51] 'I believe that every inhabitant in a kingdom has the right to be able to earn his living. ... The kingdom has no right to take this, the living he has earned, from him.'[52]

Wadenstierna unquestionably spoke for his own cause. His acknowledged zeal had promoted him to the position of elevated government official who enjoyed royal confidence. Inheritance, thrift and good business deals had also made him wealthy.[53] He saw it as his duty to bolster Swedish industries and manufactories that contributed to the country's standing and competitiveness and through his patronage to allow the arts to flourish. In that respect, his convictions were close to the thoughts presented by Carl Fredric Adelcrantz in his role as the new director of the Royal Drawing Academy in 1757 in his speech on the value and use of the free arts.[54] The major commissions from Georg Haupt or the newly established artist Pehr Hilleström can be regarded as conscious acts of patronage in line with his political standpoint. But Wadenstierna also deemed it his civil right to enjoy his successes – 'the natural right to use and utilise one's fortune for comfort and own benefit'.[55] The merchant he mentions in his inflammatory speech *Fria Tankar* was also a description of himself. And the merchant's home imbued with bourgeois virtues that he had presented as a model in one of his pamphlets in 1767, reflected his own values: '[O]n arriving home, I found the house neat and tidy, a sign of a clean and orderly life: on entering the rooms, I found them equipped with proper furniture and decorations, which characterised well-being without excessive splendour.'[56]

The well-ordered life that he planned for himself and his innermost circle at Näs could thus be justified through his significant support of artists and craftsmen in need. The construction of Näs was a good deed for the sake of goodness:

50 [Carl Eric Wadenstierna], *Fria Tankar Af* ***, Stockholm 1769, p. 5.

51 [Anonymous] Carl Eric Wadenstierna, *Bref til auctoren af Tanckar i anledning af sista öfwerflöds förordningen och desz wärckställighet*. Stockholm 1767; [Anonymous] Carl Eric Wadenstierna, *Bref til en wän innehållande swar på den af trycket utkomne skriften kallad Tankar i anledning af sidsta öfwerflöds-förordningen dedicerade til malcontenterne*, Stockholm 1767.

52 Wadenstierna 1769, p. 7.

53 His parents' inheritance is likely to have been considerable both on his father's side and especially on his mother's as his mother was the daughter of Anders Strömner, a wealthy vice president of the government authority for mining.

54 Adelcrantz, Carl Fredric, *Tal om de fria konsters värde och nytta*, Stockholm 1757.

55 Wadenstierna 1769, p. 16.

56 Carl Eric Wadenstierna, *Bref Til Auctoren Af Tanckar I Anledning Af sista Öfwerflöds Förordningen Och Dess wärckställighet*, Stockholm 1767.

> A trader, who has come into a considerable fortune, and who is tempted by a love of peace and tranquillity, wishes to spend the rest of his life within a small circle of friends and relatives and abandon trading, is he not worthy of our esteem, when he remains in his occupation, on account of the following moving reason: it would be unfailingly pleasant and good for me to abandon my business now, but if I implement this intention, it would cause suffering for many people, who should expect their livelihood from me.[57]

Näs crowned Wadenstierna's successes and united his political and private roles. Both the entrance hall's unassuming rules of life and the Swedish-made luxury of the reception rooms were expressions of the standpoints that he had pursued on the political stage and that he endeavoured to put into practice as a farming estate owner. The contradiction that can be said to exist between these – on the one hand mercantile and on the other physiocratic – dispositions also appeared here to express a middle ground. Wadenstierna belonged to the growing group of noblemen who were government officials. In this group, social status was obtained through diligent work, and values were established that later characterised the bourgeois middle class: work, integrity, utility, common sense, restraint and moderation.[58] But these virtues were also accompanied by demands for rights. It was the enlightened individual's own ability, irrespective of birth or descent and inherited fortune, that was to be given preference and that resonated in the Age of Liberty's pamphlets and debates that had shaped Wadenstierna.[59] His booklet *Fria Tankar* from 1769 was clearly in dialogue with the radical publication *Tankar om borgerliga friheten* (On civil liberty) by scientist Peter Forsskål, which had been banned in 1760. The right to 'be the master in one's cabin' as Forsskål claimed, to be allowed to utilise one's property at the same time as contributing to the prosperity of society, recurs in *Fria Tankar*, but also in the message conveyed in the overdoor decorations at Näs.[60] Wadenstierna's financial support of, and active participation in, various patriotic and charitable contexts can be viewed in the light of these values. But they can also unquestionably be set against the extensive and economically favourable lending operation that he simultaneously conducted.[61]

57 Wadenstierna 1769, pp. 42, 48.

58 Adams, Christine, *A Taste for Comfort and Status. A Bourgeois Family in Eighteenth-Century France*, Pennsylvania 2000, p. 259.

59 Among others, the periodical *Sedolärande Mercurius* by his future father-in-law Edvard Carleson, published with his brother Carl Carleson in 1730–1. On Tuesday, 23 March 1731, it stated: 'In your clothing, as with everything else, maintain a sensible middle ground.'

60 Peter Forsskål, *Tankar om borgerliga friheten*, Stockholm (1759) 2009, pp. 17, 20.

61 Wadenstierna gave financial assistance to homes for widows, homes for veterans and poorhouses, and he was also one of the nature and science supporters who financially helped the experiments

Like many of the era's members of the upper class, Wadenstierna made interest-bearing investments in the form of an extensive lending operation. The estate inventory differentiates between the receivables in the city and those in the countryside and between the ones deemed bad debts and those deemed good. The largest proportion were from the major wholesale trading houses Grill, Tottie & Arfwedsson, Hassel & Görges, Kantzow, Bohman and the ironmaster and mill owner Wahrendorf, but also from friends and colleagues within the government authorities and offices. Wadenstierna's lending business also provides good insight into his network of contacts. Alongside the traders and the industrialists involved in the export of iron, copper and tar, there were councillors of the realm, royal secretaries, senior government officials and presidents, chamberlains, court judges and county governors. However, here we also see contacts in a broader group of citizens with lower-ranking civil servants, craftsmen and small-business owners such as wigmakers, butchers, chefs, jewellers or printers. During his lifetime, wigmaker Johan Wessman managed to reduce his debt of 11,600 R.Kmnt (riksdaler copper coins) by over 9,000 R.Kmnt – which was gradually paid through wigs and hairdressing.[62] In the countryside, there were receivables from tenants, farm foremen and farmers.

Wadenstierna was hardly unique in choosing this strategic investment of his assets with the aim of increasing his capital; the phenomenon seems rather to have become increasingly common during the course of the eighteenth century, judging by the estate inventories of the elite.[63] His investments were also a way of creating economic credibility, status and influence for himself, and his successes were dependent on both his prosperity and the contact network that came with his business dealings.[64] But some people took offense by the fact that his assets had also increased substantially through royal bribes. In 1773, the same year in which Wadenstierna acquired Näs, the author and debater on economics Johan Fischerström noted: 'There is much discussion regarding *krigsrådet* WADENSTIERNA, who has now become state secretary in the war office. The military fear his self-interest, especially as he is known as one of the strongest *penningeJudar* [literally: money Jews] and money lenders.'[65]

with 'Montgolfian' hot air balloons within Sweden. Supporting scientific experiments was also seen as a patriotic deed as it bolstered the nation's reputation in the eyes of the surrounding world. *Dagligt Allehanda*, Stockholm 19 January 1784.

62 See the estate inventory for Carl Eric Wadenstierna from 1787, Riksarkivet, Näs Silverstolpeska arkivet, Personarkiven, vol. 60, Carl Eric Wadenstierna (1723–1787).

63 Andersson, Gudrun, *Stadens dignitärer. Den lokala elitens status- & maktmanifestation i Arboga 1650–1770*, Stockholm 2009, p. 140.

64 On 25 January 1779, Wadenstierna was also appointed to the group of auditors for Sweden's central bank (*Stockholms Posten*, 25 January 1779).

65 Johan Fischerström, *En gustaviansk dagbok. Johan Fisherströms anteckningar för året 1773*. Published by Gustaf Näsström, Stockholm 1951. p. 51.

Taste, cultivation and nature

Wadenstierna's position within the new nobility was undeniably helped by this capital, but an even more important factor was his ability to manage his wealth effectively, set a good example and not risk his reputation through showy consumption and an ostentatious lifestyle. His self-interest, Fischerström's biting taunt, should not obscure the view of the common good or spoil the fruits of his successes. Through the relatively modest scale of the country manor at Näs and through the strategic purchases made to furnish it, Wadenstierna was able to expand his social capital and win credibility that also increased his authority and political influence. The well-chosen furniture and the collections of art and literature that occupied an important part of the space at Näs vouched for his cultivated taste. They were investments through which his interests and insights into new thoughts and theories and new aesthetic ideals were manifested. Through these markers, Wadenstierna presented himself as a key actor on the political stage – increasingly critical of the autocracy and an advocate of a more citizen-based development of society. The status expressed by cultivated taste gave his opinions legitimacy. It was also an aspect of the complex comfort that was not to be made light of.

In a series of articles from 1772 in the women's magazine *Fruntimmers-Tidningar*, published by author and publicist Carl Christopher Gjörwell, the country estate 'Bellevue' constitutes the ideal home. A shady avenue leads to the splendid stone house surrounded by an attractive garden with meandering paths, in an elevated location affording an extensive view of the surrounding countryside.[66] The rooms in the main building are characterised by tasteful ornaments:

> They are filled with copperplate engravings and landscape paintings that enlighten the mind, as well as the rooms that nourish the imagination with new pictures, duplicate nature's beauties and refine our taste for these things, which cheer our senses when the sky is cloudy, and in our solitude they are the most instructive company for us.[67]

The description appears to be a foretaste of Linnerhielm's impressions of Näs in the early nineteenth century.

The garden and park at Näs could serve as an extension of the main building's reception rooms and the socialising for which they had been established. An English landscape garden with winding paths that offered a variety of viewing points and scenes led down to the seashore. A folly for smaller gatherings was also built here,

66 *Fruntimmers-Tidningar* 1772, part 2, p. 8.
67 *Fruntimmers-Tidningar* 1772, part 1, p. 64.

in which the furnishings alluded to the chambers and drawings rooms of the main building. The fabric wall coverings above the low wooden panelling depicted elegant flowering plants in pale colours, inspired by the paths' bellflowers, clover flowers and wild roses. The pruned and maintained garden and the free landscape park testify to the era's utilitarian thinking, but also to its emotional approach to nature. A cup of tea in the folly, or a meal in a simple summer dining room, made out of treillage in one of the manor's bosquets, could be followed by a walk in the park, where various types of memorial stones conveyed emotional messages to the walker.[68] Letters and diaries from that time illustrate how parks and gardens fulfilled an important function in social life. Count Johan Gabriel Oxenstierna gave an account of the summer months at Skenäs Manor, where walks in the park and the surrounding countryside were part of everyday life. This was also the case during visits to the Bonde family at the nearby country estates of Kesätter and Säfstaholm, which could include hours of enjoyment on the swings in the gardens.[69] But the perception of a comfortable life also played a key part in people's contact with nature. A garden temple with a sofa in a classicising style was constructed in the English landscape park of family friend Wahrendorf at the Åkers Styckebruk manor house, so that the estate owner 'surrounded by friendship and pleasures, would in this shade with more comfort, look out over the perfected works of taste and well-being'.[70] Comfortably ensconced on the sofa, the viewer was presented with a display of nature's beauty and utility. The emotional inscription in the temple wall became an instruction to the resting visitor – what to see and how to feel.

From sofas in drawing rooms and cabinets, nature was viewed in the same way. The copperplate engravings and landscape paintings that adorned the walls in the fictitious ideal home 'Bellevue' were intended to 'duplicate nature's beauties and refine our taste for these things'.[71] The pictures not only reinforced the connection between the manor's suite of reception rooms with their striking furnishings and the park's laid paths with eye-catchers, but they also reflected the cultivated gaze that was thought to distinguish the pictures' owners and viewers. The engravings' and paintings' enhancement and intensification of natural beauty was a reminder of nature's cultivating forces. Similarly, the estate owner not only saw himself as the manager of his land, but also as its refiner. On the walls of Wadenstierna's own chamber at Näs, there were no fewer than eighteen 'large and small oil-painted landscapes and other … paintings'.[72] The majority of them must have been by

68 Asplund 1960, p. 13. The park included memorial stones remembering the estate's dogs as well as a stone commemorating planted oak trees.

69 Oxenstierna (1805) 1964, pp. 57, 90.

70 Ahlund, Mikael, *Landskapets röster. Studier i Elias Martins bildvärld*, Stockholm 2011, p. 326.

71 *Fruntimmers-Tidningar* 1772, part 1, p. 64.

72 Riksarkivet, Näs Silverstolpeska arkivet, Personarkiven, vol. 60, Carl Eric Wadenstierna (1723–1787).

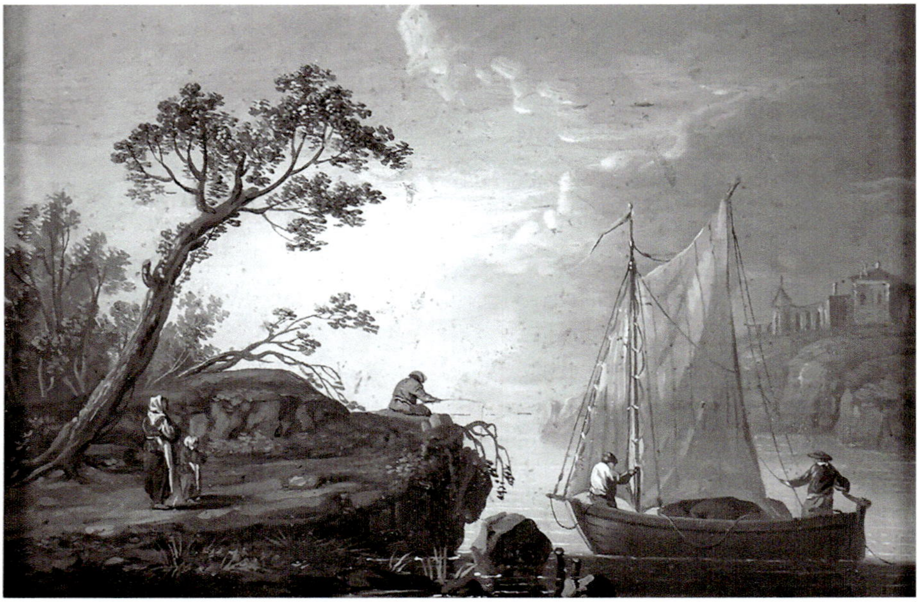

20. One of Johan Philip Korn's paintings from Näs. Oil on panel, 18 × 25 cm. Private ownership.

the landscape painter Johan Philip Korn (Image 20).[73] The paintings above all represented idealised pastoral landscapes inspired by Dutch motifs. The varied views showed landscapes with tranquil waters, at which people in simple old-fashioned garments fished and tilled the land next to their rustic cottages. The motifs hinted at new attitudes to the landscape and the rural proletariat that belonged to Näs. By regarding the surrounding reality through the filter offered by Korn's pictures – 'that nourish the imagination with new pictures' – everyday country life could be refined by being associated with a fictitious, idyllic golden age.[74]

In the same way that the walls of 'Bellevue' were covered with copperplate engravings, Näs was correspondingly embellished with a large collection of engraved pictures. The 'gentleman's drawing room' was home to '66 engravings with glass and gilt frames', and in the library in the free-standing wing, there were a further fifty-two framed engravings. The majority of these probably constituted the 191 'engravings with glass and gilt frames' that were stated in the estate inventory of Jacobina Psilanderhielm, Wadenstierna's first wife, in 1769, and that were subsequently moved from their Stockholm residence to the newly built Näs Manor.[75] Their large

73 Also see the inventory and photographic documentation work conducted by Nordiska museet in the 1960s, when a number of Korn's paintings still remained in the main building (Nordiska museet, Uppland, Rö Parish, Näs). There were also 23 oil paintings in the cabinet in the lady's suite.

74 *Fruntimmers-Tidningar* 1772, part 1, p. 64; Ahlund 2011, pp. 339–62.

75 Riksarkivet, Näs Silverstolpeska arkivet, Personarkiven, vol. 60, Carl Eric Wadenstierna (1723–1787).

number may seem remarkable, but it followed the prevailing ideal in terms of the attitudes to both cultivated taste and interior decoration, in which engravings hung close together became fashionable.[76] The eighteenth-century engravings market was considerable and connected networks of publishers throughout Europe. Swedish bookshops were also regularly filled with the latest pictures from the international market, and the newspapers were quick to advertise the new arrivals.[77] The range encompassed everything from topographic pictures to fashion plates, as well as many engraved portraits of renowned people from all over the world. Compared to paintings, the reproduced engravings were a cheaper art form and made it relatively easy to create a contemporary gallery in one's own home. The novelty value of the pictures was also significant, and the acquisition of new engravings was a way of showing informed knowledge of art, culture and politics. However, the aesthetic value and the costs of glass and gilt frames were not negligible. Wadenstierna's estate inventory states that the sixty-six framed engravings in his drawing room commanded a value that was almost as high as the room's exclusive mahogany chest of drawers made by Georg Haupt.[78]

The placing of the engravings in the drawing room used for entertaining and in the library in the southern wing, where the billiard table also stood and the majority of the guest rooms were located, also illustrates the status that they were associated with. Engraved pictures were often collected as complements to maps, books, sheet music and periodicals and appear to be a significant marker of the cultivated country estate environment. Wadenstierna's home was not only a display of the wealthy estate owner's ability to consume, but equally a manifestation of his erudite taste. His collections of art and literature and his patronage of artists and craftsmen constituted a statement about the cultivated life that he wanted to emphasise and be an active co-creator of. The library's collection of scientific and political works, as well as the latest novels and plays, harmonised with the engraved pictures on the walls. Together with the newly purchased furniture and items of applied and decorative art, the joint aim was to show Wadenstierna's participation in the era's intellectual, artistic and cultural life.[79] From this perspective, the Näs

76 Regarding the increasing prevalence of landscape pictures in the latter half of the eighteenth century, see 'Landskap och bildanvändning' in Ahlund 2011, pp. 233–9. The collection of engraved pictures can also be compared to the nearly 200 framed engravings that adorned the walls of a contemporary upper-class lady on her country estate in England; Helen Berry, 'Prudent Luxury: The Metropolitan Tastes of Judith Baker, Durham Gentlewoman', *Women and Urban Life in Eighteenth-Century England*, Rosemary Sweet and Penelope Lane (ed.), Farnham 2003, p. 140.

77 Ahlund 2011, pp. 186–201.

78 Riksarkivet, Näs Silverstolpeska arkivet, Personarkiven, vol. 60, Carl Eric Wadenstierna (1723–1787).

79 Adams 2000, p. 189. Wadenstierna's library at Näs included the scientific, economic and belles-lettres publications *Götheborgska wetenskaps och witterhets Samhällets Handlingar, Oeconomiska Handlingar, Kongl. Patriotiska Sällskapets* and *Kongl. Witterhets Academiens Handlingar, Stockholms Lärda Tidningar*

country estate – and the material culture and cultivated nature that it was in interplay with – is regarded as a representative stage that was typical of the age, designed by and for a privileged social class.

Books, socialising and silhouettes

The words in the entrance hall's overdoor decoration refer back to the idea of Näs as a place of togetherness and community for the strata of society that Wadenstierna belonged to: '[A]mong books and among good friends, to be loved more, rather than become famous.' This is where the family and friends were to gather around the tables – the dining tables, games tables, tea tables or sewing tables – but the company could also consist of the books and paintings, 'in our solitude they are the most instructive company for us'.[80] The aspiration that Wadenstierna himself had advocated was to be relegated to city life, far from Näs. Instead, country life consisted of enjoying freedom from the government official's duties and demands, but also the freedom to 'be able to use what he had honourably acquired', a theme that Wadenstierna constantly referred back to in political debate over the years.[81] The overdoor decorations at Näs proclaim this right, embedded in a pastoral family idyll.

The library at Näs – a place for both books and good friends – fulfilled a symbolically important function in the picture of the good, comfortable life. A look at Wadenstierna's library in his city residence in Stockholm provides an illustrative comparison.[82] The book collection there was much smaller than at Näs and was clearly focused on politics, economics and history. It included both old literature such as David de Constant De Rebecque's *Abrégé de politique* from 1687, and newer works such as Adrien Maurice, duc de Noaille's *Memoires politiques et militaires* from 1777. Other works included the Bible and the Swedish hymn book *Swenska Psalmboken* alongside royal ordinances, constitutions and minutes from the sessions of the parliament, the Riksdag. Publications from the Royal Patriotic Society, as well as the register of the nobility were also important for Wadenstierna's role as a government official. In contrast, it was clear that the book collection at Näs also had

and *Witterhets och Gransknings Journal* but also 'travelogues' and French and English novels (by Mercier, Marivaux, Genlis, Stern, Fielding and Burney) as well as plays. Riksarkivet, Näs Silverstolpeska arkivet, Personarkiven, vol. 60, Carl Eric Wadenstierna (1723–1787).

80 This is the description of the function of the paintings and engravings in the ideal home 'Bellevue', *Fruntimmers-Tidningar* 1772, part 1, p. 64.

81 Wadenstierna 1769, pp. 11, 17.

82 Wadenstierna's estate inventory from 1787, Riksarkivet, Näs Silverstolpeska arkivet, Personarkiven, vol. 60, Carl Eric Wadenstierna (1723–1787).

other functions. It was to provide entertaining reading for family and friends and edifying reading for the daughters. The library displayed an impressive collection of the era's best-known novels and plays, but also memoirs and a large number of 'travelogues'. In addition to the Swedish publications, leading French and English authors were represented. However, the collection at Näs certainly did not lack books and publications about history, economics and science that clearly conveyed Wadenstierna's professional role.

The fact that Wadenstierna's political standpoints were noticeable in various ways in the construction, design and furnishing of Näs, was just as self-evident as the fact that the boundary between his public and private roles was fluid. This also affected his social network, in which professional contacts were often also private ones. Services and favours as well as friendship ties comprised family and relatives, and colleagues and business contacts.[83] There was also an upper-class network that was united in everything from taste, knowledge, political standpoints and economic status to geographic proximity in the form of good neighbours. Wadenstierna's social circle thereby consisted of a heterogeneous upper-class group, including wealthy townspeople, traders, owners of foundries, mills and other industrial operations, and other business owners, senior government officials and members of the nobility who moved in royal circles.

Some of these contacts can be glimpsed in the preserved archival material about the Wadenstierna family, such as naval lieutenant Johan Snoilsky, admirals Carl Fredrik Feiff and Carl August Ehrensvärd with his wife, Sophie Sparre, and her father, Lieutenant General Johan Sparre, who were also closely connected to Wadenstierna's future son-in-law, Lars August Mannerheim.[84] Other contacts included the industrialist Fredrik Ehrenpreus, who was the director of the rifle factory in Huskvarna, Sweden's largest arms manufacturer, and works owner Joakim Daniel Wahrendorf at Åkers Styckebruk, who ran the cannon factory. But also Chamberlain Mattias Odencrantz, who took over the renowned spa Medevi Brunn, and judges of appeal Fredric Cronstedt and Fredric von Post, who became closely connected to the family.[85] After Wadenstierna's death, Cronstedt became the guardian of his daughters, and Von Post, who was also in the neighbouring area at Stora Bärby in Giresta Parish, married Wadenstierna's widow Fredrica Carleson in 1788. Councillor of the realm Sven Bunge who took over Beateberg, the largest estate in Rö Parish, in 1771 had been a member of the *sekreta utskottet* at the same

83 Adams 2000, p. 128.

84 Lars August Mannerheim (1749–1835) was the second cousin of naval officer and artist Carl August Ehrensvärd (1745–1800) and accompanied him on his trip to Italy in 1780–2.

85 These names are among the small group of people who were personally notified of Wadenstierna's death in January 1787. Riksarkivet, Näs Silverstolpeska arkivet, Personarkiven, vol. 60, Carl Eric Wadenstierna (1723–1787).

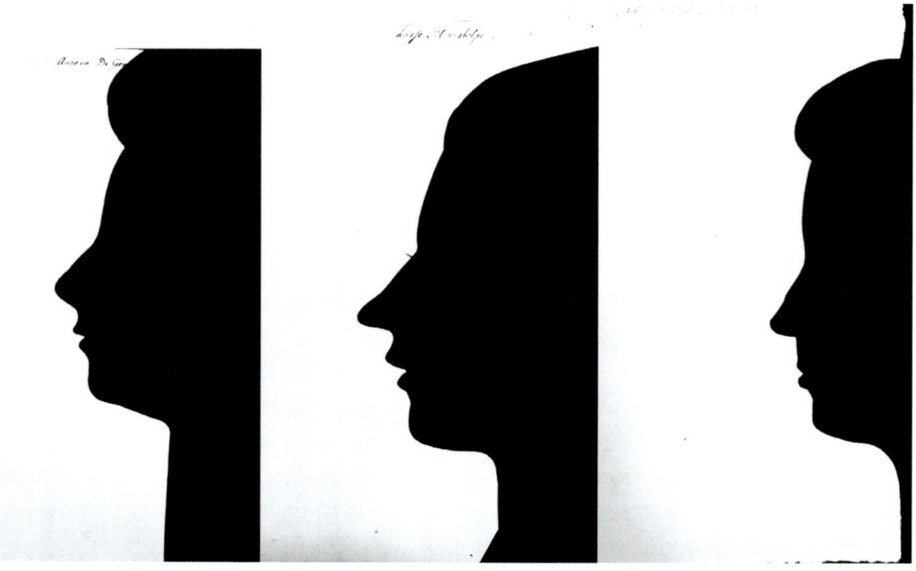

21. Part of the collection of silhouette portraits from Näs: *Fredrica Aurora Taube* (1753–1806) (SPA 1960:243), 1789; *Lars Gabriel Silfverstolpe* (1773–1832) (SPA 1960:266), 1788; *Lars August Mannerheim* (1749–1835) (SPA 1960:259), 1792. Photo: Archives of the Nordic Museum, Stockholm.

time as Wadenstierna and moreover adopted a leading position in the Hat party. Their friendship also included a loan of 1,000 riksdaler that Wadenstierna assisted with in 1781. The majority of the few letters from Carl Eric Wadenstierna that have been preserved in the Swedish National Archives are those addressed to the councillor of the realm, Fredrik Sparre, foster son of the count and politician Carl Gustaf Tessin. They are mostly about various matters pertaining to political work and give little insight into private or social life.

However, a different source tells us somewhat more about socialising and relationships. The documentation of the main building at Näs that was compiled by Nordiska museet in the 1960s includes more than thirty life-size silhouette portraits. The silhouettes are named and dated and show that the majority were created between 1788 and the first few years of the 1790s (Image 21). Together, they provide good insight into the family's social circle in the years shortly after the death of Carl Eric Wadenstierna. The silhouettes illustrate how friendship ties extended between Wadenstierna's own generation and the daughters' same-age friends and their siblings. A series of noble families are presented among the portraits. Siblings from the Silfverstolpe, Falkenberg af Bålby and Mörner af Morlanda families are those represented most. The majority of the young people depicted were students in Uppsala and seem to have visited Näs in the company of the fencing master at the academy, Carl Christopher Porath, whose profile was also rendered as a silhouette. The names tell us about friendship ties but also family relationships. Wadenstierna's eldest daughter, Sophia, got married at Näs in August 1787 to baron and politician Lars August Mannerheim (Image 21). The silhouette portrait depicts him as a forty-three-year-old estate owner at Näs in 1792, the same year that the couple's third daughter, Augusta, was born. Their elder daughter, Fredrika Carolina, married Fredrik Samuel Silfverstolpe, and they subsequently became the new owner family at Näs. His brothers and parents are also included in the silhouette collection. The portraits show how closely connected the upper-class families were, and how marriages often took place within a well-established circle of friends.

The archives do not include any preserved letters or diaries with more detailed insight into these social networks surrounding the Wadenstierna family, but Malla Montgomery-Silfverstolpe's published memoirs have certain points of contact with the circle depicted in the silhouettes at Näs. Through shared family connections, her own portrait miniature by artist Jacob Axel Gillberg later also came to be part of the portrait collection at Näs.[86] Malla Silfverstolpe grew up at the manor house Edsbergs Slott in Sollentuna outside Stockholm but spent the winter months in the capital in the same neighbourhood as the Wadenstierna family's city residence on the corner of Stora Vattugränden and Klara Västra Kyrkogata. In her descriptions of late-eighteenth-century socialising she mentions some of the names from the silhouettes at Näs. They include the renowned beauty in high society Countess Fredrica Aurora Taube (Image 21), married to Jean Jacques de Geer af Finspång, who fills Malla with unease through her brazen boldness when they gather to play games with conversation cards, or young Lars Silfverstolpe (Image 21) with his pronounced profile and beautiful mouth – the perfect person to socialise with – who instead fills her with feelings of delight. However, in 1807 she marries his brother David Gudmund Silfverstolpe.[87]

Malla Silfverstolpe's memoires also paint a good picture of social life at that time, which is likely to have had similarities with the Wadenstierna family's forms of socialising. During the mornings, everyone attended to their own tasks and occupations, while the afternoons were devoted to various social activities. The group play the clavier, dance, play blind man's buff and charades, perform pantomimes and theatricals, and draw and embroider. A neighbour's library and engravings

86 Malla Silfverstolpe's memoires contain a description from one of her visits to 'the elegant' Gillberg in 1802, *Malla Montgomery-Silfverstolpe*, I, 1908, pp. 304–5.

87 In the company of ten-year-old Wilhelmina de Geer of Leufsta, Charles de Geer's daughter, the silhouette portrait of Fredrica Aurora Taube (1753–1806) was cut in August 1789; *Malla* Montgomery-Silfverstolpe, I, 1908–20, pp. 131, 183–4. Lars Gabriel Silfverstolpe (1773–1832) is afforded significantly more space in Malla's memoires; pp. 147–9, 194, 201–3, 208, 221, 224–5, 239, 241f. The silhouette of Lars Silfverstolpe was created in January 1788, when he was fourteen years old, a quartermaster and an aide-de-camp.

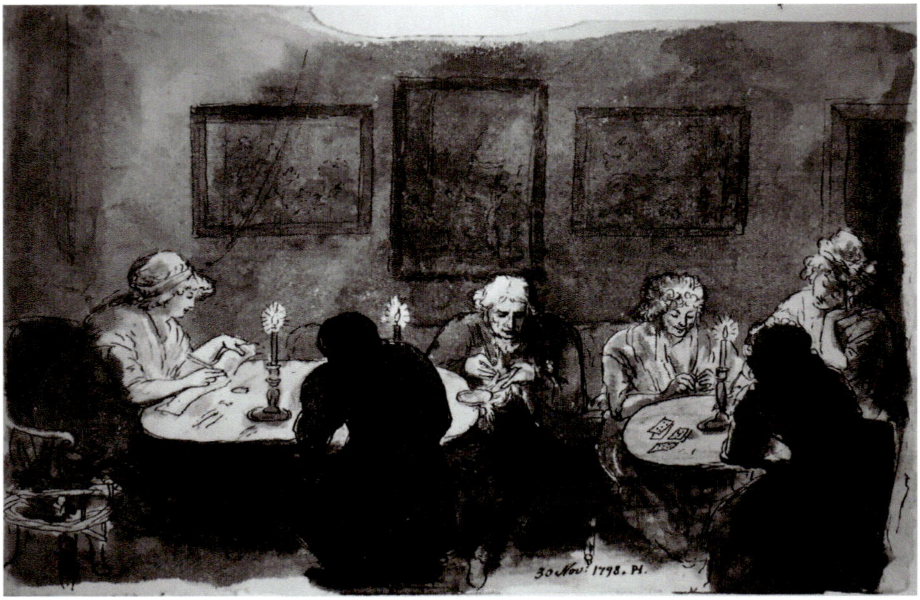

22. Pehr Hörberg, *Evening with the Family at de Geers Finspång*, 1798. Pen and ink wash on paper, 20.5 × 32.5 cm. Nationalmuseum, Stockholm (NMH 516/1884).

collection spur visits and conversations.[88] These hours could probably also have been spent on the fashionable pastime of cutting silhouettes. A small silhouette at Näs represented the artist Per Hörberg, and according to the inscription, the profile picture was cut by the artist himself.[89] Perhaps he came to Näs accompanied by Fredrica Aurora Taube, his patron and friend for many years. Several of Hörberg's drawings from De Geer's Finspång Manor show social groups spending the evening at the tables with card games, needlework, drawing and cutting (e.g. silhouettes and paper dolls) (Image 22). Everyone gathers round the flicking candlelight, while the darkness fills the unlit corners. It was probably during evenings such as these that silhouettes were created. The idea of the home as a place for unaffected, comfortable get-togethers is expressed in these friendship pictures.

Silhouette art was part of the eighteenth century's classicising trend, and these '*portraits à la mode*' were inspired by, among other things, ancient Greek black-figure vase painting. But it was Louis XV's zealously thrifty minister of finance Étienne de Silhouette who lent his name to this novelty – a *cheap* alternative to the established

88 *Malla* Montgomery-Silfverstolpe, I, 1908–20, , pp. 184, 152–4. During the city months, the visiting hour was 18:00–19:00, and on some evenings this was followed by performances at the theatre and opera; pp. 160–1.

89 Silhouette of the artist *Per Hörberg* (1746–1816), Archives of the Nordic Museum, Stockholm.

and much more expensive art of painted portraiture.[90] The silhouette picture was also a more easily accessible art form that was clearly linked to the eighteenth century's flourishing amateur culture, in which artistic activities found forms of expression in everything from drawing and embroidery to turning wood or cutting silhouettes.[91] The amateur creative activities also had a self-evident place in the social life of the era and were in that respect also expressions of the art of socialising and social networks. The silhouettes were often the result of the many and long hours spent in the company of visiting guests – a pastime that demonstrated high-class taste and deft dexterity. The silhouette pictures are therefore also a reminder that Näs was a place for social and cultural manifestation. Furthermore, they fulfilled a documenting memory function in a home where many different people came and went, as shown by the names and dates on the silhouettes. They may have been created in conjunction with a memorable event, a family or seasonal special occasion or other celebration.

The silhouettes have sometimes been called 'the eighteenth century's photographs', and their function can be said to correspond to that of the photographic portraits that were later taken for private use and often exchanged as sentimental friendship gifts.[92] Closeness to the era's passion for the cult of friendship is palpable, and the sentimental value of the pictures is what made this special form of friendship portrait so popular. The parallel with photography in later eras is also linked to the idea that the silhouette was an immediate and infallible 'imprint' of reality and not an interpretation of it. The era's physiognomic ideas were supported in the silhouette pictures as an opportunity to reach people's inner traits through their 'objective' outward appearance. The profiles of famous people were distributed with the aim of showing the connection between their physical features and inner qualities, and this became part of the era's celebrity culture.[93]

Simple silhouettes could be created by covering a silhouette frame with a thin sheet of paper and illuminating it. The model was positioned behind it, and the profile image was then transferred to the paper using a steady hand. The contour image was coloured in with black paint or traced and cut out of black paper. Using a pantograph, the silhouettes could be reduced in size to a manageable format that

90 Anne Gabrisch, *Schattenbilder der Goethezeit*, Leipzig 1966, pp. 64–6.

91 Count Johan Gabriel Oxenstierna writes in his diary on 8 September 1766: 'I have commissioned a joiner to make pantographs that one uses to [draw] silhouettes and cards.' Johan Gabriel Oxenstierna, *Ljuva ungdomstid. Dagbok 1766–8*, Uppsala 1965, p. 40 and p. 57; Brown, Carolina, 'Bilder, sällskapsliv och herrgårdskultur. Maskeradporträtt, silhuetter och andra bilder från 1700-talets Tista', *Historisk Tidskrift för Finland*, årg. 98, 2013:2, Helsinki 2013, pp. 185–215.

92 Arthur Sjögren, 'Silhuetter, 1700-talets fotografier', *Hela världen*, Stockholm 1917.

93 Leif Jonsson, 'Silhuetter ur det gustavianska musiklivet', *Svenskt musikhistoriskt arkiv*, Bulletin No. 29, June 1995, Peter Söderbäck (ed.), Stockholm 1995.

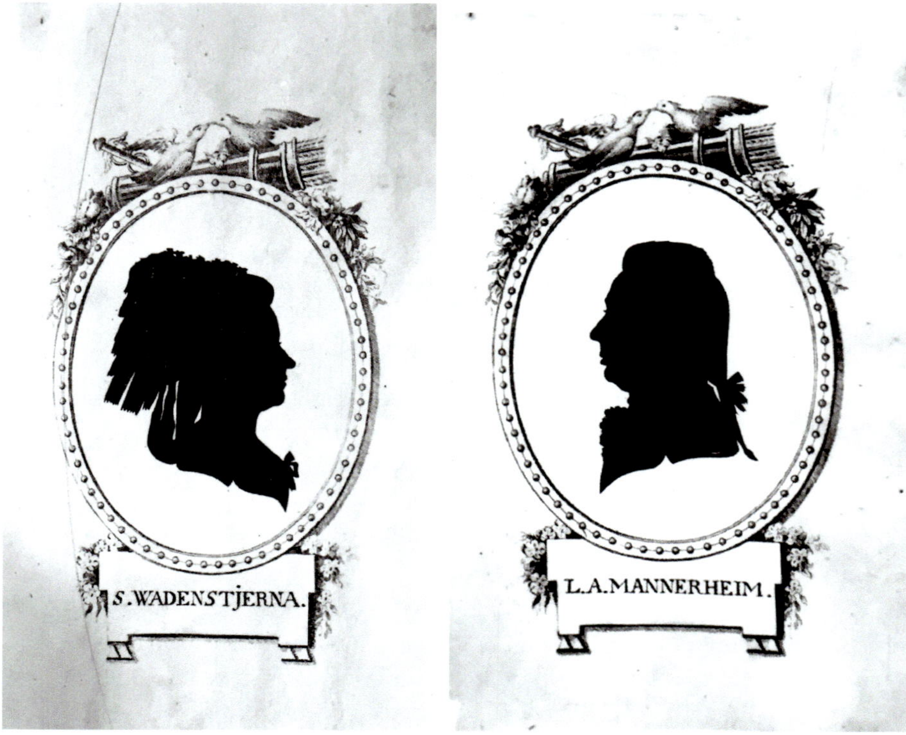

23. *Silhouette Portraits of Sophia Wadenstierna and Lars August Mannerheim*, 1780s. Possibly by Johan Ludvig Tenler. Photo: Archives of the Nordic Museum, Stockholm.

was suitable for framing or fitting into charms, rings or brooches, or they could be used to transfer the picture to decorative objects such as boxes or porcelain cups. Among the era's many professional silhouettes artists, Hieronymus Löschenkohl's silhouette factory in Vienna achieved fame. Fredrik Samuel Silfverstolpe took his parents' silhouettes with him to Vienna in 1803 and had them transferred onto a gold-rim porcelain cup – a fashionable update of Wadenstierna's older armorial tableware.[94]

In Sweden there were also silhouette artists who accepted commissions, and many of them travelled around to reach new customers. Several came from other countries, such as the German Paul Heckens, and regularly placed advertisements in the press to sell their products.[95] They included Johan Ludvig Tenler who offered

94 Photographic documentation of Näs in the 1960s; Archives of the Nordic Museum, Stockholm.

95 Another well-known figure in the social elite was the duke de Pienne, L.M.C. d'Aumont, who, after fleeing the French Revolution, found refuge with Axel von Fersen's sister Sophie Piper and who was skilled at cutting silhouettes. Collections at the Löfstad Manor; Malmborg 1978, p. 210.

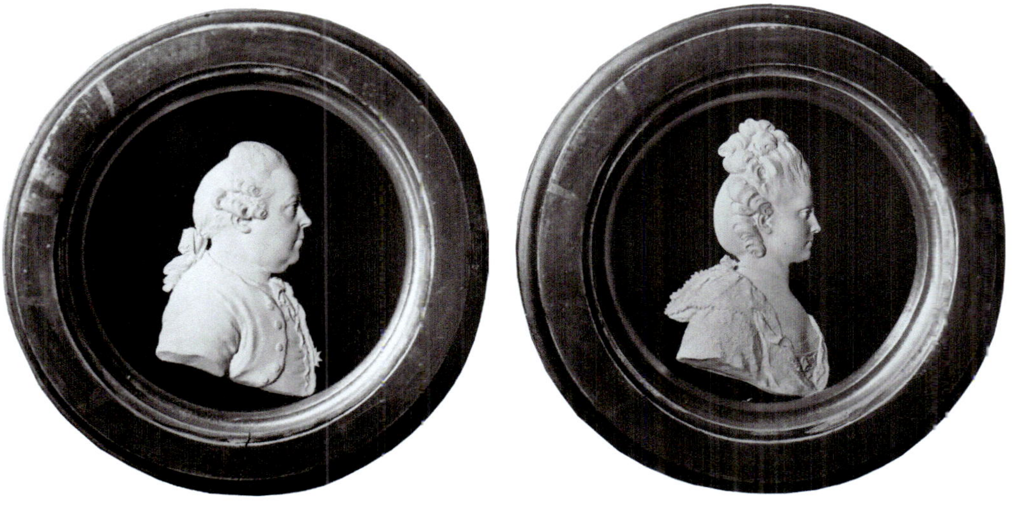

24–25. Carl Carlsson Enhörning, *Carl Eric Wadenstierna och Fredrica Carleson*, 1770s. Wax relief (SPA 1942:332). Photo: Archives of the Nordic Museum, Stockholm.

'Silhouettes on glass, ivory and paper. In rings, breastpins and lockets, etc., as well as the whole family in full-length portraits with the background of the buyer's choosing.'[96] The new trend for full-length scenes had spread from Germany during the 1780s and required both a much larger frame and a camera obscura, and the images were subsequently reduced in format.[97] Although these figure pieces often required professional equipment, they became very popular. Perhaps as they so clearly showed the actual aim of silhouette art – to preserve the memory of friendship.

The host family's own silhouettes are not among those of the visitors to Näs. Perhaps because their profile pictures were already in frames on the walls.[98] They included the portrait medallions with wax relief pictures of Wadenstierna and his wife, created by Carl Carlsson Enhörning (Images 24 and 25). The silhouettes of Wadenstiernas daughters and son-in-law were also there, possibly created by Johan Ludvig Tenler in Stockholm in the 1780s (Image 23).[99] These profile pictures also stood out from the rest of the collection of silhouettes. Fashionable hairstyles, medals, lace and bows are carefully rendered, albeit conventionally repeated,

96 Advertisement in *Jönköpings Allehanda* 1803; Ann Zätterström, 'Tenler, Johan Ludvig', *Svenskt konstnärslexikon*, Malmö 1967, p. 405f.

97 During the 1780s, the full-length silhouette scenes became fashionable through the German Johann Wilhelm Wendt, Gabrisch 1966, p. 66.

98 Carl Eric Wadenstierna had died and Fredrica Carleson had remarried and left Näs before the silhouettes were created.

99 Malmborg 1978, p. 210.

in these '*portraits à la mode*', while these elements are completely absent in the amateur portraits of friends. There, instead the profile picture has been clearly cropped by the silhouette frame, which shows how they were made. It is obvious that the home-made silhouettes were not intended to display the model's status and role but rather individual features and informal relationships. In contrast, the professionally made paper silhouettes were often glued into engraved frames, decorated in accordance with the context which was to be remembered or the status of the model. Sophia's silhouette was reused in conjunction with her betrothal to Lars August Mannerheim a few years later, and the couple's silhouettes are aptly crowned with turtle doves and arrow quivers. But unlike the decoratively framed profile pictures, the silhouettes that were drawn and cut in private provide a concrete picture of who visited the tables at Näs. Their individual features convey presence and authenticity and animate the perceptions of how the hours were spent in the company of friends. The needlework tables were perhaps intended for sewing, but could equally be used for drawing cut-out paper dolls, folding paper 'swallows' (or gliders), plaiting straw wreaths and cutting patterns or silhouette pictures. However, in contrast to most of these highly ephemeral, handcrafted items, the silhouettes have been preserved for posterity – a special way to capture moments in time that tell us about life at Näs in the late eighteenth century.

Family pictures

The silhouette pictures were also expressions of a changed relationship to the portrait genre at the end of the eighteenth century. Näs was home to older family portraits, of Wadenstierna's parents and the companion portraits from his first marriage. In comparison, they were pretentious statements about social status and position. As physical objects, they demanded space, and their formats also meant that they demanded attention. No one in the same room could avoid the portraits' message. In contrast, the amateur silhouettes could be regarded as ephemeral pictures, without high demands on quality or ostentation. Their purpose was not to be displayed for the surrounding world, and they only had value and benefit for the intimate circle in which they had been created. The portrait miniatures that Wadenstierna commissioned also fulfilled new functions compared to older portraiture. Using small gestures and perhaps for a select audience, the miniatures imparted information on relationships rather than positions. Wadenstierna's new marriage to Fredrica Carleson was not confirmed with a grand portrait commission; instead, Niclas Lafrensen was tasked with painting the three miniatures of Wadenstierna and his first and second wives (Plates 1–3).

The choice was, however, hardly for economic reasons. Lafrensen was the newly appointed royal miniature painter and had recently returned from Paris, and his exclusive miniatures painted in watercolours and gouache on ivory were expensive and coveted.[100] In that respect, the commission of the portraits was an expression of Wadenstierna's social pretensions, but equally clearly an indication of the significance that he attached to his relationship with both of his wives. The form and format of these three paintings conveyed intimacy, familiarity and closeness, and Lafrensen reinforced the mutual connections of the three depicted individuals through their gazes. In the portrait, Wadenstierna turns towards his new wife, Fredrica Carleson, in the adjacent painting. However, both of the women flanking him look straight at the viewer; they direct their gazes towards the person for which they were intended, the portraits' commissioner and owner: Wadenstierna himself. The women both meet his gaze with warm smiles. Fredrica Carleson would have possibly preferred to be the only one at her husband's side, but the same constellation was seen in other pictures. There were three additional miniatures of them at Näs, grouped and arranged within a shared frame, where Wadenstierna's first wife appears to hover above him and his new wife (Image 26).[101] Less refined than Lafrensen's skilfully created domestic triangle, these three miniatures instead constitute more of an official document, a formal statement about an evident order. The three models gaze out at the world in front of them, without mutual togetherness. Wadenstierna wearing his statesmanlike national costume, and Fredrica Carleson, through her veil, relegated to a sphere that is separate from that of her husband. Jacobina Psilanderhielm's facial features were taken – significantly – from the betrothal portrait created in her youth.

Portraits in large formats may have been ill-suited to 'the little cabin' that Näs is described as in the entrance hall's overdoor decorations. The paintings by Hilleström and Korn were all in small formats, and the framed engravings were less assuming in comparison. The miniatures and silhouettes were perhaps expressions of a corresponding more modest gesture. The wish 'to be loved more, rather than become famous' was yet another reminder of their relationships rather than their social positions, and in the 'retreat from the noise of the world' the significance of advertising oneself

100 Oscar Levertin, *Niclas Lafrensen d.y. och förbindelserna mellan svensk och fransk målarkonst på 1700-talet*, Stockholm 1899, pp. 79–80. The three portraits that Wadenstierna commissioned are likely to have originated from the time when he married Fredrica Carleson in April 1771. The miniatures can be compared to Lafrensen's portrait of the actress Magdelaine-Nicole-Julie Fromageau from around 1771, similar in style, format and framing (Nationalmuseum, Stockholm, NMB 109).

101 *Widowhood and Visual Culture in Early Modern Europe*, Allison Levy (ed.), Ashgate 2003; regarding love in marriage see Brita Planck, *Förnuft eller känsla. Adel, kärlek & äktenskap*, Stockholm 2018 and Agneta Helmius, 'Äktenskap som mål och mening. Könskonstituering i 1700-talets Sverige', in *Kjønn, makt, samfunn i Norden i et historisk perspektiv*, Dragvoll 1997, pp. 247–70.

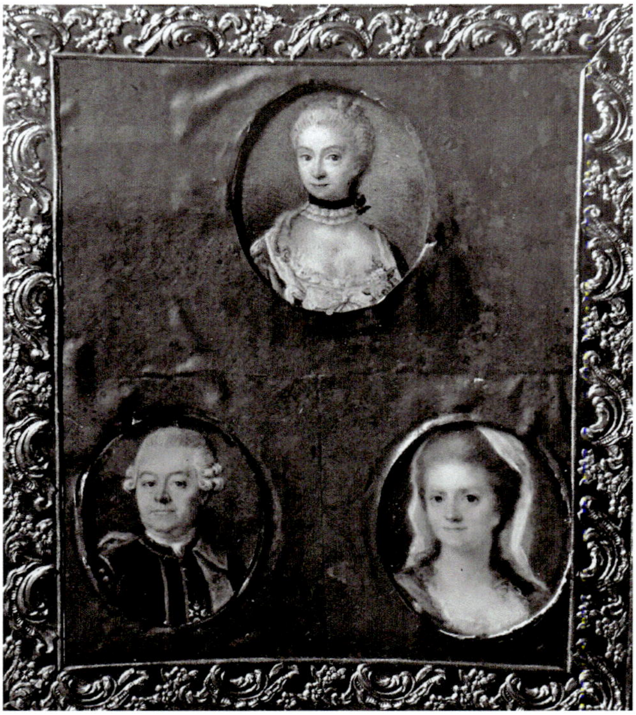

26. Unknown artist, portrait miniatures of *Jacobina Sophia Psilanderhielm von Seulenberg; Carl Eric Wadenstierna* and *Fredrica Carleson* (SPA 1942:326). Archives of the Nordic Museum, Stockholm.

was perhaps diminished. In addition, Näs did not appear to have any lavish painted portraits of Wadenstierna's daughters.[102] Anton Ulrik Berndes' small pencil portrait of Wadenstierna's youngest daughter, Carolina, was the preparatory sketch for a small portrait miniature (Image 28).[103] Next to Lafrensen's pencil drawing, which is probably the sketch for the miniature of Wadenstierna (Plate 2), they give the impression of being ephemeral and unpretentious moments captured in time (Images 27 and 28).[104] The girl with her flowing locks under a hat decorated with flowers, breathes a sense of freedom from the pretentious upper-class portraits of bygone days.

The existence of smaller – and possibly less pretentious – portraits was also linked to changes in fashion and consumption and in the attitudes to relationships, friendships and love at the end of the eighteenth century.[105] The cult of friendship

102 However, the daughters' 'portraits' are found in one of Pehr Hilleström's paintings at Näs, which is discussed in Chapter 2.

103 Magnus Olausson, 'Återfunna konstnärer, återvunna identiteter', *Athena och Ares*, Statens Försvarshistoriska Museer, booklet No. 3, Stockholm 1999, p. 243.

104 Berndes had a high reputation in the art market in the mid-1780s; Runar Strandberg, 'Berndes, Anton Ulrik', *Svenskt konstnärslexikon*, Malmö 1952, p. 164f.

105 Arne Jarrick, *Kärlekens makt och tårar. En evig historia*, Stockholm 1997; *Ljuva möten och ömma samtal. Om kärlek och vänskap på 1700-talet*, Valborg Lindgärde and Elisabeth Mansén (ed.), Stockholm 1999; Eva

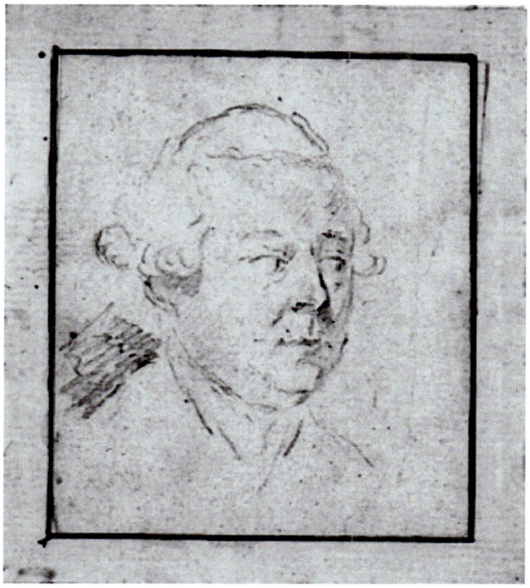

27. Niclas Lafrensen the Younger, *Carl Eric Wadenstierna* (1723–1787). Pencil on paper, 8.4 × 7.1 cm. Nationalmuseum, Stockholm (NMH 216/1891).

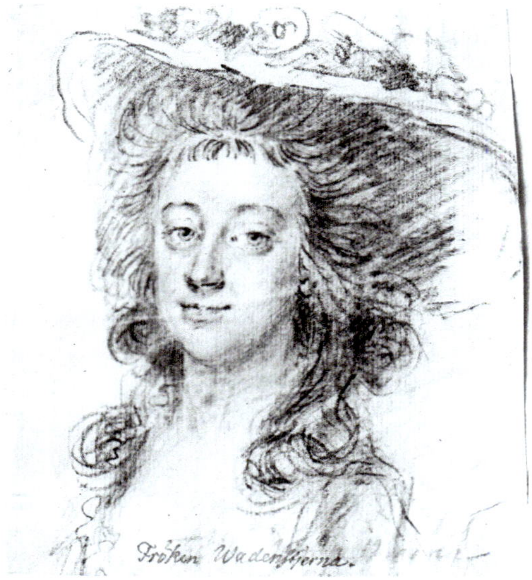

28. Anton Ulrik Berndes, *Carolina Wadenstierna* (1762–1848), 1780s. Pencil drawing, 12 × 10 cm (SPA 1920:1690).

and expectations of love within marriage accompanied the era's new currents and challenged established social duties and cultural conventions. The ideological differences between country life and urbane culture were also part of this. The formal type of entertaining that accompanied a person of rank in the city was, to a certain degree, given freer rein in the country. The old elite's established class markers such as lavish attire or large portraits had started to be questioned by a wider upper-class stratum with new values. But it was also a development that partly harmonised with new perceptions of comfortable everyday life and its ideals of informality and relaxation – of warmth and closeness in both relationships and physical rooms.[106]

In this context, Näs appears to be Wadenstierna's real 'portrait'. In the rural setting of Rö Parish, his home at Näs can be said to replace an official portrait as an identity-building form of expression. The comfortable life, the idea of a 'happy life', was expressed in the material standard: in warm and well-furnished rooms

Lis Bjurman, *Catrines intressanta blekhet. Unga kvinnors möten med de nya kärlekskraven 1750–1830*, Eslöv 1998 [diss.] and Marie Löwendahl, *Min allrabästa och ömmaste vän! Kvinnors brevskrivning under svenskt 1700-tal*, Gothenburg 2007 [diss.].

106 Prytz and Stobart 2018, pp. 234–58. The authors emphasise how social relationships and emotional values, rather than material ones, shaped the eighteenth century's view of comfort at home. See also Stobart 2022.

with comfortably upholstered furniture, in a bed made up with down bolsters and rows of pillows, in a linen cupboard that daily offered a clean shirt and clean table napkins, in a wardrobe that included informal morning gowns, in a dresser full of plates for every course, culinary creation and context, in the number of sugar lumps with one's coffee, in produce from one's own lands that filled larders and dishes. But it was also manifested in social relationships: in the wider professional network and in the private one, in the multitude of servants and in the measure of their loyalty, and in a wife's work, care and attention.[107] These different aspects are also glimpsed in Lafrensen's portrait miniatures. The small pictures, small enough to fit in the palm of your hand, summarised complex conceptions and big dreams of the happy life at Näs. The portraits of Wadenstierna's wives will therefore reappear in the following chapters.

Wadenstierna died on 5 January 1787.[108] Changes subsequently took place in rapid succession. The city residence was left to Fredrica Carleson, and the daughters received Näs and Ticksta with underlying farms as their property while they remained unmarried. The first to marry would then be entitled to take over Näs in the form of an entailed estate, while the other would be allocated a sum of corresponding value for the acquisition of an equivalent manor. As soon as in August that same year, the eldest daughter, Sophia, got married at Näs to the baron and politician Lars August Mannerheim.[109] Carolina Wadenstierna, who later became a lady-in-waiting of Queen Fredrika, married senior valet de chambre Count Jakob Gustaf Oxenstierna on 8 May the following year. It was in conjunction with this wedding that Berndes' miniature was painted. For her inheritance, Carolina acquired Ronöholm Manor, north of Stockholm. Three months later, Fredrica Carleson sold the house at Stora Vattugränd in Stockholm for 132,000 riksdaler to judicial officer Lars Segerström and married one of the executors of her late husband's estate, the latter's friend and colleague, Judge of Appeal Fredric von Post, at Stora Bärby Manor.[110] The same

107 The role of women was to provide their family and household with comfort, needlework, food management, and medical and social care and attention. These female duties and virtues are often mentioned in eulogies and epitaphs. Wadenstierna emphasises his wife's 'tenderness for her fellow human beings' and 'sincere love' in the epitaph that he commissioned to be erected in the Maria Magdalena church. The published speech given at the funeral of his daughter Sophia Wadenstierna clearly expressed how her care, attention and work aimed to benefit the well-being and comfort of others.

108 'Deaths in Stockholm. State Secretary and Knight of the Royal Order of the Polar Star, Carl Eric Wadenstjerna, died on 5 Jan. at 64 years of age. By request, family and friends are hereby notified of the death. No condolences by request.' *Inrikes Tidningar*, Stockholm 11 January 1787.

109 Fahlbeck, Erik, *Lars August Mannerheim. Politiker. Justitieombudsman. Bruksägare. Jordbrukare*, Lund 1969.

110 'Married in Stockholm. President of the Turku Court of Appeal and Knight of the Royal Order of the Polar Star Fredric von Post and Widow Mrs Fredrica Wadenstjerna, born Carleson, were married on 10 Aug.', *Inrikes Tidningar*, Stockholm 28 August 1788.

year that the Mannerheims had – and lost – their first daughter, Fredrica Carleson moved to Turku in Finland, where Von Post had taken up the position of president at the newly established court of appeal. In less than one year after Wadenstierna's death, family life at Näs had been totally reshaped.

Fredrica Carleson died due to illness in Turku in 1794.[111] The beneficiaries of her will were her husband and his two sisters-in-law who were not provided for, and her two step-daughters, Sophia and Carolina. Over the years, Mannerheim became markedly anti-Gustavian with a strong aversion to the monarchy, as a result of which he left his career as a government official in order to devote his time to farming at Näs. Nevertheless, he did not remove Wadenstierna's overdoor decoration in the entrance hall, with the line 'With your wife, children and king go contented to the grave'. His eldest daughter, Fredrika Carolina Mannerheim, married Fredrik Samuel Silfverstolpe, and Näs stayed in the Silfverstolpe family until the mid-twentieth century. A great deal at Näs had remained in a more or less unchanged state until then. The property was dissolved and dispersed during the various changes of ownership in the following decades. The silk yarn, rolled onto spools made of old calling cards and playing cards, which Bengt Söderberg found in the untouched sewing table drawers when he wrote his article about Näs in 1967, disappeared forever, along with the rest of the household goods from Näs.[112] But the next chapter unravels the threads of the story about eighteenth-century Näs anew.

111 'Deaths in the countryside. President of the Royal Turku Court of Appeal and Knight of the Royal Order of the Polar Star Fredric von Post's beloved wife, Mrs Fredrica Carleson, died on 7 Nov., 51 years of age. (By request, family and friends are hereby notified of the death. No condolences by request)'. *Inrikes Tidningar*, Stockholm 7 January 1795.

112 Söderberg, Bengt G., 'Näs', *Slott och herresäten i Sverige*, Malmö 1967, p. 12.

2. At the sewing table

Abstract

The second chapter is set at one of the tables that facilitated the comfortable everyday life of the home. The neat sewing table adhered to constructions of ideal femininity, connected to diligence and domestic virtues. The chapter has its starting point in Niclas Lafrensen's portrait of Carl Eric Wadenstierna's first wife, Jacobina Sophia Psilanderhielm, at her sewing table. Furthermore, Pehr Hilleström's paintings at Näs, whose motives mainly revolve around textile manufacturing and care, become the subject of Wadenstierna's own positioning, as a politician and a member of the government, in the luxury and commodities debate of the time.

Keywords: needle work, domestic virtues, gender, eighteenth-century portraiture, Jean Siméon Chardin

In the eighteenth century, a sewing table was small, elegant and easy for the user to move. Slender legs with brass castors facilitated its movability. The need for good lighting meant that the table had to be moved to various parts of the home depending on the time of day, but also depending on social contexts seeing as needlework was a recurring element in social life. In Sweden, the carcass of the furniture, the parts of the construction that were not visible, were generally made of pine. However, the parts that you could see were significantly more elegant. Table tops were often veneered, perhaps with Swedish maple or birch, or foreign and more exotic varieties. The combination of different kinds of woods created variation and shifts in inlays and patterns. Gilt trim and other details could also contribute to the embellishment. But the sewing table also had specific functions. Drawers with small compartments to store everything required for the work could be fitted into the apron of the table, and the table top could feature holes and attachments for sewing clamps, yarn reels and other accoutrements.[1] This was the core of the sewing table. It was an item of furniture that was both of high-class elegance and

1 Marshall Lagerquist, *Georg Haupt. Ebeniste du Roi*, Nordiska museets handlingar 92, Stockholm 1979, p. 48; Lars Ljungström, *Georg Haupt. Gustav III:s hovschatullmakare*, Stockholm 2006, p. 122.

Brown, C., *Comfortable Everyday Life at the Swedish Eighteenth-Century Näs Manor.*
Taylor & Francis Group, 2024
DOI 10.5117/9789048562374_CH02

practical. It was a table to display and gather around, but also to work at. Narrow table legs and a stretcher made of pieces of wood curving inwards created space for feet and dresses and enabled you to get close to the table from several sides. Sewing was a social activity and a task that was included in the ideals of utility and cultivation in the Age of Enlightenment. The documents about the Wadenstierna family also mention the sewing tables. According to the estate inventory drawn up after Wadenstierna's death in 1787, there was '1 rectangular sewing table with inlays' in his city residence, and '1 small round sewing table' as well as '1 ditto rectangular in mahogany' at Näs.[2] We do not know which craftsman or craftsmen made the sewing tables that appear in the family documents or anything about the tables glimpsed in Hilleström's paintings. But this item of furniture is the starting point for this chapter.

The tables also feature in the portraits of the family. Jacobina Sophia Psilanderhielm leans her arm on an elegant sewing table in Lafrensen's portrait (Plate 1). She is sitting comfortably in the silk-upholstered armchair, and her clothing is draped in soft folds. The peignoir with lace and ribbons and the silk dress adorned with bows stand out against her white complexion and pink lips. In her hand she holds a piece of embroidery, and her workbag and sewing scissors are on the table next to her – but at this moment she has taken a break from her work. The portrait is undeniably a display of contemporary fashion. Next to the delicate silk and tulle of her attire and the striking golden edging of her workbag, the painting highlights the chair's upholstery with its patterned woven fabric and the sewing table's marquetry and gilt trim. Here, there is a clear aim to sensually convey the material culture that surrounds the lady in the painting. But her active presence, her smiling expression and needlework in progress were also important to accentuate, even though the portrait was painted posthumously – five years after her death.[3]

Why did Carl Eric Wadenstierna decide that a portrait of his deceased wife would also form part of the commission that he ordered from Niclas Lafrensen, when Wadenstierna, who had recently married Fredrica Carleson, was about to start a new chapter in life at the newly built Näs Manor? And why did he want her to be depicted in her daily work, in the clothing she wore during the mornings in their home? What associations did the sewing table on which she was leaning convey, and how was it linked to her as a person and her position in life?

If Lafrensen's three portrait miniatures are placed in a row with the gentleman in the middle, his first wife on the left discreetly turns her back on the newlyweds. She differs in the composition through the choice of colours and her informal

2 Riksarkivet, Näs Silverstolpeska arkivet, Personarkiven, vol. 60, Carl Eric Wadenstierna (1723–1787).

3 Niclas Lafrensen the Younger probably used an earlier portrait as a model, presumably the companion portrait attributed to Johan Henric Scheffel, SPA 1942:311 (Image 30).

clothing, yet remains linked to the portrait of Wadenstierna's new wife. They are both depicted as being of the same age and equal in merit. Wadenstierna could proudly position himself between both of his exemplary wives, who in the ordered world of portraiture honour him with a display of female skills, beauty and grace, at the same time that they are surrounded by the material prosperity that he has provided them with. And both are equally present, even though time and life had moved on.

The recurrent sessions at the sewing tables were key parts of the women's everyday life – in the Wadenstierna family's Stockholm residence and later also at Näs. But these activities were also firmly anchored in the era's ideas of a woman's roles in the family and society. The sewing table thereby represents a combination of everyday life, new thoughts on comfort, and older, deeply rooted perceptions of the nature and duties of women. Everyday activities had an important symbolic dimension. This mix of utility, relaxation and ideology is the subject of this chapter.

Jacobina Sophia Psilanderhielm af Seulenberg

Jacobina was the daughter of Jakob Psilanderhielm, a recording clerk and civil servant at the fortifications office, and Christina Catharina Strobell, the daughter of an apothecary. Jacobina had played an important part in Wadenstierna's life, and he clearly wanted to keep her by his side even after her death.[4] They had both been orphaned at a young age, and after they got married in October 1756, they built up the home and family life that they had both been deprived of early on. Just under two years later, little Sophia was born, named after her mother, and their second and third daughters Charlotta and Carolina were born in 1761 and 1762, respectively.

In 1761, the couple also acquired the considerable and centrally located property in Stockholm, next to the Klara church.[5] The first owner of the house was the *krigsråd* (senior government official for military matters) Jakob Rök Andersson. He had purchased it the year before Wadenstierna himself was appointed to the position of *krigsråd*, so perhaps Wadenstierna took over Andersson's position and home. It was a residence that suited both a growing family and an industrious government official who was often summoned to contribute to various matters. In addition to a basement and an attic, the house had 11 rooms on the first floor and 8 on the second.[6] The property also included four outbuildings made of stone. There

4 Carl Eric Wadenstierna took up the position of clerk at the war office just under two years after Jakob Psilanderhielm's death in 1741. *Kultur- och personhistoriska anteckningar*, I, p. 154. http://runeberg.org/strokirk/1/0158.html, accessed: 12 January 2020.

5 Stockholms Stadsarkiv, *Brandförsäkring* (fire insurance), 6 February 1760.

6 An advertisement in *Dagligt Allehanda* on 9 September 1772 to sell 'a fairly beautiful and good riding and sleigh horse' states that prospective buyers could register their interest at Wadenstierna's house,

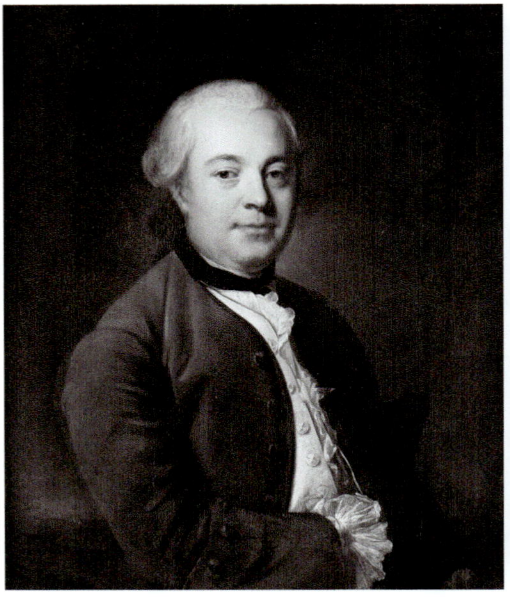

29. Johan Henric Scheffel [attrib.], *Carl Eric Wadenstierna*. Oil on canvas, 79 × 64 cm (SPA 1942:32). Private ownership. Photo: Bukowskis.

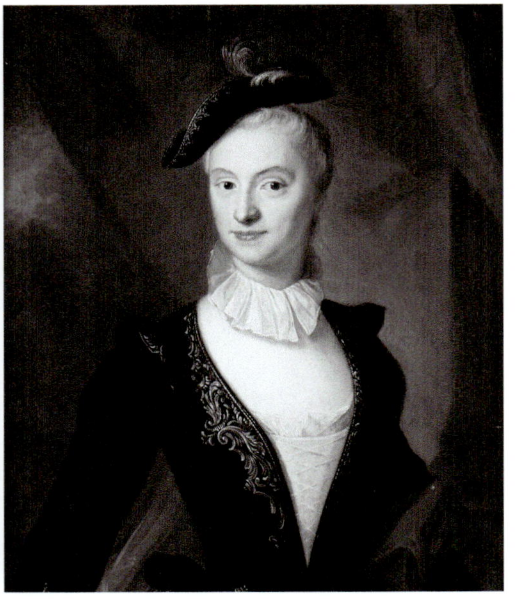

30. Johan Henric Scheffel [attrib.], *Jacobina Sophia Psilanderhielm von Seulenberg*. Oil on canvas, 79 × 64 cm (SPA 1942:311). Private ownership. Photo: Bukowskis.

were stables, a carriage house, woodsheds, a wash and mangle shed, three rooms for servants, and a bakehouse with a baking oven and built-in copper boiler – all together valued at 96,200 daler copper coins.[7] The couple probably had the financial means from both of their families. Wadenstierna had effectively managed his inheritance from his affluent maternal aunt Christina Tungelfelt, and Jacobina's brother, Johan Fredrik Psilanderhielm, who was a vice president at the government authority for mining, died unmarried in 1759 and probably left a bequest to his only sibling.[8]

The portraits of the couple in the early years of their marriage have been ascribed to Johan Henric Scheffel (Images 29 and 30). Wadenstierna is wearing unassuming upper-class clothing, and a rosy glow of dawn is glimpsed in the background. His hand is resting securely inside his white waistcoat, and the delicate linen of his shirt cuffs and ruffles stands out against his unadorned grey-blue coat. The image appears to be deliberately restrained, without eye-catching

specifically the ground floor, which perhaps indicates that the family only used the lower floor of the house.

7 Stockholms Stadsarkiv, *Brandförsäkring*, 6 February 1760.

8 During his lifetime, Johan Fredrik Psilanderhielm had bequeathed a sizeable sum of money to each of Wadenstierna's daughters, Asplund, Karl, 'Näs i Rö', *Fataburen*, Nordiska Museet, Stockholm 1960, p. 9.

lace or other lavish embellishments. In the companion portrait, his wife steps in from the landscape backdrop and stops, straight-backed, mid-movement. She is dressed for the city's winter amusements in a black fancy-dress costume. Compared to her husband's tranquil portrait, hers has greater intensity, with black velvet and draped red silk fabrics against her white complexion and powdered hair. The silver embroidery on her costume forms dancing borders, and there is a hint of a smile on her lips. The half-length portraits by one of the era's leading portraitists were in themselves pretentious manifestations, and the gazes and gestures of the models demonstrate the self-confident role that they adopted. The portraits were probably displayed in a prominent place in their new home in Stockholm.

Their home also became filled with a great many household items that were representative of the couple's status, while horses, carriages and servants occupied the outbuildings. Family life ran in parallel with Wadenstierna's intensive working life as a government official in the midst of the turbulence between the political parties and the monarchy. But as time went on, the unease in the political sphere was accompanied by misfortunes in the family's private life. In May 1768, almost exactly two years after the couple's five-year-old daughter Charlotta died, Jacobina also passed away, aged just thirty-five. Biographies and obituaries convey Wadenstierna's devastation.[9] Her epitaph in the Maria Magdalena church was erected by 'a husband grieving until his death'. The lapidary style inscription on the large marble plaque emphasises: 'PIOUS. DECENT. AND. GOOD. SHE. POSSESSED. ALL. THE. VIRTUES. OF. HER. SEX. WITHOUT. FAULT.' The inscription asks everyone to stop at the tomb and share the grieving husband's emotion. Wadenstierna's strong feelings are also shown in a letter to his remaining daughters after his wife's death. He writes, '[A] lthough my heart is troubled and broken, ... the most blissful marriage on earth was entered into and was founded on unaffected esteem, the most tender love and pure respect.' In the short rules of life that he draws up, he urges the girls to endeavour to emulate their mother, so that they may be honoured in life, missed after death and blessed in eternity.[10]

The estate inventory of Jacobina Psilanderhielm presents a picture of the affluent home that she left behind. The densely written folios mention showpiece mirrors, chests of drawers with marble tops, walnut slant-top desks, eight games tables, sofas upholstered in silk damask, sixty-two chairs, cupboards with glass doors, an ornately upholstered 'Imperial' bed, 191 engravings with glass and gilt frames, family portraits, a chandelier with enamelled flowers, bird cages, silver tea and coffee

9 Fahlbeck, Erik, *Lars August Mannerheim. Politiker. Justitieombudsman. Bruksägare. Jordbrukare*, Lund 1969, p. 59.

10 Riksarkivet, Näs Silverstolpeska arkivet, Personarkiven, vol. 60, Carl Eric Wadenstierna (1723–1787).

services, armorial tableware, tableware from the Marieberg factory in Stockholm and English tableware.[11] Hat party politician Wadenstierna's support of Swedish manufactories can be discerned in the wealth of belongings in his home, but there are indications that he also supported trade with distant countries. The many pieces of jewellery embellished with rose-cut gems, brilliants and natural pearls also testify to inheritance and capital in keeping with upper-class status. Jacobina Psilanderhielm's gold watch with twenty-five brilliants and a chain commanded a value of 1,500 daler copper coins, and her twelve *'robe de ronde'* dresses in her considerable collection of clothes, were of corresponding value.[12]

The significance of textiles

There is, however, another category of objects that constitute part of Jacobina Psilanderhielm's estate inventory: seven spinning wheels and seven yarn winders (yarn swifts) with spools, reels and cards, as well as embroidery frames and sewing tables, which indicate that the home produced a considerable volume of textile items. The large number of *'hus lärfts'* (literally: house linen) sheets has been clearly marked in relation to the small number of sheets made of the finest Dutch linen fabric.[13] Many ells of silk and calico intended for 'clothes for the young ladies' were also included in the possessions left by Jacobina. The inventory states that Jacobina's gold thimble and sewing rings had been given to her eldest daughter, Sophia. This was an important indication. The gift symbolised that the eldest daughter would, in due course, take over the responsibility for the house's textile work.

In one of the paintings that Wadenstierna commissioned from Pehr Hilleström, the significance of needlework is emphasised particularly clearly (Plate 5). The artist titled the painting *2ne Fröknar Wadenstiernas portraiter – i Conversation* (Portraits of two young Wadenstierna ladies – in conversation), but in the picture, the daughter Sophia Wadenstierna averts her gaze from 'the conversation' and looks out of the picture towards the viewer. In the same way that her mother was depicted by Lafrensen, Sophia has momentarily stopped sewing in order to smile and meet the viewer's gaze. Perhaps she is using her mother's thimble. On the adjacent small veneered *bonheur du jour* writing table, we glimpse a book and possibly also a workbag next to the ball of yarn. The chair she is sitting on is also

11 Estate inventory, Jacobina Sophia Psilanderhielms bouppteckning, 4 December 1769, Riksarkivet, Näs Silverstolpeska arkivet, Personarkiven, vol. 60, Carl Eric Wadenstierna (1723–1787).

12 Ibid.

13 The expression *'hus lärft'* does not show that the fabric was necessarily produced within the household, but rather that it was Swedish-made in relation to the imported fabrics.

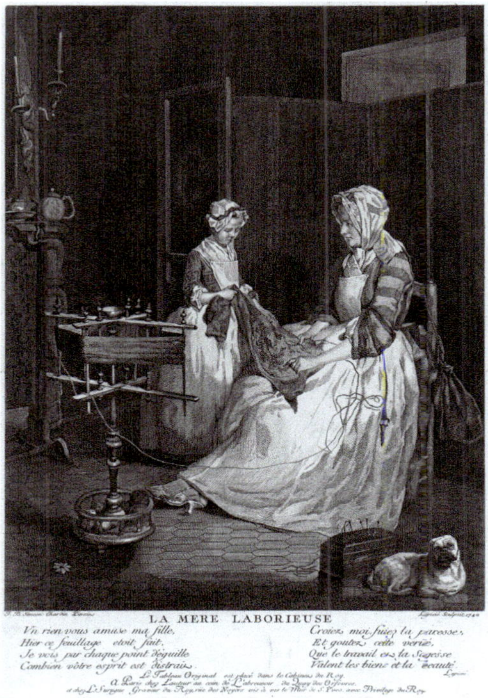

31. François-Bernard Lépicié after Jean-Baptiste Siméon Chardin, *La mère laborieuse*, 1740. Engraving, 37.6 × 26.9 cm. Rijksmuseum, Amsterdam (RP-P-1952-637).

reminiscent of her mother's blue-upholstered armchair in Lafrensen's portrait miniature (Plate 1).

In Hilleström's painting *Tillrättavisningen* (The telling-off), which was commissioned at the same time, the older girl is urged to be industrious with her sewing (Plate 6). The girl positioned on the blue-upholstered armchair, wearing a blue dress and holding her linen needlework in her hands, also bears a slight resemblance to Sophia in this genre scene. But that *2ne Fröknar Wadenstiernas portraiter – i Conversation* was intended to specifically be a *portrait* is shown from Hilleström's title, included on his own handwritten list of his artworks from 1810.[14] Sophia and her younger sister, Carolina, have gathered around the yarn winder at which a woman is sitting and winding yarn. It is a 'yarn winder with reels' of the type stated in the estate inventory of the girls' late mother. They had probably sat with her by the yarn winder on countless occasions during her lifetime. Hilleström's scene is bound to have evoked emotions of recognition and togetherness in Wadenstierna and his daughters. But Hilleström's title does not

14 According to the list that Hilleström compiled of the works that he created between 1773 and 1810. The list is kept at the Royal Swedish Academy of Fine Arts but has also been reproduced in Gerda Cederblom, *Pehr Hilleström som kulturskildrare*, I, Stockholm 1927.

state who the woman in the painting is. When it was commissioned, in around 1774, Wadenstierna had already married his new wife, Fredrica Carleson, and their shared life at Näs was about to start. Perhaps the painting aimed to show that the home and girls had now gained a new 'mother', who is continuing to wind the thread that their late mother had left behind. Or maybe, as was the case with Lafrensen's portrait, it was a picture that Wadenstierna had in his mind of his deceased wife and found difficult to let go of.

The theme of a woman engaged in needlework was, in both cases, in accordance with prevailing expectations. Throughout the ages, it had symbolised the view of women and their roles as wives and mothers. The Lutheran instruction book *The Small Catechism* included a section called 'Hustavlan [Household chart]' that stipulated the order of duties and responsibilities within households, and subsequent tracts that served as moral mirrors and stipulated female behaviour, brought up girls and women to be diligent and obedient in compliance with the stated order.[15] *Husfrudömet* was the sphere of power and authority of the lady of the house and included responsibility for the household's material items and their production, care and maintenance.[16] She was expected to contribute to the household's economy, above all by making, sewing, labelling, washing and mending the textiles that were needed in the home by her husband, children and employees.[17] The work often required knowledge of all stages of textile production, from the raw materials to the finished items, which we are reminded of by the cards, spinning wheels and weaving looms in the estate inventories. The stock of textile items encompassed everything from curtains, bed linen, cloths, napkins and towels to everyday clothes, underwear, handkerchiefs, collars, cuffs and other items of clothing. More intricate, decorative sewing in the form of embroidered garments and accessories or sewn and bobbin lace details also required time and skill. 'Plain' needlework, such as household linens, was a particularly

15 These moralistic and didactic booklets presented the good examples that women could mirror themselves in and adapt themselves to, and they emphasised female virtues such as humility, piety, moderation, modesty and submissiveness; *Unga Fruentimbers Hushålls Spegel*, Stockholm 1754, reissued in 1773 and 1788.

16 The worldly order of the Lutheran *hustavlan* (household chart) differentiated between the spiritual, earthly and household realms, and in the latter the responsibility was divided up between the master and the lady of the house. The keys symbolised the lady's responsibility for the household's property (in the sense of items, belongings), of which textiles constituted an important part.

17 Unmarried adult sons could also count on benefiting from the care that their mothers bestowed on looking after their sons' linens and clothes. Märta Helena Reenstierna sewed and mended the shirts of her son Hans Abraham, even after he reached adulthood. Reenstierna, Märta Helena, *Årstadagboken*, I–III, Stockholm (1985) 1993, p. 191; Pernilla Rasmussen, *Skräddaren, sömmerskan och modet. Arbetsmetoder och arbetsdelning i tillverkningen av kvinnlig dräkt 1770–1830*, Nordiska museets handlingar 136, Stockholm 2010, [diss.], pp. 71–3.

time-consuming occupation for the women. The large number of linen shirts listed on eighteenth-century estate inventories testifies to the importance of constantly having changes of clothes in an era of limited laundry facilities. Carl Eric Wadenstierna's estate inventory mentions three dozen linen shirts and a dozen nightshirts, twenty-five pairs of various kinds of cuffs and twenty-five cravats. Jacobina Psilanderhielm's multitude of peignoirs, petticoats, handkerchiefs and *engageantes* are expressions of the same needs.[18] The extensive stock of linens and clothes was therefore not only a measure of wealth but also a measure of a privileged cleanliness that was a marker of class.[19] Comfort required large volumes of linens and clothes.

To maintain comfortable everyday life, continual work at the sewing tables was required. Proficiency in a series of different sewing techniques was therefore regarded as an extremely important skill for women and was to be trained from a young age. Samplers, engagement gifts for fiancés and bridal bed covers were proof of the skills that women were expected to develop over the years. There were above all two occasions in life, in conjunction with childbirth and in preparation for marriage, that demanded more extensive acquisition of linen and undergarments. The most extensive was the trousseau – the collection of clothing and other items that accompanied a girl into marriage. François-Alexandre de Garsault's book *L'art de la lingerie* from 1771 presents the recommended contents of an *état d'un trousseau.*[20] The incredibly long lists of the many different textile items that were to be included probably felt like a weighty demand on all unmarried daughters and their families. The work on the contents of the trousseau had to be started well in advance as many years of sacrificing time and money were required to complete it. Perhaps this was also something that Wadenstierna realised when his wife died and left him alone with two young daughters.[21]

Wills, estate inventories and other inventories and lists are reminders of the significant value of the textiles, as is the care devoted to looking after them. Expensive fabrics were inherited and reused for generations and gained new functions. A cover for a child's bed at Näs in the eighteenth century, sewn from various saved

18 Jacobina Sophia Psilanderhielms bouppteckning, 4 December 1769, Riksarkivet, Näs Silverstolpeska arkivet, Personarkiven, vol. 60, Carl Eric Wadenstierna (1723–1787). *Engageantes* were the thin, often lace-trimmed ruffles or flounces on the end of the sleeves of women's clothes.

19 Carolina Brown, 'Den vita lyxen. Spetsar i 1700-talets visuella och materiella kultur', *Det svenska begäret. Sekler av lyxkonsumtion*, Paula von Wachenfeldt and Klas Nyberg (ed.), Stockholm 2015, pp. 98–100.

20 François-Alexandre de Gersault, *L'Art de la lingerie*, Paris 1771, pp. 11f.

21 'What we know is that the task of taking care of our upbringing, especially in the earliest years, falls to the mother in particular. We spend our childhood under her eye, but her care must often also extend to our youth and our more mature years, at least regarding her daughters.' *En fullkomlig Ägta Hustrus Bild,* Gothenburg 1787, pp. 31–2.

scraps of silk, such as from an old cloth and a cravat, is an example of reuse in which nothing was wasted.[22] A well-stocked linen cupboard was therefore a concrete measure of the household's wealth, but also of the skill of the lady of the house in making, utilising and preserving the textile items. The high economic value of the textile goods was shown in the owner's monograms that were neatly embroidered onto the fabric – a stamp of ownership which guaranteed that nothing would end up in the wrong hands during laundry, when moving house or in the distribution of an estate. Male owner's monograms signify the high status of the textile goods and indicated who had ultimate authority over the use of the items. For example, Carl Eric Wadenstierna's estate inventory from 1787 meticulously specifies which of the 629 linen damask napkins had been marked with the initials C.E.W. The hierarchy expressed through the household's bed linen can also be deduced from the estate inventory.[23] The items for the bed of the master and lady of the house comprising mangled and marked bed linen, a bolster, eight down pillows, three long pillows and a silk bed cover are followed by the daughters' smaller number of pillows and calico bed cover, and the servants' individual pillows and simpler 'Wäst göthe Täcke' (bed cover with fabric made in Västergötland Province). In barn kitchens and farm hands' quarters, sheepskins were used instead of bed covers. The Wadenstiernas at Näs were no exception. In his will dating from 1804, the diplomat Ulric Celsing drew particular attention to his exclusive damask linen, purchased in Saxony: 'by me, on site in the factory, ordered and purchased for 960 R:dr, as the finest to be made and more valuable than my heirs could probably imagine' – a statement that emphatically underlined the importance of the linen and that it was also a matter for men.[24]

The choice of portrait pose for Jacobina Psilanderhielm and her daughters, in Lafrensen's and Hilleström's portraits, was not only a marker of the socio-economic significance ascribed to textiles and the women's responsibility for this part of the larger structural order that the household constituted. It was even more clearly a visualisation of the virtues that were associated with an ancient notion of the ideal woman. The large numbers of pictures and portraits that displayed women engaged in needlework and that absolutely inundated the pictorial world of the eighteenth century wanted to convey something important about the women and girls depicted.

22 Nordiska museets arkiv, KU 3542, Uppland, Sjuhundra hd, Röö sn, Näs.

23 The significance of bed linen emerges in both wills and estate inventories; Riksarkivet, Näs Silverstolpeska arkivet, Personarkiven, vol. 60, Carl Eric Wadenstierna (1723–1787).

24 Ulric Celsing's will, *Testamentariska Fideicomiss-Förordnanden af Framl. Envoyén och Commendören af Kongl. Nordst. Orden, herr Ulric Celsing Gustafson; af d. 1 mars och 3 Dec. 1804 samt d. 5 och 22 Nov. 1805*, 1806, p. 43.

The exemplary women of the eighteenth century

To show that the women were keeping busy was crucial in this context. Sloth (laziness) – *Acedia* – was one of the seven deadly sins, while industriousness – *Industria* – was its virtuous opposite. Both occupy their allotted place in the eighteenth century's varied literature on how to bring up women.[25] Boudier de Villemert's *L'ami des femmes* (translated into Swedish in 1763) expounds on the eighteenth century's thrifty versus wasteful types of women, where the latter is consumed with her laziness and thoughtlessness, only enlivened by a new precious stone or 'a monkey made of porcelain'.[26] In the spirit of the Age of Enlightenment, under the heading 'The occupations of womenfolk' there was instead an emphasis on the importance of following 'nature' and the order that had assigned women their place and role. Women of all classes and ages are urged to occupy themselves daily and incessantly with useful work in order to fill their life in an exemplary manner.

With the rise of new, bourgeois-tinted values in the late eighteenth century, the gender-coded activities became symbols of an original 'natural' order ranked higher than the hierarchical class society that the era started to distance itself from. References to bygone days, when each individual took care of their own tasks, recurred as a socially critical trope throughout the eighteenth century.[27] Earlier, Molière's *L'école des femmes* (School for wives, 1662) was a reminder of how the women in the development of the consumer society all wanted to live in luxury and laziness, like ladies in Paris. As an antithesis, the former golden age was emphasised when a natural order kept chaos in check, such as here in the Swedish edition from 1738 when Molière's *L'école des femmes* was performed in Stockholm:

> Alas! Blessed be bygone days, when decency reigned!
> Then one heard nothing but silence, virtue and honour;
> Then a woman's work was to sit at the spinning wheel,
> And her daughter was raised with a needle and lace bobbin.[28]

25 Also see the visual art in this respect. Many of the eighteenth century's widespread engraved images with moral themes illustrated the two opposites, with the lazy and vain woman devoting her time to gazing at her reflection at her dressing table, while her virtuous sister is diligently bowed over her sewing, for example 'Graveur de quatre sujets apres Etienne Jeaurat: La dévote, L'econome, La savante et La coquette, gravés par Michel Aubert,' *Mercure de France*, vol. 799, October 1734, p. 2267.

26 Boudier de Villemert, Pierre Joseph, *Qwinno-könets wän. Öfwersatt ifrån fransyskan*,Västerås (1758) 1763, pp. 28–30.

27 One example is the quote 'When each and every person takes care of their task, all will be well, whatever we encounter' (*The Small Catechism*, Household Chart, 15). Compare with this statement by medieval clergyman John Ball: 'When Adam delved and Eve span, who was then the gentleman?' (from the sermon delivered at Blackheath after the Peasants' Revolt in 1381).

28 Jean Baptiste Molière, *Qwinno-Skolan, Eller: Den Enfaldige Agnes, i Fem Acter, Föreställd på den Swenska Theatren i Stockholm Anno 1738*, translated into Swedish by Gustaf Palmfelt, Stockholm 1739, p. 5.

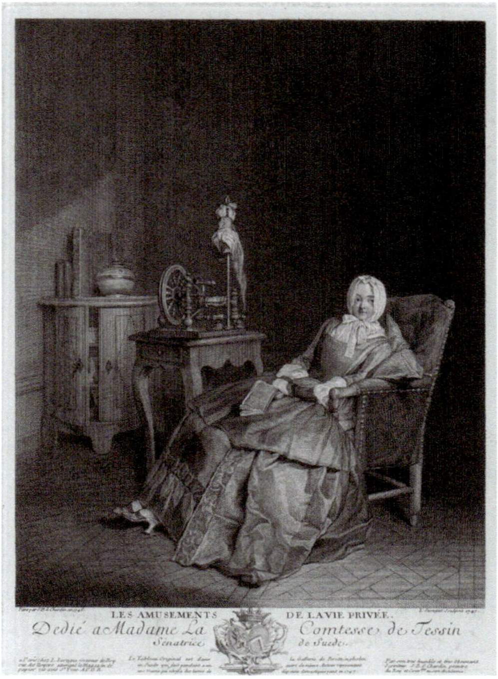

32. Pierre Louis Surugue after Jean-Baptiste Siméon Chardin, *Les amusements de la vie privée*, 1747. Copperplate, 37.6 × 27.2 cm. The Metropolitan Museum, New York (61.591.20), the Elisha Whittelsey Collection, the Elisha Whittelsey Fund, 1961.

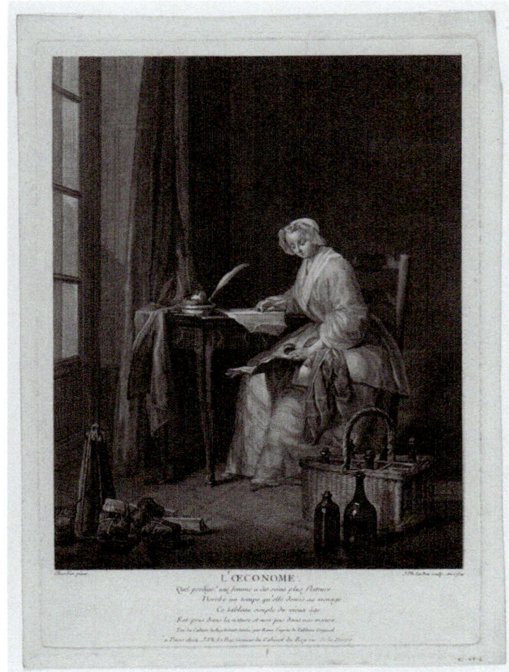

33. Jacques-Philippe Le Bas after Jean-Baptiste Siméon Chardin, *L'économe*, 1754. Copperplate, 38.4 × 27.3 cm. Philadelphia Museum of Art, gift of Henry P. McIlhenny, 1942.

A woman doing needlework in pictorial art was the symbol of good housekeeping, for the well-functioning home and for the virtuous wife.[29] The two paintings by Jean Siméon Chardin that Carl Gustaf Tessin commissioned on behalf of Queen Lovisa Ulrika in 1745 came to play an important part in the development of the theme during the eighteenth century. The paintings were originally intended to show *L'éducation sévère* and *L'éducation douce et insinuante*, the strict and mild forms of upbringing, respectively. But when they arrived in Stockholm in 1747, they showed other albeit parallel subjects, which could be interpreted in a wider sense.[30] *Les amusements de la vie privée* illustrated relaxation from household chores, in which the woman sinks into the armchair with a book, while the spinning wheel has to wait

29 As moralising contrasting images, there were also examples of women and girls who had fallen asleep over their needlework. A Swedish woodcut print from 1759 shows a woman who has fallen asleep at a spinning wheel, while a pig spins yarn with a spindle, a second pig hackles linen, a third reels and a fourth winds the spun yarn (see Bringéus 1995, p. 198).

30 Pontus Grate, *French Paintings, II, Eighteenth Century*, Nationalmuseum, Stockholm 1994, p. 95.

on the adjacent table. And *L'économe* showed the administrative work involved in housekeeping, portrayed by a woman writing and reviewing lists and bills at a small table (Images 32 and 33). Chardin's own wife, Françoise-Marguerite Pouget, was the model in the paintings of the exemplary wife, and when *Les amusements de la vie privée* was engraved that same year by Louis de Surugue de Surgis, the engraving was dedicated to Carl Gustaf Tessin's wife, Countess Lovisa Ulrika Sparre.[31] Via the engravings, the message spread like ripples in water – from the realm's 'first lady', wife and mother Queen Lovisa Ulrika, to the women of the elite and the bourgeoisie.

François-Bernard Lépicié's epigram for the engraving *L'instant de la méditation* states that both repose and work are aimable – 'this lovable work, this pleasant reading'.[32] Morally and didactically, utility, enjoyment and relaxation are united here by the hearth of the home. For the woman who loyally and dutifully adheres to her assigned lot, her life is whole and harmonious, and she can enjoy her well-deserved rest. In *Les amusements de la vie privée* rest is also depicted as fashionable. Relaxed and elegant, with crossed legs, the woman leans against the soft cushions of the armchair. The woman's household duties are here united with the ideal of modern comfort. Everything in this well-ordered existence meets all the needs for *kommoditet* (*commodité* – comfort, amenity) and convenience in everyday life. Chardin's motif became very widespread in the following decades.[33] Paintings by Swiss artist Johann Caspar Heilmann displayed variations on the theme, where the woman had resumed her tasks (Images 34 and 35).[34] In the subsequent engravings by Juste Chevillet from 1762, the depicted women are titled as *Melle.* [*Mademoiselle*] *sa soeur* and *Le bon exemple*.[35]

In the same way as in the Christian literary moral mirrors for girls and women, women were here able to engage in self-reflection by looking at their exemplary fellow women in the engravings.[36] Marie Christine of Austria, Marie Antoinette's

31 Louis de Surugue de Surgis' engraving after Chardin's *Les amusements de la vie privée* was widely disseminated, and the motif recurred in many different contexts. The dedication to Countess Tessin was replaced by, for example, an equivalent one to Baroness Eva Sofia Stenbock, when Fredrik Wilhelm Hoppe interpreted the motif in the form of a Découpure in around 1766–70 (Image 92).

32 'Cet amoureux travail, cette lecture aimable / De la sage Philis occupent le loisir, / Quand on sçait joindre l'utile à l'agréable / L'innocence est toujours la baze du plaisir.' Chardin's now lost portrait of Madame Lenoir from 1743 was engraved by Louis de Surugue de Surgis in 1747.

33 In the 1750s, Johann-Joachim Kändler also created porcelain figurines after Chardin's well-known motif (Victoria & Albert Museum, London [C.976-1919 and C.977-1919]).

34 Compare the rather similar composition in Jacques-André-Joseph Aved's portrait of Chardin's second wife, Françoise-Marie Pouget, from around 1760 (Musée Carnavalet, Paris [P49]).

35 The model is thought to have been Heilmann's sister; see information on Juste Chevillet's engraving *Melle. sa soeur* from 1762, after Heilmann's original, Victoria & Albert Museum, London (E.3784-1922).

36 Freya Gowrley's article 'The Sister Arts: Textile Crafts between Paint, Print, and Practice', *Journal for Eighteenth-Century Studies*, Vol. 53, No. 2, 2020.

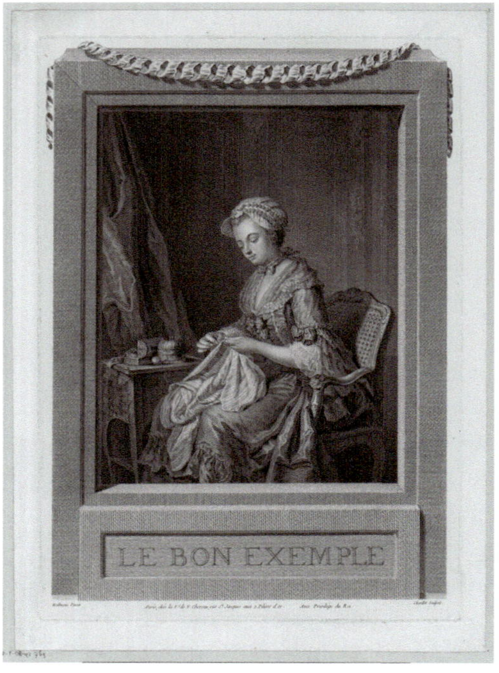

34. Juste Chevillet after Johann Caspar Heilmann, *Le bon exemple*, 1762. Engraving, 45.7 × 32.4 cm. Rijksmuseum, Amsterdam (RP-P-OB-42.769).

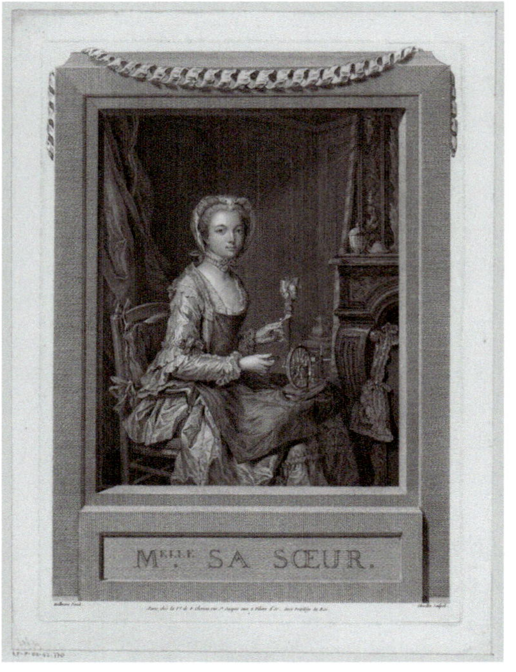

35. Juste Chevillet after Johann Caspar Heilmann, *Melle. [Mademoiselle] sa soeur*, 1762. Engraving. Rijksmuseum, Amsterdam (RP-P-OB-42.770).

sister, chose the spinning 'sister' as the starting point to copy for her own self-portrait in 1765. She transferred her own facial features to the pose that she deemed suitable to identify herself with, albeit distinguished with aristocratic jewellery. On the wall panel in the background, she added a varied collection of engravings in accordance with the fashion at the time.[37]

James Wilson's (or James Watson's) mezzotint engravings from the mid-1760s, after Heilmann's pictures, referred to Chardin's *L'amusement de la vie privée* in the titles *Domestick Amusement. The Lovely Spinner* and *Domestick Amusement. The Fair Seamstress* (Images 36 and 37). The exemplary woman is presented as 'lovely' and 'fair'. Her fashionable clothing and figure made her virtue not only tempting for the viewer but an aspiration for every woman. And the woman does not appear to need to rest from her work in order to experience 'amusement'. The usefulness itself gives her contentment, and thereby also beauty, as stated in a contemporary handbook on beauty care:

37 Marie Christine of Austria (1742–1798), *Selbstporträt mit Spinnrad*, 1765, gouache, Kunsthistorisches Museum, Vienna.

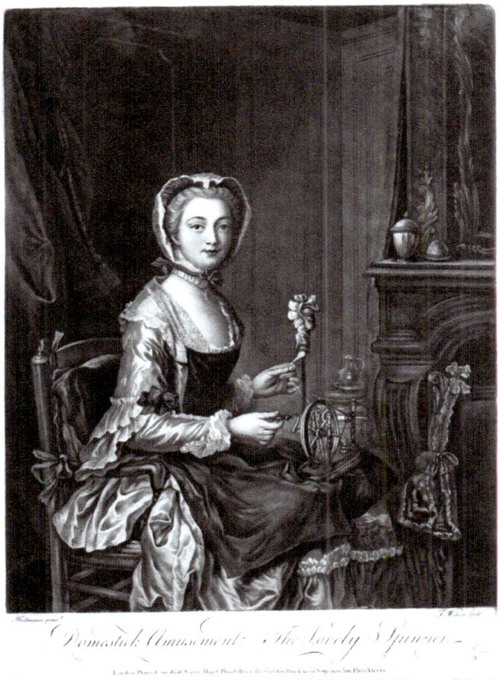

36. James Wilson after Johann Caspar Heilmann, *Domestick Amusement. The Lovely Spinner*, c. 1764. Mezzotint, 35 × 25 cm. Lewis Walpole Library, Yale University.

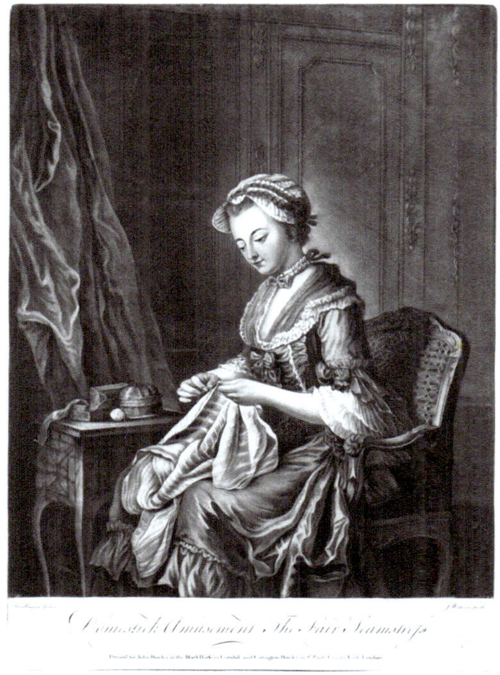

37. James Watson after Johann Caspar Heilmann *Domestick Amusement. The Fair Seamstress*, c. 1764. Mezzotint, 35 × 25 cm. Lewis Walpole Library, Yale University.

> The useful and necessary tasks that women accomplish as wives, mothers and housewives are the most suitable for health and beauty, as the awareness of having fulfilled one's duties in these three specific respects must give them wonderful satisfaction, and this serene glad contentment has more effect on beauty and health than many would believe.[38]

The engraving by Nicolas Arnoult from Nicholas Bonnart, *Recueil des modes de la cour de France* (1687), illustrates how eighteenth-century pictures were rooted in an older tradition (Image 38). In addition to the motif's distinctive needlework, the comfortable chair, the informal apron and the lace bonnet *en déshabillé* were already recurring elements in the seventeenth century.

38 *Om medlen att förhöja qwinliga skönheten. Handbok för damer*, Lund 1806, p. 15. However, the fact that work was moderate was stressed as being important: 'The Graces do not love perspiration and suntan. Excessively hard work deprives a woman's body of its pleasant curves and beautiful colour, makes the body angular and muscular, and the skin uneven', pp. 14–5.

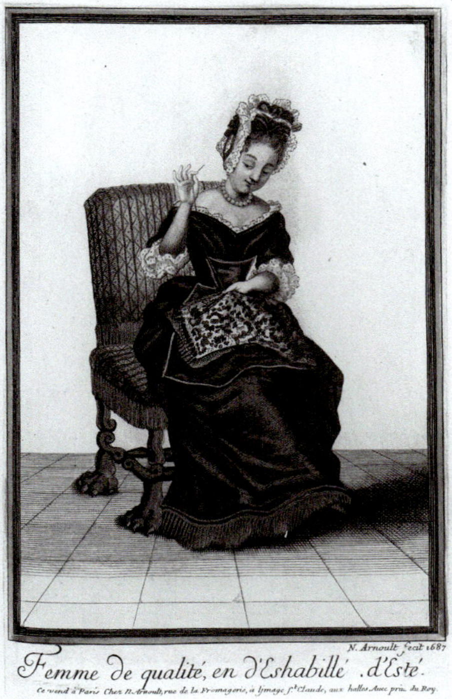

38. Nicolas Arnoult, *Femme de qualité en d'eshabillé d'esté*. Engraving, 36.51 × 23.81 cm. From Nicholas Bonnart, *Recueil des modes de la cour de France*, Paris, 1687. Los Angeles County Museum of Art (LACMA), purchased with funds provided by the Eli and Edythe L. Broad Foundation, Mr and Mrs H. Tony Oppenheimer, Mr and Mrs Reed Oppenheimer, Hal Oppenheimer, Alice and Nahum Lainer, Mr and Mrs Gerald Oppenheimer, Ricki and Marvin Ring, Mr and Mrs David Sydorick, the Costume Council Fund, and member of the Costume Council (M.2002.57.116).

Pehr Hilleström's painting of the mother winding yarn and the daughter sewing next to the elegant sewing table seems in this respect to be a version of Chardin's *L'amusement de la vie privée* – a picture of the household's happy order and harmony, in which each individual has their task and each object has its place; where the order is also regarded as the prerequisite for the beauty of the women and the comfort of the home. Hilleström also appears to have been influenced by Chardin's earlier motifs on a similar theme, focusing on the mother–daughter relationship (Image 31). Back in 1741, Carl Gustaf Tessin had dispatched a painting by Chardin to Sweden. It was a copy of *La mère laborieuse* (The diligent mother), with which Chardin had garnered success at the 1740 Salon in Paris, and which he subsequently donated to the French king as a gift.[39] Tessin describes the motif as '[a] girl showing her haircloth embroidery to her mother'.[40] The mother in her apron by the yarn swift is holding a ball of yarn in one hand while critically scrutinising her daughter's handiwork.[41]

39 Paula Radisich, *Pastiche, Fashion, and Galanterie in Chardin's Genre Subjects*, Maryland 2014, p. 14. This copy also ended up in Queen Lovisa Ulrika's collections.

40 Fredrik Sander, *Nationalmuseum. Bidrag till taflegalleriets historia*, Stockholm 1872, appendix 1, p. 54.

41 The epigram on the engraving is also signed Lépicié: 'Un rien vous amuse ma fille, / Hier ce feuillage étoit fait. / Je vois par chaque point d'éguille / Combien votre esprit est distrait – Croiez moi fuiez la paresse

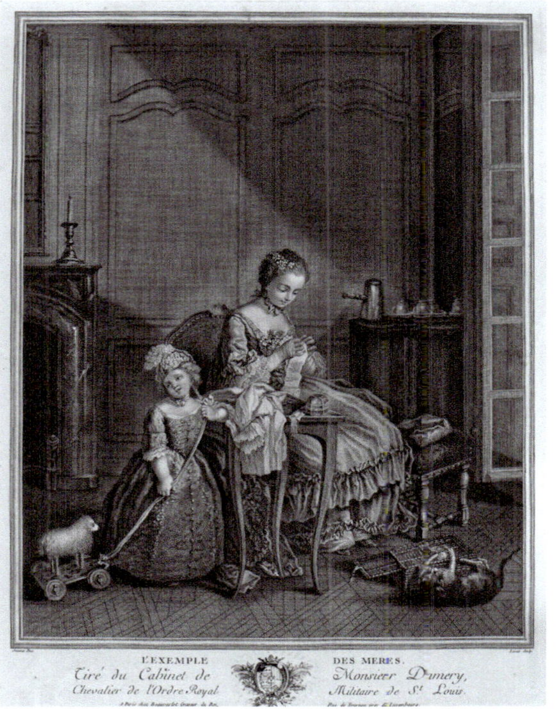

39. François Lucas after Étienne Jeaurat, *L'exemple des meres*. Engraving, 44.6 × 33.6 cm. Widener Collection, National Gallery of Art, Washington, DC (1942.9.2185).

In Hilleström's painting, Carolina Wadenstierna is also wearing an apron, but her jewellery and hairstyle indicate that she is a young lady of the nobility in contrast with Chardin's humble bourgeois daughter. She does not look down and instead looks the woman directly in the eye when she shows her the lace she has been working on. Hilleström has opted for a more cautious approach and a less admonitory tone. The woman in the painting is also depicted with a posture of class awareness, and displays similarities with other portrayals of Wadenstierna's new wife, Fredrica Carleson. In the painting, she has adopted the mother's role, in clothes that also relate to those worn by Jacobina Psilanderhielm in Lafrensen's portrait.

The woman engaged in needlework as a symbol of motherhood appears time and time again in the wealth of European engravings from that era. In Étienne Jeaurat's *La mère laborieuse*, the woman is hemming a shirt, while a child and a cat are playing beside her. The subsequent engraving by François Lucas was given the title *L'exemple des meres* (Image 39). Correspondingly, *A Wife – Une femme mariée*

/ Et goûtez cette vérité, / Que le travail et la sagesse / Valent les biens et la beauté.' The final part translates as: 'Work and wisdom are what impart virtue and beauty, that is what the girl should understand.'

is depicted in John Raphael Smith's engraving from 1791.[42] It was in accordance with this tradition that Wadenstierna chose to allow Jacobina Psilanderhielm to be depicted at the sewing table in Lafrensen's posthumous portrait. Through Hilleström's painting he probably wanted to portray Fredrica Carleson as the new mother in the home.[43]

However, hints of a conflict between the different roles of women and between needlework and education were also discernible at that time. The library at Näs included works by Hedvig Charlotta Nordenflycht, with the poem 'Fruentimbers Plikt, At Upöfva Deras Wett [Women's duty to practice knowledge]' from 1741, in which Nordenflycht refers to women's right to education.[44] The men's 'stupid law' and 'blind custom' deprived women of the right to study; instead they were to be raised to be good housewives.[45] According to a source from 1782, she constantly had a book hidden under her apron when duties in her youth forced her to do needlework.[46] Consequently, Nordenflycht was declared as being unusual and deviating from the norm. Author Anna Maria Lenngren revisited the problem in the poem 'Några ord till min kära dotter, ifall jag hade någon [A few words to my dear daughter, if I had one]'. Half a century had passed by the time it was 1798, but the role of women prevailed. With the lines 'Do not waste time reading – Our sex needs it so little', she summarised the era's female ideal and resignedly adds; 'Stay at your embroidery, your ribbons.'[47] The young woman with a thirst for knowledge who hides her book or writing under her needlework apron was also a recurring rhetorical figure in contemporary literature.[48] The woman doing needlework

42 John Raphael Smith, *A Wife – Une femme mariée*, 1791, engraving, 45.3 × 32.7 cm, British Museum, London (1877, 0512.618).

43 For a cultivated audience, there were also associations between the sewing woman and the virtuous wife, through Homer's example in *The Odyssey*. Awaiting the return of her husband, Odysseus, from the Trojan War, Penelope kept her suitors at bay by not receiving any of them before the funeral shroud had been woven; each night she unravelled it, and each day she wove it again. The varied pictorial world of the eighteenth century recurrently referred to Penelope. When François-Hubert Drouais portrayed the ageing Madame de Pompadour at her embroidery frame in 1763–4, it was an emotional allusion to her loyalty to Louis XV (National Gallery, London [NG 6440]).

44 This probably refers to *Fru Hedvig Charlotta Nordenflychts Utvalda arbeten*, published by Johan Fischerström in Stockholm in 1774; second edition 1781.

45 The poem on women's duty to use their senses is included in the hand-written Cronstedtska Poemboken from 1741, but was published in Hedvig Charlotta Nordenflycht, *Qwinligit Tankespel för Åhr 1744*, Stockholm 1744.

46 Johan Fredrik Martin, 'Fru Hedvig Charlotta Nordenflycht', *Svenska Galeriet, eller portraiter af märkvärdige svenske herrar och fruntimer*, Stockholm 1782, p. 1–19.

47 The poem was published in *Stockholms Posten*, 25 April 1798.

48 In Samuel Richardson's *Pamela, or Virtue Rewarded* from 1740, the heroine hides her letter-writing in her clothes and quickly picks up her needlework when the master of the house Mr B approaches. He expects diligence from his subordinates: 'You mind your pen more than your needle: I don't want such idle

represented order in the home and, from a wider perspective, a social order in which every individual adhered to their assigned role.[49] Wadenstierna's daughters were hardly barred from the contemporary fiction that filled the shelves of the library at Näs, but when they were depicted in Hilleström's painting, they are occupied with needlework. Instead the book has to rest on the adjacent sewing table.

Needlework, conversation and gender

But at the same time that these occupations centred on diligence and utility, they were also influenced by the era's culture of comfort. A well-filled wardrobe and a well-stocked linen cupboard constituted a key part of the comfortable life, and sewing tables and their accoutrements were designed to be practical and comfortable pieces of furniture and tools, adapted to both industriousness and pleasant socialising.

In Pehr Hilleström's painting *2ne Fröknar Wadenstiernas portraiter – i Conversation*, the eldest daughter, Sophia, meets the viewer's gaze (Plate 5). She is possibly turning to face her father, who was probably the commissioner and first viewer of the portrait. Perhaps he entertained the gathering by reading aloud. Hilleström's indication in the title of the painting 'in conversation' underlines the social context that the scene conveys. The participants not only exchange glances over balls of yarn and seams, but also thoughts, feelings and confidences that were included in their conversation. Everyone involved understood that bringing up children to become polite noblewomen not only required practical dexterity but also social skills that encompassed both correct behaviour and engaged conversation and active listening. The art of conversation is just as important in the scene as the needlework. Hilleström presents them as closely linked art forms.

He revisited the motif in the painting that was commissioned by Gustaf III in 1779 and that was described in the artist's own list as *A Picture with Sixteen People*

sluts to stay in my house,' he threatens. Samuel Richardson, *Pamela, or Virtue Rewarded*, I, Manchester 1811, *p. 36*.

49 This division of roles should not be simplified in terms of subordination and superiority in an unequal distribution of power between the sexes. The needlework did not necessarily prevent women from developing creativity and cultivation. Elaine Hedges' article 'The Needle or the Pen' ('The Needle or the Pen. The Literary Recovery of Women's Textile Work' in *Tradition and the Talents of Women*, Florence Howe, (ed.), Illinois 1991) is met in more recent research with the statement 'the needle *as* the pen', about how women create their own spheres of power within an established order. See also Heather Pristash, Inez Schaechterle and Sue Carter Wood, 'The Needle as the Pen. Intentionality, Needlework, and the Production of Alternate Discourses of Power' in Maureen Daly Goggin and Beth Fowkes Tobin, (ed.), *Women and the Material Culture of Needlework and Textiles, 1750–1950*, New York 1999, pp. 13–30.

Representing a Conversation at Drottningholm (Plate 7). In the pictorial space, the positioning, gestures and gazes of the people portrayed create a social game resembling a theatrical scene. The actors in the scene interact (and perhaps secretly plot) in their roles, well-versed in ingrained actions and movements. While the women keep their hands busy with embroidery, passementerie and frivolities, gazes and smiles are exchanged. Low-voiced conversations and discrete whispers accompany the person reading aloud. The props, in the form of clothes and furniture, are in interplay with the varied importance of their roles. Gilt detailing, silk fabrics and table veneers are illuminated for maximum effect. The needlework, carried out with graceful gestures and upright postures, is just one of the many expressions of the conversation. Hilleström created a smaller 'conversation piece' on the same theme for the architect Carl Fredric Adelcrantz in 1775, shortly after his commission for Wadenstierna.[50] A woman is making passementerie in the company of a friend and a reader. The interior decoration of the drawing room is meticulously rendered, the gilding on comfortable armchairs and framed oil paintings gleams against the backdrop of silk-clad wall panels. A small table with a book and ball of yarn is recognisable from Wadenstierna's corresponding painting. Here, needlework is also presented as something more than a virtuous skill. It is part of the drawing room's cultivated socialising and cultivated conversations, and is carried out in interplay with the lavish interior decoration and expensive clothes.

A description of a moment in time at Tista Manor in the 1760s confirms the authenticity of Hilleström's paintings. Fredrik Wilhelm Hoppe captured an everyday scene from one of the cabinets at Tista with the help of his camera obscura, a manual predecessor of early cameras. In an elegantly furnished cabinet, Eva Sofia Stenbock, Countess Rosenhane, sits at her lace-making pillow, while her good friends Councillor of the Realm Melker Falkenberg af Bålby – reading aloud from a book – and his wife, Hedvig Eleonora Wachtmeister, keep her company (Image 40).[51] There is a glimpse of the wall's dense rows of framed paintings and etchings behind the armchairs and sofa. As in Hilleström's paintings, the needlework is presented as a self-evident part of social life and is framed by drawing room interior decoration with upholstered and comfortable furniture which was characteristic of the elite. Diderot and D'Alembert's illustrated *Encyclopédie* also demonstrated the functions of the yarn-spinning tools in a drawing room with elegant furniture against landscape paintings and a mirror on the walls.[52] It was not therefore unusual in the eighteenth

50 Cederblom, Gerda, *Pehr Hilleström som kulturskildrare*, I, Stockholm 1927, Image 31, *Förmiddagsunderhållning* (Morning entertainment), 74 × 62 cm.

51 The Falkenberg family at Bålby were also part of the social circle that Wadenstierna's daughters belonged to, as shown by silhouettes cut at Näs.

52 Louis-Jacques Goussier after A.J. Defehrt, *Fil, roiiet, dévidoirs*, Denis Diderot and Jean-Baptiste Le Rond d'Alembert, *L'Encyclopedie*, vol. 4 (plates). Paris, 1765.

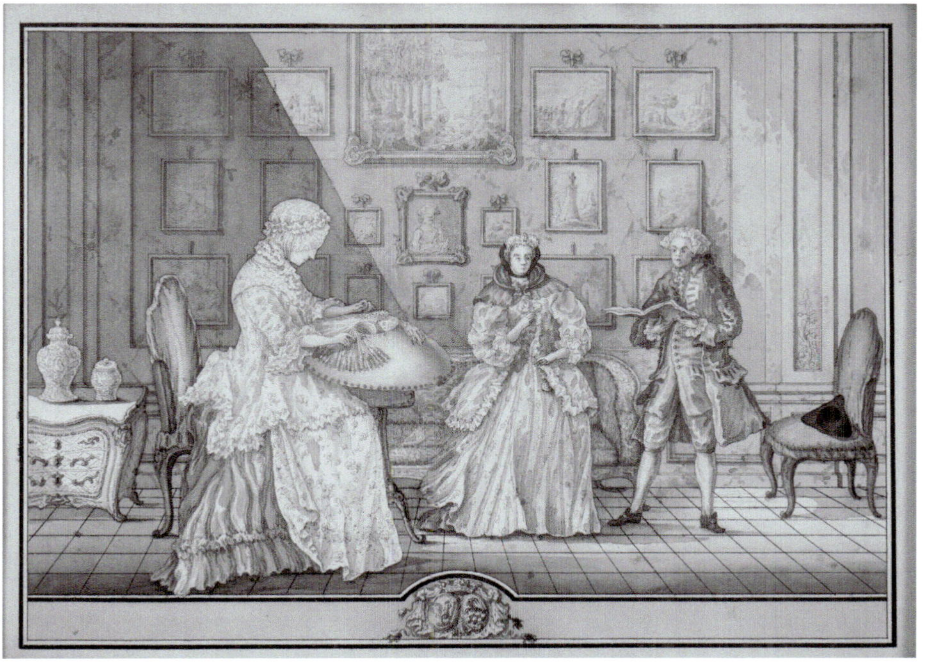

40. Fredrik Wilhelm Hoppe, *A cabinet in the west wing in Tista garden, where Countess Rosenhane mostly spent the day, before the manor house was built. . . . [T]his piece was drawn using the camera obscura by Lieutenant Colonel: Hoppe. Countess Rosenhane, née Stenbock, is sitting making lace. The wife of Councillor of the Realm Falkenberg, née Baronness Wachtmeister, is standing in front of the sofa, her husband is holding a book in his hand*, 1767–8. Pen-and-wash drawing, 19.8 × 27 cm. Private ownership. Photo: Hans Thorwid.

century for the spinning wheel to stand in the drawing room. According to Carl Gustaf Tessin's inventory of Åkerö Manor, Countess Ulla Tessin also had the spinning wheel (and butter churn) in her lavish small cabinet room.[53]

Pehr Hilleström's rendering of the Wadenstierna sisters doing needlework in a representative drawing room milieu followed the conventions of the pictorial genre and the era's forms of upper-class social life. Various elements in the picture, such as paintings and engravings on the wall, patterned oak parquet flooring or a patterned veneered sewing table, as well as doors in the background that open up onto a formal enfilade of rooms, place the activity in its expected context. The discrepancy between, on the one hand, coarse aprons and robust yarn winders and, on the other hand, the jewellery and silk bows of the young noblewomen and the drawing room's elegant furniture, was not a contradiction but entirely in keeping with the social and material culture – and women's everyday role in it.

53 Tessin's inventory of Åkerö Manor, 1757, is discussed in Gösta Selling, *Svenska herrgårdshem under 1700-talet*, Stockholm (1937) 1991, p. 127.

The idea of women as 'sensual objects', which was rooted in the sensuous, material world, in contrast to men as intellectual subjects, is not only seen in visual art but is also reflected in other contexts of that time. Women's areas of responsibility centred on the family's material world, in the physical objects, the management and handling of these objects and economic and financial matters associated with them. The tactile feeling of various materials and qualities often accentuated in eighteenth-century portraits of women – the sheen of silk fabric, fragile and delicate lace, the shimmer of silk thread or the glint of embroidery scissors – constituted references to the sphere in which women had been appointed as experts. The objects referred to her taste as well as her areas of knowledge and were ultimately symbols of social and cultural continuity and stability. The sensibility and connoisseurship associated with women of the elite were regarded in the eighteenth century as signs of their competence and traits. Scientists in the Age of Enlightenment explained the connection on the basis of, among other things, a more easily moved and fine-fibred nervous system.[54]

This characteristic was often emphasised in portraiture – from finely chiselled facial features and thin white hands, to the sheer fabrics and delicate embellishments of the clothing. The women's manner of sensitively touching lace and pieces of embroidery or small sewing needles or dainty shuttles made of ivory, tortoiseshell, mother-of-pearl or silver, was a recurring element in the era's portraits of women. The gesture visualised their informed knowledge of the material culture as well as the visual and sensual aspect of luxury. Their connoisseurship was in their gaze but also in their tactile ability to feel the quality of the expensive materials when handling them. International eighteenth-century research has also pointed out that women's work was often associated with their bodies.[55] The apron that protects the woman's body and clothes when she winds the coarser yarn is another expression of this attitude. Delicate intricate sewing did not require this, as seen in Hilleström's portrait of the Wadenstierna sisters.[56] The work that could be carried out 'in conversation', in presentable clothing in the drawing room, was appropriate and exemplary.

This sensibility undoubtedly also encompassed the men within the elite, and many sources convey that male engagement in the wood-turning room and at the

54 One advocate of this view was the Scottish doctor George Cheyne (1671–1743), an eighteenth-century physician in Bath; George Cheyne, *The English Malady; or, A Treatise of Nervous Diseases of All Kinds, as Spleen, Vapours, Lowness of Spirits, Hypochondriacal and Hysterical Distempers*, Dublin 1733.

55 Chloe Wigston Smith, *Women, Work, and Clothes in the Eighteenth-Century Novel*, Cambridge 2013, p. 13.

56 The eighteenth century's fashionable attire for women also included 'decorative aprons' as an accessory with clear connotations to the role of women at that time, *An Elegant Art, Fashion and Fantasy in the Eighteenth Century*, Edward Maeder (ed.), Los Angeles 1983, pp. 28ff.

embroidery frame was perceived as an activity suitable for the upper class during which sensibility was honed.[57] But although the socialising around needlework also included men, this is a motif rendered less often in paintings and engravings.[58] The normative purpose of art was, however, to underline the traditional allocation of roles in the home, and by extension the overall ideal social order, even though real life was obviously much more differentiated and nuanced. Towards the end of the eighteenth century, shifts in gender constructions slowly started to shape new perceptions of men's and women's work, side by side.[59] The memoirs of author Malla Silfverstolpe from 1797 provide insight:

> [Wilhelm] Lilliehöök was as before at Mrs Rudbeck's nearly every day and often helped Gustava and Malla with embroidery for their clothing. He drew patterns and also embroidered quite well. It was ridiculous to see him in his equerry or hussar uniform with large boots and spurs, sitting at the embroidery frame.[60]

But the items of needlework equipment were not just practical and functional; they were often luxuriously made and harmonised with the conventions surrounding gender, sensibility and connoisseurship. The estate inventories of Wadenstierna and his family show how scissors, thimbles, needle cases and other accessories in gold and silver were the elegantly designed work of goldsmiths and highly valued possessions. As part of their inheritance, the daughters each received a lavish pair of scissors with gold decorations and a scissors case.[61] In Lafrensen's portrait of Jacobina Psilanderhielm, the scissors on the sewing table are a reference to both her productive skills and her exquisite possessions, where the sewing scissors could be assigned the same level of importance as her jewellery and gems. The noblewoman's role as both a consumer of luxury *and* a producer of luxury in relation to the context of the needlework is shown in research conducted by historian

57 Oxenstierna, Johan Gabriel, *Journal*, Stockholm (1805) 1964, p. 38: 'I have today started to make lace, which Albertine is teaching me, and can already make the common square filet'. See also Ilmakunnas, Johanna, 'Adelns arbete och vardag på 1700-talets svenska herrgårdar. Johan Gabriel Oxenstiernas och Jacobina Charlotta Munsterhjelms dagböcker', *Historisk Tidskrift för Finland*, årg. 98 2013:2. Helsinki 2013, pp. 156–84.

58 However, one exception is a watercolour by Isak Kjölström from 1797 representing the large drawing room at Brunnby, Vreta Abbey, Östergötland Province, where two women and a young man sit together working at a large embroidery frame, Näsström , Gustaf, *Forna dagars Sverige*, III, *Kulturhistorisk bilderbok om frihetstid och gustaviansk tid*, Stockholm 1962, p. 101.

59 In 1805, Count Oxenstierna points out that he is engaged in women's work during his summer sojourn at Skenäs: 'During the rainy part of the day, I continued my women's work; I am making weak progress in knitting, but I am making lace correctly', Oxenstierna 1964, p. 77.

60 *Malla Montgomery-Silfverstolpes memoarer*, utgifna af Malla Grandinson, I, Stockholm, 1908, p. 181.

61 Riksarkivet, Näs Silverstolpeska arkivet, Personarkiven, vol. 60, Carl Eric Wadenstierna (1723–1787).

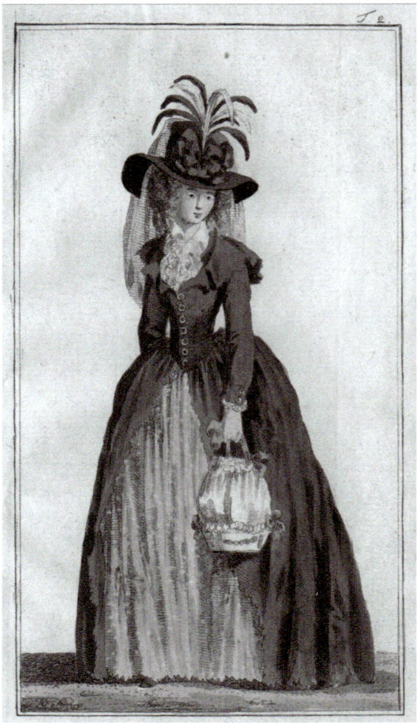

41. Fashion engraving from *Journal des Luxus und der Moden*, vol. 3, January 1788, image 2, published by Friedrich Justin Bertuch and Georg Melchior Kraus, Weimar. Rijksmuseum, Amsterdam (BI-1967-1159B-2).

Johanna Ilmakunnas, for example. Noblewomen's consumption behaviours are exemplified in Countess Charlotta Sparre's troubles regarding the order of a pair of sewing scissors from Paris.[62] The women's informed knowledge of qualities, available products and contacts demonstrates the importance attached to what were not only practical work tools but also aesthetically and symbolically charged objects.

The workbags that often feature in eighteenth-century portraits of women and in genre scenes and conversation pieces are similarly a reminder of women's areas of responsibility and skills as well as their role as fashionable consumers. The same applies to the ostentatious 'decorative aprons' in women's fashion. The workbag did not just fulfil its obvious function for storage of pieces of needlework and sewing accessories such as yarn, scissors and needles; it was also an eye-catching fashion accessory – a practical predecessor of the present-day handbag. It was often made of exclusive silk taffeta, embroidered and decorated, and in itself proof of the woman's skill and taste, as well as reflecting the value of its intended contents. Women generally owned several of these workbags, so that they were suitable

62 Ilmakunnas, Johanna, *Ett ståndsmässigt liv. Familjen von Fersens livsstil på 1700-talet*, Stockholm 2012, p. 205.

for different occasions and matched various outfits.[63] Preserved bills show that when Fredrica Carleson purchased mourning bands, mourning aprons, veils and gauze in conjunction with the death of her husband, Carl Eric Wadenstierna, in January 1787, she simultaneously ordered two workbags to provide his daughters with correct and suitable accessories.[64] Märta Helena Reenstierna also proudly noted in her diary when her new 'expensive and pretty workbag', decorated with 'coats of arms and heraldic devices', arrived from the city.[65] In January 1788, a fashion image in *Journal des Luxus und der Moden* depicted a woman wearing a black coat and hat and equipped with a large workbag (Image 41). The picture caption informs us that 'ein eleganter Englischer Ladys Work-Bag, oder Arbeits-Beutel, à la Gondole, der meist von Taft, gemacht, und mit Blumen decorirt ist, an den Arm' belonged to the fashionable French outfit, which was influenced by the era's anglomania.[66] The workbag clearly completed the look of the fashionably dressed woman, even when she intended to leave her house – the functional home comfort accompanied her on walks or visits. In the paintings by Pehr Hilleström on the walls at Wadenstierna's Näs Manor, the workbag accompanied the depicted women in highly varied contexts: during their work at the spinning wheel but also during a visit to a fortune teller.

The workbag as a decorative accessory in fashion images was hardly new. In the 1750s, Boudier de Villemert complained about the fact that what had once been a symbol of female diligence and virtue had become a superficial fashion with other associations:

> A woman always carries a closed bag with her, with work, that hangs by her side, in company, at the theatre, it is to provide assurance that she is occupied. She views it as a obligation. For my part, I find her lamentable that she adheres to a vain semblance, which cannot free her from suspicions of laziness.[67]

63 Artist Alexander Roslin's French wife, the pastellist Marie Suzanne Giroust, owned more than ten silk workbags, embellished with embroidery and ribbons, 'Inventaire après décès d'Alexandre Roslin, Paris, A. N., M.C.XXXI, 271, 17 juillet 1793', *Art Bulletin of Nationalmuseum Stockholm*, Vol. 7, Stockholm 2000, p. 80.

64 The bill for wages to Christina Erengren is dated Stockholm, 13 January 1787. The mourning aprons are included on a bill for wages to Maria Carlström, dated Stockholm, 10 January 1787. Riksarkivet, Näs Silverstolpeska arkivet, Personarkiven, vol. 60, Carl Eric Wadenstierna (1723–1787).

65 Reenstierna, I, 1993, p. 81.

66 But the reporter points out that the question of whether the bag refers to fashion or the woman's inclination to work cannot be answered: 'Ob diess nur ist um der Figur mehr Maintien zu geben, oder obs wirklich Mode wird, dass di eleganten Damen auch arbeiten wollen, kann ich nicht sagen' *Journal des Luxus und der Moden*, Jahrgang 3, Weimar, January 1788, p. 26; *Cabinet des modes 1785–6*.

67 Boudier de Villemert 1763, p. 24.

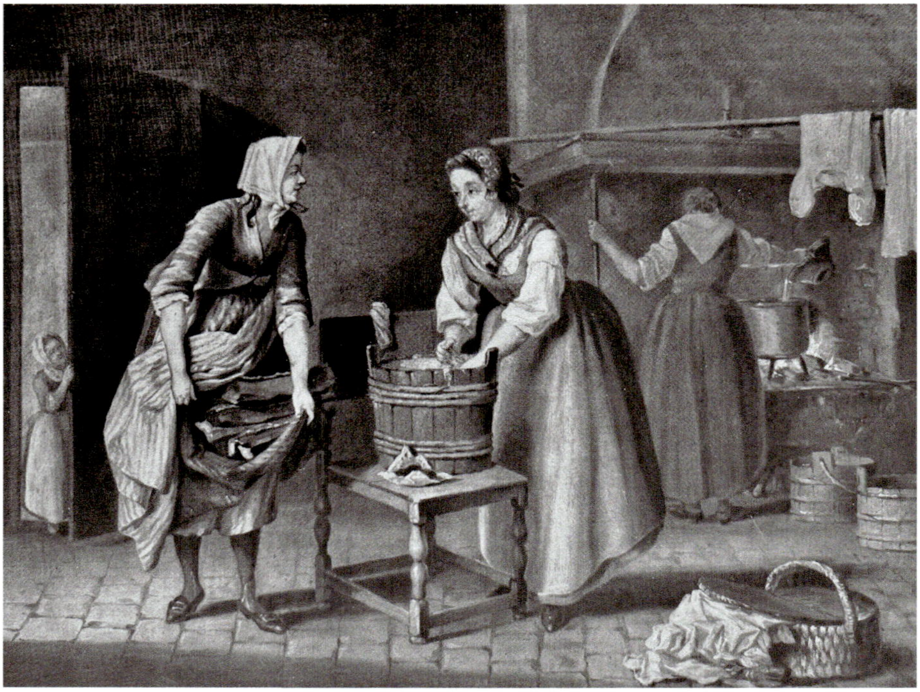

42. Pehr Hilleström, *Ett qvinfolk som kokar, en som öser vatten i en gryta en som bär ved och en som tittar i dören* (A woman cooking, one pouring water into a pan, one carrying firewood and one looking through the doorway). Oil on canvas, 40 × 51 cm. Private ownership.

The satirical advertisement about a lost workbag in *Stockholms Posten* in 1781 was just one of other similar verses.[68] The lost bag admittedly did contain a started piece of lace, but a larger proportion of its contents consisted of sweets and love letters. This figure of thought almost became a cliché in the late eighteenth century, in which the traditional symbol of female diligence and virtue was reduced to a triviality of fashion.

These different examples show how the era's pictures and texts reflect the fashionable connotations that needlework accoutrements had come to embody. Exclusive sewing accessories and fashionable workbags became indispensable during the elite's conversations in drawing rooms, both at the royal court and in bourgeois homes. Chardin's and Hilleström's motifs with scenes taken from 'the home' belonged to the genre *le goût moderne* – the modern taste – where the image of comfortable and informal life was combined with elements of *galanterie*

68 *Ur den gamla Stockholms Posten. En samling artiklar, valda och utgivna av Elof Ehnmark*, Stockholm 1931, p. 115. Also compare the sequel in *Stockholms posten* in 1795, 'Förlorade saker' (lost things) by Anna Maria Lenngren.

and *esprit*.[69] Hilleström closely followed Chardin's method of appealing to the elite by harnessing the potential of fashion. The novelty was not the motifs, which on the contrary referred to old established conventions and a pictorial world that had often taken shape in the Dutch seventeenth century, but the way of presenting them to the discerning urbane consumers of the eighteenth century, who were keen to express their informed taste. The woman keeping the Wadenstierna sisters company in Hilleström's painting not only adopts the role of mother, but is also fashionably *modern*, busy with tasks in the drawing room that could in several ways be associated with contemporary fashion at that time and a lifestyle in keeping with their class status. Today's viewer might miss the small details and subtleties that would catch the eye of viewers in that era: a workbag or a lace bonnet, '*coëffure demie négligée*', known from a fashion magazine, or a fashionable table, a '*bonheur du jour*', or the thin black ribbon around the woman's neck. Details that conveyed a message which people at that time could immediately interpret.

The utility of luxury: Wadenstierna and the debate on luxury

The hot, well-polished flat iron glides heavily over the white shirt (Plate 8). In the chiaroscuro, the fire crackles in the tiled stove where the base of the iron had just been heated. The door of the linen cupboard is ajar and waiting for the newly ironed laundry that the woman is working on. She leans forward slightly over her task while turning towards the woman who is knitting a sock in the armchair next to her. The latter has crossed her legs under her long apron and has wedged the ball of yarn under her arm to prevent it from rolling away on the floor. The tone of conversation between the lady's maids seems to be one of calm accord, in keeping with their everyday clothing and the unassuming furniture of the room. Conversation is also in progress in the painting that depicts the interior of a scullery, where the kitchen maids are washing the linens and clothes that will later be ironed (Image 42). Coifs and kerchiefs indicate that the heavy work was performed by lower-ranking servants. One of the women brings wood for the stove where the water for the laundry is being heated. She has folded her coarse skirt upwards and filled it with an armful of firewood, and she stops to chat with the woman at the wash tub. The tub has been placed on one of the kitchen chairs to make the work easier, and next to it there is a dollop of soap on a sheet of newspaper close at hand. The water splashes onto the damp brick floor.

69 Radisich, Paula, *Pastiche, Fashion and Galanterie in Chardin's Genre Subjects. Looking Smart*, Plymouth 2014, pp. 13ff.

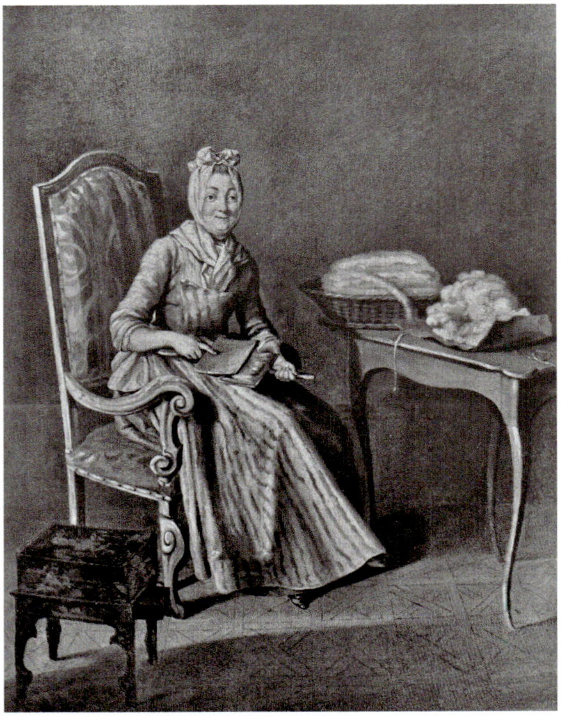

43. Pehr Hilleström, *Ett d:o som kardar bomull* (A ditto carding cotton). Oil on canvas, 51 × 40 cm. Private ownership.

The scenes recur in the suite of paintings that Wadenstierna commissioned from Pehr Hilleström in connection with the move to Näs in the mid-1770s. These 'conversation pieces' also centre on textile handicrafts and work. But these paintings do not portray the handicrafts as a social skill; instead they convey the utility and meaning of a household's own production and maintenance of textile goods. The theme is reinforced in a further two paintings that show how the textile raw materials are handled, where one woman is carding and the other is spinning (Plate 9 and Image 43). Together, the paintings tell us about the production of textile items within the household and the maintenance – washing and ironing – of the finished garments, as well as the distribution of tasks concerning what were perhaps the home's most important possessions. In terms of theme, composition and format, the paintings were designed to form pairs, and they were probably also intended to be viewed in a shared context.

The carding and spinning women were undeniably symbols of good housekeeping and of a hierarchical order that guaranteed a well-ordered, comfortable life. The female servants in the paintings who are working with the textiles or helping family members get dressed were visible proof of privileged comfort. But pictures of beautiful servant girls at work had also long constituted a genre of their own. The popular engravings that disseminated the pictures more widely

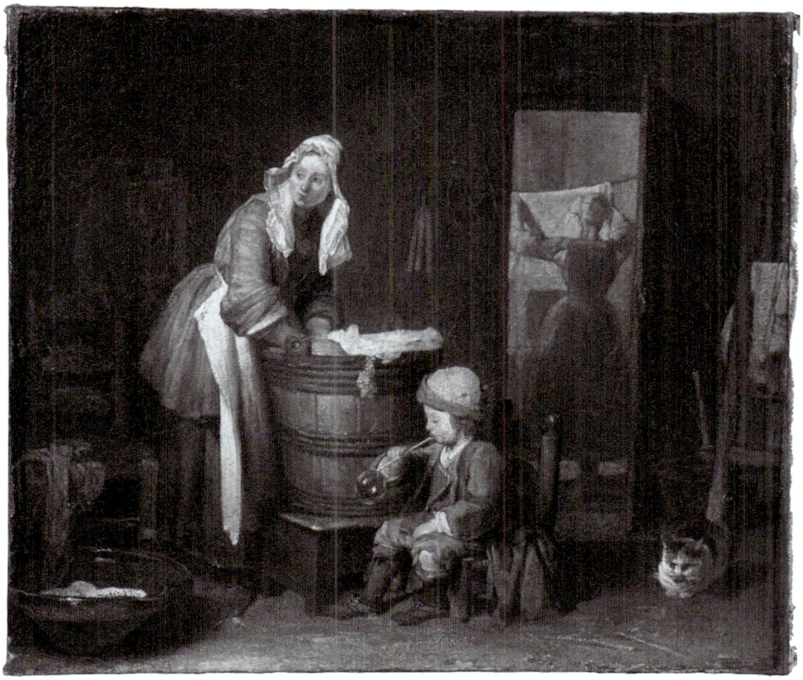

44. Jean Siméon Chardin, *La blanchisseuse*, 1733. Oil on canvas, 37 × 42.5 cm. National Museum, Stockholm (NM 780). Photo: Cecilia Heisser (CC BY-SA).

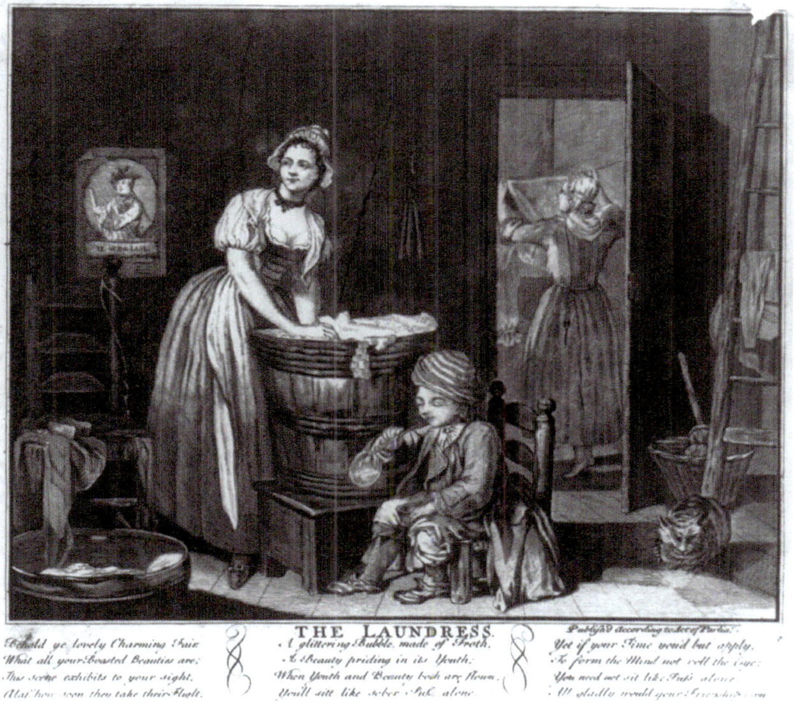

45. Unknown artist after Jean Siméon Chardin, *The Laundress*. Engraving, 24 × 30 cm. Library of Congress, Washington, DC.

emphasised in their well-chosen titles the specific beauty that was associated with women who in simple linen garments performed the housework that they had been assigned.[70] There was often an erotic undertone in these pictures, especially in the scenes that showed work with the soft linen, which was associated with corporeality and intimacy.[71] An engraved version of Chardin's laundress – *La blanchisseuse* from 1733 – has been modified with the aim of emphasising the woman's physical attractiveness (Images 44 and 45). With a deeper neckline, short sleeves on her blouse and a distinct smile, the woman turns towards the engraving representing a man on the wall behind her. Like the depicted man, the viewer is urged in the accompanying verse to 'Behold ye lovely Charming Fair'.

Chardin's modern maids and governesses who in high-heeled shoes and dazzlingly white aprons were made part of the elegant urbane culture, are also glimpsed in Hilleström's pictures. Motifs and details in his paintings have in several cases been loaned directly from Chardin's pictorial world. However, in one or two of Hilleström's paintings, the social context may be elusive – Is the woman spinning yarn in her shimmering silk jacket a lady's maid or a noble relative? (Plate 9). But there we see nothing of the coquettish ambiguity that could lurk in the engravings which were inspired by Chardin. The titles that Hilleström gave to his paintings are fastidiously descriptive compared to those by Chardin's engravers and were unquestionably created for a different purpose.[72] The painting of the woman at the large spinning wheel was described by the artist succinctly and precisely: *Ett Fruent: spinner bomull* (A woman spinning cotton). But here, the emphasis on the exclusive cotton is the significant element and is what gives the scene a certain importance. The woman at the spinning wheel is accordingly better dressed than the others in the suite of pictures and is portrayed in a room that has a more genteel style. The expensive table with its urns made in the Marieberg factory and the strategically placed workbag on the tabouret in the foreground, of which there were similar ones in the Wadenstierna family's home, show that the woman's skills with the delicate cotton thread were of the highest class. She possessed the connoisseurship that was distinctive for the elite.

70 See, for example, Johann Jakob Haid, *La belle fileuse*, 1770s, mezzotint, 24.5 × 32.7 cm, British Museum, London (1885, 1212.14). 'The beautiful spinner' smilingly casts down her eyes while, with elegant gestures, she handles the yarn and exposes her bare forearms.

71 Colin Bailey, *Jean-Baptiste Greuze: the Laundress*, J.P Getty Museum, Los Angeles 2000.

72 'Beskrifning öfver de ämnen som föreställes på alla taflor som Hilleström, sedan 1773, till och med 1810, målat i oljeferg (Description of the subjects depicted on all pictures that Hilleström painted in oils from 1773 to 1810). (After the artist's own list. The archive of the Royal Swedish Academy of Fine Arts), Cederblom, I, 1927. Hilleström came up with the titles to enable him to remember the works he had created, not to inform a wider audience.

The scene belongs together with the painting of the carding woman (Image 43). In his list the artist states that this also involves cotton. The work using the cards required dexterity, but was comparatively less advanced, and the woman performing this task is consequently rendered in simpler clothing and in a more vaguely defined room.[73] The armchair is an older model, and a games table has been used as a side table for the cotton and the carded cotton in the basket. However, a richly embellished box is displayed in the foreground. In this context it is an odd object that stands out with its expensive and exotic design. According to tradition, it was to have belonged to Wadenstierna.[74] The box and the expensive raw cotton elevate the scene from its genre-like context and seem to define it in relation to Wadenstierna himself. It is certain that the cotton, and possibly also the box, were high-quality commodities from far away. Few households at this time had the opportunity to handle the exclusive raw cotton. But perhaps there were additional reasons why Wadenstierna placed the motifs in his own specific context?

These paintings can possibly be interpreted as being part of the upbringing that Wadenstierna wanted to give his daughters, who were twelve and sixteen years old when the paintings were commissioned. The motifs that surrounded the family and servants in their everyday life were supposed to remind them of and urge them to comply with their obligations and areas of responsibility. The suite of pictures clearly conveys which tasks were assigned to kitchen maids and lady's maids and which were suitable for young noblewomen. They not only demonstrated the nature of the tasks, but also how they were supposed to be performed in the correct context and company, and in the correct relationship to one's body, clothes and room. The pictures set a tone that confirms that this interplay takes place in harmony, in accordance with an order and a mutual agreement. But the paintings can also be interpreted in an even larger context, outside the walls of the home – as manifestations of an ideology that concerned the civil free right to own and consume and the obligation to contribute to Swedish production.[75]

The political debates during the Age of Liberty had been strongly permeated by these economic issues and involved the repeated sumptuary laws that also aimed at the upper classes. It was in the light of the speech on the utility of luxury, by

73 Maybe the scene is taking place in a room that corresponds to the dressing room at Näs, which also had older furniture. For example, consider the interior decoration of the dressing room at Tessin's Åkerö Manor, where the room had mainly been furnished with older and unfashionable furniture that was no longer suitable in the reception rooms. Selling (1937) 1991, p. 128.

74 Cederblom, Image 87. Wadenstierna's estate inventory includes two boxes – '1 Turkish box with a stone and mother-of-pearl inlay' and '1 wooden box, with brass fittings', which may refer to the depicted object. Riksarkivet, Näs Silverstolpeska arkivet, Personarkiven, vol. 60, Carl Eric Wadenstierna (1723–1787).

75 Wadenstierna viewed England as a good example, with its motto 'Liberty and Property' [Carl Eric Wadenstierna], *Fria Tankar af ****, Stockholm 1769, p. 8.

politician Anders von Höpken, which was given in 1740 at the Royal Swedish Academy of Sciences, and the particularly strict sumptuary law of 1766 that Wadenstierna appeared in the public debate. Höpken was not only a fellow political party member but also a colleague and friend of Wadenstierna's future father-in-law, Edvard Carleson. Strongly influenced by the intensive discussions within his political and private networks, Wadenstierna set out the text in his anonymous publication *Fria Tankar* (Free thoughts) in 1769. He stated that the sumptuary laws were depleting the nation in the long term and that they

> deprive craftsmen and artists of the cheap profit that they should expect from the richer people, deprive the rich, yes, everyone in society, of their natural right, to use and utilise their fortune for comfort and own benefit. ... If a rich person is prohibited from decorating his house and his farms, this impoverishes a few thousand workers, craftsmen and artists, the state and its income, causing much damage and loss.[76]

The project to build Näs and decorate it with art and furniture made by Swedish craftsmen and artists can be seen as a manifestation of Wadenstierna's political programme. He gave work to those who had the right to expect their bread and butter from him and his equals. Näs was furnished by the cabinetmakers Haupt and Eckstein, the dresser was full of tableware made by the Marieberg factory in Stockholm, and portraits painted by Scheffel and Lafrensen next to landscapes by Korn adorned the walls. And, becomingly, the manor's women contributed to stemming the flow of expensive imports by weaving and sewing items themselves to meet the household's needs. The linen cupboards' '*Hus lärft*' (house linen) was evidence of everyone doing their share to help.[77] This entire chain – with home-made and Swedish-made products, from shirts to tiled stoves – was documented by Pehr Hilleström in the suite of paintings commissioned by Wadenstierna. Viewed from this perspective, the paintings primarily seem to be party political propaganda pictures in the service of the Hat party, and Wadenstierna appeared to practise what he preached.

The era's heated debate about the perdition or profits of excess largely concerned women and their role. There was a widespread perception that women's taste for fashion and 'trinkets' was the driving force behind the imports of luxury goods, and this applied especially to the demand for clothes, textiles and fashion accessories.[78]

76 *Fria Tankar*, p. 16.

77 See note 13.

78 Berry, Helen, 'Prudent Luxury. The Metropolitan Tastes of Judith Baker, Durham Gentlewoman', *Women and Urban Life in Eighteenth-Century England*, Rosemary Sweet and Penelope Lane (ed.), Farnham 2003. pp. 130–150 and Ann Öhrberg, 'Françoise Marguerite Janiçon: en kvinnlig aktör på frihetstidens

The cities' shops and traders in luxury items advertised when they had received new products, and consumer goods from abroad were those deemed most coveted.[79] In the same way that Charlotta Sparre knew which traders she should address in Paris, her fellow women also had informed knowledge of the range of products on offer in their vicinity and often established personal contact with traders who they revisited over the years. In Stockholm, the shops were concentrated around Mynttorget and Riddarhustorget Squares. They included the trinket and fashion trader Adolf Collin, the silk and clothing retailer Wilhelm Mauritz Schvardz, and the trading house Knigge & Brandel, which sold textiles and luxury goods from Germany and the Netherlands. This was also the location of Barbara Pauli's large fashion shop Temple du Goût, which sold imported French fashion in the 1770s and 1780s. The king had also granted her exemption from the obligation to belong to a guild, which enlivened the debate.[80]

The luxury consumption could be regarded as an elite virtue, a way of taking responsibility for the nation's economy, if it took place in the form of supporting the country's own crafts and manufactories. Many women from a wider social stratum made a living by receiving commissions and selling items that they produced at home.[81] The newspapers' advertisements indicate that the manufacture of luxury decorative items was widespread. The following characteristic advertisement was published in *Stockholms Posten* in March 1779: 'On Holländaregatan Street, in the farrier's house, on the first floor, caps, collars and similar finery for women are made, in the newest taste.' And preserved bills that belonged to Fredrica Carleson show that she recurrently commissioned women in Stockholm to do various kinds of sewing tasks.[82]

The moral, useful consumption was also surrounded by a utilitarian approach that was described in words such as *restraint, thrift, common sense* and *diligence*.[83] They were virtues that were linked to being a good lady of the house, according to the norms of the Lutheran *hustavlan* (household chart), and that no sumptuary laws in all the world could have any impact on. At least, according to Wadenstierna and his mercantile-minded political party colleagues. It was hardly the foreign finery that contributed to a woman's beauty. Whether the woman as a consumer

politiska arena', *Riksdag, kaffehus och predikstol. Frihetstidens politiska kultur 1766–1772*, Marie-Christine Skuncke and Henrika Tandefelt (ed.), Stockholm 2003.

79 *Dagligt Allehanda*, 19 June 1786, and *Stockholms Posten*, 10 April 1780 and 17 August 1781.

80 Johan Elers, *Stockholm*, I, Stockholm 1800, p. 97.

81 Britta Hammar, 'Modebubblor – kvinnlig fägring under två sekel', Britta Hammar and Pernilla Rasmussen, *Kvinnligt mode under två sekel*, Lund 2001, pp. 34–5. Also see advertisements in *Stockholms Posten*, 3 November 1779, and *Dagligt Allehanda*, 11 October 1784.

82 Riksarkivet, Näs Silverstolpeska arkivet, Personarkiven, vol. 60, Carl Eric Wadenstierna (1723–1787).

83 Berry 2003, p. 150.

was useful and thrifty or wasteful was a matter of upbringing and morals. For these matters, the man, with his authority, had the ultimate responsibility.[84] It was the man's task to ensure that the resources in the form of money, time and work were distributed correctly and that what the household could produce was not due to laziness purchased elsewhere. *Unga Fruentimbers Hushålls Spegel* from 1754, a 'moral mirror' stipulating young women's correct behaviour, which was reprinted on popular woodcut prints in 1773 and 1788, stated how 'trinkets, pleats, plumes, collars, neck ribbons, bows, finery and fripperies', if they were deemed indispensable, should be made by the young women themselves to avoid unnecessary expenditure in the cities' shops.[85] It was work that should preferably not steal time from the essential utility sewing, which is also discernible in an occasional poem written by Wadenstierna, in which his daughters' crafting of fashion items takes place in the expensive light of the candle-ends at night. Wasting resources on a small and large scale plagues the economically minded master of the house:

> But soon there will be things to put in order,
> When the sun is caught by the darkness' warder,
> And all gather indoors for the night,
> And all, all demand light. Then calls come from all corners and nooks:
> Light in your stable, for card players' hooks.
> I must with ribbons my bonnet adorn
> And then do my sewing at night all forlorn.
> Light to darn all your socks,
> Light to deflea old pug Mops, light for tending your ox and ass,
> Light for dancing the *polska* – alas,
> A stub of a candle to stick by the stove,
> And one for cards telling Lena's fortune – by Jove.[86]

In 1730, the clergyman Petrus Törnevall in Skara formulated his criticism of how diligence was applied to unnecessary things: 'To knit and make swirls and rosettes shaped like roses and lilies, criss-crossed and checked, and all that can be used as finery and fripperies around the neck or on the head secured with a hair pin.'[87] But in his publication *Fria Tankar*, Wadenstierna pointed out the significance of women

84 'A beautiful woman does not need to use foreign ornaments, her attractiveness is sufficient embellishment.' See Runefelt 2015, pp. 117, 125, where Wadenstierna's involvement in a planned sumptuary law at the 1766 session of the parliament is discussed.

85 *Unga Fruentimbers Hushålls Spegel*, Stockholm 1788.

86 Gustaf Näsström, *Forna dagars Sverige*, III, Stockholm 1962, p. 158.

87 Petrus Törnevall, *Dygdz och Odygdz Spegel i hus-håld och Algemena Lefwernet, allom i hwart stånd til nyttig påminnelse, och vnderwisning*, Skara 1730, pp. 22–3.

in the development of economically sound Swedish industries in these particular art forms as these elaborate products would otherwise be eagerly acquired in the international market. The art form's decorations could only be developed and be in demand in a country where women had 'beauty and intelligence', that is, had informed taste, which was regarded as one of the distinctive characteristics of urbane upper-class women.[88] These decorative items not only encompassed fashion's 'fripperies' but also the wall coverings and furniture upholstery, cloths, curtains and fireguards that embellished upper-class interiors and to which the women of the house were expected to contribute.

It can therefore be perceived as a deliberate decision to commission Hilleström to also include the Wadenstierna sisters in the suite of paintings for Näs, busy with precisely this type of artistic handicrafts 'in conversation'. It was a scene that demonstrated handicrafts that were suitable for young noblewomen, work that thereby fulfilled a key function for the wider social order. 'A honourably thinking party is the one that through useful statutory instruments helps agriculture; establishes handicrafts; encourages industries; enlivens the competition,' politician Wadenstierna wrote in 1769.[89] Everyone was supposed to take part in this competition, each person according to their abilities and position in life. To not only train one's daughters in household tasks, but also train their skills in artistic handicrafts was a way of showcasing them as role models in this competition. This was also the art form in which women were allowed to participate and express themselves in the public art world. Women's embroidered pictures were exhibited alongside the 'male' history paintings of the Royal Swedish Academy of Fine Arts.[90] Embroidery was generally regarded as a form of painting created with needles, and literature on raising children underlined the importance of women learning this art form so that they could spend their time meaningfully and usefully, both alone and in company.[91] Sophia Wadenstierna's neat sewing conveys a clear message in Hilleström's painting, as does the shimmering embroidery in her mother's hands in Lafrensen's portrait. Mother and daughter are depicted as good examples in the most well-ordered of worlds.

88 *Fria Tankar*, pp. 27f.

89 *Fria Tankar*, p. 17.

90 Anna Lena Lindberg, *En mamsell i akademien. Ulrica Fredrica Pasch och 1700-talets konstvärld*, Lund 2010, p. 48. Hilleström's paintings also show upper-class women working on embroidery based on models consisting of engraved landscape pictures and *vedute*.

91 Erasmus Darwin, *Plan for the Conduct of Female Education in Boarding Schools*, London, 1797, p. 27. Compare the discussion in Pristash, Heather; Schaechterle, Inez; Carter Wood, Sue, 'The Needle as the Pen. Intentionality, Needlework, and the Production of Alternate Discourses of Power', *Women and the Material Culture of Needlework and Textiles, 1750–1950*, Maureen Daly Goggin and Beth Fowkes Tobin (ed.), New York 1999, pp. 13–30.

Never being unoccupied

Softly upholstered chairs and practically designed sewing tables and tools undeniably facilitated the tasks and contributed to comfort. But the tasks nonetheless formed an occupation that was to be characterised by diligence and utility. Work with textiles constituted a recurring theme in the suite of paintings that Carl Eric Wadenstierna commissioned from Pehr Hilleström in 1774 (Plates 5, 8 and 9; Images 42 and 43). Here we see the production of textile goods (the women card, spin, knit, sew and embroider), the care and maintenance of the items (washing and ironing), and their use, such as dressing and the showcasing of clothes and home furnishings (Plate 15 and Image 71). The textile qualities are rendered through the connoisseur's eyes: shimmering silk fabrics and coarse linen, heavy brocades or the thinnest tulle. All the fashion accessories – fans, workbags, gloves, ribbons, hats and lace bonnets – complement the scenes. Pehr Hilleström painted according to his client's requests but was also particularly well-suited to the motifs he was commissioned to portray. He had started his career in the 1740s as a student of the fan painter Christian Fehmer and the high-warp tapestry weaver Jean Louis Duru and was engaged in the textile decoration of the Royal Palace in Stockholm.[92] When he was sent to Paris with the task of learning more about the work at the Savonnerie and Gobelins manufactories, he also used part of the time to develop his painting skills. When Gustaf III admitted Hilleström as a member of the Royal Swedish Academy of Fine Arts in 1773, it was for his merits as a weaver, even though his painting commissions started to constitute a growing proportion of the artist's output at that time.[93] Wadenstierna therefore became one of Hilleström's early clients while the artist was still highly active as a weaver. The feeling for the textiles that he depicted was consequently firmly rooted in his skills. He probably knew how the yarn would be positioned at the spinning wheel and how the needle would be angled at the embroidery frame. In the paintings that he delivered, this concrete knowledge was combined with the era's notions of ideal home life. Hilleström's understanding of the special properties of the textiles corresponds to the client family's connoisseurship in this subject.

The textile theme was possibly also an obvious choice as a suite of paintings was intended to depict everyday life in Wadenstierna's home, where his wife, teenage

92 Osvald Sirén, *Pehr Hilleström d.ä. Väfvaren och målaren, hans lif och hans värk*, Stockholm 1900; Mikael Ahlund, *Pehr Hilleström. Att se vardagen*, Konstmuseet Sinebrychoff, Helsinki 2014, pp. 28–36; Mikael Ahlund, 'Konsten att försörja sig som konstnär. Pehr Hilleström och konstmarknaden i 1700-talets Stockholm', *Ekonomisk kulturhistoria. Bildkonst, konsthantverk och scenkonst 1720–1850*, Klas Nyberg (ed.), Stockholm 2017, pp. 55–8.

93 Ahlund 2014, *ibid*; Ahlund 2017, *ibid*. Also see 'Pehr Hilleström', *Svenskt biografiskt lexikon* (article by Gustaf Hilleström).

daughters and the lady's maids spent their time. The textile items accounted for a large part of the daily work and a considerable part of the household's overall wealth. Hilleström's paintings fulfilled educational functions as well as being status symbols, and his motifs could be interpreted as ideological and political messages. But there were probably also more personally directed messages, aimed at Wadenstierna's daughters and wife. Far from being generally arranged genre scenes alluding to a wide and vague pictorial tradition concerning female virtues, the paintings at Näs were more specific and directly linked to the female members of the household and their everyday tasks. When the eldest daughter, Sophia, with her needlework looks out from the painting, it is with the dignity of the person who has inherited the gold thimble (Plate 5). In this group of people, she is the person carrying out the most advanced work, and her sewing does not require an apron. She would one day take over the responsibility for the textile work in the home, and would be the person who took over Näs after her father's death.

At Näs, in her marriage with Lars August Mannerheim, Sophia would give birth to four daughters, three of whom survived to adulthood. In turn, they would also learn from the work order in Hilleström's paintings. It is possible that her eldest daughter, Fredrika, also took over the gold thimble. The female responsibility for the home's textiles did not diminish during the nineteenth century. On the contrary, it became an allocation of roles that was further cemented in the era's clear distinction between male and female spheres and tasks. When Sophia died in January 1830, the funeral eulogy focused on the virtue of 'the little world'. A perfect woman was one who did not seek affirmation from the wider world, and her life was perfect in her useful work by the hearth in the home, which kept her occupied right up to the end:

> She need not therefore seek joy in the world's amusements, what she inherently possesses is much better, or a diversion that would merely distract the mind from the most precious and holiest duties, or attention that would eventually make her a stranger to her dearest friends. *One* name, *one* delight, *one* happiness in her heart outweighs everything that the world can offer: and she hears this name, and she enjoys this delight, this happiness in her own home every day. ... She willingly denied herself all comforts, so that she could thereby bring joy to others. Indefatigable in the care of her house, she loved the most considerate order, and right up to the final days of her life, she was never unoccupied for a single moment.[94]

94 *Tal vid Förste Expeditions-Secreteraren m.m. Friherre Lars Aug. Mannerheims Kära Makas, Friherrinnan Sophia Mannerheims, född Wadenstjerna, Jordfästning, Den 17 Januarii 1830, Hållet af Johan Jacob Hedrén*, Stockholm 1830, pp. 9–11.

She endeavoured to make life comfortable for others, and that she had never been unoccupied in this 'for a single moment' was one of her foremost merits and showed that she fulfilled her duty throughout life, as a daughter, wife and mother. The similarity between Sophia and her mother, Jacobina Psilanderhielm, in the introductory portrait by Niclas Lafrensen was intentional in every respect. (Plate 1). In the portrait of her mother, Sophia would see her role model, and she would take over where her mother left off. Jacobina Psilanderhielm had been dead for five years when Lafrensen received the commission for the painting from Wadenstierna, but in the portrait her sewing work remains ongoing. Her role as a wife and mother did not cease with her death. The textile items that she left behind, in the fine cotton and linen fabrics of the dresses or the monograms on the bed sheets, carried her legacy forward. Her epitaph in the Maria Magdalena church reminded not only her close family but a wider contemporary social circle of her tenderness and care: 'SO. THAT. THE. MEMORY. OF. THE. BEST. AND. MOST. VIRTUOUS. WIFE. WILL. NOT. DISAPPEAR. TOO. QUICKLY. FROM. THE. WORLD.'

Finally, Lafrensen's portraits of both of Wadenstierna's wives can again be viewed in the light of Chardin's pictures of good and virtuous wives and mothers. When Jacobina Psilanderhielm in that eternal moment looks up from her embroidery, she becomes the symbol of '*l'amusement de la vie privée*', resting in the knowledge that she followed her calling in her loving care of her home and family, whereas Fredrica Carleson at her writing desk with her quill pen in her hand, represents '*l'économe*', administrating the household (Plates 1–3). While Jacobina Psilanderhielm, dressed in informal *déshabillé*, is presented as the home's protector, Fredrica Carleson, in a formal *robe*, directs her gaze out towards the social world that surrounded the family. Through the portraits, the women have been assigned their respective roles in the household, both equally necessary for the whole. When the new family life takes shape at Näs in the mid-1770s, the sewing tables are placed in the lady's cabinet. This room was home to a small round sewing table and a rectangular one made of mahogany, and they shared the space with Fredrica Carleson's '*skrif bureau*' (a secretaire desk).[95] Both aspects of being a good lady of the house therefore had their place in the lady's 'study'. Näs was to be furnished to meet the needs of Wadenstierna and his new wife and for their comfort, and they are united in Lafrensen's portraits through concordant attire and gestures, each of them in keeping with the responsibilities and tasks that the era's norms demanded of men and women. While the memory of his first wife was preserved in the portrait's warm rosy shimmer and the never-finished embroidery.

95 Riksarkivet, Näs Silverstolpeska arkivet, Personarkiven, vol. 60, Carl Eric Wadenstierna (1723–1787).

3. At the writing table

Abstract
Wadenstierna's second wife, Fredrica Carleson, was depicted by Niclas Lafrensen at another type of table and this portrait from the early 1770s is the starting point for the third chapter. The diminutive desk became an example of contemporary women's furniture that both encouraged and restricted female writing. It corresponded to a widespread culture of letter writing, but may also reflect the view on female education. The room layout at Näs Manor and the location of the family's various writing furniture further reflect the view of male and female roles and spheres, as exemplified in their fashionable Gustavian home.

Keywords: letter writing, *marchands-merciers*, books and reading, portraiture, education, Niclas Lafrensen

In Niclas Lafrensen's suite of portraits from around 1773, Carl Eric Wadenstierna is turning towards his second wife, Fredrica Carleson (Plates 1–3). He married her on 19 April 1770, nearly two years after the death of his first wife, Jacobina Psilanderhielm. The women in the portraits are each positioned at a table where they represent two of the era's expected female skills. Jacobina's needlework at the sewing table corresponded to Fredrica's letter writing at her writing table. The portrait of Fredrica Carleson writing a letter is small yet encompasses a whole world of beautifully painted details. The young woman with the quill pen in her hand turns, smiling, towards the viewer. Her posture is both straight and elegantly relaxed, and behind her back we glimpse a gilt armchair upholstered in patterned woven red silk fabric. She rests her arms on an exclusive small table with brass edging, ornamental fittings and black-checked plaited veneer decoration. Close at hand are an ink pot and sand shaker (pounce pot), as well as a small bell with which to summon a servant if the ink runs out or she would desire a cup of coffee. The shade on the candlestick means that she can have the light source very close to her to obtain comfortable lighting without the risk of burning her lace bonnet when she bends over her letter. '*Kommoditet*' (*commodité*, comfort) and functionality were conscious expressions of a modern culture of comfort. Her clothing was well

Brown, C., *Comfortable Everyday Life at the Swedish Eighteenth-Century Näs Manor.*
Taylor & Francis Group, 2024
DOI 10.5117/9789048562374_CH03

chosen for the occasion. Admittedly, she is wearing a *bonnet négligé,* an informal head covering that indicates the morning hours in a home environment, but lace, silk bows and starched tulle show that it is following the latest fashion. She has finished her morning toilette, and rows of sheer lace, pearl bracelets and a necklace complete her *robe à la français* in greyish blue silk that rustles slightly against the backrest of the chair.

The glimpses of silk-upholstered chairs and veneered tables in the portraits hint at the environment that surrounded the family and at their ideas of a life in keeping with their upper-class status. Every meticulously rendered detail in the paintings is a element in the narrative that Wadenstierna wanted to convey about their life. Jacobina Psilanderhielm was the mother of Wadenstierna's daughters, and her embroidery in the portrait served as a reminder of her care for her family and home. What duties now awaited his new wife and which virtues should she represent in the portrait role that Lafrensen had created for the world to see? Was the letter writing something characteristic of Fredrica Carleson or was it an accepted expression of her social identity? And what were the conditions for comfort at the writing tables at Näs in real life, outside of the portrait frame?

Letter writing and comfort: Women's furniture à la mode

Fredrica Carleson's writing table is a clear marker of class.[1] Veneered writing tables or upholstered chairs and sofas were virtually non-existent in eighteenth-century lower-class homes. The specialised pieces of furniture, and the opportunity to use them at any time of day or night, were characteristic of upper-class environments.[2] In Stockholm at that time, there were unquestionably skilled cabinetmakers (*ébénistes*) who created, among other things, fashionable 'women's furniture'. But their role models were on the Continent.[3] Particularly influential were the

1 Here, the assumption is that the table at which Niclas Lafrensen depicts Fredrica Carleson is a writing table, although its design also resembles sewing tables of that time. See, for example, a sewing table made by Georg Haupt from 1775 in Lagerquist, Marshall, *Georg Haupt. Ebeniste du Roi*, Nordiska museets handlingar 92, Stockholm 1979, p. 48 and p. 122 in Lars Ljungström, *Georg Haupt. Gustav III:s hovschatullmakare*, Stockholm 2006.

2 The homes of the lower classes were dominated by furniture and storage that was attached to the wall; Gösta Berg and Sigfrid Svensson, *Svensk bondekultur*, Stockholm 1969, p. 92 ff.

3 Torsten Sylvén, *Mästarnas möbler. Stockholmsarbeten 1700–1850*, Stockholm 1997, pp. 13–31. French furniture was generally not available for purchase in Sweden, but items similar to the French designs were. When Carl Gustaf Tessin ordered French furniture to be shipped home from Paris, it was an exceptional event. For a thorough review of how drawings, models and finished pieces of French furniture did reach the uppermost elite in Sweden; Bo Vahlne *Frihetstidens inredningar på Stockholms slott. Om bekvämlighetens och skönhetens nivåer*, Stockholm 2012. Outside the Swedish capital, the chances of finding furniture that

cabinetmakers who collaborated with *marchands-merciers* in Paris, who traded in luxury and *commodité* goods and who also worked as interior decorators and designers for the French aristocracy.[4] Well-known *marchands-merciers* such as Simon-Philippe Poirier and Dominique Daguerre worked closely with cabinetmakers including Martin Carlin, Jean-François Oeben or the father and son both named Pierre Migeon.[5] This cooperation resulted in new types of furniture that not only represented superb artisan skill, with elements of luxurious materials such as lacquered panels or plaques of Sèvres porcelain. They were also designed with a new lifestyle and an increasingly female-dominated clientele in mind.[6]

As shown, eighteenth-century upper-class homes were decreasingly furnished on the basis of large-scale formality and grand displays of representative status, and increasingly with an emphasis on intimacy and comfort. The French capital's *hôtel particulier* set the tone, the private city palaces that the elite commissioned to be designed as their modern, urban homes in contrast to the rigid court life dictated from Versailles. Bedchambers, cabinets and boudoirs were made smaller, and practical alcove beds were complemented with sofas, armchairs and small, lightweight tables. It was in these informal rooms that their occupants spent the mornings dressing, doing their morning toilette, drinking coffee, reading, and writing letters. This special context that took shape in close collaboration between craftsmen, traders and the elite created an expanding market for new types of furniture, in which *commodité* was a key common denominator. *Meuble volant* was the collective name for the lightweight, movable new pieces of furniture on brass castors that could easily be rolled up to the edge of the bed or the warmth of the fireplace. Lightness and daintiness were the distinctive characteristics of

followed Continental fashion were even smaller, largely due to the guilds' view of their own self-sufficiency, *Hushållnings Journal*, Stockholm 1777, p. 448; *Kommers. Historiska handelsformer i Norden under 1700- och 1800-talen*, Gudrun Andersson and Klas Nyberg (ed.), Gävle 2010.

4 Mimi Hellman, 'Furniture, Sociability, and the Work of Leisure in Eighteenth-Century France', *Eighteenth-Century Studies*, Vol. 32, No. 4, 1999, p. 418.

5 Jean-François Oeben developed new types of furniture with innovative, technical functions known as mechanical furniture, which were also distinctive for their intricate patterned veneer details. Oeben's and Pierre Mignon's style was adopted by a wider upper-class stratum through 'copies' by other craftsmen.

6 Olof von Dalin's occasional poem 'Med en så kallad Secretaire, Skickad Som Jul-Klapp til Fru … [With a so-called secretaire, sent as a Christmas present to Mrs …]' reflects the fashion in the mid-eighteenth century: 'A friend seems to reasonably be astonished, that his wife does not have a secretaire of her own, when her husband has nearly one hundred *De consequence & de bel air*. Now this one is applying to serve in that position. It is not witty, cannot make judgements about politics, beauty and ugliness, and does not understand how to praise itself, but it can hide good paperwork rather than bad bills at Christmas.' From *Framledne Hof-Cancellerens och Riddarens af Kongl. Maj:ts Nordstierne-Orden Herr Olof von Dalins Witterhets-Arbeten, I bunden och obunden Skrif-Art*, Vol. 6, Stockholm 1767, p. 248. See also Berry, Helen, 'Prudent Luxury. The Metropolitan Tastes of Judith Baker, Durham Gentlewoman', *Women and Urban Life in Eighteenth-Century England*, Rosemary Sweet and Penelope Lane (ed.), Farnham 2003, pp. 132–4.

this furniture and created a material and visual feeling of comfort. The especially diminutive items of furniture were also associated with the female consumer. This undoubtedly reflected a female ideal, where small hands were expected to perform small tasks at the tables – read novels in small octavo volumes, embroider pretty seams or write short notes and letters.[7] In Diderot and D'Alembert's *Encyclopédie* it is specifically the *small* tables that are associated with women. The word *tablette* informs us of the decorative small work table that was an embellishment for a woman's cabinet room and on which she placed her books, but also small ornaments – 'des porcelaines, & des bijoux de toutes sortes'.[8]

The multitude of different types of writing furniture that were launched was also the result of the major breakthrough of letter writing in the eighteenth century, and the genre's connection with women thereby contributed to special writing tables being designed for the female consumer. The many models illustrate the specialisation but also how furniture was now intimately associated with fashion and lifestyle. Each specific task, depending on place, time – and gender – required its own special piece of furniture in order to be carried out with '*commodité*'. It is clear how the development of this furniture that was especially for women follows a general 'gendering of fashion' that gradually takes shape during the eighteenth century.[9] To differentiate between a *liseuse* and a *bonheur du jour*, insight into international fashion and its market was required. One illustrative example is a short news item in *Mercure de France* in July 1755, in which the writer refers to the need for a new phrase book or dictionary that could bring order to all the new names for everything from furniture to hairstyles and culinary dishes that fashion presented.[10]

The fashionable words not only intended to help the consumer navigate the multitude of choices, they also served as effective markers that differentiated between people who were well-informed about the latest fashion and those who were not. They marked a clear boundary between old and new – from a time when a table was a table to a completely new way of looking at the world. 'Nos meubles, grace aux recherches des heureux du siécle & à l'art ingénieux de nos ouvriers,

7 The design of small work tables for ladies could sometimes normatively reinforce these tasks, for instance, with decorative veneer inlays on the table top that depicted the objects linked to the expected use for the table: balls of yarn, scissors, jewellery, quill pens, letters and books.

8 'Tablet', *Encyclopédie,* 1 re èd., Paris 1751, Tome 15 pp. 806–10.

9 See the discussion in, among others, Jones, Jennifer Michelle, *Sexing La Mode. Gender, Fashion and Commercial Culture in Old Regime France*, Oxford 2004.

10 'Dictionnaire portatif de tous les termes nouveaux & en usage parmi un certain monde, concernant la table, les équipages, les ameublemens, les ajustemens, tant d'hommes que de femmes, & les modes de toute espece, pour servir de monument à la constance & au bon goût de la nation; ouvrage extrêmement utile à tous ceux qui veulengt se répandre & paroître bonne compagnie, avec des anecdotes, &c', *Mercure de France, dédié au Roi*, Paris July 1755, p. 14.

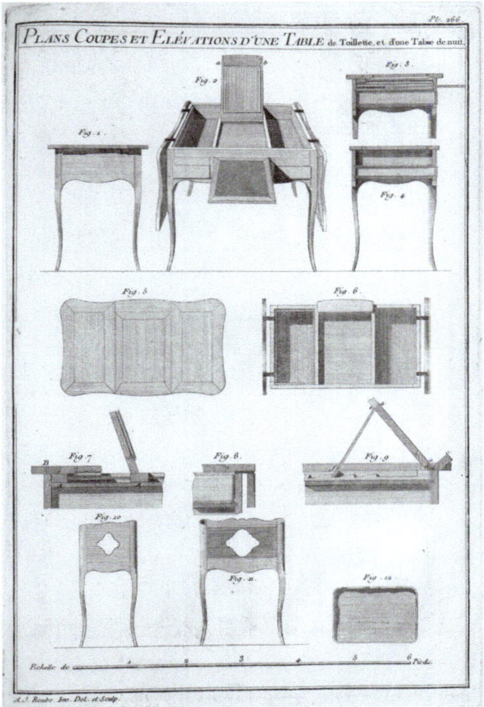

46. Drawings for a dressing table and bedside table by André Jacob Roubo. From Roubo, *L'art du Menuisier*, Paris, 1769. Photo: The New York Public Library.

ne ressemblent plus à ceux de nos peres [Our furniture, thanks to our century's fortunate development and our craftsmen's ingenious art, no longer resembles that of our fathers]', the writer explains in *Mercure de France*.[11]

The names also reflected the intended function of the specialised furniture, and there appears to have been a piece of writing furniture for every moment of the privileged upper-class woman's day. With a small *écritoire*, a box with a sloping lid, the letters could be written when you were half-lying in bed, and at a *poudreuse* the writing could be combined with the morning toilette. Moreover, a *bonheur du jour* indicated how the small and sometimes collapsible writing table could easily be moved to follow the daylight. Jacobina Psilanderhielm's estate inventory from 1769 also states '1 ink pot and sand box in a briefcase' for use during travel.[12] The large range of products offered comfort at all times. But the movability of the furniture and the objects was also designed for a new and healthy approach to people's need for mobility. In the spirit of the Age of Enlightenment, authors and scientists wrote about

11 *Mercure de France*, July 1755, p. 11.

12 Jacobina Sophia Psilanderhielms bouppteckning, 4 December 1769, Riksarkivet, Näs Silverstolpeska arkivet, Personarkiven, vol. 60, Carl Eric Wadenstierna (1723–1787). Perhaps it is the briefcase made of red Morocco leather with green lining, and with writing sand still in one of the glass boxes, that today remains among the property from Näs.

the danger of an excessively monotonous sedentary lifestyle that could adversely affect a woman's posture and facial expressions. Freethinker and scientist Erasmus Darwin (grandfather of Charles Darwin) proposes early training in holding the pen (or sewing needle) in a relaxed way and with 'an agreeable moderate attention of the countenance'.[13] A special table, which should preferably be sloping so that the body does not need to bend excessively and which offers good access to light, is intended to facilitate comfort and support health and beauty. The movable small table reduced the risk of constantly sitting with the same side of your body turned towards the fire or the window, which could lead to lopsidedness in a young person whose bone structure was still being formed. Flexibility was the new era's cure for old rigid ways of life – just like in today's ergonomic advice.

In this context, the *poudreuse* was a piece of multifunctional furniture ingeniously designed to meet all of a woman's specific needs. Outwardly, it resembled an elegant veneered writing table, but it was equipped with a hidden mirror that was opened up out of the table top, side leaves that could be folded out to reveal velvet-clad interiors with compartments for both make-up compacts and stationery, and a table frame with lockable drawers for storage of private correspondence (Image 46). Cabinetmaker Georg Haupt created a version where a pull-out leaf had also been designed as a chessboard.[14] The combination of different functions associated with a female sphere also proved to be a commercial success. It generated an increasingly extensive market for luxury and fashion items – from furniture to ink pots and pen-wipers, from dressing jackets to trinket boxes.[15] This also effectively anchored women's writing activities to a specifically assigned time and place. The sentimental letters that were associated with the era's ideal role of women were most suitably written during the morning toilette.

A portrait from 1787 by the French miniature painter Pierre Nöel Violet depicts a young woman who has sat down at her *poudreuse* (Image 47). She is still only wearing a corset and an undone dressing jacket *en déshabillé*, and smilingly she plays with curls of her hair with one hand.[16] The woman has opened up the mirror out of the table top to complete her morning toilette, and a perfume bottle can

13 The scientist Erasmus Darwin also offers the precise measurements for the perfect writing table for a woman, Erasmus Darwin, *Plan for the Conduct of Female Education in Boarding Schools*, London, 1797, section 4, pp. 15, 77. Compare how mobility and softness in the late eighteenth century appear as upper-class ideals that follow the English fashion, Christopher Daniel Bunth, *An Essay on English Lecture, Selected for the most part from late Authors*, Lund 1792, p. 189. *Malla Montgomery-Silfverstolpes memoarer*, utgifna af Malla Grandinson, I, Stockholm 1908, p. 213, declared that the older generation's formally rigid body language was old-fashioned.

14 Uppsala Auktionskammare, 2013.

15 Auslander, Leora, *Taste and Power. Furnishing Modern France*, London 1996, pp. 55f.

16 In the eighteenth century, it was fashionable to portray male authors in morning gowns *en déshabillé*, which symbolised both privileged, informal lifestyle and intellectual freedom. Compare Louis Michel

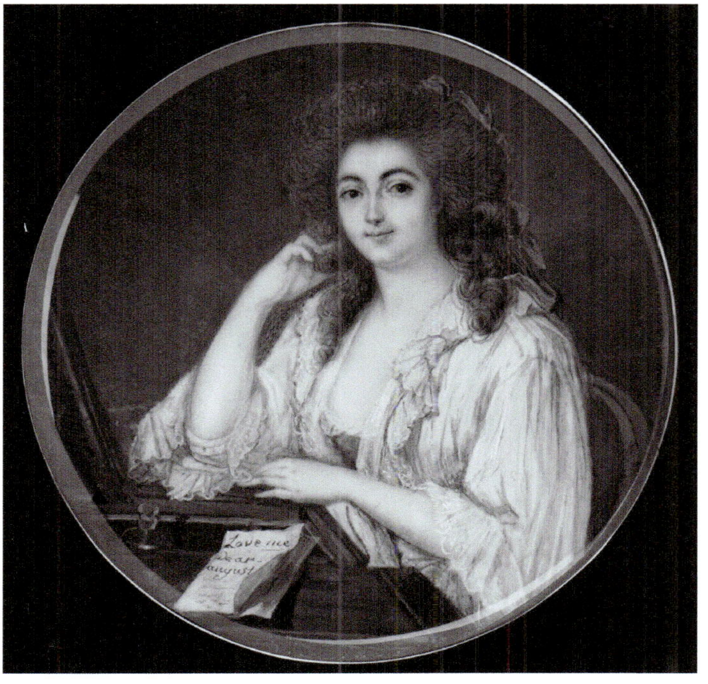

47. Pierre Nöel Violet, *Unknown Woman*, 1787. Gouache on ivory, 6.6 cm. Tansey Collection, Celle, Germany.

be glimpsed in the blue-clad box. She seems to have just finished a letter that has been turned towards the viewer to be read.[17] The portrait renders the woman as young, beautiful and loved, and with time, money and taste for both fashion and love letters – an ideal image for all women within the era's social elite – including Fredrica Carleson.

Words such as *liseuse*, *poudreuse* or *bonheur du jour* bring to mind Lafrensen's pictorial world, in which the era's new, intimate rooms are populated by elegantly relaxed women who demonstrate how reading, needlework and letter writing were arranged on the basis of the latest modern comfort. Fashion plates, but also engraved pictures that were widely disseminated, served as a form of eighteenth-century product placement, in which the newest inventions of *marchands-merciers* were presented to a clientele among the consumption-centred women of the social elite. The pictures not only showed what was required to be *à la mode*, but also how the fashionable items were to be used, and by whom and where. For example,

van Loo's portrait of Denis Diderot from 1767 (the Louvre). A parallel to this consists of the women who were portrayed writing letters *en déshabillé*.

17 On the letter the text states: 'Love me Dear August.' The woman wants to assure the viewer and recipient of both the letter and portrait of her heartfelt love. Although the letter and portrait miniature were intended for a specific recipient called August, the message also follows an expected pattern in the eighteenth century.

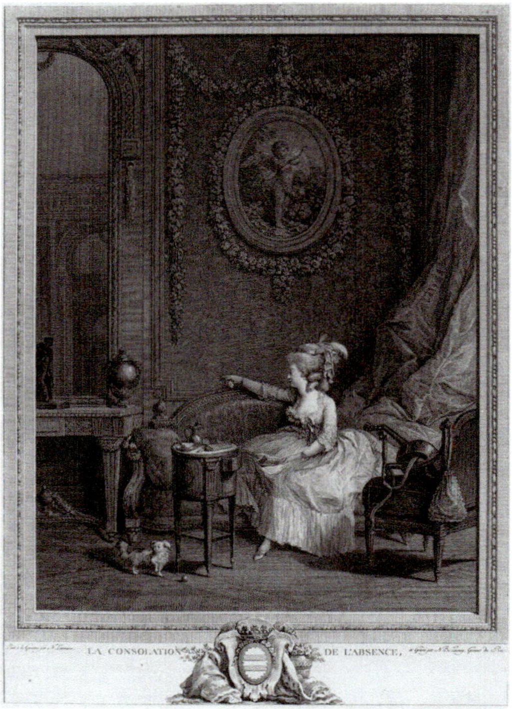

48. Nicolas Delaunay after Niclas Lafrensen the Younger, *La consolation de l'absence*, c. 1785. Engraving, 32.3 × 40 cm. Widener Collection, National Gallery of Art, Washington, DC (1942.9.2402).

the engraved version of Lafrensen's painting *La consolation de l'absence* (Plate 10 and Image 48) was updated with the latest fashionable piece of multifunctional furniture – its functions are demonstrated through the pulled-out drawer and the arrangement with the coffee service.

The specialised tables reappear in the eighteenth century's pictorial world and illustrate how the letter-writing culture was interwoven with fashion, consumption and a privileged lifestyle. The connoisseurship of reproducing the correct table and the correct writing accessories for the context seems to be a key element in the pictures. The table glimpsed in Fredrica Carleson's portrait was possibly a *bonheur du jour* – she has now left her morning toilette and meets the viewer's gaze fully dressed. Lafrensen was able to find models of 'women's furniture' in the era's engraved pictorial world as well as in the furniture that surrounded his clientele. In the Wadenstierna family after her death, Jacobina Psilanderhielm left a writing table and two slant-top desks for use in the family's city residence.[18] Perhaps one of these could also complement the furniture at the newly built Näs Manor, in the study and library.

18 Jacobina Sophia Psilanderhielms bouppteckning, 4 December 1769, Riksarkivet, Näs Silverstolpeska arkivet, Personarkiven, vol. 60, Carl Eric Wadenstierna (1723–1787).

Writing and reading: The Wadenstierna sisters and the library at Näs

The library at Näs was in the large room that dominated the manor's southern wing. It included the collection of books, engravings and maps along with writing tables and a billiard table. The library was flanked by four guest rooms equipped with writing tables, but also with games tables and tea tables. When the Wadenstierna family began using the manor in 1775 and the varied book collection could be arranged in the bookcases and on the shelves of the room, the library must have encouraged gatherings as well as reading and writing in solitude.

In April 1770 when forty-seven-year-old Carl Eric Wadenstierna married Fredrica Carleson, who was twenty years younger, his daughters Sophia and Carolina were aged twelve and eight. Wadenstierna's care for the girls was probably partly why he now chose a new wife who could assist him in raising the girls to become young ladies. He shows his tenderness and care for the girls in the letter with rules of life that he wrote to them in conjunction with the death of their mother in 1768. He urges them to never forget their parents' love for each other and their children and to always trust in divine providence.[19] But his care is also demonstrated in the choices that he made when ordering the pictures and books that would contribute to the environment that the girls would grow up in at Näs and that in a concrete and instructive way illustrated the rules of life that he had stipulated for them. There was perhaps also an unspoken thought that it would also benefit his young wife.

When Wadenstierna commissioned Niclas Lafrensen to paint the portraits of both of his wives, his ambition was probably that both women would appear to be equal role models for his daughters. A detail from *Tillrättavisningen* (The telling-off), one of the paintings that Wadenstierna concurrently commissioned from Pehr Hilleström, highlights the relationship between the girls and their female role models (Plate 11). The two young girls in the picture are not referred to as portrait representations, but they do represent the daughters' equivalents in the era's normative pictorial world. The girls are urged to be diligent – at sewing, reading or writing – so that they gain the virtues and skills that would subsequently be expected of them as adult women. The girls' clothes are also influenced by the adult world's ideals.

Correspondingly, Wadenstierna's library can be said to display equal proportions of ambition and care concerning the girls. The estate inventory provides a detailed picture of the extensive book collection. The library in the city residence at Stora Vattugränden in Stockholm above all reflected Wadenstierna's political profession, whereas, fiction, plays, memoires and 'travelogues' were grouped in the library

19 Riksarkivet, Näs Silverstolpeska arkivet, Personarkiven, vol. 60, Carl Eric Wadenstierna (1723–1787).

wing at Näs. The choice of good reading material was also deemed crucial for the development of good written language skills. Child-rearing literature from that time stresses the importance of reading the good examples again and again to develop one's feel for language. Erasmus Darwin thought that the ear had to become accustomed (which is also a reminder that reading aloud remained common), so that the 'musicality' of the language was absorbed, and that the young woman thereby developed an ability to create her own, similar compositions.[20] The role models were essential so that the girls would develop an assured taste and become fully fledged letter writers.[21]

Some of the titles in the library at Näs comprised the era's well-known epistolary novels, and a notably large number of the library's books were written by women – from Hedvig Charlotta Nordenflycht to Fanny Burney. There were also reviews such as *Histoire litteraire des femmes françoises* and Aublet de Maubuy's *Les vies de femmes illustres de la France*. According to Darwin, the good and cultivating literature should both entertain and educate, and several of the titles he presents as suitable for young women were also within reach for the sisters at Näs. These included the Marquise de Genlis' plays, *Théâtre d'éducation à l'usage des jeunes persones* (with subjects thought to engage young women): *La marchande de modes*, *La lingère*, *Le libraire* or *Le portrait ou les rivaux généreux*; Henry Fielding's *Tom Jones* (although Darwin did not deem it suitable for minors); Samuel Richardson's *William Harrington* and Fanny Burney's *Evelina, or the History of a Young Lady's Entrance into the World*.[22] The library's many plays also included comedies by Sébastien-Roch-Nicolas de Chamfort and Niccolò Piccinni, expressions of the 1770s' fashionable theme *à la turque*.[23] In this respect, the Wadenstierna family seem somewhat liberal and modern and do not shun the entertaining literature that people usually issued warnings about in households with daughters.[24] The number of books by English-speaking authors also testifies how British attitudes and ideals gained ground within the more progressively minded elite in the latter half of the eighteenth century.

The library at Näs thereby tells us about the family's attempts to navigate between new and old ideals and about the view of the girls' cultivation and future roles. The era's approach to child rearing advocated that the girls should learn through good

20 Darwin 1797, section XIV, p. 39.

21 Darwin 1797, pp. 25–6.

22 Darwin 1797, p. 31.

23 Carolina Brown, *Liksom en herdinna. Litterära teman i svenska kvinnoporträtt under 1700-talet*, Stockholm 2012 [diss.], pp. 261–347.

24 '[...] the mischievous trash which the circulating library pours forth for the entertainment of a mind unaccustomed to reflection.', Thomas Gisborne, *An Enquiry Into the Duties of the Female Sex*, London 1797, p. 353.

role models and warning examples in the form of cautionary tales and through the familiar confiding tone of address in epistolary novels. This is how female virtues such as love, empathy and humility were shaped. The girls' reading was therefore intended to develop their social skills rather than their intellectual ones.[25] The latter half of the eighteenth century also entailed increasingly clear domestication of the role of women, and thereby a narrowing limitation of women's sphere to the home and family life.[26] This was based on both changed gender constructions and social and structural changes between groups in society as a whole, and it entailed consequences for attitudes to women's education, to love and to marriage. The clear boundaries that came to separate the nineteenth century's male and female spheres developed from these ideological changes, formulated by representatives of the Age of Enlightenment led by Rousseau, among others.[27]

The funeral eulogy after the death of Wadenstierna's eldest daughter, Sophia, in 1830 was a result of the attitudes that raised her generation. Here, a picture is painted of a woman whose only needs were the placid, unassuming virtues in the home, in her family circle, following 'nature's life-giving outlook'.[28] The starting points for Fredrica Carleson's own upbringing had been formulated by her father in *Sedolärande Mercurius*, the magazine that he published together with his brother Carl Carleson in 1730–1. It was admittedly over a decade before any of his daughters were born, yet the magazine stresses the importance of never neglecting a girl's upbringing so that she could develop into a useful wife and mother and a self-assured person of rank. The girl must be kept away from the servants, but must also be protected from developing a taste for conceit and extravagance. 'The children should also become accustomed to trivial and useful as well as valuable and artistic work. But work must in all ways be made out to be play, or to be easy and pleasant.'[29]

A large number of the novels and plays in the library at Näs could therefore, from the era's perspective, serve as instructive reading for Sophia and Carolina Wadenstierna and their young stepmother, Fredrica Carleson. This literature included the epistolary novel *Sophronie ou leçon prétendue d'une mère à sa fille* by Françoise-Albine Puzin de la Martinière Benoist, in which Sophronie, a young widow and loving mother, guides her teenage daughter, Adèle, on the enlightened path

25 Boudier de Villemert, Pierre Joseph, *Qwinno-könets wän. Öfwersatt ifrån fransyskan,* Västerås (1758) 1763, p. 23.

26 *Journal för allmänna upplysningen och sederne*, Twelfth part, Stockholm 1797, pp. 385–7.

27 Jennifer J. Popiel, *Rousseau's Daughters. Domesticity, Education, and Autonomy in Modern France,* New Hampshire 2008.

28 *Tal vid Förste Expeditions-Secreteraren m.m. Friherre Lars Aug. Mannerheims Kära Makas, Friherrinnan Sophia Mannerheims, född Wadenstjerna, Jordfästning, Den 17 Januarii 1830, Hållet af Johan Jacob Hedrén,* Stockholm 1830, p. 11.

29 Edvard Carleson, *Sedolärande Mercurius*, Stockholm 1 Dec. 1730.

of virtue through the dark thicket of emotions. And there was also *Le mariage du siècle* by André-Guillaume Contant d'Orville, a correspondence between a woman in the city, surrounded by attentive admirers, and her friend in the countryside. The decadent city life, where the days are spent moving between dressing tables, writing tables, coffee tables and games tables, is contrasted with simple, tranquil country life.[30] The country home was where true happiness could be found, according to the novel's heroine, Sophie – also a recommendation to Sophia Wadenstierna reading at Näs.

The epistolary novels instructed the Wadenstierna sisters in how they should formulate their letters, how confidences were conveyed and what standpoints were suitable for their social position, gender and disposition, on everything from love to consumption. But perhaps above all the novels represent manuals in how to handle emotions. In the battle between sense and sensibility, the fictional female letter writers tremble, gasp, cry and rage. The novels also revealed the significance of the room – how it was used and furnished. The heroines retire to their chambers and cabinets to write and reflect; they have private meetings in their dressing rooms and they seek solace among their sofa cushions. The engraved illustrations in the library's books also had an instructive function. They showed both how emotionality was dealt with and how rooms were furnished.

The library wing at Näs must have been an inviting place for this type of reading. In addition to the books, there were tables, a large sofa and eight comfortable armchairs to sink into, and the walls were covered with a map of Lake Mälaren and fifty-two engraved pictures with gilt frames. The pictures hung close together and provided views of a wider world, which could also be read about in the books' letters and depictions of travels: Siberia, Iceland, the Netherlands, Italy and Turkey. Guided by the authors Sparrman, Hulphers, Björnståhl, Von Troil or Cook, the girls could travel around the world from their corner of the sofa, without leaving home. The library wing was also a place for socialising, and in the large room the billiard table was a focal point around which people could gather. The books, pictures and billiard table were all central expressions of the Wadenstierna family's status and aspirations. The collection displayed the ambition of being part of the era's intellectual and cultivated climate – at the same time that the environment encouraged comfortable and informal gatherings.

In the book collection at Näs, fiction and the books for enjoyment and recreation occupied a particularly prominent position. Titles such as Élie Bertrand's *Essai sur le plaisir* or Ducry's *Amusement curieux et divertissant propre à égayer l'esprit* set the tone. One of the overdoor decorations in the entrance hall of the main building

30 André-Guillaume Contant d'Orville, *Le mariage du siècle, ou lettres de Mme la Comtesse de Castelli à Mme la Baronne de Fréville*, 1767, pp. 6, 9–10.

clarified in the same vein of thought that Näs was the place where Wadenstierna intended to enjoy his *otium honestum*: 'Free of the noise of the wider world, among books and among good friends, to be loved more, rather than become famous, enables you to feel the force and right sweetness of life.' It was in this spirit that the daughters – through their reading and writing – were also to be moulded into a social role. Sophia Wadenstierna's 'poetry book' or 'friendship book' (*album amicorum*), that she wrote herself and that probably dated from the late 1770s or early 1780s, is a clear example of this class affinity and the expectations it was associated with (Image 49). The small red Morocco leather volume starts with a neat verse that closely follows the rules of life that her father had written to her in connection with her mother's death. The first lines, like a psalm, encourage contentment and patience:

> Be satisfied with the gifts of good fortune
> do not judge the faults of others harshly
> share the gifts that
> heaven has bestowed upon you
> be properly loyal to your friend
> tender-hearted towards a harmless soul
> mature in decisions and deliberations
> do not think ill, but speak well.[31]

The verses, poems and stanzas that follow show that the purpose of the book was also to be an exercise in beautiful handwriting and in fluently mastering language – also French. Errors and corrections, misspellings and rewrites demonstrate Sophia's development and probably also that of other writers who had contributed to the book. The fact that the written language in both form and content closely resembled spoken language is seen in the many songs and verses that resonated from the era's popular broadside ballads, dance songs, vaudeville and drinking songs. The majority of these, such as the free reproductions of Carl Michael Bellman's 'Fredmans epistlar', Olof von Dalin's verses or various broadside ballads, illustrate the oral tradition, but also how women's spelling, more often than men's, included elements of spoken language.[32] The library's book collection was probably also

31 It is conceivable that the introductory verses were written by Wadenstierna himself when he gave the book to his daughter as the handwriting closely resembles Wadenstierna's own. Riksarkivet, Näs Silverstolpeska arkivet, Personarkiven, vol. 61, Sophia Wadenstierna (1758–1830), Carolina Wadenstierna (1762–1848).

32 Although some of Fredman's epistles were disseminated as broadside ballads and manuscripts in the early 1770s, they were not published until 1790, and Sophia Wadenstierna's 'poetry book' is likely to have been based on an oral rendition. Riksarkivet, Näs Silverstolpeska arkivet, Personarkiven, vol. 61, Sophia

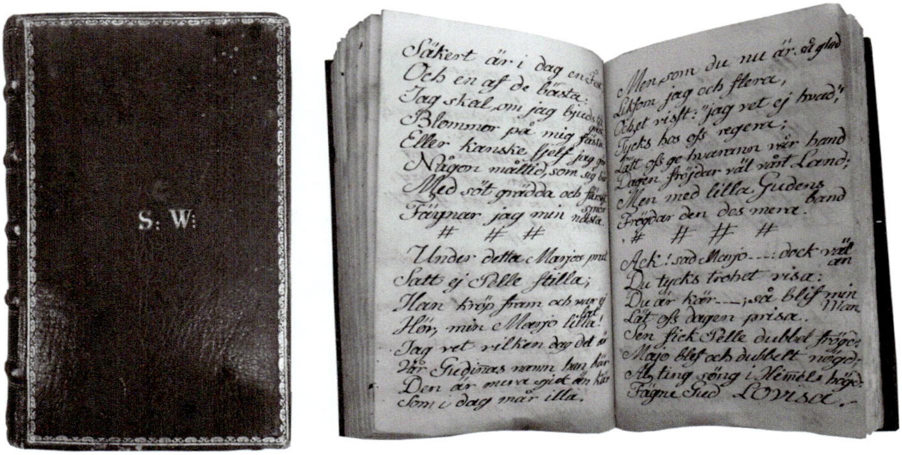

49. Sophia Wadenstierna's (1758–1830) 'poetry book', 1770–80s. The open book shows lines from Olof von Dalin's pastoral poem for Her Majesty the Queen's name day: *Herdevisa (På Hennes Maj:ts Drottningens Namnsdag, den 26 Aug. 1781)*. The National Archive, Stockholm.

used as a source of inspiration. Here, Sophia Wadenstierna can be compared to fourteen-year-old Jacobina Charlotta Munsterhjelm, who writes the following in her diary in May 1800: 'In the morning I wrote a verse for sister Ulla from Dalin's works, and for dear mother I wrote three verses.'[33]

Sophia Wadenstierna's poetry book is full of drastic contrasts in a varied mix. One of the pages reproduces the polite conversation between the amorous shepherd and shepherdess Annette and Lubin. On the other page there are eye-catching exclamations such as 'Ma Maitresse infidelle, aime le grand Calas, ha ha ha' and '[S]ee, here is a snifter, stretch out your hand, our schnapps with gold and gems, enriches your tongue and teeth.' Songs from theatres and ballrooms, noisy bellowing from celebrations and parties, or shouts from markets and coffee houses emanate from the pages of the book. The general public's street language, in French known as *en poissarde*, had become a fashionable component with which to spice up the era's theatre language. It shaped a literary genre with elements of slang, spoken colloquial language and imitations of sounds – which Bellman excelled in – and

Wadenstierna (1758–1830), Carolina Wadenstierna (1762–1848). Regarding women's written and spoken language, see Löwendahl, Marie, *Min allrabästa och ömmaste vän! Kvinnors brevskrivning under svenskt 1700-tal*, Gothenburg 2007 and Forselius, Tilda Maria, 'Min nådiga pappas Uprigtiga Vän och fiolliga flicka. Julie Ekerman/Björckegrens brev till Carl Sparre lästa utifrån frågor om makt och identitet', magister thesis at Department of Literary Studies, Stockholm University 2002. Carina Burman, *Bellman. Biografin*, Stockholm 2019, pp. 178–9.

33 *Jacobina Charlotta Munsterhjelms Dagböcker, 1799–1801*, Bo Lönnqvist (ed.), Svenska Litteratursällskapet i Finland, Helsinki 1970, p. 59.

was used in popular songs and dance songs of the time. Sophia Wadenstierna's book contains traces of the jargon *en poissarde* as well as eloquent preciosity.[34]

The books in the library and Sophia Wadenstierna's poetry or friendship book both thereby remind us how closely the era's texts followed the oral tradition. The novels developed the art of conversation of the epistolary genre, and librettos reproduced dialogues in the performing arts. Some of the books in the library at Näs compiled all these different expressions within their covers – reading that was deemed especially useful and suitable for women. Volumes such as *Lettres à Myladi***, et autres œuvres melées* from 1773 by Pierre-Antoine de La Place offered excerpts from letters, plays, epigrams and songs.[35] The poetry book's verses and songs had probably also been created and used in social contexts – it was Sophia's own collection of what was sung and danced to at gatherings and verses that could be used for tableaux and charades. Reciting, singing and reading aloud were part of the culture of socialising, and it was in the art of conversation's wide variety of expressions and forms that women were thought to have a natural advantage. The poetry book was thereby not only a pastime but also part of a young woman's journey towards cultivation.

'The young ladies' chamber', probably situated next to the entrance hall at Näs, was dominated by a shared bed with a blue and white linen bed cover, along with a sofa, six armchairs and an old armchair. But the room had no designated writing furniture. There was one small lady's walnut 'bureau', which possibly had a pull-out writing surface in addition to its storage function, and the simple square pine table that was also in this room may have been used for writing exercises, but the girls were not expected to have their own writing table.[36] Instead, they may have been summoned to the adults' writing furniture in chambers and the library when they were to practise their writing and reading skills. Moreover, much of the training probably consisted of oral language exercises. The girls' room thereby differs from the cabinet of their step-mother in one key respect. Fredrica Carleson's '*skrif bureau*' (writing bureau, secretaire) clearly stated in her estate inventory shows that this piece of writing furniture was the privilege of the lady of the house.

34 The street language *en poissarde* (which refers to the fishwives of the markets in France) was enjoyed by the social elite from theatre stages and became a fashionable element in the era's various forms of culture. In *The Other Enlightenment. How French Women Became Modern*, Princeton 2003, Carla Hesse states how this phenomenon, alongside preciosity, formed an independent linguistic space for women at the time around the French Revolution.

35 The book included epigrams regarding the artist François Boucher's portrait roles (p. 70) as well as for the literary portraits that Jean de la Bruyère created in his classic anecdotes *Les caractères* (p. 18) – a reference to edifying reading for young ladies.

36 This 'bureau' differed from the 'clothes bureau' that was also in the room and had its function specified in the estate inventory (Riksarkivet, Näs Silverstolpeska arkivet, Personarkiven, vol. 60, Carl Eric Wadenstierna (1723–1787).

'The cabinet': A room of her own for Fredrica Carleson

In his portrait by Niclas Lafrensen, Carl Eric Wadenstierna pauses his reading for a brief moment and lets his gaze drift from his open book to his wife beside him (Plates 1–3). The portrait commission was perhaps not only a loving manifestation of his new marriage and a commemoration of his first wife, Jacobina Psilanderhielm. The task he put to the esteemed Niclas Lafrensen may also have been a way for Wadenstierna to show his new wife that he was knowledgeable about fashion and taste.

Fredrica Carleson came from a cosmopolitan family. She was the daughter of the widely travelled city commissioner and president of the board of trade, Edvard Carleson, and his Dutch wife, Clara Leytstar. Together with Carl Fredrik von Höpken, Carleson had travelled far on behalf of Sweden to become more familiar with industries and sectors.[37] Fredrica was born in Constantinople in 1743, where her father worked as an envoy. He was knighted the same year for his work for Swedish manufactories and sciences.[38] Carleson established himself in grand style after his return to Sweden in 1746. He acquired Malmvik Manor with considerable land not far from the royal palace at Drottningholm on the outskirts of Stockholm, as well as Vårby Gård, which was known at the time for its health spring. Over several years, he assiduously invested in new properties, farms and manufactories. Raised in the Age of Liberty's thoughts on the utility of luxury, Fredrica Carleson probably fully understood the luxury required for a life in keeping with her class status and how fashion's latest '*kommoditeter*' (*commodités*) were to be best arranged, both inside and outside of the frames of portraiture.[39] Through her family's and her father's interests, she was part of the era's cultural and material cosmopolitanism. Luxury consumption was an expression of active participation in this larger identity-building international network.[40] Wadenstierna is likely to have had several points of contact with his future father-in-law and the latter's business activities a long time before he contemplated marrying Carleson's daughter.

37 Hat party politician Carleson was driven by the thought of establishing manufactories and long-distance trade in an age when manufactories constituted a subject of contention between the parties. One of his contributions to the debate was the 1731 booklet *Möjeligheten At i Swerige inrätta Fabriquer och Manufacturer* (The possibility of establishing factories and manufactories in Sweden), Stockholm 1731.

38 Carleson and Höpken's activities in Turkey are reported in Carleson, E & Höpken, C. F. von, *Relation, om herrar envoyéernes och cancellierådens, herr baron v. Höpkens och herr Carlesons hafde audience wid Ottomanniske porten 8/19 julii 1740*, Stockholm 1740 and *Biographiskt lexicon öfver namnkunnige svenska män*, III. Uppsala 1837, pp. 183–7.

39 Carl Fredrik von Höpken's brother, the politician Anders von Höpken, wrote a famous speech on the utility of luxury in 1740 with the aim of promoting Swedish luxury production, Britta Allzén and Ingemar Tunander, *Yppighets nytta. Liten encyklopedi över människor, idéer och dyrbarheter i svensk rokoko*, Malmö 1979.

40 *A Taste for Luxury in Early Modern Europe. Display, Acquisition and Boundaries*, Johanna Ilmakunnas and Jon Stobart (ed.), London and New York, p. 9.

Artist Niclas Lafrensen was also part of this cosmopolitan network. He had recently returned home from Paris in the early 1770s, was soon to be appointed court painter and was a direct agent for French upper-class culture and its fashion and lifestyle. The multitude of engraved pictures distributed after his paintings were also furnished with pretentious dedications to prominent names within the contemporary international elite and thereby gave the idealised scenes an enticing element of authenticity. Who would not want to belong to the world that Lafrensen produced in his pictures? People wishing to confirm their social position and manifest their identification with high society could have it all through a portrait commission by 'Nicolas Lavreince', which became the artist's French alter ego. Although only part of the table edge is glimpsed in the portrait miniature of Fredrica Carleson, it is a direct reference to this exclusive, privileged and consumption-centred world. This was a writing table specially designed for the fashionable correspondence of an elegant woman and was as if taken from Lafrensen's Parisian environments. Fredrica Carleson is presented here as being knowledgeable about cultivated correspondence and taste and as a participant in contemporary international culture.

Fredrica Carleson's cabinet consisted of the southern corner room in the main building at Näs, with a view of the manor's separate wings, while Wadenstierna's room was situated in the northern part of the building. The interior decoration was in the style of the architect Carl Hårleman, with wooden wall panelling, above which winding leaf and flower tendrils spread out on the pale fabric-covered wall panels. Along with a mirror, no fewer than twenty-three oil paintings jostled for space on the walls, hung closely together within the painted frames of the wall panels. The room was not large and was filled with the most essential pieces of furniture: '1 woman's writing bureau with inlay' (secretaire), two sewing tables, six chairs upholstered in cotton and a small sofa. In the inner corner stood a tiled stove with chinoiserie decoration.[41] The cabinet was embellished with two potpourri urns made by the Marieberg factory and a late-Baroque mantel pendulum clock by clockmaker Vincent Schultz in Stockholm – the black lacquered chinoiserie pattern on the case followed the theme on the tiled stove (Image 51). The windows were decorated with curtains, and three rugs kept floor draughts at bay. The room was in all respects cosy and comfortable – situated between the bedchamber and the dressing room, where two maids slept at night – and furnished to suit the tasks of the lady of the house.

Perhaps the 'woman's writing bureau' that according to the estate inventory stood in the room was the one made by Johan Niclas Eckstein in 1773.[42] Eckstein's secretaire

41 Riksarkivet, Näs Silverstolpeska arkivet, Personarkiven, vol. 60, Carl Eric Wadenstierna (1723–1787).

42 The assumption about which rooms the pieces of furniture were placed in at Näs is based on Wadenstierna's estate inventory from 1787, in which the furniture and effects are stated room by room. However, the meagre description of the furniture does create a degree of uncertainty.

was distinctive with its marquetry featuring floral intarsia in various coloured types of wood, and its modern function with a roll top that concealed a pull-out veneered surface and a series of small shelves and drawers (Plate 12). The embellishment with *'marqueterie à fleurs'* was reminiscent of prominent French *ébénistes* such as Jean-François Oeben or Léonard Boudin, whose work Eckstein here skilfully succeeded in resembling.[43] But the estate inventory does not specify the piece of writing furniture in Fredrica Carlesson's cabinet in detail. The secretaire with floral decoration could be equally appropriate in Carl Eric Wadenstierna's suite of rooms.

But the information that the piece of writing furniture that stood there was especially for a *'fruntimer'* (woman), sufficed as reference to the fashionable furniture and its given place in the home. There was a long history of having separate gentleman's and lady's suites, but the eighteenth century's items of furniture specially for women, *'fruntimers möbler'* for the women's rooms, were an expression of the era's gender-coded distribution of roles in the home and the growth of a determined target group-oriented market.[44] Fredrica Carleson's *'fruntimers skrif bureau'* (literally: woman's writing bureau) defined her cabinet as a particularly 'female' room, as well as defining her as being well-versed in the era's fashion and taste. The piece of writing furniture that stood there, its shape and function and its suitability for female activities such as correspondence, made it especially apt for her cabinet. The table in Lafrensen's portrait of Fredrica Carleson perhaps does not depict a specific one, but in the same way it is a reference to international models, through the meticulous rendering of the veneer work and ornamentation and its location in a female sphere.

Lafrensen's portrait thereby conveys a glimpse of the reality that surrounded Fredrica Carleson at Näs. Just as she is depicted well dressed and presentable together with objects that were representative of the latest fashion, neither Fredrica herself nor her cabinet were isolated from the eyes of the surrounding world in everyday life at the manor. The oldest floor plan for the main building at Näs shows that the cabinet was not to be connected to the suite of reception rooms but was instead to be linked to the manor's practical rooms and overlooking the comings and goings of servants and activities at the kitchen. But later drawings show how a door opened her cabinet into the adjacent and lavish bedchamber. The building was small enough for you to be constantly reminded of the proximity to the more formal rooms. However, the position of the room also refers to the duties and responsibilities of

43 In 1772, Léonard Boudin (1735–1807), whose training included instruction in the Migeon brothers' studio, also became a marchand-mercier, Sylvén 1997, p. 102. Eckstein's secretaire is described in detail in Marshall Lagerquist's article 'Blomstermålning i trä', *Fataburen, Nordiska museets och Skansens årsbok*, Stockholm 1962, pp. 51–62.

44 Cynthia Wall, 'Gendering Rooms: Domestic Architecture and Literary Acts', *Eighteenth-Century Fiction*, Vol. 5, iss. 4, 1993 and Appadurai 1986.

the lady of the house, where closeness to the front of the building was crucial. The view of the courtyard and the free-standing wing buildings, especially the kitchen wing, related to her responsibilities. It was important that she could constantly keep a watchful eye on the activities that took place there, even when she was busy at her writing and sewing tables in her cabinet. She was expected to maintain dialogue concerning the distribution of tasks with the servants, and she should be able to quickly summon employees to her room to give instructions and orders. The man's responsibility was 'the outdoor housekeeping' and the woman's 'the indoor housekeeping'.[45] This is clearly stated in the book on the ideal wife from 1787: 'She knows everything that occurs in the house, all work must be performed for her eyes.'[46] The position and design of the cabinet guaranteed this order and thereby comfort in everyday life.

According to the view of 'women's education' at that time, her area of responsibility therefore comprised the home, household, children and servants, and it was her duty to constantly control this sphere. Or, as it is worded in one of the era's popular journals:

> Women's obligations are many and considerable; their stipulations are great and important. The felicity of the entire household depends on them. The maintenance of order and prosperity within the home, supervision of all parts of the housekeeping, care of the delicate beings that they have given life to, are according to nature's order the tasks that they should occupy themselves with.[47]

Rousseau's attitude permeates the exhortations. In the same way, it was expected that the work she engaged in at her writing table in her cabinet should be associated with her special areas of responsibility.[48] Jacques-Philippe Le Bas' engraving from 1754 after Chardin's painting *L'économe* illustrates the expectations (Image 33). The engraving's epigram praised the thrifty lady of the house who, in the old virtuous manner, busied herself with housekeeping instead of superficial fashionable pastimes.[49]

At this little table, time is not spent on vain love letters but on writing shopping lists and laundry lists and on the household's bookkeeping. A sewing table next to a

45 *En fullkomlig Ägta Hustrus Bild. Tecknad Efter den målning, som finnes i Ord-språks-Bokens sidsta Capitel.* Transl. by Eric Forssén, Gothenburg 1787, p. 17.

46 Ibid.

47 *Journal för allmänna upplysningen och sederne*, 1797, part 12, p. 382.

48 Brown 2012, pp. 94, 149–73.

49 Gunnar W. Lundberg, *Svenskt och franskt 1700-tal i Institut Tessins samlingar*, Malmö 1972, p. 112. 'L'oeconome. Quel prodige! Une femme a des soins plus flateurs. Derobe un temps qu'elle donne au menage. Ce tableau simple du vieux âge. Est pris dans la nature et non pas dans nos moeurs.'

writing table in Fredrica Carleson's cabinet are correspondingly two of the exemplary wife's useful possessions – which also symbolically accompanied Wadenstierna's two wives in the portraits. Perhaps she is not busy with letters written in French in Lafrensen's portrait, but rather lists of the number of pounds of cheese and soap, or the ball of silk thread, that she needed to order.[50]

The home's gender-coded disposition of rooms had been clearly stated, for example, in François Blondel's architecture treatise from the late seventeenth century – *Cours d'architecture* (1675–83) – and was further developed in equivalent eighteenth-century texts.[51] Jean-François de Neufforge's *Recueil élémentaire d'architecture* (1757–68) states how the woman's '*boudoir*' corresponds to the man's '*laboratoire*' (where, among other things, scientific experiments could be performed as an upper-class pastime) in their respective parts of the home.[52] Fredrica Carleson's cabinet can hardly have been characterised as an aristocratic boudoir; it was rather her study and corresponded to Wadenstierna's study at the other end of the building. Wadenstierna's room could not live up to the definition of a French '*laboratoire*' either. In 'Mr state secretary's own chamber' there was a large telescope and a set of weights, but what above all differentiated his room from that of Fredrica Carleson was that it was furnished with both a writing bureau (secretaire) and a writing table, with a matching desk chair, all made of mahogany and highly valuable (Image 50).[53] The estate inventory also includes pen cases made of gold and ebony with silver trim.[54]

50 Compare with Jonathan Swift's *Verses wrote in a Lady's Ivory Table-Book*, 1698, where the person secretly reading the woman's notes does not find the love poems that reveal her heart, but rather notes on how much she has spent on purchases of shoes and lace.

51 *Cours d'architecture*, Paris 1675–83. A hundred years later, a similar work was published, by the seventeenth-century architect's namesake Jacques-François Blondel, *Cours d'architecture ou traité de la décoration, distribution et constructions des bâtiments contenant les leçons données en 1750, et les années suivantes*, Paris 1771–7.

52 Jean François de Neufforge, *Recueil élémentaire d'architecture*, IV, Paris 1761. Cheng 2011, pp. 319–20.

53 Wadenstierna's corresponding study in his city residence contained two globes, a barometer, a telescope, gold weights, weighing scales and a microscope. Riksarkivet, Näs Silverstolpeska arkivet, Personarkiven, vol. 60, Carl Eric Wadenstierna (1723–1787). In comparison, according to a 1796 inventory, Count Clas Julius Ekeblad's library room at Stola Manor contained an English 'Thelescoph', an 'Electricitets Machine', an hourglass, 'Mathematiska Instrumenter', two barometers and a thermometer, two globes, a 'Camra Clara' and a compass, William Karlson, *Ett svenskt herremanshem på 1700-talet. Clas Julius Ekeblads inventarium över Stola 1796*, Lund 1940, pp. 68–70. Regarding the secretaire that stood in Wadenstierna's room, see p. 34 in Asplund, Karl, 'Näs i Rö', *Fataburen*, Nordiska Museet, Stockholm 1960. A similar secretaire, in the style of Lars Nordin, was sold by Bukowskis in Stockholm in 2019: *Important Spring Sale* 617. This model, equipped with a folding toilet mirror in the top drawer, shows how these items of writing furniture fulfilled several functions. See Vahlne, Bo, *Frihetstidens inredningar på Stockholms slott. Om bekvämlighetens och skönhetens nivåer*, Stockholm 2012, pp. 187f., where King Adolf Fredrik's cabinet at the Royal Palace of Stockholm is described as a study.

54 Riksarkivet, Näs Silverstolpeska arkivet, Personarkiven, vol. 60, Carl Eric Wadenstierna (1723–1787).

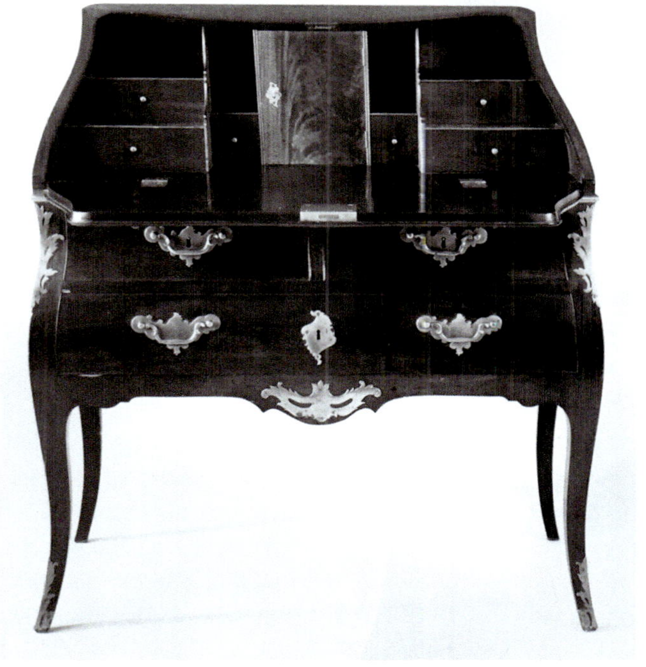

50. According to the estate inventory, a mahogany *'skrif bureau'* (writing bureau or secretaire), stood in Wadenstierna's own chamber. It may well have been this one. Photo: Märta Claréus, 1958, Archives of the Nordic Museum, Stockholm.

Wadenstierna's adjacent drawing room, which belonged to the suite of receptions rooms, was also furnished with both a secretaire and a writing table. The furniture that he commissioned from Georg Haupt, 'Ebeniste du Roi à Stockholm', in 1775 with its lavish veneer inlays could have been well suited to this room, although these items were not specified in the estate inventory.[55] The secretaire and chest of drawers by Haupt were embellished with a 'W' crowned with a laurel festoon and the correspondingly crowned Wadenstierna family's star (Plate 13).[56] His silver writing tools, comprising an ink pot, a sand box (pounce pot) and a bell on a special mahogany tray, would have looked stylish on the writing furniture. His room had been equipped with two items of writing furniture, while the two sewing tables instead complemented Fredrica's 'woman's writing bureau' in her cabinet.[57] Their

55 Stina Odlinder Haubo, 'Georg Haupt. Sekretär', in *Från Makalös till Haupt*, Åmells konsthandel, Stockholm 2006, no. 28.

56 Haubo 2006, p. 28ff. and Lagerquist, Marshall, *Georg Haupt. Ebeniste du Roi*, Nordiska museets handlingar 92, Stockholm 1979, pp. 137, 157.

57 Wadenstierna's city residence included four writing bureaus, a writing table with inlays and a combined secretaire and beside table with a mirror. The fact that there were more pieces of writing furniture here than at Näs possibly indicates the proximity of the city residence to Wadenstierna's professional life. Jacobina Psilanderhielm's estate inventory, of which the contents also belonged to the city residence, also

respective rooms clarified the differences in their tasks and the expectations of their different roles, according to the same pattern as in the portraits. In Lafrensen's portraits, Wadenstierna's book represented the professional, publicly printed word, while his wife's handwritten letters (or housekeeping lists) represented what was amateur, private and intimate.[58] The little writing table's multitude of small objects are trinkets within the homely environment, while the royal order in Wadenstierna's portrait is a single item that summarises his achievements in the outside world.

Fredrica Carleson's cabinet facing the front of the manor was thereby a room that was linked to female letter writing, and during the latter half of the eighteenth century this activity became increasingly clearly associated with seclusion and privacy.[59] Seeking seclusion in a private sphere developed into an ideal that was no longer only associated with religious devotions or prayers but rather with the cultivation of upper-class sensibility.[60] The cabinet became the room that the lady of the house could retire to in order to write, read, sew and rest from an existence that constantly meant closeness to other people, family, servants and guests. In contrast, the lady's drawing room in the suite of reception rooms was entirely furnished for socialising, with a large sofa and rows of comfortable chairs. Architect Nicodemus Tessin the Younger had pointed out that rooms for '*retraite*' were essential for daily comfort, and he was probably referring to the rooms that followed on from the bedchamber: smaller cabinets and dressing rooms.[61]

The floor plan and the position of the cabinet at Näs can be regarded as a modern and updated successor to the comfortable room functions found in the homes of the elite during Tessin's era. Queen Lovisa Ulrika's cabinet in the royal palace Kungshuset on the islet of Riddarholmen in Stockholm was furnished with bookcases

listed two slant-top desks and one writing table. Riksarkivet, Näs Silverstolpeska arkivet, Personarkiven, vol. 60, Carl Eric Wadenstierna (1723–1787).

58 On male and female writing, see Gisborne, Thomas, *An Enquiry Into the Duties of the Female Sex*, London 1797, p. 110.

59 The increase in privacy associated with the letter writing culture coincides with the widespread practice of reading in silence and solitude that becomes noticeable in the latter half of the eighteenth century. References to letters as mirrors of the soul are found in descriptions from the era; Löwendahl, Marie, *Min allrabästa och ömmaste vän! Kvinnors brevskrivning under svenskt 1700-tal*, Gothenburg 2007, p. 39.

60 'I am never more happy than when I am alone. Oh! If I then have a beautiful book, a beautiful picture to look at, or on an agreeable walk, I feel as though I possess a heaven within me. Often tears of pure pleasure flow from my eyes, that is how happy I feel in my solitude, which I always choose rather than so many gatherings, where the ear and heart are often wounded!' These are the words of Carl Christopher Gjörwell's daughter Gustafva in a letter to her father in 1798 (Löwendahl 2007, pp. 294–5; Anne Thérèse de Marguenat de Courcelles, Marquise de Lambert, *Reflexions nouvelles sur les femmes, par une dame de la cour de France*, London 1730, pp. 27–9; Cheng, Diana, *The History of the Boudoir in the Eighteenth Century*, Montreal and Quebec 2011, pp. 77–8.

61 Vahlne 2012, p. 105.

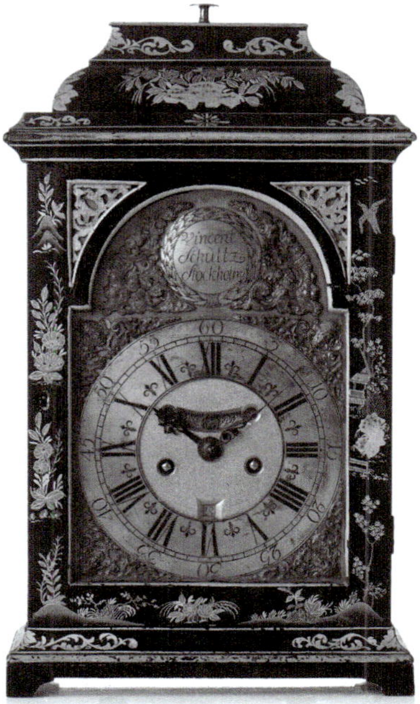

51. The clock that kept track of the time in Fredrica Carlesson's cabinet at Näs. Vincent Schultz, mantel pendulum clock, first half of the eighteenth century. Black lacquered with chinoiserie bronzed decoration, 41 × 25 cm. Private ownership. Photo: Bukowskis.

and writing tables, as was the cabinet of Ulrika Lovisa Sparre, the wife of Carl Gustaf Tessin, at Åkerö country manor. There, Olof Fridsberg portrayed her in her cabinet, sitting at her writing table and surrounded by her various personal effects.[62] These cabinets resembled studies, from the term *cabinet d'étude*: it was a room for a moment's secluded contemplation but could also be used for socialising with a small group of people.[63] According to Carl Gustaf Tessin, the family liked to gather in the cabinet of the countess during the mornings to write and draw and to teach the young girls.[64] Fredrica Carleson's cabinet probably also fulfilled a similar function. In her private cabinet she could gather her thoughts for her correspondence and read letters undisturbed, while *simultaneously* being available for her duties within the home. The presence of an old mantel pendulum clock is a reminder of her responsibilities.[65] Although the cabinet was her own room, it was not associated with laziness or freedom from responsibilities.

In Wadenstierna's drawing room, where the two pieces of writing furniture stood, there were also sixty-six engraved pictures with glass and gilt frames on the walls. However, the most distinctive artworks were copperplate portraits of the king and

62 Olof Fridsberg, *Ulrika Lovisa Sparre, grevinna Tessin i sitt kabinett på Åkerö*, 1762, watercolour and gouache, 22 × 17 cm, Nationalmuseum, Stockholm, NMB 6.

63 Vahlne 2012, p. 131.

64 Gösta Selling, *Svenska herrgårdshem under 1700-talet*, Stockholm (1937) 1991, p. 128.

65 Riksarkivet, Näs Silverstolpeska arkivet, Personarkiven, vol. 60, Carl Eric Wadenstierna (1723–1787).

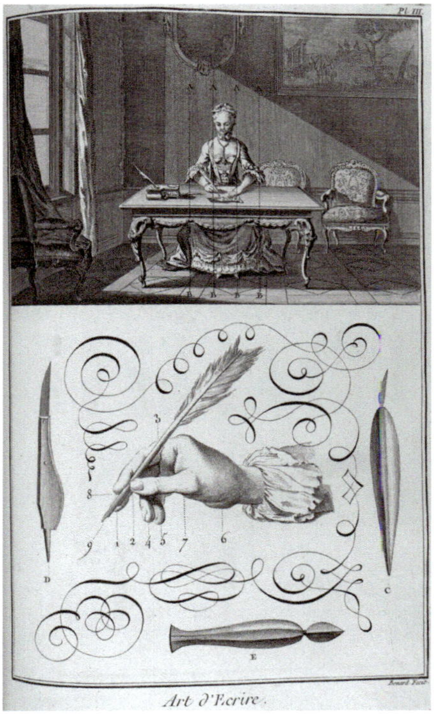

52. Alessandri et Scattaglia, *Sur la position des jeunes demoiselles pour écrire*. Engraved plate. From Charles Paillasson, *L'art d'écrire réduit à des démonstrations vraies et faciles, avec des explications claires pour Le dictionnaire des arts, par Paillasson expert écrivain juré*, Paris, 1763.

queen, which could be deemed well chosen in relation to the writing furniture and the shining silver of the inkstand. Everyone who entered the 'gentleman's drawing room' was to be reminded of Wadenstierna's many years of royal service and his successes. His room was about the outside world; hers about the home and private domestic life.

Some of the many landscape paintings that Wadenstierna commissioned from Johan Philip Korn may have also been among the small oil paintings on the walls in Fredrica Carleson's cabinet. The motifs provided a connection with the country life taking place outside her window as well as a distancing or civilisation of the same nature when it was viewed through the artist's eyes. Arcadian landscapes with ruins or idealised pastorals, like the entrance hall's epigrams, could serve as reminders of the unaffected and character-building virtues of country life. The depictions of nature were possibly chosen to evoke the sensibility associated with upper-class sensitivity and inspire Fredrica Carleson in her letter writing or encourage her to do her needlework diligently in accordance with what was regarded as a nature-bound order. The picture of an exemplary letter-writing woman in Charles Paillasson's *Art d'écrire* from 1763 displays certain similarities with Fredrica Carleson's portrait (Image 52). It is not just her figure, with her clothing and posture, or the way in which she holds her quill pen and paper, that make Fredrica Carleson a role model in relation to the ideal image. Her real-life cabinet followed the ideal, furnished with a lady's writing table and landscape paintings on the walls.

Letter writing: A female genre

The portrait of Fredrica Carleson can be generally regarded as a reminder of the significance of letters and letter writing in the eighteenth century. Today's constant flow of electronically transmitted words has a parallel in the eighteenth century's letters and notes that were exchanged in a steady stream, delivered by the postal service and servants. The correspondence linked the era's social networks, which even extended far and wide around the world. Calendars and almanacs not only provided information on the dates of full moons or exchange rates, but also the times for the postal service in various towns and cities and whether deliveries were made by horse riders or horse-drawn mail carts.[66] The letters constituted the hub of a life that often included long distances between family and friends. The contact with often protracted periods of time between in-person gatherings gained presence and continuity through the daily correspondence. But eighteenth-century letter culture also became strongly associated with a modern lifestyle, in which fashion, consumption and privileged comfort became central elements.

Early on, letters were already regarded as the literary genre that was closest to women.[67] The direct and spontaneous tone of a letter, comparable with an easy-going and lively conversation, chimed with what was thought to be women's emotionally driven nature.[68] However, the significance of emotion to the genre did not make it exclusively for women. The ability to express emotions or convey tenderness and confidences was hardly gender-specific in the eighteenth century but was rather seen as a sign of birth, descent and cultivation.[69] But it was women's 'naïve' nature that made them particularly well suited to letter writing, especially to letters written for reasons of friendship or love. In contrast, male writers were permitted to work in a wider field. Occasionally, women purposely used 'childish' wording to reinforce the naïve expression in the letters, and they were consequently sometimes answered

66 *Almanach de Gotha* states 'Cours des Postes' with details of 'à Cheval' or 'en Chariot'.

67 Isobel Grundy, 'Women and Letters', *Women, Popular Culture, and the Eighteenth Century*, Tiffany Potter (ed.), University of Toronto Press 2012, pp. 133–49; Cheryl Nixon and Louise Penner, 'Materials of the 'Everyday' Woman Writer: Letter-Writing in Eighteenth-Century England and America.' *Women & Things 1750–1950. Gendered Material Strategies*, Maureen Daly Goggin and Beth Fowkes Tobin (ed.), Routledge, New York 2009, pp. 157–88.

68 Alenius 1993, vol. 1, pp. 364ff.

69 Brown 2012, p. 142.

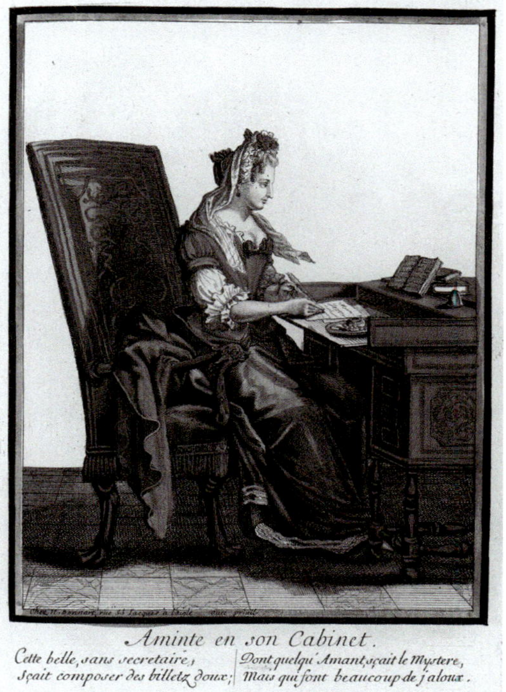

53. Nicolas Bonnart, *Aminte en son cabinet.* Engraving, 36.5 × 23.5 cm. From Bonnart, *Recueil des modes de la cour de France*, Paris, 1678–93. Los Angeles County Museum of Art (LACMA) (2002.57.8322).

in a corresponding tone.[70] It was a rhetorical gesture that above all recurred in love letters or tender closing phrases. As a phenomenon, it may appear contradictory as letter writing was also an important part of young girls' education and was practised with the help of printed sample letters. Over time, manuals in the art of writing love letters were also published.[71] Additionally, conversation games could be used to practise this skill, where cards with various questions and answers created both instructive and entertaining conversations. At the Wadenstierna family's Näs Manor, there was an equivalent game with French phrases, where the game simultaneously became an exercise in the art of conversation in French. The

70 Löwendahl 2007, pp. 37, 266; Forselius 2002.

71 Most eighteenth-century Swedish guides to letter writing were translations of foreign originals, such as Johan Biurman's short yet clear guide from 1729 which included advice on punctuation and various types of letters and was published in several editions during the eighteenth century. One manual in the art of writing love letters was *The New Lover's Instructor; or, Whole Art of Courtship. Being the Lover's Complete Library and Guide; and Containing ... Love Letters, ... Cards of Compliment, ... Love Epistles in Verse, Written in an Elegant Style;* [etc.] London 1780. Nixon, Cheryl and Penner, Louise, 'Materials of the 'Everyday' Woman Writer: Letter-Writing in Eighteenth-Century England and America.' *Women & Things 1750–1950. Gendered Material Strategies*, Maureen Daly Goggin and Beth Fowkes Tobin (ed.), New York 2009, pp. 164–73.

love-themed games were particularly popular with emotionally charged questions and elegantly formulated answers such as: 'Lead me to the temple of domestic bliss' or 'Are you happy in all respects?'[72]

Exercises in the art of writing built social skills. Letters were saved, circulated and often read aloud in large or small gatherings of family members, friends or more distant acquaintances. In his diary in 1744, Baron Carl Axel Hugo Hamilton af Hageby describes a visit to his friends Ulrika Eleonora and Ebba Margareta Ribbing at Hörningsholms Manor south of Stockholm, where they entertain themselves while they drink coffee by reading a bundle of letters written by Charlotta Fredrika von Fersen to her brother Carl Sparre.[73] The insight into – and recognition of – the various social relationships and contexts are probably what gave letter writing and letter reading their piquancy. Both family relationships and friendships as references to shared polite ideals and values linked the social networks. The significance of the letters for this class-based togetherness also extended over time and space.

But female letter writing could also have literary ambitions that rose above the fleeting, emotionally driven tone. As a female literary genre, its roots were in the seventeenth century's reading, writing and social customs.[74] The pictorial world that reflected the eighteenth century's letter writing was also formed during the previous century. Nicolas Bonnart's engraved plate from *Recueil des modes de la cour de France*, published in 1678–93, illustrates the French court fashion and the era's aristocratic lifestyle in the more informal *appartements de commodité* of upper-class homes (Image 53). The engraving's title *Aminte* alludes to Torquato Tasso's famous pastoral drama *Aminta* from 1573, which regained topicality in the French literary salons where the courtly pastoral love was a recurring theme of discussion. The beautiful woman has retired to her own private cabinet to pick up her quill pen and write a love letter. The open book on the desk shows how she is allowing herself to be inspired by the literary fiction. When the seventeenth-century engraving is viewed next to the portrait of Fredrica Carleson, the similarities stand out rather

72 The quotation 'Are you happy in all respects?' is from a game found among the effects from Carl Linnaeus' (Carl von Linné's) household in Uppsala, Linnémuseet.

73 Carl Axel Hugo Hamilton (1722–1763); 'Utdrag ur Carl Axel Hugo Hamiltons Dagbok år 1744', *Personhistorisk tidskrift*, Svenska autografsällskapet, Stockholm 1900, p. 64.

74 Letters were often written with a wider readership in mind and thereby became closer to resembling literary epistolary fiction. Novels in the eighteenth century also adopted the form of fictitious letter correspondence. The art of letter writing was associated with the French literary salons, where the letter as a female literary genre took shape in the seventeenth century. Several of the women associated with the salon culture were known for their novels, letters and lifestyles, and women's letter collections were published and used as good examples within the elite. Madame de Sévigné occupies an exceptional position in this respect. The art of written conversation shaped the seventeenth and eighteenth centuries' upper-class ideals and codes of behaviour within the elite, Michèle Longino Farrell, *Performing Motherhood. The Sévigné Correspondence*, Hanover 1991 and Auslander 1996, p. 64.

than the contrasts, despite the changes in fashions over the nearly one hundred years that separate the pictures (Plate 3). Writing tables with veneer inlays and silk-upholstered chairs are equally important status symbols in both cases. When the women with upright postures and graceful gestures pose with the symbolic letter, both images want to convey the cultivated and fashionable context that letter writing was associated with and the heroines engaged in correspondence in literary fiction – the seventeenth century's *Princesse de Clèves* or the eighteenth century's *Julie*.[75]

A pictorial world full of letters

The art of letter writing accordingly developed into a genre with many offshoots in a contemporary culture that gained increasingly clear female overtones. Women were not only the protagonists in most fictitious and real-life correspondence, but also in a multifaceted pictorial world that portrayed the writing and reading of letters; a pictorial world that clearly reflects the roles that were assigned to women, socially and culturally. The images defined a female sphere – where she could be, what she should feel and how she should act in different contexts. What were regarded as the foremost female characteristics – beauty, sensibility, social skills – were represented in a gender-normative way in the pictures. The eighteenth century's genre pictures were filled with beautiful women in love who posed holding letters and demonstrated the entire register of love-related emotions in various ways (Image 54).

The images also convey other aspects of the era's social and material culture in which women played a prominent part. Dressing tables, movable small writing tables, armchairs and sofas, thick drapes and soft down cushions frame the women's writing and reading of letters. The pictures clearly manifest the culture of comfort and consumption that developed during the eighteenth century. Informal clothing and relaxed untidy rooms where the coffee awaits demonstrate that letter writing and letter reading were often associated with everyday morning activities and with a sphere shielded from the eyes of the surrounding world. The screened-off cabinet or the separate boudoir are presented as rooms for seclusion, own thoughts and private matters – and as a pronounced female sphere.[76] In her research into the creation of a separate female intellectual culture, literary scholar and critic Elaine

75 Madame de La Fayette's novel *La princesse de Clèves* (1678) is about a love plot in which a letter plays a crucial part, and Jean-Jacques Rousseau's epistolary novel *Julie, ou la nouvelle Héloïse* (1761) was a paraphrase of the letter correspondence between the medieval lovers Héloïse and Abélard.

76 The word *boudoir* stems from the French *bouder*, 'to sulk', and hints that it was a room to which women could retire with their private emotions (Cheng 2011, p. 4). Before the seventeenth century, the

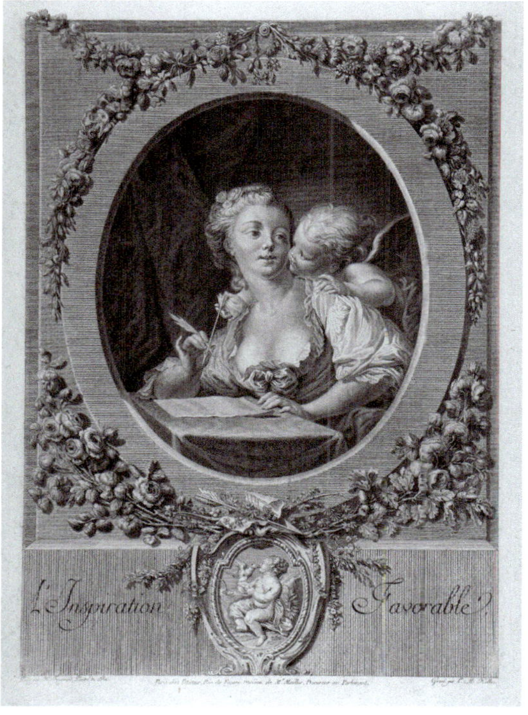

54. Louis Michel Halbou after Jean Honoré Fragonard, *L'inspiration favorable.* Engraving, 40.5 × 26.2 cm. The Metropolitan Museum of Art, New York. The image shows the sphere within which women's writing was generally expected to be contained. An amorino (cupid) sneaks up on the letter-writing woman. When the woman distractedly turns round, the amorino takes the opportunity to touch her quill pen with his love arrow, as a result of which her writing had to follow the feelings of her heart.

Showalter has drawn attention to the strategies that women developed to shape their own intellectual sanctuaries through their writing.[77] These perspectives have also been deepened by Dena Goodman, who has highlighted writing as a way for women to create a socially accepted literary room and thereby also a socially defined 'self' – a space for self-reflection and the shaping of own identity.[78] Letter writing offered a way and an opportunity for women to develop their own literary genre in which they did not need to compete with the men.[79] Goodman states that this driving force is also visible in pictures of letter-writing women. According to Goodman, upper-class women played an active part in the creation of their social roles, where specifically the choice of portrait role was a key stage in this identity-building process.

The pictures of women reading letters and writing them thereby summarises a series of central eighteenth-century socio-cultural themes. As the letter genre

private room was instead a place for studies and solitary prayer (Cheng 2011, pp. 11, 37ff.; Philippe Ariès and Georges Duby, *A History of Private Life*, Cambridge, Massachusetts and London 1989.

77 Elaine Showalter, *A Literature of Their Own: British Women Novelists From Brontë to Lessing*, Princeton 1977 and *Inventing Herself: Claiming a Feminist Intellectual Heritage*, New York 2001.

78 Dena Goodman, *Becoming a Woman in the Age of Letters*, Ithaca 2009. Löwendahl 2007.

79 Löwendahl 2007, p. 10.

was deemed female, there was an opportunity here to represent notions of female beauty, emotionality, friendship and intimacy, but also notions of the desire for comfort and consumption that was assigned female undertones. Details in the pictures underline the importance of fashionable clothing, and accessories and objects that belonged to a fashionable lifestyle – a modern sofa or an open novel could be elements in the pictures that pointed the viewer's associations in the right direction. The letter not only symbolised the social glue that bonded the upper-class network together; in visual art it also became a concrete visual expression of *politesse*, a coveted social and cultural skill in which women were assumed to be exceptional. The real-life women who allowed themselves to be portrayed while writing letters should not automatically be equated with the daydreaming women reading letters in the genre scenes. Portraits and genre pictures had different aims, and different types of pictures complied with different rules. The real-life women in the portraits had their own specific life stories and contexts that had to be differentiated from those in fiction. But many of the norms and ideals expressed in the genre scenes were also implied in the portraits. In the same way that guides to letter writing and sample letters illustrated how the perfect letter should be worded, the genre and fashion pictures showed what the ideal female letter writer should look like.

With detailed clarity, Niclas Lafrensen's portrait of Fredrica Carleson presents the material world that surrounds her and her role in it (Plate 3). The painting is simultaneously in a borderland between a portrait and a fashion image. Lafrensen had successfully established himself as both a genre painter and portraitist, and Fredrica Carleson's portrait shifts elegantly between these different types of picture. In one way, the depicted woman seems to be an anonymous model, similar to the fashionable ideal woman in genre images. However, to her contemporaries, Fredrica Carleson also appears portrait-like and identifiable in all respects in her specific social context. This shift must have been a desirable quality for Lafrensen's clients. Admittedly the portrait had to resemble the model, but it should also evoke associations with a wider world of fashions and ideals in the era that the person depicted in the portrait wanted to be associated with.

In the portrait of Fredrica Carleson, the artist obviously wanted to emphasise the young woman as an informed letter writer. Under her hands there are several densely written sheets of paper, and she is equipped with accoutrements in accordance with the era's upper-class fashion and taste. There are no preserved letters by Fredrica Carleson in the archives. However, whether she actually wrote often or rarely is of lesser importance in the realm of the portrait. What the portrait shows is a statement with a specific aim – in accordance with her social identity, letter writing was an expected part of her daily life. The pile of sheets of letter paper defined what she was – although not necessarily who she was.

Niclas Lafrensen was a master of rendering these activities *à la mode*. He had spent most of the 1760s in Paris, and through his paintings he conveyed the ideas of the luxury and comfort of modern life. The pictures formulated the norms for an ideal existence where beauty and love were actively placed in an active relationship with the latest fashion and the most comfortable lifestyle, a relationship that was maintained by the rising culture of consumption in the latter half of the eighteenth century. The engravings after Lafrensen's pictures also came to be printed by the company Esnauts & Rapilly in Paris, the same publisher that published the most widespread fashion plates in the last few decades of the eighteenth century.

Lafrensen's example thereby demonstrates how the eighteenth century's portraits of women were in a borderland between various types of pictures, where fashion images, genre scenes and portrait ideals meld together. Identities were dissolved or recast, shifted between personal identification and more general fashionable ideal images. Portraitists copied each other and borrowed freely from the multitude of pictures distributed in the international engravings market. In Paris, Alexander Roslin was well established when Niclas Lafrensen arrived there, and like many other portraitists, Roslin's feel for trends, fashion and social networks had contributed to his successes. In his 1779 portrait of Marie Emilie, the daughter of artist François Boucher, Roslin seems to have found inspiration for the fashionable clothes and hairstyle and his depiction of the fashionable activity of letter writing from an engraving in *Galerie des modes et costumes français* (Images 55 and 56). Marie Emilie is similar to the woman looking up from her letter in the fashion plate, but Roslin has added the addressee very visibly on the letter that his model is holding out: 'à Monsieur Cuvillier', Marie Emilie's husband as of 1773. Through the personal letter, an individualisation of the portrait emerges and thereby also the manner in which she addresses her husband or the feelings she is directing at him through the letter. Here, Roslin undoubtedly conveyed a likeness to the portrait's model, but it was also closely linked to the fashion's ideal image.

The portrait of Fredrica Carleson probably also encompassed personal references which for its owner and viewers evoked a particular likeness with the model. Additionally, the miniature format and delicate gouache painting technique are indicative of a type of picture intended for a more private sphere and a more intimate circle of viewers. In the same way that letter writing was readily associated with love and friendship, memories and longing, portrait miniatures were often exchanged as emotionally charged gifts.[80] Small pictures demanded closer inspection – in the same way that a letter is held close in order to be read. The recurring references to how women hold both love letters and portrait miniatures in their hands, examine

80 Various types of portraits were represented in miniature formats. For example, official portraits of regents could serve as less emotionally and more politically charged gifts.

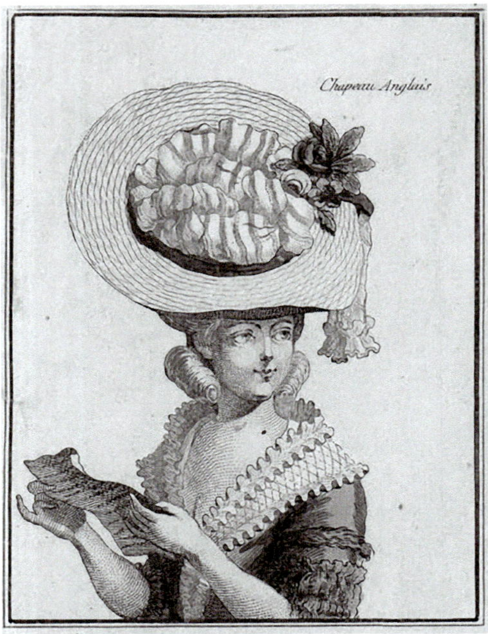

55. Jacques Esnaut and Michel Rapilly, *Chapeau anglais*. Engraving from *Galerie des modes et costumes français*, Paris, 1778, 5e.

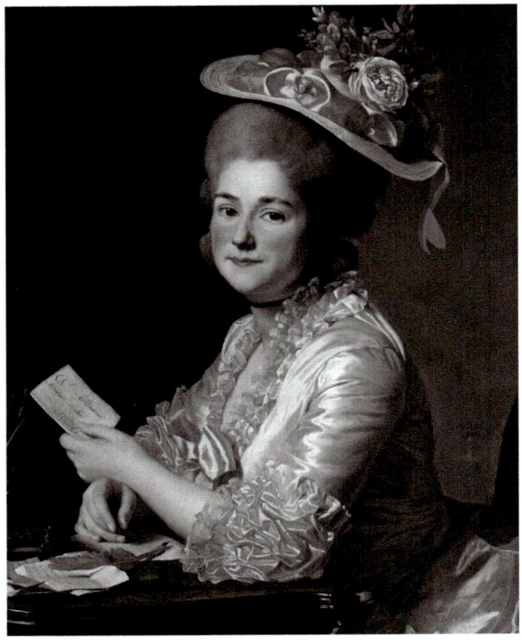

56. Alexander Roslin, *Marie Emilie Boucher*, 1779. Oil on canvas, 80 × 64.5 cm. Photo: Bukowskis.

them and kiss them in private, demonstrate the close connection between the letter genre and the portrait miniature genre.[81] Like many artists at that time, Lafrensen combined letters and portrait miniatures in his genre motifs and thereby utilised the relationship between them to strengthen the emotional impact of the pictures.[82]

The picture of Fredrica Carleson at her writing table obviously aims to express a feeling of affinity with the close circle that her letters and portrait were intended for. Just as her gaze is assumed to be directed at the recipient of the portrait miniature, the letters she writes are possibly also intended for the same person – according to the same pattern as in Roslin's portrait. But the feeling of affinity is also directed at her wider social circle consisting of the upper-class society around her. In the same way that Mme Cuvillier can be compared to the ideal woman of fashion images, the associations with the shared ideals were intended to reinforce the sense of a wider class-based community and confirm the depicted woman's successes in her

81 Depictions of people in love who are kissing a portrait miniature are seen in works by artists such as Jean-Frédéric Schall or Pierre Alexandre Wille, but also in letters and diaries: '[H]ow I love you and everything about you, I can sit for long whiles and talk to your portrait and kiss it, too,' 4 July 1785 . Carl August Ehrensvärd, a selection by Holger Frykenstedt, *Brev till Kickan*, Stockholm 1971, p. 30.
82 *Intimate Encounters. Love and Domesticity in Eighteenth-Century France*, New Jersey 1997.

social and cultural role. In this endeavour expressed by the portrait, the furniture rendered in detail played a key part.

In the studies and cabinets at Näs

As shown, the normative ideas that differentiated between male and female writing activities in the eighteenth century also divided up the home into male and female spheres. 'The state secretary's own chamber' differed from Fredrica Carleson's cabinet, just as the pictorial space of the portraits explained the era's gender-specific conventions. Scenes in genre painting also clarified this division. One of the rooms at Näs was home to Pehr Hilleström's painting of two women in conversation at a coffee table (Plate 16). The ball of yarn has been put in its place on the yarn winder while the women drink their coffee. Perhaps the letter that the younger woman is holding has been read aloud during the coffee break, as a result of which the cloth has been pushed aside and the coffee grounds in the cup are now being consulted to determine the continuation of the letter's news. The painting wanted to show how women's letters concerned 'the small world', the everyday chores in the home or the quandaries of the heart, and how gossip and superstition also played their parts. Perhaps certain elements of the picture reflected real life at Näs – the older woman recurs in a couple of the paintings at the manor, and a pug is also thought to have lived there as a pet. Furthermore, both a yarn winder and a pelisse lined with squirrel fur, similar to the one the woman is wearing, are included in the estate inventories.[83]

However, Hilleström's painting ought have been regarded as a genre-like comment on the ideas that were generally associated with women's letter writing. The yarn winder placed in the foreground aims to serve as a reminder of thoughtlessness and neglected duties. Lafrensen's portrait of Fredrica Carleson displays a clear contrast. A writing table replaces a coffee table, and formal garb replaces loose and wide morning attire. In turn, the differences created different contexts for women's reading and writing of letters. Perhaps Hilleström's painting also belonged to the room where letters were read and coffee was drunk, in a drawing room or bedchamber, rather than forming an eye-catching image for Fredrica Carleson in the cabinet where she wrote her letters. But the different pictures also display

83 According to an inventory of the painting collection at Näs, the older woman is stated as being 'Miss Schürer von Waldheim'; Cederblom 1927, image 9. The pug at Näs is also presented in Carl-Eric Wadenstierna's poem about light, reproduced in Näsström, Gustaf, *Forna dagars Sverige*, III, *Kulturhistorisk bilderbok om frihetstid och gustaviansk tid*, Stockholm 1962, p. 158. The furniture and effects are entered in the estate inventories at Riksarkivet, Näs Silverstolpeska arkivet, Personarkiven, vol. 60, Carl Eric Wadenstierna (1723–1787).

how the presentation of female letter culture was not unambiguous. The objects, clothes and environments in the pictorial spaces could be associated with widely different notions and expectations.

Correspondingly, Carl Eric Wadenstierna's and Fredrica Carleson's separate cabinets at Näs were designed to fulfil many different functions, which is not apparent from the simplified structure of the floor plan. 'The state secretary's own chamber' included writing furniture, but also objects that related to everyday toilette, and in both Wadenstierna's and his wife's respective rooms, sofas and chairs encouraged both conversations and solitary repose. Alongside Wadenstierna's presentable drawing room with expensive writing furniture, his smaller chamber primarily resembled a more private study. His wife's cabinet was also a place to retire to but also a room in which contact with the surrounding world was maintained – by writing letters and keeping an eye on the servants. Lafrensen's portraits of Wadenstierna and his wife reflect all these functions.

The relationship of the companion portraits to each other also shows somewhat of a contradiction. Despite the symbolic and aesthetic harmony that the couple display, Fredrica Carleson is nonetheless independently depicted, in her own room and busy with her own writing. When regarded as a separate portrait, it connects with a significantly larger context than the prescribed conventions of the companion portrait. Instead of only being interpreted as a loving greeting to her husband, what she is writing can serve as a reminder that she was also a cosmopolitan woman. The portrait role proves multifaceted and was in interplay with the different and often contradictory expectations of her actual roles, as a beloved wife, exemplary mother and presentable member of the upper class. If her letters had been saved for posterity, they could have told us more about these roles and how they interacted with everyday life at Näs.

Carl Eric Wadenstierna's rooms had been furnished with four pieces of writing furniture, compared to his wife's single 'writing bureau'. From what is hidden behind the wording of the estate inventory, however, Georg Haupt's monogrammed showpieces probably stood in the rooms of the lady's suite.[84] The drawing room of the gentleman's suite was instead home to cabinetmaker Eckstein's secretaire embellished with flowers. The majority of Haupt's furniture – a tea table, a chest of drawers and two bedside cabinets – stood in the home's most lavish reception room, the large bedchamber in the lady's suite, and the matching elegant secretaire stood in the adjacent lady's cabinet. Perhaps Wadenstierna had commissioned

84 In the estate inventory, the Haupt furniture has been listed in the same way, specifying that each item includes *inlaid work*, while Eckstein's secretaire has been stated differently: '1 walnut writing bureau with inlaid wood *in several colours*'. The smaller format of the Haupt secretaire (width 81 cm) compared to Eckstein's (94.5 cm) may also hint at its function being a lady's secretaire. Riksarkivet, Näs Silverstolpeska arkivet, Personarkiven, vol. 60, Carl Eric Wadenstierna (1723–1787).

the furniture as a gift to his young wife, with which to decorate her rooms at the newly built Näs Manor. His monogram decorated with laurel thereby appears less pretentious and more loving.

Male and female norms and constructions again prove more multifaceted than first meets the eye. Although the man's secretaire was larger, floral bouquets adorned its rounded shapes. The woman's secretaire was admittedly smaller, but in contrast it had an austere, classicising design. The positioning of her piece of high-status writing furniture also illustrates that the cabinet not only met practical, everyday needs but also represented her class and status. In 1775, Haupt had achieved successes in Stockholm, and ownership of his furniture signalled informed knowledge of contemporary fashion and a financially and materially comfortably appointed life.[85]

With a gentle smile, Fredrica Carleson meets the viewer's gaze as she sits elegantly at her lavish piece of writing furniture in Lafrensen's portrait. The room around her refers to a female sphere and a comfortable everyday environment. But the portrait also refers to the era's international upper-class culture and to wider social and cultural contexts. Through the portrait's message and through the letters she writes, the small cabinet at Näs is connected with the wider world beyond.

85 Ljungström, Lars, *Georg Haupt. Gustav III:s hovschatullmakare*, Stockholm 2006; Lagerquist, Marshall, *Georg Haupt. Ebeniste du Roi*, Nordiska museets handlingar 92, Stockholm 1979, p. 37.

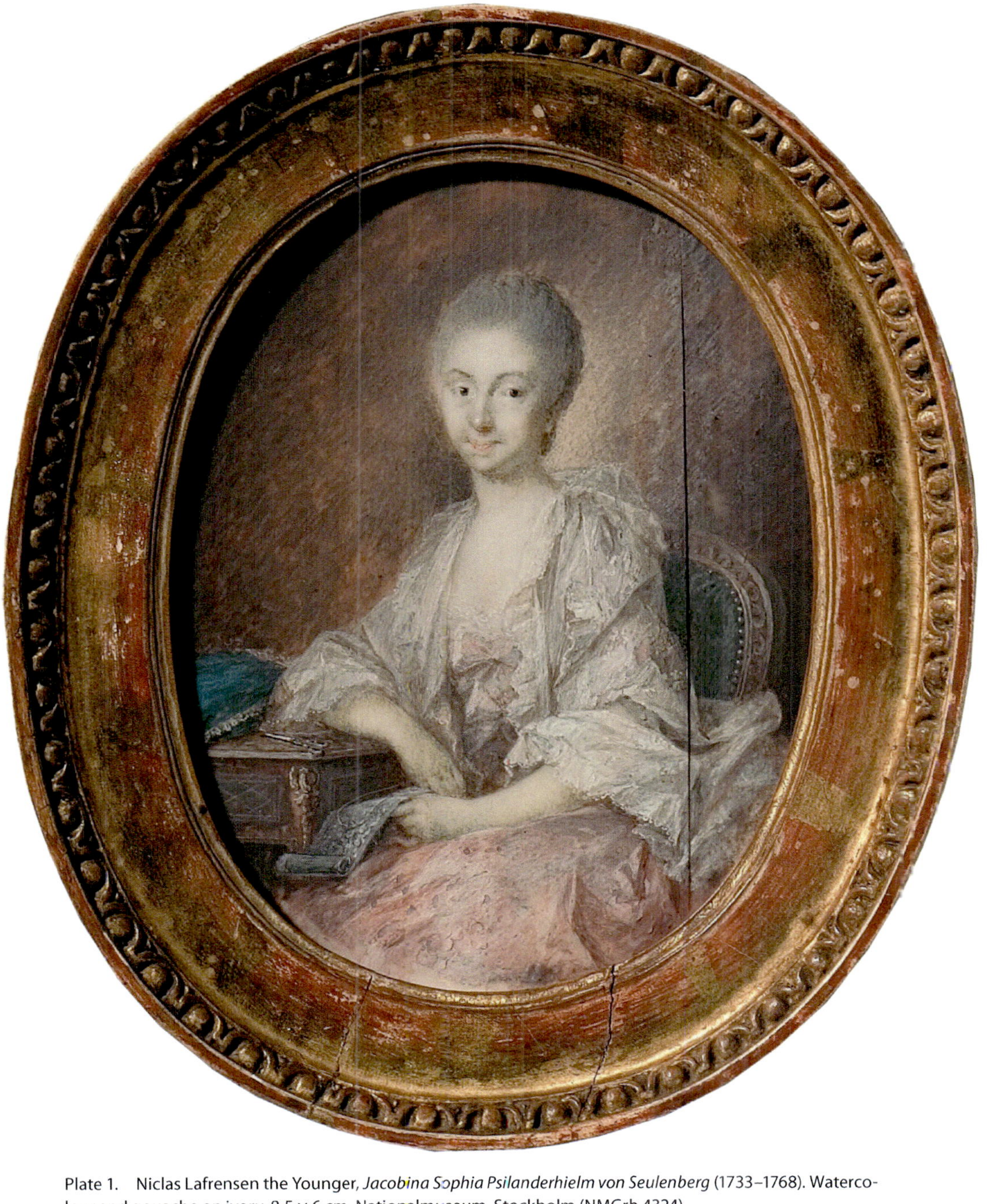

Plate 1. Niclas Lafrensen the Younger, *Jacobina Sophia Psilanderhielm von Seulenberg* (1733–1768). Watercolour and gouache on ivory, 8.5 × 6 cm. Nationalmuseum, Stockholm (NMGrh 4324).

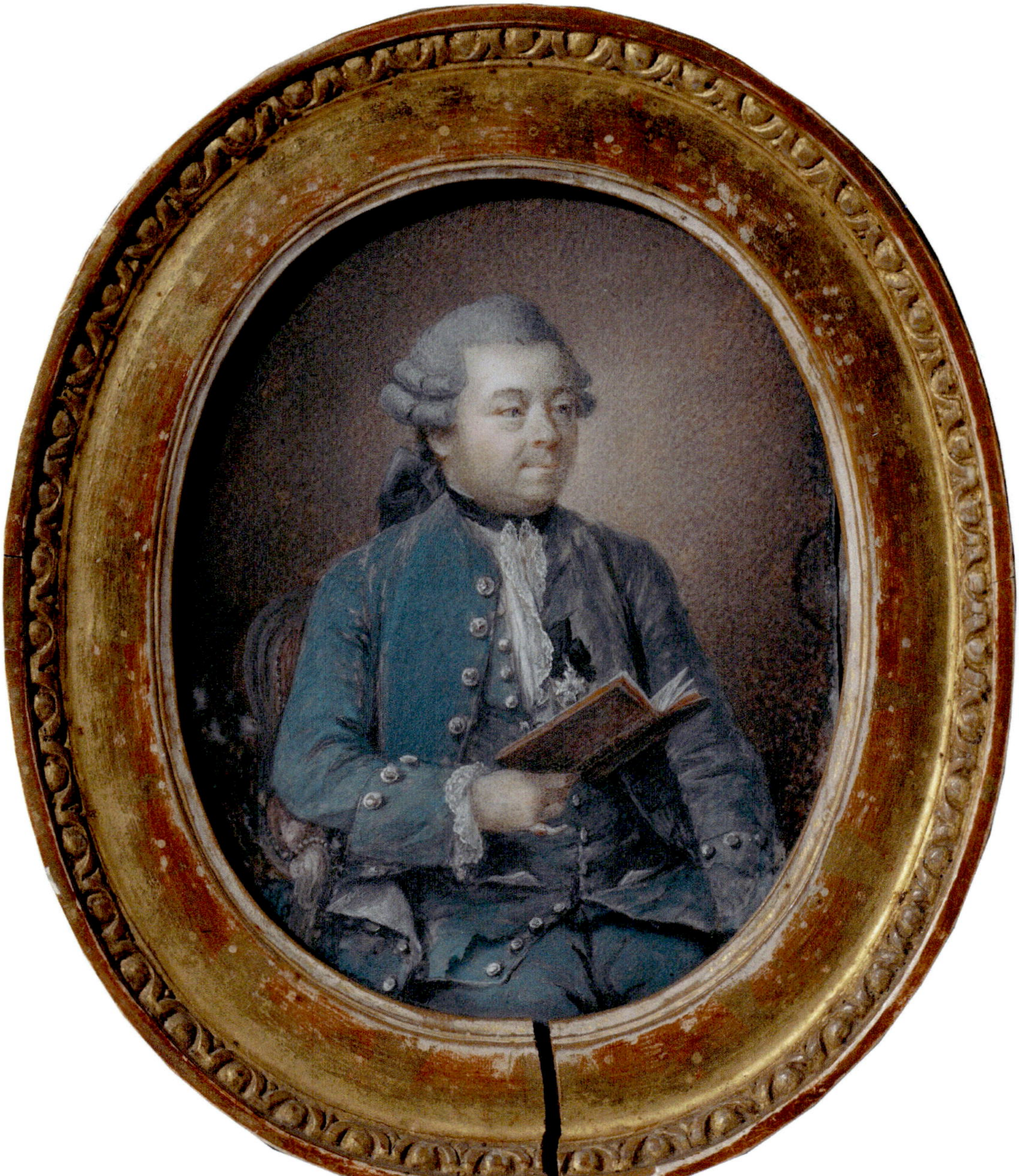

Plate 2. Niclas Lafrensen the Younger, *Carl Eric Wadenstierna* (1723–1787). Watercolour and gouache on ivory, 8.5 × 6 cm. Nationalmuseum, Stockholm (NMGrh 4323).

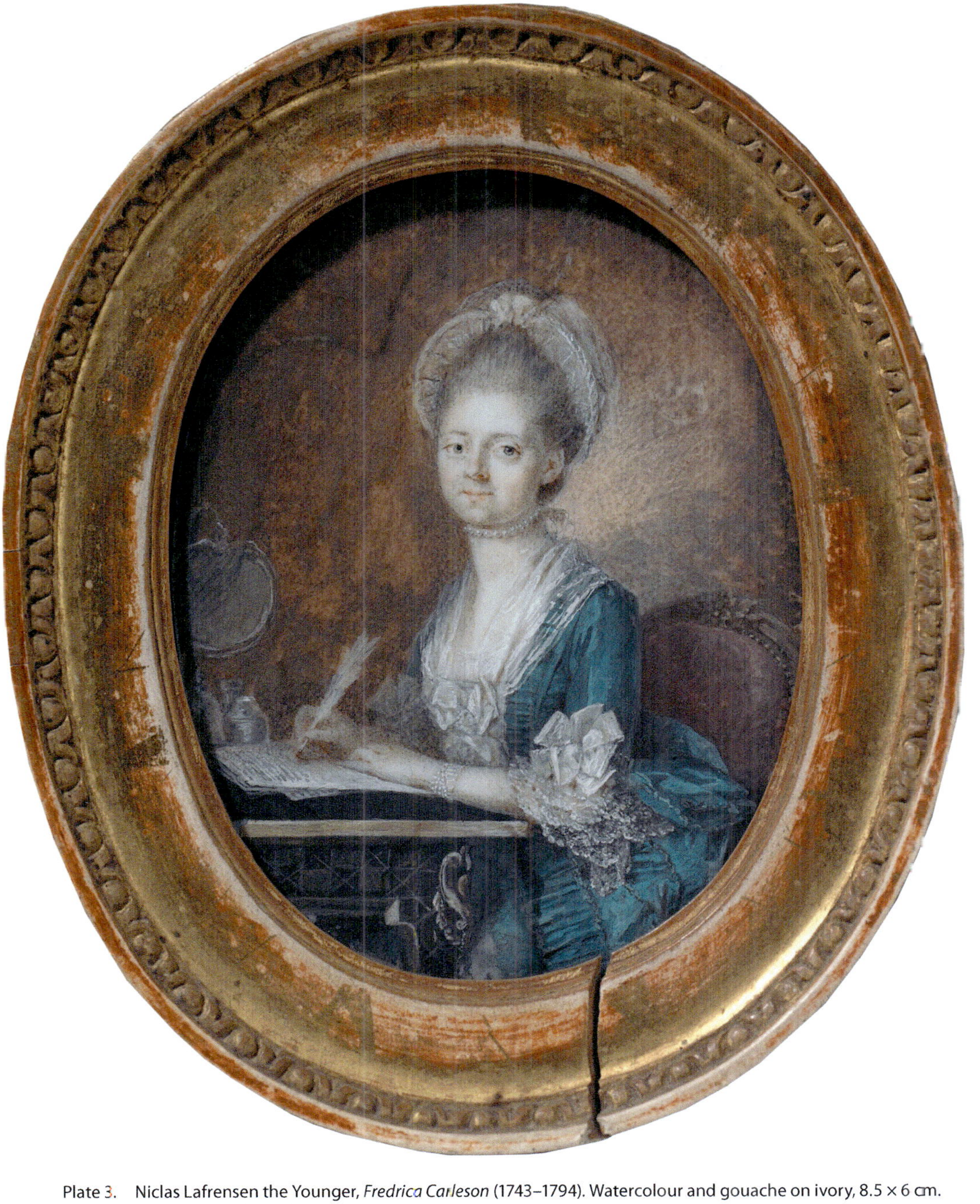

Plate 3. Niclas Lafrensen the Younger, *Fredrica Carleson* (1743–1794). Watercolour and gouache on ivory, 8.5 × 6 cm. Nationalmuseum, Stockholm (NMGrh 4325).

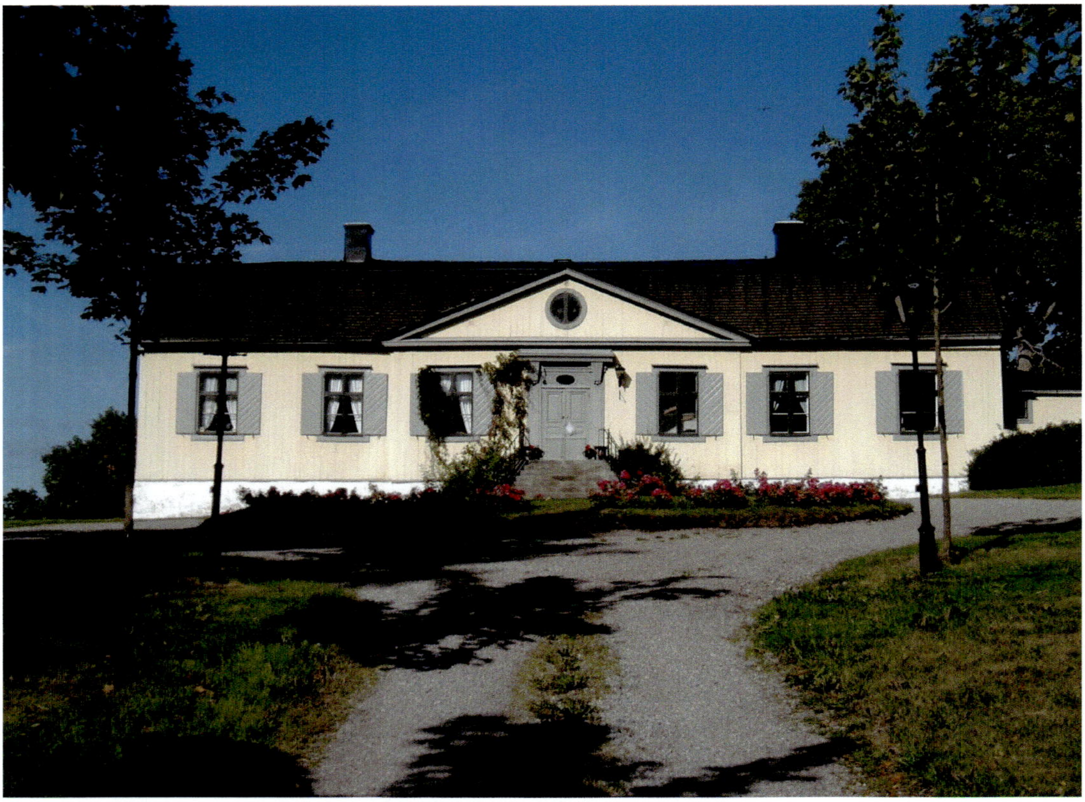

Plate 4. The main building at Näs. Photo: Udo Schröter. Wikimedia Commons.

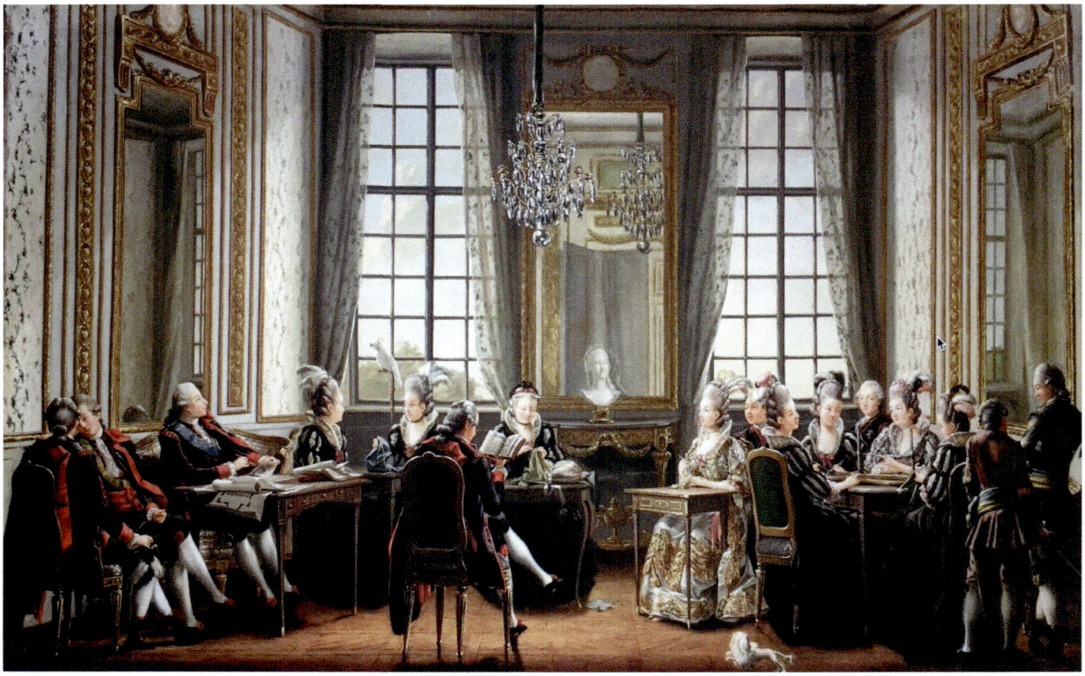

Plate 7. Pehr Hilleström, *En tafla med 16 personer föreställande en Conversation på Drottningholm*, 1779. Oil on canvas, 74.5 × 117 cm. Nationalmuseum, Stockholm (NMDrh 751).

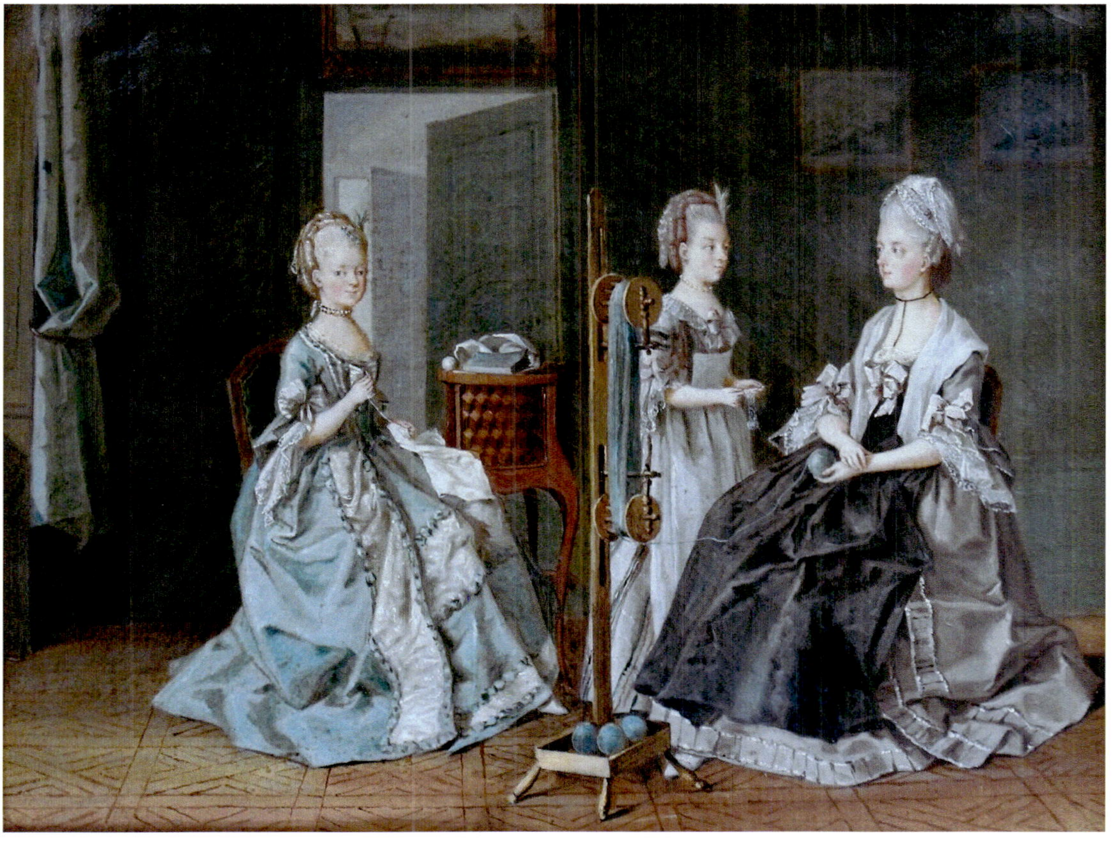

Plate 5. Pehr Hilleström's portrait that was commissioned for Wadenstierna's Näs Manor, *2ne Fröknar Wadenstiernas portraiter – i Conversation*, c. 1774. Oil on canvas, 32 × 41 cm. Private ownership.

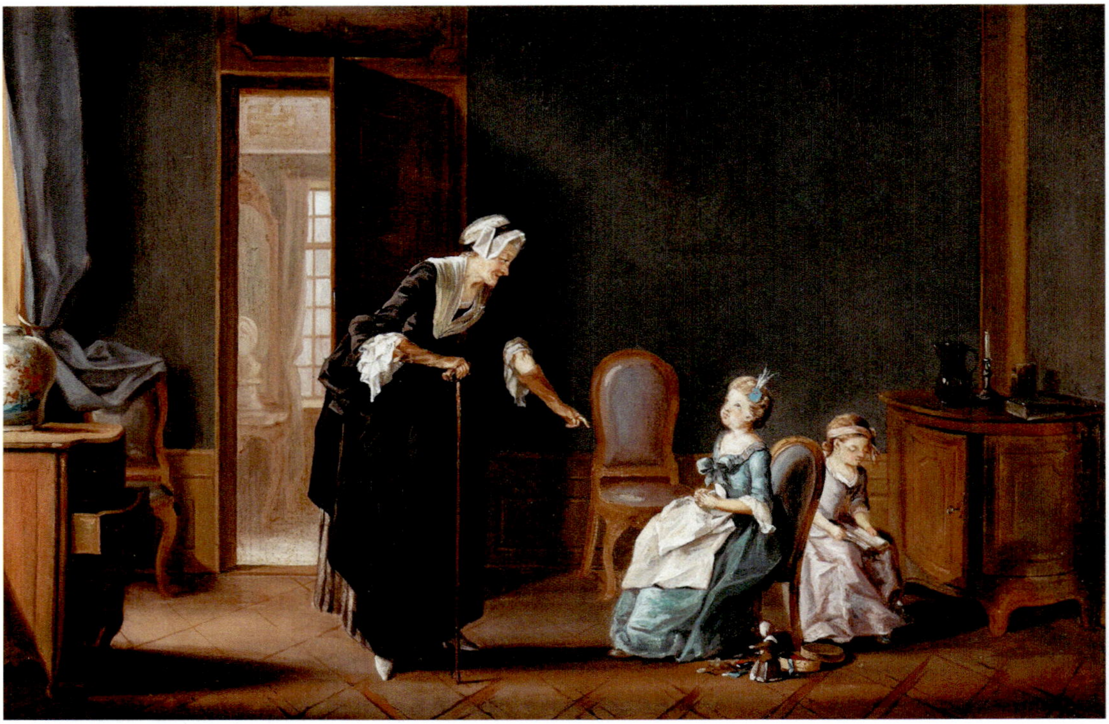

Plate 6. Pehr Hilleström, *En gumma med 2ne flickor* (later called *Tillrättavisningen*), *c.* 1774. Oil on canvas, 33.5 × 49.5 cm. Private ownership. Photo: Bukowskis. The painting belonged to Wadenstierna's Näs estate.

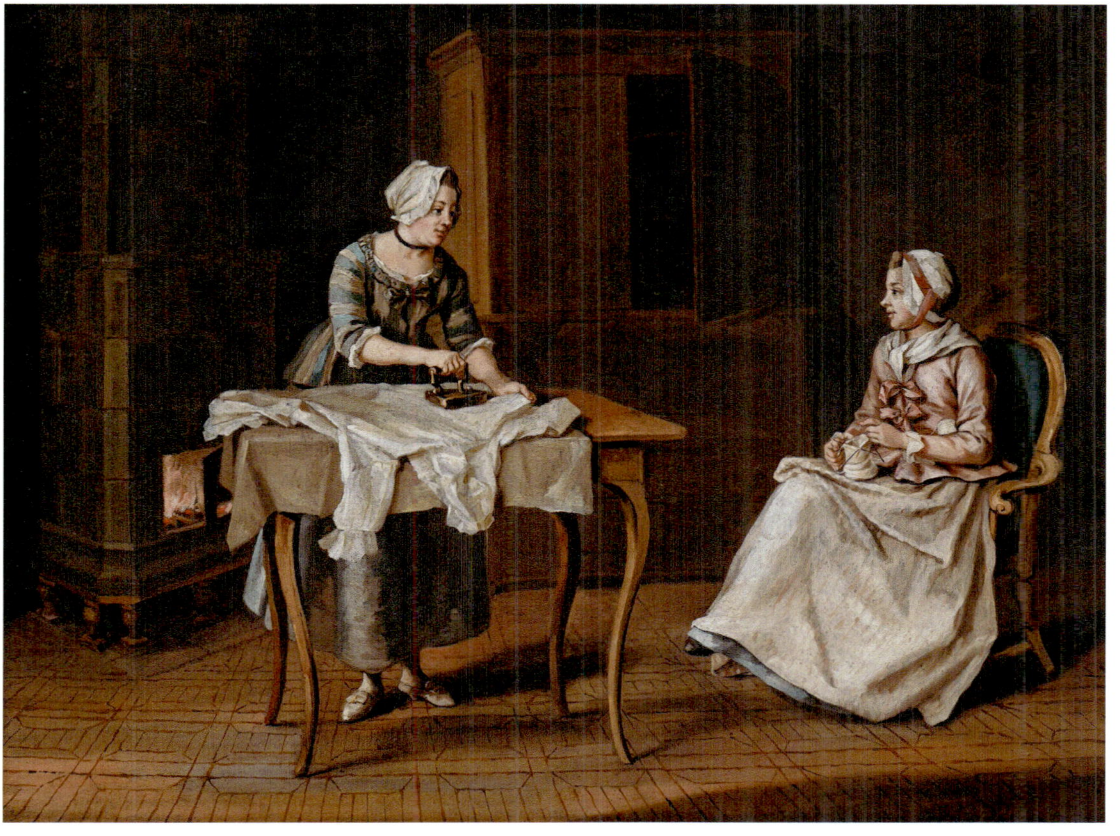

Plate 8. A suite of paintings at Wadenstierna's Näs Manor tell us about everyday work with the home's textiles: Pehr Hilleström, *En som stryker och en som sticker* (one ironing and one knitting). Oil on canvas, 40 × 51 cm. Private ownership. Photo: Bukowskis.

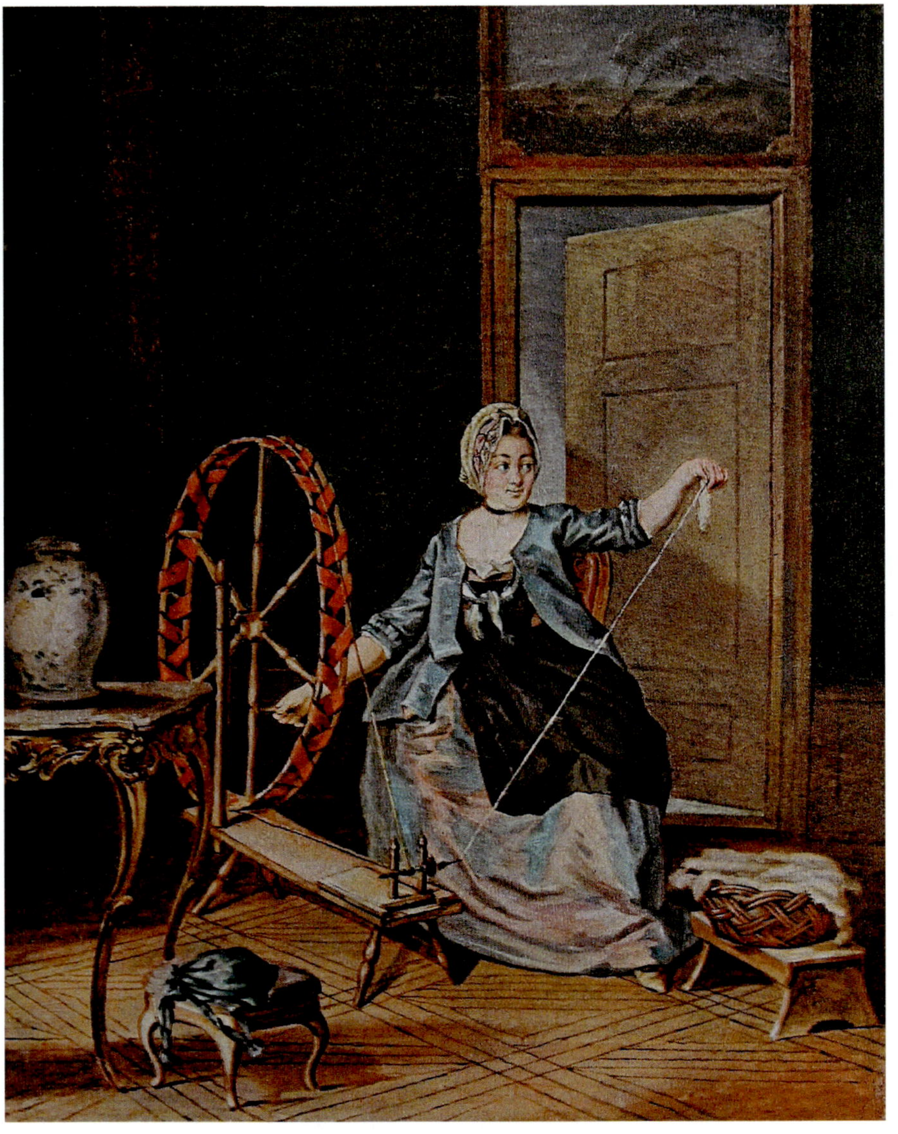

Plate 9. Wadenstierna's commission for Näs also included Pehr Hilleström, *Ett Fruent: spinner bomull* (A woman: Spinning cotton). Oil on canvas, 51 × 40 cm. Private ownership.

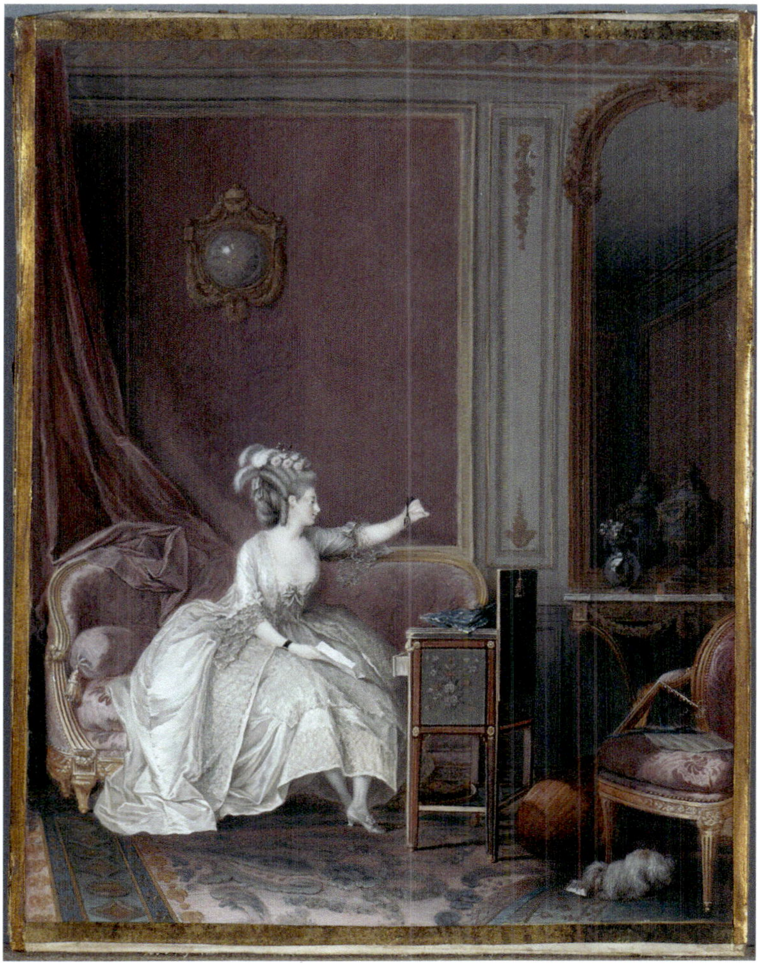

Plate 10. Niclas Lafrensen the Younger, *La consolation de l'absence*, *c.* 1785. Gouache, 26 × 20.5 cm. Paris Musées/Musée Cognacq-Jay, Paris (J 156).

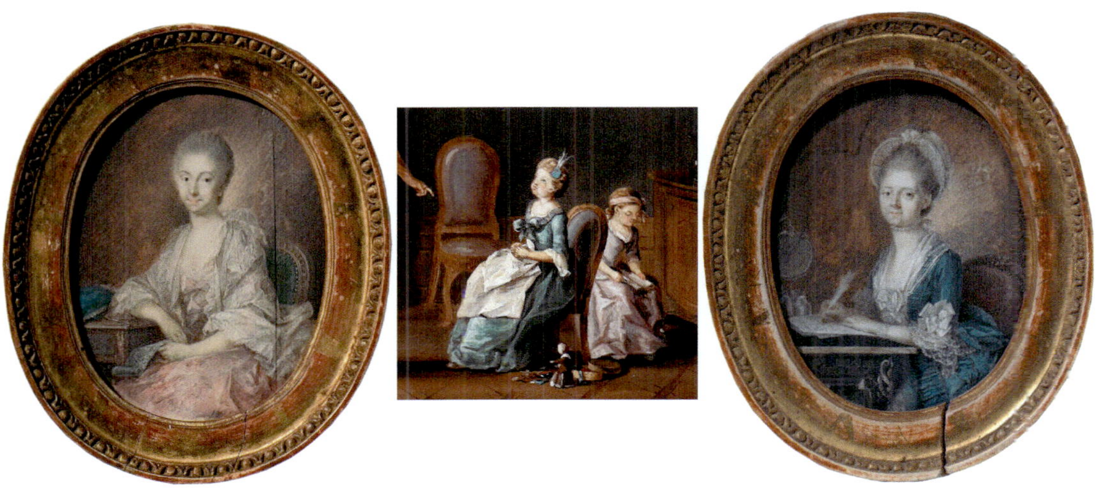

Plate 11. Niclas Lafrensen the Younger, *Jacobina Sophia Psilanderhielm von Seulenberg* (1733–1768) and *Fredrica Carleson* (1743–1794). Watercolour and gouache on ivory, 8.5 × 6 cm. Nationalmuseum, Stockholm (NMGrh 4324); Pehr Hilleström, *En gumma med 2ne flickor* (detail), *c.* 1774. Oil on canvas, 33.5 × 49.5 cm. Private ownership. Photo: Bukowskis.

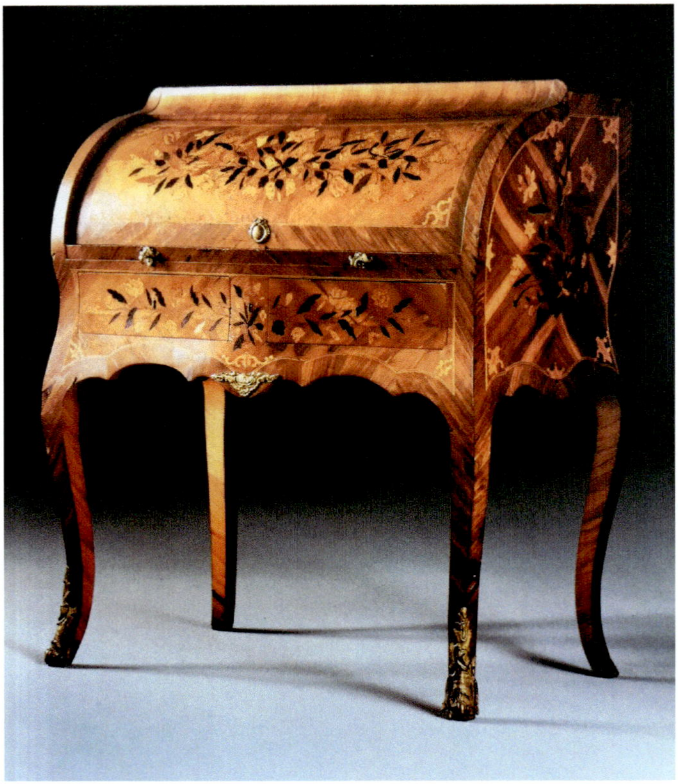

Plate 12. Johan Niclas Eckstein, Wadenstierna's secretaire, signed 1773. Veneered with jacaranda, plumwood, citron wood, maple, dark poplar and amaranth (purpleheart wood). W 94.5 cm, H 106 cm, D 49.5 cm. Private ownership. Photo: Christie's.

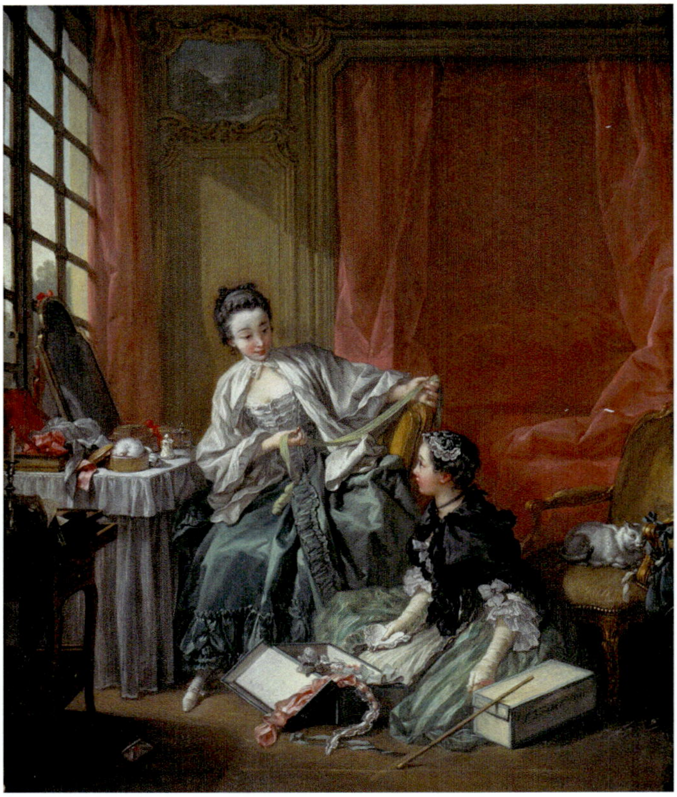

Plate 14. François Boucher, *La marchande de modes*, 1746. Oil on canvas, 64 × 53 cm. Nationalmuseum, Stockholm (NM 772). Photo: Cecilia Heisser.

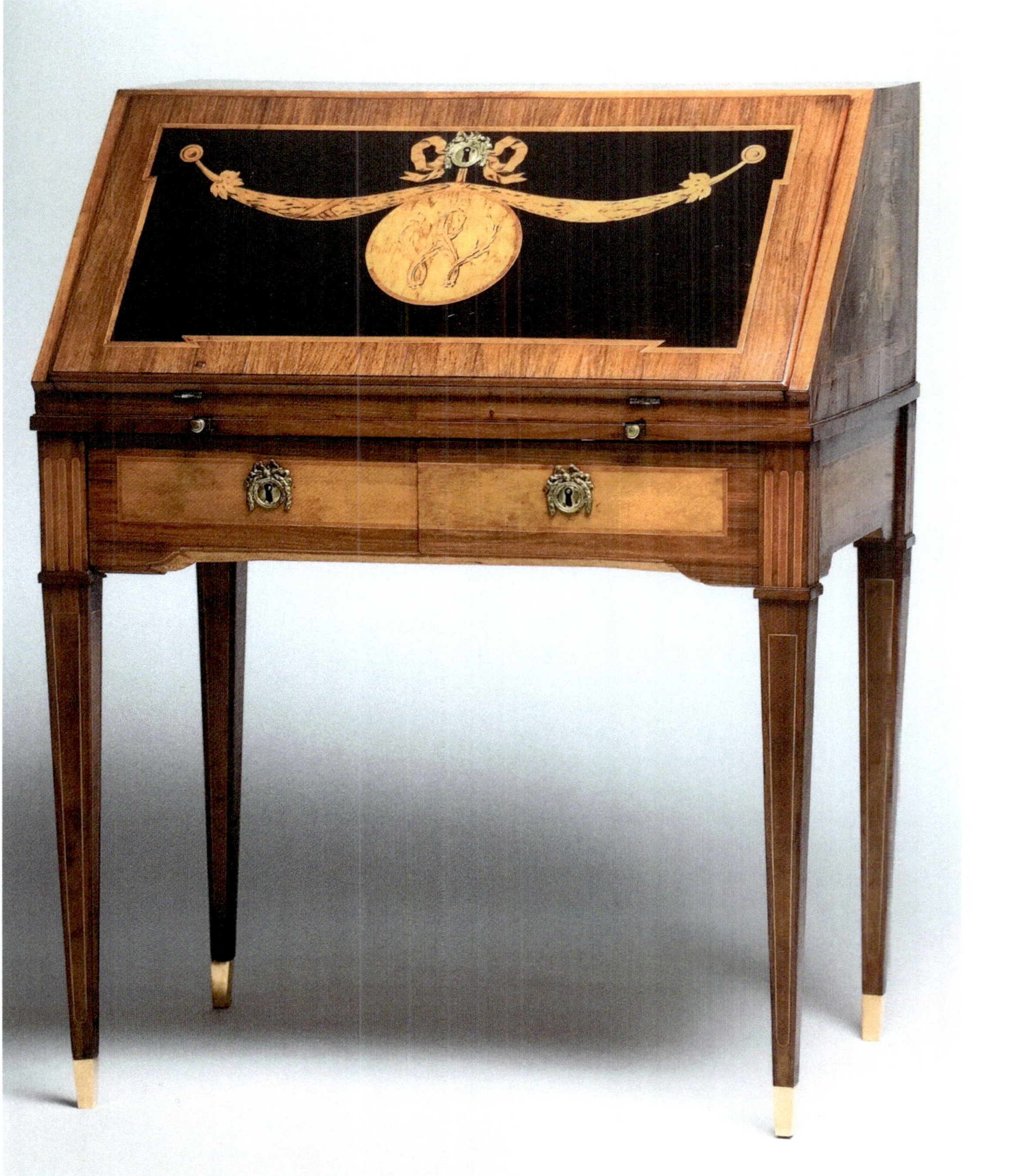

Plate 13. Georg Haupt, secretaire completed for Wadenstierna, signed 1775. Veneered with coloured birch, maple, walnut and possibly mulberry wood. W 82 cm, H 106 cm, D 55 cm. Private ownership. Photo: Åmells.

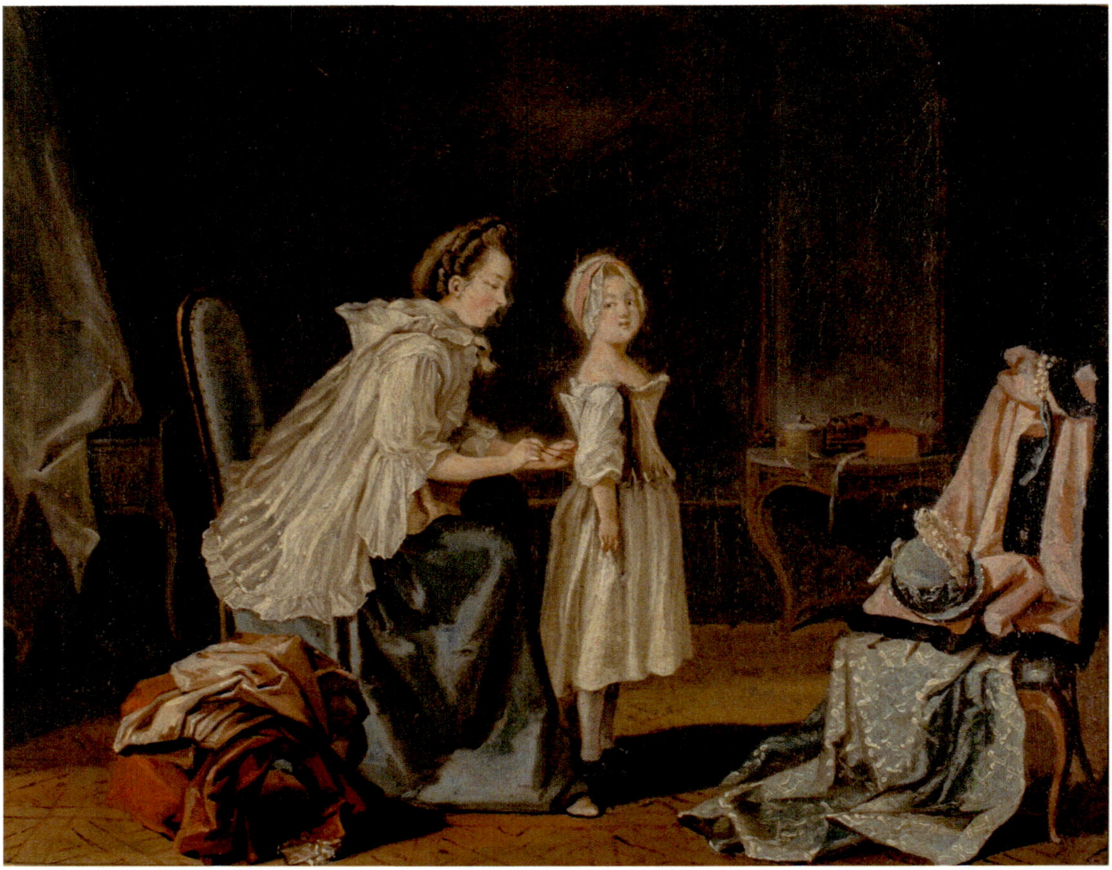

Plate 15. Pehr Hilleström, *Ett Fruent: som snör en flicka* (A woman lacing a girl's corset). Oil on canvas, 32 × 41 cm. Private ownership. The painting was part of Wadenstierna's commission of Hilleström's works in the 1770s.

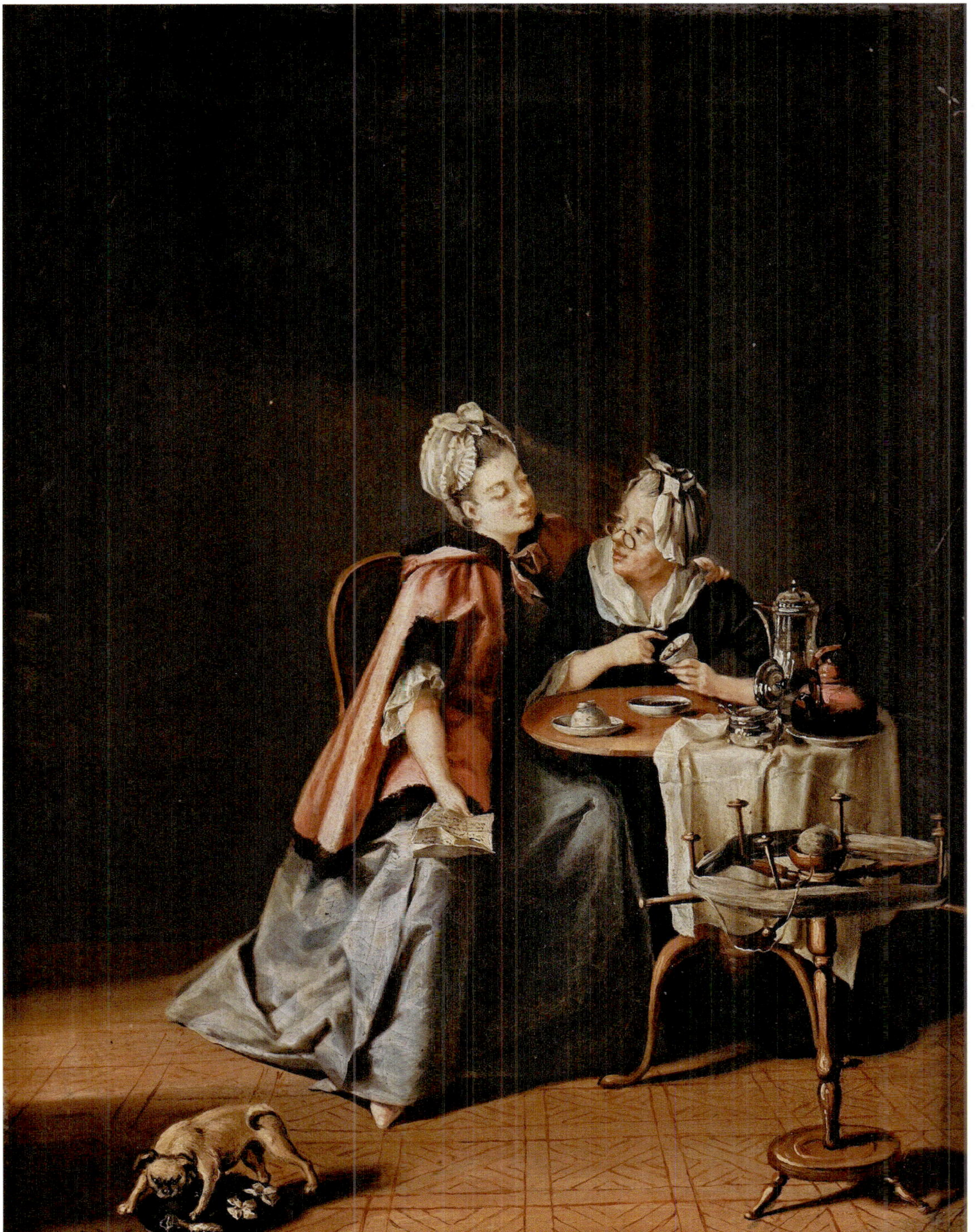

Plate 16. In the eighteenth century, Näs was home to Pehr Hilleström's painting *Interiör med ung dam och gumma som spår i kaffesump* (Interior with young lady and old woman reading coffee grounds), from *c.* 1775. Oil on canvas, 38.5 × 30 cm. Private ownership. Photo: Bukowskis.

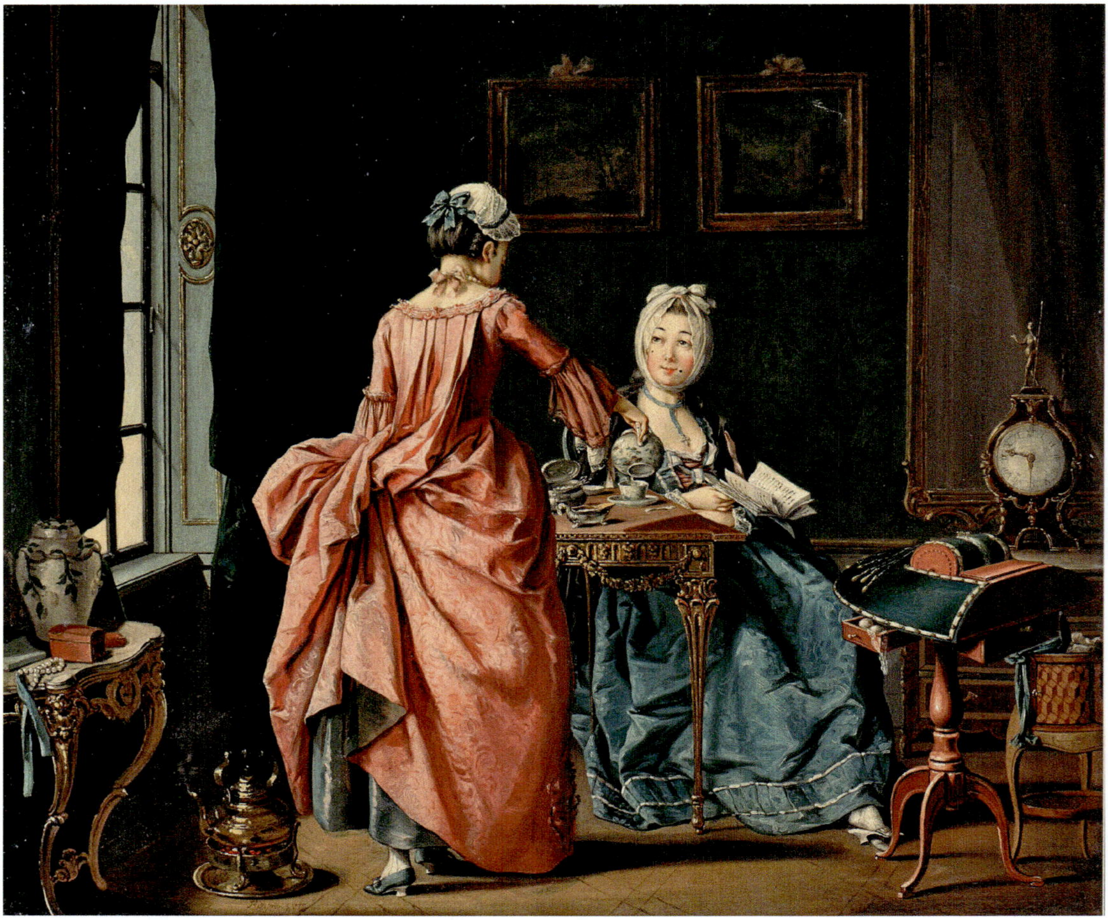

Plate 17. Pehr Hilleström, *Ett fruentimmer sitter och läser, kammarjungfrun kommer med Thé* (A woman sits reading, the lady's maid brings tea), 1775. Oil on canvas, 53 × 62 cm. Nordiska museet, Stockholm (NM.0177655*1).

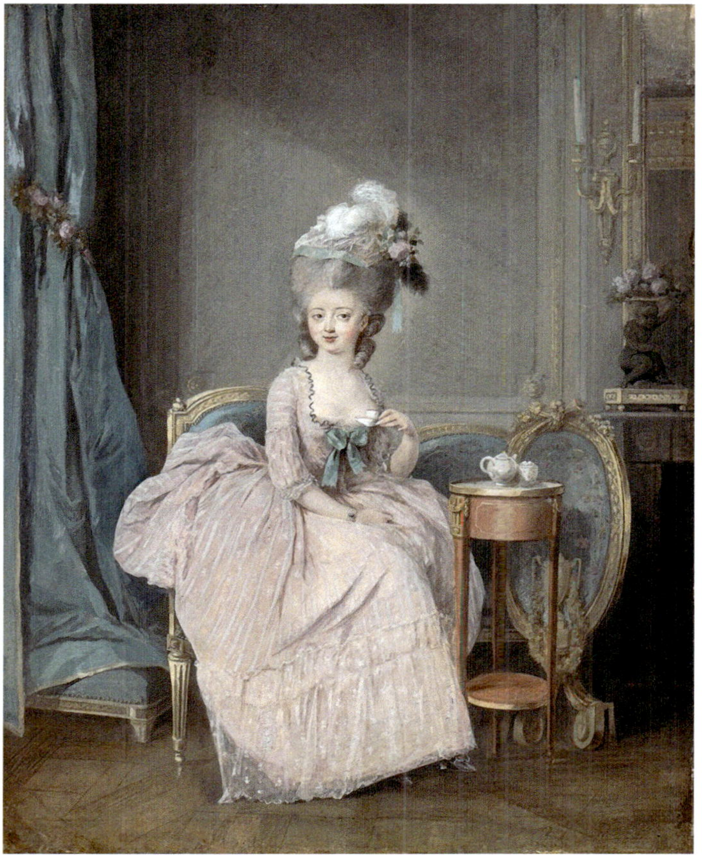

Plate 18. Niclas Lafrensen the Younger, *Lady Drinking Tea*, *c.* 1780. Gouache on paper, 28 × 21.9 cm. Harvard Art Museums/Fogg Museum, Gift of Charles E. Dunlap (1956.248).

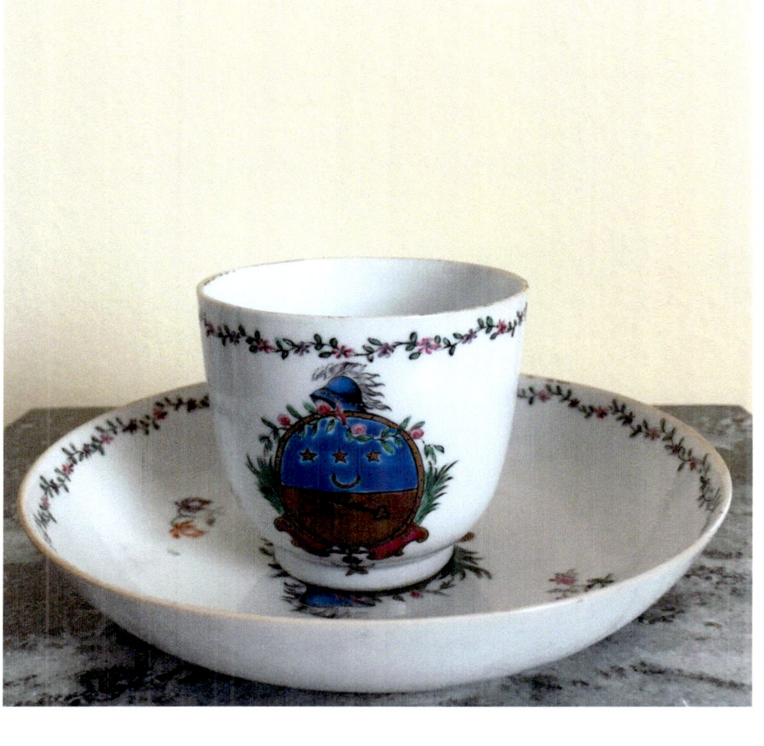

Plate 19. Cup from Wadenstierna's armorial tableware. Polychrome decoration with the cross of the Royal Order of the Polar Star hanging around the coat of arms after Wadenstierna was awarded the distinction in 1767. Private ownership.

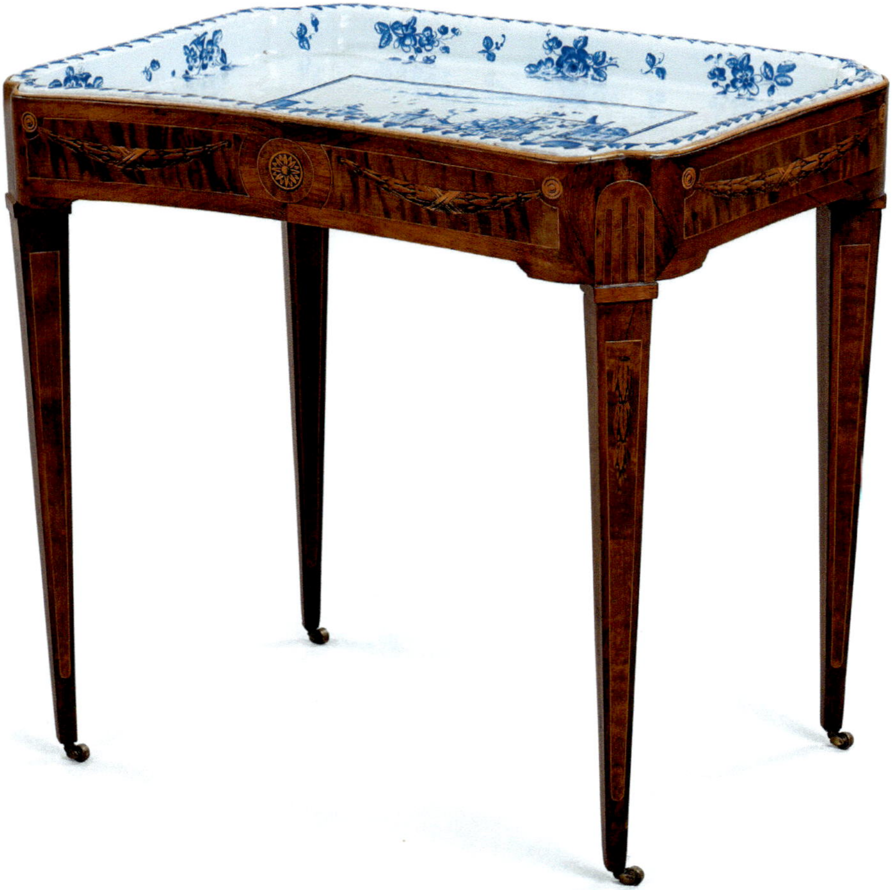

Plate 20. Georg Haupt, Wadenstierna's tea table, 1775. L 80 cm, W 57.5 cm, H 75 cm. Private ownership. Photo: Bukowskis.

4. At the dressing table

Abstract
The chapter highlights the dressing table, a piece of furniture that perhaps most clearly links the eighteenth-century image of women with views of luxury consumption, commodities and comfort. European portraiture of the time often depicted women at dressing tables, yet these portraits as well as regular dressing tables were missing at Wadenstierna's Näs. What does this absence signify and how was it compensated for? Does the lack of dressing tables in Swedish portraiture in general and at the Wadenstierna manor in particular tell us anything about the Swedish identity during the eighteenth century?

Keywords: boudoir, French fashion, *table de toilette*, luxury consumption, portraiture, François Boucher

The table is cluttered with boxes and cases. A swansdown powder puff lies in an open powder box in front of a large mirror and a tangle of ribbons spills out of the red interior of a box (Plate 14). The table that is most reminiscent of eighteenth-century upper-class culture is perhaps the dressing table. Many complex issues of the era concern this particular table – about beauty ideals and the roles of women, about eroticism and virtue, about politics and consumption. The dressing table constituted a hub in the era's fashionable lifestyle, and a material culture developed regarding the table, in which fashion and upper-class manifestation excelled. The traces of this dressing table culture are found everywhere in eighteenth-century visual culture – in fashion images and paintings or as motifs on decorative objects, fabrics or ceramics. The history of the dressing table is about the woman as a consumer and about comfortable leisure life during the mornings. But the narrative about *la table de toilette* also encompasses tensions, complications and contradictory ideals.

La toilette developed during the eighteenth century from a cloth (*la petite toile*) to a table (*la table de toilette*) and subsequently to comprise an entire room in privileged homes. The necessary accoutrements consisted of not only the make-up and cloths, mirrors and boxes but also the clothes and the furniture. Both men and women used dressing tables in eighteenth-century upper-class circles, and

Brown, C., *Comfortable Everyday Life at the Swedish Eighteenth-Century Näs Manor.*
Taylor & Francis Group, 2024
DOI 10.5117/9789048562374_CH04

men also participated in the multifaceted dressing room culture. They were also sometimes depicted in dressing gowns during their morning toilette, but in the era's pictorial world, women occupy a significantly more prominent position. This chapter is therefore mainly devoted to the female side of the phenomenon.

French role models and complications

In the *Almanac de Gotha* under the heading 'Inventions de luxe & de commodité', at the end of the eighteenth century, readers could obtain information about all of the modern toilette's necessary *'eaux'*, *'esprits'*, *'essences'*, *'aluns'*, *'esponges'*, *'huiles'*, *'vinaigres'*, *'pâtes'*, *'savonnettes'*, *'mouches'*, *'fard'*, *'pastilles'*, *'pommades'* (in fantastic colours such as yellow, red and purple) or *'poudres'* (in pink and cerise).[1] The heading 'Connaissance de différentes marchandises' informed of prices and qualities of new versions of dressing tables, washstands and bidets. The latest style of negligee was also featured, which simply and elegantly concealed unkempt morning attire and which you could easily put on while still in bed. The garment was created by the milliner 'Madl. Alexandre' for Madame la Comtesse d'Artois and, as its name suggested – 'Déshabillé à la Henri IV' – was inspired by the French Renaissance, but also by Turkish attire.[2] It was thereby also connected with various themes in the fashionable reading material deemed suitable for the dressing room.[3] In *Mercure de France* on 4 July 1789, the perfumer Caron advertised his beauty products at Rue du Four in Paris. Clients who lived far away were urged to write and order; it was no trouble to dispatch products to the most remote countries.[4] The range of items in these and similar publications demonstrated a constant stream of new products. In Swedish newspapers advertisements were placed by the boutiques that sold the new French and English goods or the bookshops that had received the latest fashion plates from Paris.[5] The ever expanding availability of the fashion items, and the opportunity to choose from a continually growing range, made such items increasingly significant during the eighteenth century for the era's identity-building consumption.[6]

1 *Almanach de Gotha pour l'année MDCCXCI*, Gotha 1791, pp. 58–63.

2 Princess Marie-Thérèse de Savoie (1756–1805).

3 The perfume advertised under the heading 'Inventions de Luxe' was also linked to the theme: 'Guzelleck ou Ekmecq, nom arabe', *Almanach de Gotha* 1776, p. 100.

4 *Mercure de France*, Paris, 4 July 1789, p. 47.

5 *Stockholms Posten* 9 January 1779 and 25 September 1781 and advertisements in *Dagligt Allehanda* 28 November 1782.

6 Morag Martin, 'A Market for Beauty', *Selling Beauty. Cosmetics, Commerce, and French Society, 1750–1830*, Baltimore 2009, pp. 32–51.

Estate inventories and other inventory lists provide insight into real-life dressing rooms, from the royal palaces to bourgeois homes. The sources inform of the multitude of objects, but also of an increased significance of comfort. In addition to a dressing table with accessories, various pieces of comfortable furniture for relaxation such as daybeds, sofas and armchairs were often included in these rooms.[7] Countess Ebba Margareta Bonde, married to Councillor of the Realm Carl Bonde, had a folding bed, chairs, a lacquered tea table and a 'Turkish floor rug' in her 'toilette' in the 1780s. In her dressing room at Sturehovs Manor outside Stockholm, Ottiliana Liljencrantz, married to Gustaf III's newly ennobled finance minister, Johan Liljencrantz, had an expensive 'toilette büreau av mahognÿ', but also a silk-upholstered sofa and four armchairs.[8] Dressing rooms evidently intended to be for both privacy and socialising, where comfortable but also high-status furniture and objects were displayed.

The designated dressing room furniture that was developed in the latter half of the eighteenth century was both a result of the growing culture of comfort and an expression of a female sphere. Just as the *poudreuse*, which combined the functions of a writing table and dressing table and had space for make-up containers as well as ink pots and sand shakers (pounce pots), they were often designed to be practical multifunctional furniture (Image 46). In visual art, there is often a glimpse of a letter or open book on the dressing tables or in the folds of the peignoir, as a hint that the women not only represented youth and beauty, but that politeness and cultivation also belonged to the female upper-class ideal that was connected with these pieces of furniture and objects.[9] The acquisition of the new and comfortable dressing room furniture, or the decision to be portrayed in the latest style of peignoir, thereby became key social and cultural markers.[10] On their dressing tables, Ebba Bonde or Ottiliana Liljencrantz could display a novel or other suitable light reading, and identity, ideals and comfort were united in the many different activities associated with this item of furniture.[11] This was possibly

7 Vahlne, Bo, *Frihetstidens inredningar på Stockholms slott. Om bekvämlighetens och skönhetens nivåer*, Stockholm 2012, p. 130.

8 Estate inventory of Ebba Margareta Bonde (1746–84): Svea Court of Appeal. Nobility estate inventories of Carl and Ebba Margareta Bonde drawn up in 1796, E IX B: 129–52; estate inventory of Ottiliana Vilhelmina Transchiöld, married Liljecrantz (1741–88): Svea Court of Appeal. Nobility estate inventories, drawn up in 1789, SE/RA/420422/01/E IX b/131.

9 Many engraved pictures were published on the theme, such as Louis Surugue's engraving *L'ornement de l'esprit et du corps*, after Jean-François de Troy's original from 1747 or Claude Duflos the Younger's *Le billet doux* and *La revendeuse à la toilette*, after Jean Ernest Aubert's original, which were advertised in *Mercure de France*, December 1755, pp. 215–16.

10 On 'la sociabilité': Daniel Gordon, *Citizens without Sovereignty. Equality and Sociability in French Thought 1670–1789*, Princeton 1994.

11 For example, *Toilette-lecture för fruntimmer och herrar*, Stockholm 1798 with free translations of French fables, stories and poems. Other suitable reading included fashion magazines published in the

why images from dressing rooms became so common in the eighteenth century, even when they were presented in a more restrained way in Sweden.

A woman has sat down at a comfortably set up dressing table and is absorbed in examining a light-green silk ribbon in her hands (Plate 14). At her feet sits a milliner, whose black pelerine and gloves show that she has just arrived to offer her coveted products. Both she and the viewer of the painting are visiting this private, female world during the morning's activities. The woman at the table is well dressed but not fully dressed, and a loosely tied peignoir is spread out over her shoulders. Her red cheeks and powdered hair illustrate that she has just finished her toilette. Warm hues from the red silk-clad alcove bed and the long window curtains bathe the room in an enveloping atmosphere.

François Boucher's painting *La marchande de modes* (The milliner) – or *Le matin* (The morning), as it also came to be known – conveys all the superficialities of fashion – what government official Carl Reinhold Berch called 'des brimborins' in a letter to Count Carl Fredrik Scheffer, when the negotiations with Boucher about the royal commission were at their height.[12] The painting from 1746 was also disseminated to a wider audience. The artist soon painted a replica, which in turn formed the basis for a series of engravings.[13] But the image of luxury that imbued the everyday life and environments of the elite could also be interpreted as the bearer of a moralising message – a message that here creates a contradiction. At the same time that the motif represents frivolous, modern life, it could be interpreted as an objection to the artificiality that characterised this lifestyle. The epigram added to René Gaillard's contemporary engraving juxtaposed the simple and original life ('la simple nature'), with the life unnaturally decorated with 'ces vains ornemens'.[14] The motif depicted the lifestyle of the elite but also questioned it through a link to one of the Age of Enlightenment's recurring figures of thought, namely placing modern, urban civilisation in the light of pure, unaffected nature. The theme was repeated by various artists throughout the eighteenth century, in pictures where beautiful women and well-filled dressing tables symbolised the moralising content.

Boucher's painting was intended for the royal family's palace, Drottningholm, where it formed part of a complex visual context among the rooms' wealth of portraits, engravings and genre paintings. In this environment, among royals

last few decades of the eighteenth century. But 'livres du boudoir' above all comprised popular novels. Suggested reading was stated in Marquis de Paulmy's *Mélanges tirés d'une grand bibliothèque: Manuel des châteaux, ou, Lettres contenant des conseils pour former une bibliothèque romanesque, pour diriger une comédie de société & pour diversifier les plaisirs d'un salon*, Paris 1779.

12 Grate, Pontus, *French Paintings, II, Eighteenth Century*, Nationalmuseum, Stockholm 1994, p. 66.

13 Engravings were advertised for sale in, for example, *Mercure de France*, May 1755, p. 133.

14 René Gaillard after François Boucher, *La marchand de modes*, 1746–55, engraving, 37.5 × 25.7 cm, Metropolitan Museum of Art, New York (53.600.1107).

and ladies-in-waiting, this pictorial world could undoubtedly create recognition and associations with their own experiences of the era's culture of consumption.[15] However, in the circle of educated and cultivated members of the upper class, the paintings were probably also reminders of other ideals that gave the motifs double meanings. The woman at her dressing table in *La marchande de modes* was perhaps reminiscent of the meaning of *l'art de plaire*, the art of pleasing, and the virtues expected to belong to this art, with a reminder that artificial beauty can never manage to emulate genuine, true beauty.[16] The same message was formulated in the text for Gaillard's engraving. The paintings that Carl Eric Wadenstierna commissioned from Pehr Hilleström belonged to the same set of motifs and probably aimed to express the same exhorting ideals – but here not directed at the ladies-in-waiting at Drottningholm, but at his teenage daughters at Näs.

Wadenstierna's own voice in the contemporary Swedish luxury debate is also linked to Hilleström's pictures. In his pamphlet *Fria Tankar*, addressed to Queen Lovisa Ulrika, Wadenstierna praises her 'invaluable tenderness for the fine arts, for sciences and for handicrafts, her tender and compassionate heart for her poor and needy subjects'.[17] Here, Wadenstierna argues for the utility of luxury. Limiting luxury, for example, through sumptuary laws, entailed depriving the poor of their livelihoods. In the light of Wadenstierna's political and economic opinions, Hilleström's paintings thereby gained an additional dimension. The pictures of comfortable, lavish rooms ultimately constituted a way of visualising a social order that aimed to benefit everyone. But the debate also included a moralising tone, which in Wadenstierna's words referred back to the message in Boucher's painting. 'A beautiful woman does not need to use foreign ornaments, her attractiveness is sufficient embellishment.'[18] The profitability of luxury was one thing, but beauty was disfigured by borrowed feathers. This was an attitude that also had consequences for the design of women's portraits.

The social elite who commissioned and admired these paintings must have nonetheless found the beauty, material luxury and inviting comfort conveyed by the pictures appealing. The interior shown in Boucher's *La marchande de modes* also illustrated how the milliners could provide these wealthy circles with everything needed for the modern lifestyle. The motif is like a sensuous sample

15 In the early 1750s, Ulla Sparre, the wife of Count Carl Gustaf Tessin, gifted a French dressing table to Queen Lovisa Ulrika; Vahlne 2012, pp. 130f.

16 Merit Laine, 'Skönhetsgalleriet på Drottningholm', in Merit Laine and Carolina Brown, *Gustaf Lundberg 1695–1786. En porträttmålare och hans tid*, Stockholm 2006, p. 186 and Runefelt 2015, pp. 119–27.

17 Wadenstierna, Carl Eric, *Fria Tankar*, Stockholm 1769, p. 2.

18 *Sveriges ridderskaps- och adels riksdags-protokoll*, 1765–6, part 2, p. 90, and Runefelt, Leif, *Att hasta mot undergången: anspråk, flyktighet, förställning i debatten om konsumtion i Sverige 1730–1830*, Lund 2015, p. 125.

card of the range of furniture and objects available for purchase from the French capital's *marchands-merciers*: the comfortable alcove bed, the elegant writing furniture or the richly equipped dressing table. When Gaillard's engraving was marketed in *Mercure de France*, the same magazine included advertisements for the products ('les brillans colifichets') sold by the milliners.[19] In the midst of this zeal for consumption, there were also misgivings in the era about the dangers of this tempting range of products. The allegories of modern life, which Boucher's painting belonged to, not only reflected the pleasurable upswing in the whirlwinds of fashion, but also contained a message of safeguarding more moderate virtues. The women who aspired to belong to the upper echelons of society were expected to observe this underlying meaning and find a balance between the two force fields, not least if they chose to portray themselves in similar environments.[20]

The eighteenth century's dressing table was therefore encircled by a cloud, not only of powder, but also of complex and contradictory notions of excess, comfort, artificiality and naturalness, be it in the French elite in Paris or in the court culture at Drottningholm. But the question is, How were these notions disseminated in the wider Swedish upper-class culture? How were the French pictures and ideals interpreted at Swedish manors? And how were the messages modified in the portraits that depicted the women and daughters of the Swedish nobility? To understand the motives behind the Swedish portraits and behind the Wadenstierna family's commissions from artists such as Pehr Hilleström and Niclas Lafrensen, it is necessary to place the pictures in a wider contemporary context. This study will therefore now look at some of the eighteenth century's pictorial worlds before we return to Näs in Roslagen.

Dressing tables, fashion images and portraits

Pictures of women at mirrors were obviously not a novelty in the eighteenth century. They had featured in art since time immemorial – as representatives of various virtues or vices, or as illustrations of the hours of the day or people's ages; they could originate in religious or mythological tales, such as that of the toilette of Venus or Susanna in the bath. The mirror and dressing table could also serve as a *vanitas* motif and as a symbol of the inexorable transience of time, youth, beauty and love.

19 *Mercure de France*, May 1755, p. 133.

20 For example, the artist François-Hubert Drouais reused Boucher's well-known scene in 1756 when he painted a monumental family portrait on the theme (oil on canvas, 244 × 195 cm, National Gallery of Art, Washington, DC, 1946.7.4).

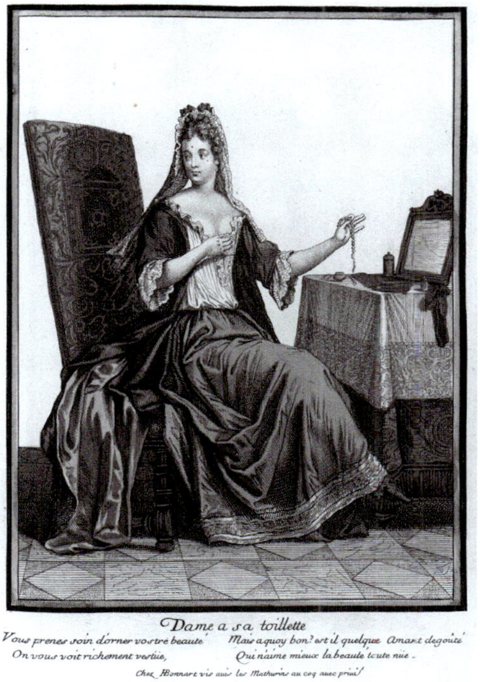

57. Henri Bonnart, *Dame a sa toillette*, 1687. Engraving, 36.5 × 23.8 cm. From Nicholas Bonnart, *Recueil des modes de la cour de France*, Paris, 1678–93. Los Angeles County Museum of Art (LACMA) (M.2002.57.81).

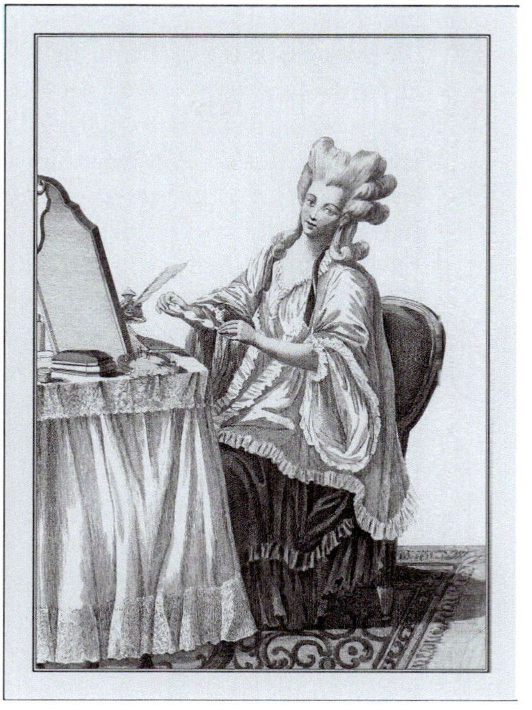

58. Nicolas Dupin after Pierre-Thomas Leclerc, *Femme galante à sa toilette ployant un billet*, Engraving. From *Galerie des modes et costumes français*, 1778, 10e.

From the latter half of the seventeenth century onwards, the motif was found in an additional type of picture, the engraved fashion plate, which was distributed in the form of illustrated almanacs or in publications such as *Mercure galant*.[21] The Bonnart firm's engravings from Paris depicted everything from the latest court fashions and court parties to interiors from fashion boutiques and aristocratic boudoirs.[22] The pictures of scantily dressed women at dressing tables not only informed people of new fashions but also how to lead a modern and comfortable

21 *Mercure galant* 1672–1724, subsequently under the name *Mercure de France*.

22 The dressing table in Bonnart's engraving was a reminder of formal court life where rank and position were expressed in visual codes, where clothes, accessories and make-up marked social status. Just as the formal and complicated court fashion required servants to assist with the hairstyling or dressing, the application of make-up became an act that demonstrated the upper-class role. Louis XIV developed the *lever* ceremony at Versailles, where selected guests were permitted to attend when the king got out of bed and performed his morning toilette, Richard Corson, *Fashions in Makeup. From Ancient to Modern Times*, London (1972) 1989, pp. 214–22 and Kimberly Chrisman-Campbell, 'Dressing to Impress. The Morning

life. In Bonnart's engraving *Dame à sa toilette* from 1687, the woman is posing at the dressing table while wearing a *robe de chambre* and a *chemise* with lace trim and a low décolletage (Image 57). This clothing allowed new freedom of movement and represented a new comfort and informality. But the scene did not lack social pretensions. The dressing gown has been draped so that the lining in its contrasting colour harmonises with the expensive fabric of the chair. Exclusive lace embellishes the table and frames the woman's artistically styled hair and made-up face. This was a scene directed at a viewer – the woman looking away from the mirror now waits to be admired. This tradition lived on in the eighteenth century, as clearly shown in Leclerc and Dupin's fashion plate from 1778 (Image 58).

The establishment of the rituals of make-up and toilette in an elite culture and its close connection with material luxury and upper-class comfort continued to develop throughout the eighteenth century, which is seen in eye-witness accounts conveyed through letters, diaries and memoirs.[23] These sources do not describe the toilette as a purely private or intimate phenomenon. The dressing table was not only used for personal hygiene but was also associated with socialising and the display of lavish possessions.[24] The more private aspects of the toilette, such as washing armpits or combing lice out of hair, were not intended for public view.[25] In *Tableau de Paris*, Louis-Sébastien Mercier makes a clarifying distinction between private and public toilette in Paris in the 1780s.[26] Mercier passes over the first toilette in silence – the fact that it is very 'secret' suffices as an explanation. However, 'la seconde toilette' is described as a carefully rehearsed social event, not only with the aim of demonstrating status and position, but also as a coquettish game between the sexes, in which everything is arranged and carried out in a calculated manner.[27] Social calls and receptions around the dressing tables developed into a coveted form of socialising. The Countess de Genlis, who liked to comment on the era's customs and taste in her writing, was

Toilette and the Fabrication of Femininity', in *Paris. Life & Luxury in the Eighteenth Century*, Charissa Bremer-David, (ed.), Los Angeles 2011, p. 54.

23 One example is when the ambassador Count Gustaf Philip Creutz introduced the young Count Axel von Fersen, during his sojourn in Paris in 1773–1774, to Countess de Brionne during her toilette. Nils Erdmann, *Ur rokokons liv. Typer och seder*, Stockholm 1925, pp. 132–3.

24 The Countess de Genlis describes the admiration and envy that Madame de la Reynière's lavish toilette evoked among the women of the elite. *Memoirs of the Countess de Genlis*, I, London 1825, p. 153.

25 The 'real' toilette is only glimpsed sporadically in eighteenth-century sources. This includes the private depiction of a female relation's louse-infested and malodorous hair-restyling in London in the 1770s (Richard Corson, *Fashions in Hair*, London 1965, pp. 337f.) or the artist Sergel's sketches from Stockholm in the 1790s of 'Anna Rella', whose hair is styled next to the pans in the kitchen, and Count Ehrenfalk, who is shaving with a small mirror balanced on a chest of drawers (Cederlöf 1997).

26 'Une jolie femme fait réguliérement chaque matin deux toilettes. La premiere est fort secrette, & jamais les amans n'y sont admis; ils n'entrent qu'à l'heure indiquée' (Mercier 1783, vol. 6, pp. 148ff.).

27 Mercier 1783, vol. 6, pp. 131–2, and Candid 1782, pp. 11–12.

hardly shocked that women tightened their corsets in front of male visitors, but was shocked that this now also took place outside of the privileged royal court.[28]

In eighteenth-century French visual art, dressing tables appear in different contexts and for different purposes. They constitute a recurring motif in portraiture but also in more ambiguous genre scenes. Jacques-André-Joseph Aved's portrait of Baroness Marguerite-Françoise-Bernard de Reims – one of many similar betrothal portraits from the first half of the French eighteenth century – was displayed at the Salon in Paris in 1739.[29] The woman, sitting in a silk-covered armchair, leans her elbow on a dressing table covered with lace cloths and adorned with silverware. *Mercure de France* presented Aved's portrait as being clearly historicising ('Portrait fort historié').[30] The audience was supposed to associate the scene with the well-known mythological motif 'the toilette of Venus' and see the parallel with the young bride's beauty, virtue and moral stature. A portrait commission was one of several gestures that marked the importance of entering into marriage.[31] This also included the exchange of gifts and transfer of the dowry. The portrait that shows the bride-to-be at her luxurious dressing table was thereby also a ostentatious display of the excess of the comfortable life. The expensive wedding gift often included a dressing table service, and the painting also shows some of the costly textiles that belonged to the dressing table.[32] François-Alexandre de Garsault's *L'art de la lingerie* from 1771 states what is needed for a well-equipped dressing table in the uppermost stratum of society: in addition to the tablecloth, a *petite toile*, a stock of forty-eight towels, six comb cases, thirty-six cloths (*frottoirs*) with which to remove rouge and thirty-six for removing powder, forty-eight handkerchiefs, forty-eight linen cloths for washing one's arms, six pairs of linen muffs for cleaning one's hands, twenty-four special aprons (*tabliers de toilette*), six peignoirs and eighteen scarves (*fichus*), eighty-four different types of caps and hair coverings (bonnets and *coeffes*), seventy-two blouses (*chemises*) and seventy-two pairs of slippers.[33]

28 Stéphanie Félicité Brulart de Sillery, Comtesse de Genlis, *De l'esprit des étiquettes de l'ancienne cour et des usages du monde de ce temps*, Paris 1996, p. 105.

29 Jacques-André-Joseph Aved, *Françoise de Reims, Baronne de Vanne*, 1739, oil on canvas, 130 × 97 cm, the Israel Museum, Jerusalem (B69.0175).

30 *Mercure de France*, September 1739, p. 2225: 'Portrait fort historié, de Mad. Duplex de Baquancourt, en deshabillé galant à sa Toilette'.

31 Entering into marriage was usually the foremost shift in status in a woman's life, a transition to a new phase in life that was given a virtually ritualistic framework and that was often followed by a portrait commission; Brown, Carolina, *Liksom en herdinna. Litterära teman i svenska kvinnoporträtt under 1700-talet*, Stockholm 2012, pp. 44ff.

32 Chrisman-Campbell 2011, pp. 56–9.

33 The French word '*toilette*' actually referred to this special cloth, which consisted of an upper cloth, '*le dessus*', and a lower one, '*les volants*', which was made of lace for the city residence and muslin for the country home. Gersault, François-Alexandre de, *L'Art de la lingerie*, Paris 1771, pp. 11f.

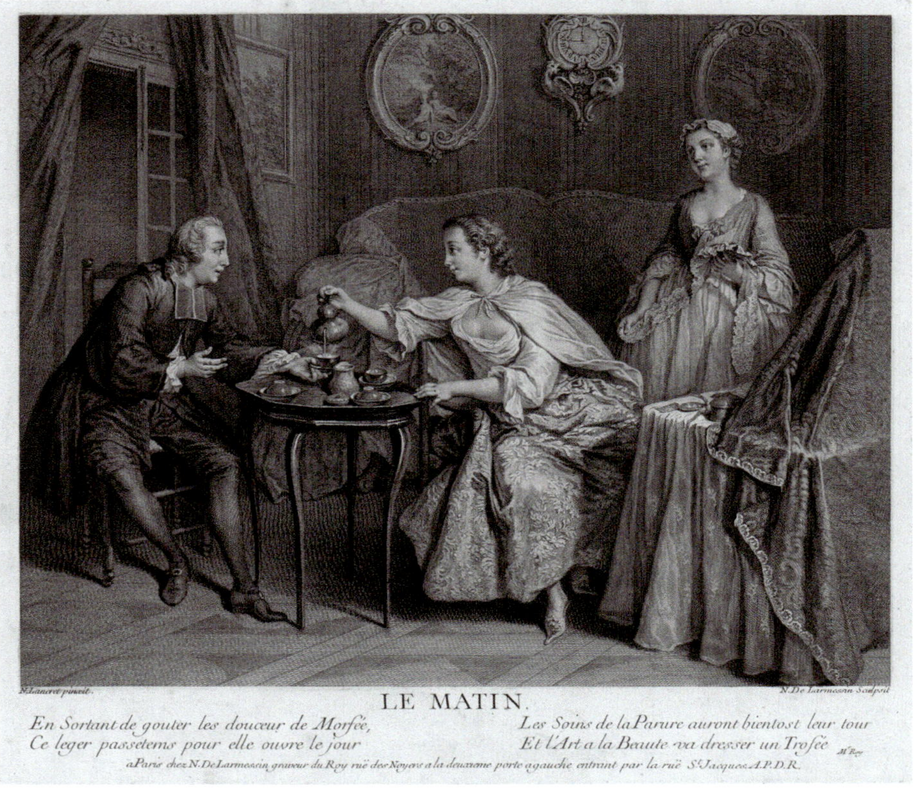

59. Nicolas de Larmessin after Nicolas Lancret, *Le matin*, 1741. Engraving, 33 × 37.4 cm. Rijksmuseum, Amsterdam (RP-P-OB-43.961).

In the portraits where the model is depicted next to the dressing table a glimpse of this material excess is conveyed.

But at the same Salon in 1739, Nicolas Lancret's painting *Dame à sa toilette, prenant du caffé* was also on show.[34] Compared to the portrait, Lancret's genre picture offered a freer and more ambiguous rendering of the motif. In Nicolas de Larmessin's engraving of the motif from 1741, the title *Le matin* (The morning) and an appurtenant epigram strengthened the feeling of a bed-warm boudoir and lazy comfort (Image 59).[35] At the same Salon, visitors could therefore see two very different presentations of the motif.

34 *Mercure de France*, September 1739, p. 2222; Nicolas Lancret, *The Four Times of Day: Morning*, 1739, oil on copper, 28.3 × 36.4 cm, National Gallery, London (NG 5867).

35 Larmessin's engraving from 1741 was given an epigram by 'Monsieur Roy': 'En Sortant de gouter les douceur de Morfée / Ce leger passetems pour elle ouvre le jour / Les Soins de la Parure auront bientost leur tour / Et l'Art a la Beaute va dresser un Trofée.' In de Larmessin's engraving, the décolletage has been

When Count Carl Gustaf Tessin took up his position as ambassador in Paris in 1739, he brought his wife, Ulrika Lovisa Sparre, and her cousin's children, Carl and Charlotta (Lotta) Sparre, with him. The sojourn in Paris made a strong impression on the twenty-year-old Lotta Sparre, who eagerly participated in the French capital's range of amusements. She also probably had the opportunity to attend prestigious toilette receptions there.[36] After returning home to Stockholm, she quickly placed orders for a series of coveted French products – stockings, gloves, shoes, jewellery, pomade and perfume.[37] During her years in Paris, she had acquired specialist knowledge of which retailers sold which items and which contacts needed to be activated to carry out the orders.[38] A portrait of her from 1746, by Swedish pastellist Gustaf Lundberg, includes clear echoes of her time in France (Image 60). Admittedly, there is no dressing table in the picture, but the thin peignoir she is wearing nevertheless creates associations with this set of motifs. Her casual pose and informal clothing indicate that she was depicted during her morning toilette, but in the background we can glimpse a sundial which shows that it is already approaching midday.[39] The epigram attached to the portrait hints that the lazy woman is comfortably following the path of the sun and doing as she pleases, from *levér* to *dinér*.[40]

made less visible, Paul Ackroyd, Ashok Roy and Humphrey Wine, 'Nicolas Lancret's The Four Times of Day', *National Gallery Technical Bulletin*, Vol. 25 London 2004, p. 54.

36 Gunnar W. Lundberg, 'La charmante rose Carl Gustaf Tessins nièce', *Vision och gestalt. Studier tillägnade Ragnar Josephson*, Stockholm 1958, pp. 150–4. Lotta Sparre had her portrait painted by Donat Nonotte and Jean Marc Nattier in 1741, and was drawn by François Boucher and Jean Baptiste Massé. On her way home from Paris, she was also portrayed by Antoine Pesne; Lundberg 1958, pp. 153–61.

37 Johanna Ilmakunnas, *Ett ståndsmässigt liv. Familjen von Fersens livsstil på 1700-talet*, Stockholm 2012.

38 Ilmakunnas 2012, p. 209. The Von Fersens had five daughters, who were brought up to live in an inherited upper-class role and engage in corresponding consumption behaviour. The daughters got married between 1770 and 1774, and their dressing table items made of silver stood out in their dowries, both symbolically and economically. Christina Augusta's silver dressing table wares commanded a high value: 7,600 daler copper coins, p. 230. Carl Gustaf Tessin also utilised his contacts to continue making purchases after returning home to Sweden; Karl Asplund, 'En gammal mans dröm om Paris', *Gustavianskt. Studier kring den gustavianska tidens kulturhistoria tillägnade Sigurd Wallin på hans femtioårsdag*, Stockholm 1932, p. 342.

39 The painting can be compared to Gilles-Edmé Petit's engraving *Le midy*, in which the woman is correctly fully dressed for the day, while Lotta Sparre is comfortably and *à la mode* still wearing the peignoir seen in *Le matin*. See the engraving *Midday. A Lady Setting Her Watch*, 31.1 × 21.7 cm, Metropolitan Museum of Art, (53.600.1043).

40 Both Tessin and his friend from his years in Paris, author Alexis Piron, wrote epigrams for the portrait. See Lundberg 1958, p. 166, and Sander, Fredrik, *Nationalmuseum. Bidrag till taflegalleriets historia*, Stockholm (1872) 1878, p. 41: 'One sees the sundial but wishes to glimpse the beautiful woman. Such a long time left until the toilette hour. Alas, the hour for dinner and for the siesta's nap are well marked here with the narrow shadow, but not the time for the pleasures of the heart.'

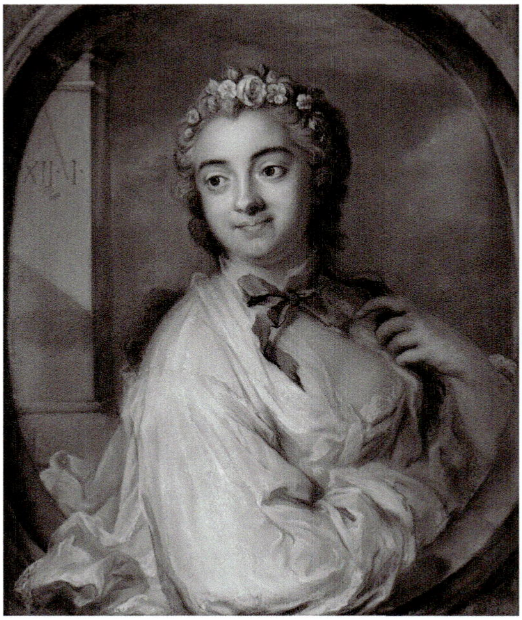

60. Gustaf Lundberg, *Charlotta Fredrika Sparre, grevinna von Fersen* (1719–1797). Pastel, 67 × 53 cm. Private ownership. Photo: Stockholms Auktionsverk.

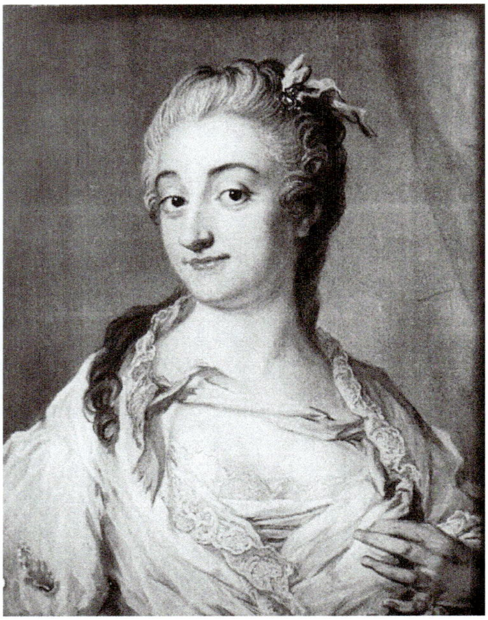

61. Gustaf Lundberg, *Christina Helena Löwen* (1724–1764). Pastel. Private ownership. Photo: SPA.

The portrait was intended to be displayed in Carl Gustaf Tessin and Queen Lovisa Ulrika's planned gallery of beauties at Drottningholm Palace.[41] The maids of honour included Christina Helena Löwen, and she was also portrayed *en déshabillé* by Gustaf Lundberg in 1746 for the gallery of beauties (Image 61). According to the painting's epigram, she is portrayed as a milliner in her boutique, and the gesture is an allusion to the coquettish frivolity that they were associated with in the eighteenth century.[42] In a letter from Charlotta Fredrika Hamilton af Hageby to Tessin's niece Brita Christina Sparre in July 1746, it emerges that the portrait's epigram was deemed accurate and amusing, but also worthy

41 Laine, Merit, 'Skönhetsgalleriet på Drottningholm', Merit Laine and Carolina Brown, *Gustaf Lundberg 1695–1786. En porträttmålare och hans tid*, Stockholm 2006, pp. 182–9; Ragnar Josephson, *Tidskrift för konstvetenskap*, Stockholm 1922, p. 27.

42 Alexis Piron, *Oeuvres Complettes d'Alexis Piron*, VII, Paris 1776, p. 131; Sander 1872, p. 42. Tessin's epigram is reproduced in Sander 1878, pp. 42 and 118; Laine 2006, p. 186. In contemporary eighteenth-century sources milliners were associated with youth, beauty, sensuousness and desire; Jones, Jennifer Michelle, *Sexing La Mode. Gender, Fashion and Commercial Culture in Old Regime France*, Oxford 2004, pp. 155–60. Without merchandise and alone in the picture, the encounter appears to be exclusively between the portrayed woman and her viewer, and thereby also an ambiguous signal that what she has to offer is what the viewer sees, as clarified by her gesture.

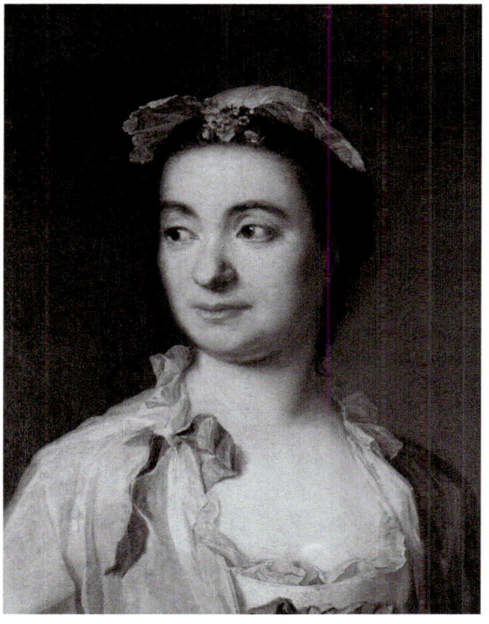

62. Johan Henrik Scheffel, *Anna Helena Celsing* (1725–1795). Oil on canvas, 49 × 38 cm. Private ownership. SPA (1925:1178).

of admiration and respect.[43] The portraits of the maids of honour referred to French dressing table culture, yet they were restrained statements about it. The cluttered dressing table and the lavish fashion items have been left outside of the pictorial space.

Lundberg's portraits are in that respect representative of a Swedish version of the elegant French dressing table genre within portraiture. Another example is the portrait created by Johan Henrik Scheffel in the 1750s of Anna Helena Celsing wearing a peignoir, in the morning's casual state of undress, *déshabillé* (Image 62). She turns away, deep in thought, perhaps to look at a mirror or dressing table outside of the scene. The peignoir indicates that she belongs to an elegant upper-class culture, but the portrait also expresses a distinct unpretentiousness. Another Swedish portrait that is linked to this set of motifs is Johan Joachim Streng's painting of Ulrica Stenbock from 1753 (Image 63). The young countess is leaning on a dressing table while balancing a beauty patch (mouche) on her extended forefinger. The artist has borrowed the composition from one of the era's more widespread pictures (Image 64). Gilles-Edmé Petit's engraving *Le matin. La dame à sa toilete* was in turn created after one of the paintings in the suite of the hours of the day

43 'The milliner amuses me greatly.' Brita Stina Sparre (1720–1776), Riksarkivet, Börstorpsamlingen (RA/720132.014), E 3099.

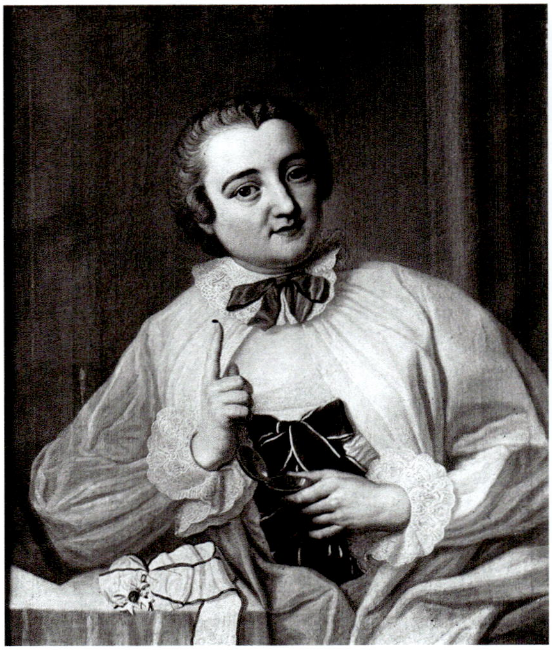

63. Johan Joachim Streng, *Ulrica Stenbock* (1732–1783), 1753. Oil on canvas, 74 × 62 cm. Private ownership (SPA 1919-411).

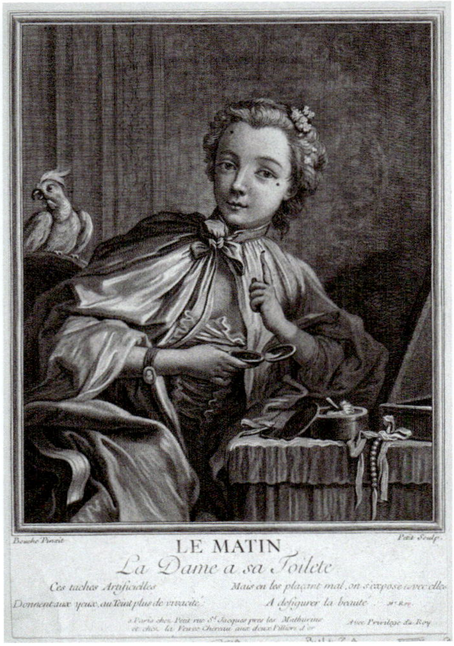

64. Gilles-Edmé Petit after François Boucher, *Le matin. La dame à sa toilete*. Engraving, 31.5 × 21.6 cm. The Metropolitan Museum of Art, New York (53.600.1042).

by François Boucher from 1734.[44] Streng's portrait follows this model closely but has also been simplified and altered. The powder box and powder puff, comb and necklace have been removed from the dressing table and replaced by the star of an order with a white ribbon in the foreground of the painting.[45] The Vadstena Noble Maiden Diocese offered unmarried noblewomen a secure annual pension, and in the portrait, the star of the order is highlighted as an important status symbol.[46] Although the portrait poses were borrowed from Continental upper-class fashion,

44 At the auction held in 1771 after Carl Gustaf Tessin's death, a painting was sold in a gilt ornamentally carved frame: 'A women performs her toilette, with a parrot on the armrest of her chair, original. Painted in grisaille or grey on grey by Boucher' (Sander 1872, p. 63; Ananoff 1976, vol. 1, nos. 111–14).

45 There is a brief comment on the portrait in Roosval 1910, p. 38.

46 As a member of the Vadstena Noble Maiden Diocese, Ulrica Stenbock was less dependent on a man or relatives. Boucher's model displays another relationship – next to the hand holding the mouche box, the woman's naked arm is adorned with a miniature medallion. When Boucher revisited the motif in 1758 in a portrait of the Marquise de Pompadour, the marquise's bracelet featured the king's portrait, directly next to the rouge box that she is holding. In an additional variation on the motif from 1769, the mouche box features a portrait miniature of a man. These were the men who the depicted women aimed to please, but the 'diocese maiden' Ulrica Stenbck is free of these allusions in her portrait.

in Sweden they were characterised by more clearly marked restraint and perhaps also by a different ideal of virtue.[47]

Criticism of dressing table culture

Swedish portraits appear somewhat subdued in relation to French dressing table culture. Contradictory perceptions of the fashionable French lifestyle also developed in the course of the eighteenth century. The portrait commissions involved a series of deliberations; the pictures of the young women were to manifest their own and their families' ambitions and expectations of the future, yet stay within the framework of the convention. For these women, the biblical moral mirror for women *Biblisk Qwinno=Spegel* from 1750 by the clergyman Olof Kolmodin was possibly a more truthful and real mirror than that of French fashion. The well-directed receptions in dressing rooms in Paris belonged to a distant world, whereas the norms and values at the heart of the Christian ideal of virtue about what constituted a good daughter, wife and mother, were more influential in their Swedish everyday life. In the book's eighth edifying conversation between the 'daughter-in-law' and the 'mother-in-law', which concerns girls' education, it is stated that all wise and sensible men value diligence, virtue and decency higher than beauty in a wife: 'without artificial twists and turns, yes, without affected facial expressions and gestures'.[48] When the daughter-in-law wonders how a girl should deal with the natural urge to be beautiful, the mother-in-law's answer echoes the Age of Liberty's utilitarian approach: 'It is best to turn this desire into something good, to such an extent that she may gladly be as beautiful as she wishes, provided that she only embellishes herself with things that she has made.'[49] The words also included a reminder of the dangers that lurked in this wish to please through beauty. Pride – *Superbia* – was one of the seven deadly sins, in visual art often represented by an attractively dressed woman, spellbound by her own reflection.[50] When Ulrica Stenbock let the star of the Vadstena Noble Maiden Diocese take the place of the make-up jars, this was a sign in accordance with the educational exhortations that also characterised political debate. The portraits conformed to an older tradition, at the same time that they became part of a contemporary context.

47 Choices of portrait poses could also be a pecuniary issue: a half-length portrait, where the composition often avoided the depiction of hands, lowered the price. This concrete significance of the number of depicted hands in paintings is stated in the magazine *Svenska Parnassen*, 1784, p. 63.

48 Olof Kolmodin, *Biblisk Qwinno=Spegel*. Stockholm 1750, pp. 48f.

49 Kolmodin 1750, p. 52.

50 Carolina Brown, *Skönhetens mask. Historia om kropp och själ, ideal och verklighet*, Stockholm 2011, pp. 14–39; *Sedolärande Mercurius*, II, No. 23. 4 May 1731.

Paintings and engravings thereby illustrated an ambivalent relationship with fashion consumption in general and with the dressing table and its superficial make-up in particular. Cosmetics were associated with an upper-class privilege but could also be regarded as a false art of dissembling. The made-up face was a mask behind which the woman could hide her true self and thereby manipulate the world around her, seize power or set hearts on fire on dishonest grounds. Writers vented their concern in everything from religious educational literature to theatrical plays.[51] For example, a collection of useful conversations in a French–Swedish phrase book includes a conversation about 'a woman's beauty'. One of the men asks about a beautiful woman he has seen, while the other points out that the 'beauty' was only painted and stuck on, the body was corseted and padded, and even the beautiful blue eyes were made of glass.[52] The phrase book's sample conversation highlights norms surrounding female beauty but also displays a critical attitude to the French fashion that dominated the century that was now coming to an end. The perceptions of the French fashion were conveyed through the eyes of the outside viewer, in everything from travel phrase books, 'travelogues' and newspaper articles to epistolary novels. The narratives about the French nation's manners and customs were now joined by the depictions of the fashion and luxury consumption and their relationship with the morals and character of the French.

A recurring theme in these descriptions comprised the cultural contrasts between France and England, where the use of cosmetics recurred as an illustrative example. The extremes in the French court culture's use of make-up were compared to the English culture's more 'bourgeois' and 'natural' ideals.[53] In her article 'Cosmetic Differences: The Changing Faces of Britain and France', Lynn Festa shows how national identity was expressed in concrete terms in relation to the use of cosmetics in the eighteenth century and highlights observations made by people on their travels during that era.[54] In the depictions, the pure and 'natural' face was often

51 *Mercure de France*, 2 September 1786, pp. 6–18, published the characteristic story 'La toilette, conte poétique, imité de Pignotti, Florentin'. The aged beauty tries to revive the beauty and love of her youth with the help of make-up, while the man eventually realises that he has been worshipping a false image. The story is a paraphrase of the work by the popular poet Lorenzo Pignotti (1739–1812).

52 David Krutmejer, *Fransk parleur, eller vald samling af fransyska och svenska samtal, innehållande en praktisk vägledning för begynnare att tala franska språket,* Stockholm 1811, pp. 100f.

53 Martin 2009, pp. 75–6.

54 In 1718, Lady Mary Wortley Montagu claimed that Frenchwomen looked monstrously unnatural through all the make-up they used, Lynn Festa, 'Cosmetic Differences. The Changing Faces of Britain and France', *Studies in Eighteenth Century Culture*, Vol. 34, p. 27. Author Tobias Smollett described what he thought were the dirty make-up habits of the French in the account of his travels from 1766; Tobias Smollett, *Fransoserne Äro ej Hvad De Utropas För, Eller Utdrag af några strödda Bref. Författade Under en resa genom Frankriket,* Stockholm 1784, pp. 27–8; Tobias Smollet, *Travels through France and Italy*, London 1766, p. 61.

linked to what were seen as modest and innocent virtues in their own culture, and the made-up face to what were perceived as vices and faultitudes in the other culture. French aristocratic luxury and formality were contrasted with British informal and equal comfort.[55] Urban culture was contrasted with rural culture. The national traits were explained by, among other things, the differences in climate, which were also thought to explain the differences between the classes, their appearance and their actions in the different countries. Like English 'naturalness', corresponding Swedish modesty was ascribed a similar quality on the basis of the era's climatology.[56] Although Sweden was strongly influenced by French ideals, there was opposition to the extremes of French fashion among both Swedes and the British. An article in the newspaper *Stockholms Posten* on 8 July 1779 explained why the French influences that were spreading in Sweden were so unseemly:

> Here in the Nordic countries, where modesty has its real residence, refinement is not as free, perhaps undisciplined, as in other locations. Yet, it varies. The further from the capital city, the more modest. ... Nature has enveloped Swedes' virtue and seriousness so much, that they become ridiculous when they want to be anything other than Swedes. What is steadfast, decent and pure in a Nordic girl's mind and face, cannot withstand to be mixed with what is free, coquettish, lively and slightly impudent, which suits the composition of a girl born in the south.

According to the author, the coquettish game – 'un jeu inventé par la coquetterie' – which Mercier associated with the toilette of privileged Frenchwomen, clearly did not suit Swedish women's unassuming nature.[57] By 1779, the criticism of fashion's 'fuss and fripperies' had been expressed over and over again for a long time.[58] It was already an issue in the latter half of the seventeenth century, when French court fashion became established in Swedish upper-class culture.[59] In the

55 Marie Odile-Bernez, 'Comfort, the Acceptable Face of Luxury: an Eighteenth-Century Etymology', *Journal for Early Modern Cultural Studies*, 14, 2 (2014), pp. 3–21.

56 Climatology was developed by Charles-Louis de Secondat Montesquieu in *De l'esprit des loix*, Geneva 1748; Carl Frängsmyr, *Klimat och karaktär. Naturen och människan i sent svenskt 1700-tal*, [diss.], Stockholm 2000.

57 Olof von Dalin made ironic remarks about the applied coquetry associated with French fashion; *Then Swänska Argus*, N:o XXIX, Stockholm 1733.

58 Carl Michael Bellman, *Tankar om flickors ostadighet*, Stockholm 1758.

59 At the same time as the first French fashion plates started to be disseminated in Sweden, satire and criticism were formulated on the same theme. When government official and poet Israel Holmström emphasised natural beauty over the new artificial fashion in 1694, Georg Stiernhielm's poetry had already paved the way 40 years earlier. Israel, Holmström, *Samlade dikter*, I, *Kärleksdikter, förnöjsamhetsvisor, sällskapspoesi, dansvisor, burleska dikter, fabler, gåtor, spådomar, epigram*, Bernt Olsson, Barbro Nilsson & Paula Henriksson, Svenska Vitterhetssamfundet, Stockholm 1999, p. 223.

1730s, author Olof von Dalin sharpened the tone in the paper *Then Swänska Argus*. Strongly influenced by English but also contemporary French texts, he rephrased the international criticism for a Swedish context.[60] Carl Gyllenborg's play *Swenska Sprätthöken* (The Swedish fop) premiered in Stockholm in 1737. The satire showed how the French influence on fashion and lifestyle had consequences for the lives of the various characters, but also how it affected the relationships between the old and the new nobility. The play was performed again in 1752, with apparently maintained topicality. In an era that became increasingly characterised by social mobility and accessible consumer goods, luxury imports not only seemed to be a moral threat but also drained the nation's finances and in the long run threatened the very foundations of social order. Sumptuary laws and mercantile endeavours to curb the imports and facilitate domestic production and exports became burning political issues. The nobility, whose ultimate duty was to represent the nation, was to set an example of good judgement and demonstrate moderation and thrift in the consumption of foreign luxury.[61] Politician Anders von Höpken's speech on the utility of luxury in 1740 was an attempt to turn the luxury consumption into an advantage.[62] Without consumption, there was a threat of stagnation. The key was to find different routes, preferably within the country, for upper-class consumption. Powdered wigs differentiated the upper class from the lower class, but instead of taking the bread out of people's hands, the indispensable powder that was taxed as a luxury could be extracted from the newly discovered potato flour.[63]

As a young clerk at the war office in 1747, the twenty-four-year-old Carl Eric Wadenstierna published his translation of Florent Carton Dancourt's comedy *Le chevalier à la mode* from 1687.[64] The play is about a bourgeois woman who is driven by desire for social advancement, and in her superficial world, where a name, a carriage adorned with a coat of arms and a liveried footman blind you to reality, it is easy to be seduced by the 'fashionable dandy'. Wadenstierna translated the plot for the Stockholm stage concerning high society in the pleasure garden at Kungsträdgården. Dancourt's farce was well chosen for the era. Highly influenced

60 Also compare with Dalin's contemporary Carl Reinhold Berch (1706–1777) and his experiences during his youth in England in the 1730s: 'He arrived with the preconception, that many shared with him, to not regard anything as good that was not French. ... He saw a well-cultivated land, its people with well-being and cheer, who, without frippery and fuss, were polite and service-minded; without ostentation and finery, but smartly and properly dressed.', *Biographiskt Lexicon öfver namnkunnige svenska män*, II, Upsala 1836, p. 121.

61 Ilmakunnas 2012, p. 394.

62 Leif Runefelt, 'Från yppighets nytta till dygdens försvar – den frihetstida debatten om lyx', *Historisk Tidskrift*, 124:2, 2004, pp. 203–23.

63 Countess Eva De la Gardie was elected to the Royal Swedish Academy of Sciences in 1748, when she discovered the new areas of use for potatoes.

64 Florent Carton Dancourt, *Then A la Modiske Cavallieren. Comoedie uti Fem Öpningar*, Stockholm 1747.

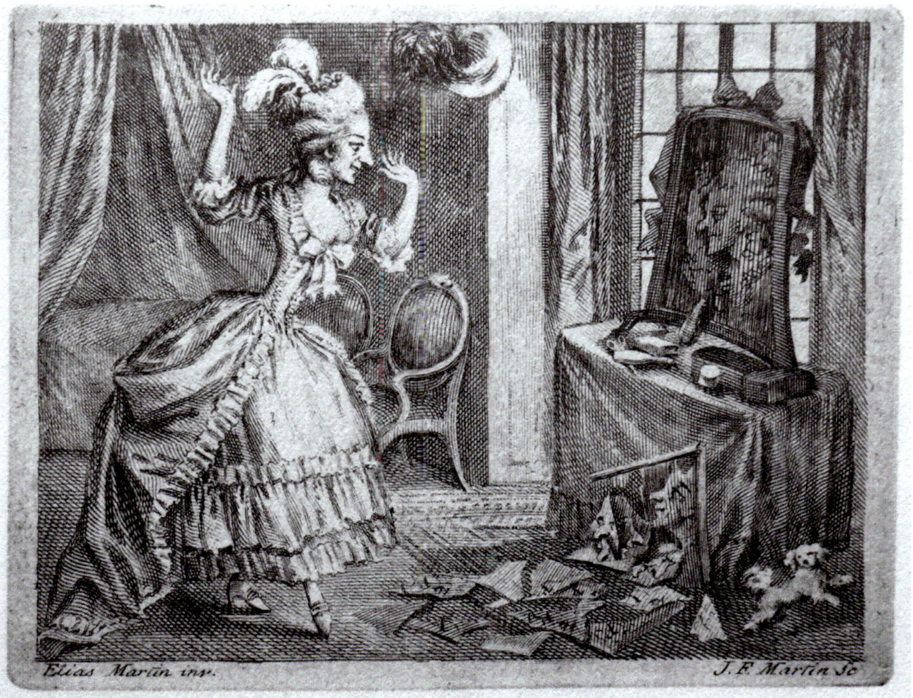

65. Johan Fredrik Martin after Elias Martin, vignette to Olof von Dalin's poem 'Den sanna Critiquen [The true critique]'. Engraving, 7.2 × 9.4 cm. From Olof von Dalin, *Poetiska arbeten*, Stockholm, 1783.

by the prevailing political debate, Wadenstierna probably regarded the play as a suitable contribution following on from the play *Swenska Sprätthöken*.

Criticism was also expressed in the era's multifaceted pictorial world. Dressing tables, make-up, powder and trinkets, as symbols of a francophile, superficial and materially obsessed upper-class culture recurred in many motifs (Image 65). The pictures contributed to creating frames of reference for the eighteenth century's various, and increasingly consumption-driven, social groupings, but they also highlighted the ambivalent role of the elite in an era imbued with growing criticism of consumption.[65] The dressing table mirror was a charged metaphor in the era's debate on luxury and subsequently also in the portraits of the Swedish social elite.

During the 1770s, King Gustaf III reintroduced the *levé* ceremony as one of several highly traditional and symbolically charged ways of staging his royal power. This

65 Morag Martin, *Selling Beauty. Cosmetics, Commerce, and French Society, 1750–1830*, Baltimore 2009 and Berg and Eger, 'The rise and fall of the luxury debates', in *Luxury in the Eighteenth Century*, Maxine Berg and Elizabeth Eger (ed), London 2003; Patrik Steorn, 'Modebilder i det svenska 1700-talets trycksakskultur: migrerande motiv och produktiva instabiliteter', *Biblis*, 2015 (69), pp. 10–8.

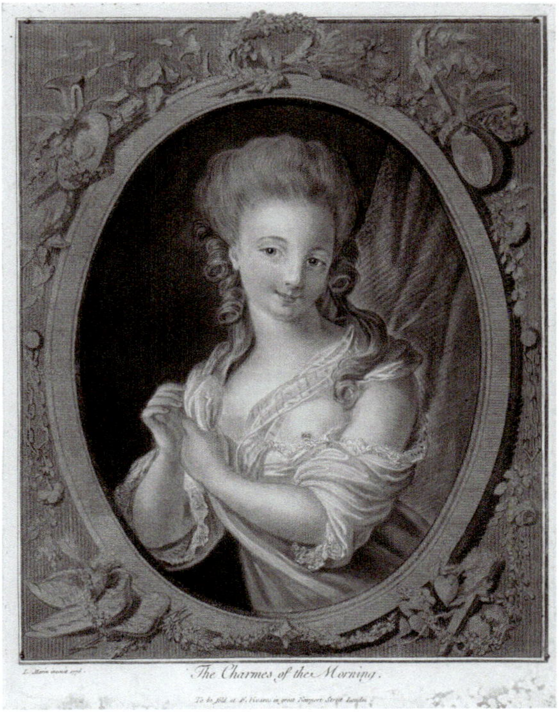

66. Louis-Marin Bonnet, *The Charms of the Morning*, 1776. Etching, 32.2 × 24.9 cm. Rijksmuseum, Amsterdam (RP-P-1959-362).

royal variation on '*la seconde toilette*' was a gesture towards French court rituals and the power of the ever-present French fashion. However, it was also criticised by the opposition. The lavish, exclusive court life was a drain on financial resources, and the *levé* ceremonies intensified the currents of opposition to the king. The fact that the normative French fashion was criticised in various respects could also be problematic in a wider upper-class circle that lacked close connections with the court. The commission of a portrait included expectations of representing the virtues and ideals of the class society, by being knowledgeable about French culture and by being a patriot. The portraits often struck a subtle balance between both of these roles. Being depicted at a dressing table could refer to an international upper-class culture, but also risked challenging the idea of unaffected 'Swedishness'. Although Frenchwomen contemporary with Charlotta Sparre had portraits painted that depicted them at well-stocked dressing tables, corresponding Swedish portraits were not as self-evident.[66]

66 There are a few exceptions, but these have a clear French link. These include the portrait miniature that Carl Gustaf Tessin commissioned of his sister-in-law Augusta Törnflycht, Countess Wrede-Sparre (oil on copper, 17 × 13.5 cm, private ownership), which Olof Arenius in 1737 based on a painting by Charles-Antoine Coypel from 1730. Coypel's painting titled '*La toilette*', was later engraved by Simon Duflos, 1747; Gunnar W Lundberg, 'Ett rokokoporträtt och dess tillkomst', *Fataburen*, Nordiska museet, Stockholm 1960, pp. 138–41.

In Niclas Lafrensen's portrait, Jacobina Psilanderhielm wears a thin peignoir over her soft silk dress (Plate 1). The viewer is likely to have associated this with the pictorial world that depicted mornings at the dressing table and the privileged comfort and French luxury that it was connected with. Wadenstierna's wife is also remarkably similar to the ideal woman in the contemporary fashion image (Image 66). However, the table that she is leaning on is not a dressing table but a sewing table. The virtue and utility that the literary 'moral mirrors' for women wanted to emphasise also appear to be relevant in this portrait. The beauty ideal that the peignoir evoked is here accompanied by the woman's diligence – she is making the decorations prescribed by fashion herself. She is presented as a good example with a complete lack of idleness and frivolity. But the symbols of pastoral love that frame the woman in the fashion image did not lack resonance in the real-life portrait. The unaffected attire evoked ideas of genuine emotion and unspoiled love. The pure, white linen became the symbol of innocent nature.[67] In the fashion image, eroticism lurks in this undressed and supposed naturalness, but in the portrait of Wadenstierna's exemplary wife, the informal attire instead symbolises the sincerity of the emotions.

'*Toilette kammaren*': The dressing room at Näs

The estate inventory for Wadenstierna's Stockholm residence mentions a lavish dressing table with veneer inlays and equipped with boxes of gold, silver, tortoiseshell and enamel. The table also had scent bottles embellished with gilt trim, soap boxes, hair tongs, toothpicks of gold and cut glass cologne bottles with silver stoppers.[68] The arrangement testifies that the era's dressing table culture also formed part of the Wadenstierna family's everyday life during their stays in the capital. Here, the piece of furniture created the conditions for participating in the city's social life with visits during the mornings and gatherings around the dressing table in the French manner. With its expensive materials and many functions, the table was created for both comfort and entertaining. There was also a combined secretaire and beside table with a mirror – an item of furniture that combined various functions and was possibly reminiscent of the fashionable *poudreuses* that elegantly met changing needs.[69]

At rural Näs Manor, the patterns of socialising appear to have been somewhat different. Recurring and daily visits by outsiders were here replaced with more

67 Brown 2012, pp. 202–3.

68 Riksarkivet, Näs Silverstolpeska arkivet, Personarkiven, vol. 60, Carl Eric Wadenstierna (1723–1787).

69 Ibid.

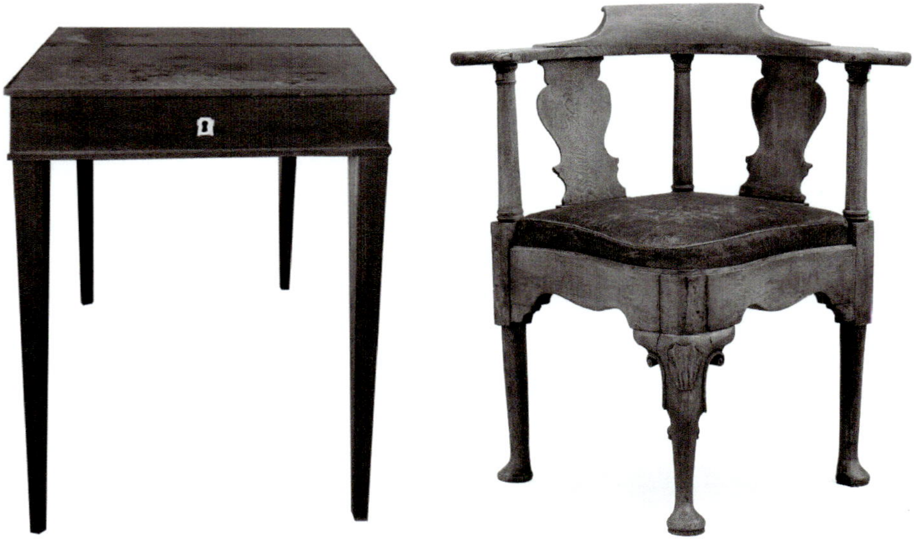

67. Multifunctional table and writing/dressing table chair from Näs, latter half of the eighteenth century. Private ownership.

informal socialising within the family and with the guests who visited the manor. The family undoubtedly also led an upper-class social life in the country, but it seems to have differed from that in the city. Through preserved documents, objects and furniture, a modified version of the era's dressing table culture emerges in their new home in Roslagen. An unassuming table is included among the effects at Näs (Image 67). The lid conceals drawers and possibly space for a mirror, while the table top is stained with a great many ink blots; perhaps it was used both when dressing and when doing writing exercises.

Wadenstierna's estate inventory from Näs mentions a dressing room with related furniture and objects.[70] This room included six armchairs, three chests of drawers for clothing, two pine tables, a linen cupboard, a washstand and a bench-bed where two of the maids slept.[71] But there is no mention here of an extravagant dressing table of the type found in the family's Stockholm residence.[72] The room instead

70 In Wadenstierna's estate inventory, the rooms follow an order that starts with the room to the right of the entrance hall. The dressing room follows after the cabinet, which was at the opposite southern gable end of the house. Riksarkivet, Näs Silverstolpeska arkivet, Personarkiven, vol. 60, Carl Eric Wadenstierna (1723–1787).
71 Riksarkivet, Näs Silverstolpeska arkivet, Personarkiven, vol. 60, Carl Eric Wadenstierna (1723–1787). In royal environments it was also common that the closest servant slept in the dressing room. See Vahlne 2012, pp. 189–91; ChengDiana, *The History of the Boudoir in the Eighteenth Century*, Montreal and Quebec 2011, p. 35.
72 At Count Claes Julius Ekeblad's country manor, Stola, there was admittedly a dressing table in the dressing room, but additional dressing tables were found in the 'Salon' and in the count's small drawing

appears to have served as a type of wardrobe room, in which garments and linens were ironed, starched and stored. It was also located in the lady's suite of rooms, adjacent to Fredrica Carleson's cabinet. A comparison can be made with Count Carl Gustaf Tessin's manor, Åkerö, where a similarly furnished room was located beyond Countess Tessin's cabinet and was used as a combined wardrobe and dressing room, as well as being a bedroom for the lady's maid.[73]

But despite the lack of a specific dressing table, preserved receipts show that there were purchases of powder, Venetian soap and lavender essence oil.[74] At Näs, the various dressing room functions seem to have been spread out in the manor's bedchambers and cabinets. The chests of drawers and tables of the dressing room could no doubt be equipped with mirrors and used for various phases of morning hygiene, make-up and dressing. Other parts of the morning toilette could take place elsewhere in the home. Carl Eric Wadenstierna himself stored a shaving case with razors, a mirror and a shaving box in his own chamber, which was also home to a mahogany washstand with space for a jug, basin and chamber pot. His desk chair could equally function as a dressing table chair (Image 67). In the billiards and library wing, the writing tables in the guest rooms were equipped with mirrors for equivalent needs.

Due to the lack of specific dressing tables, the bedside tables appear to have played an important role for comfort at Näs (Image 68). There were at least six lavish bedside cabinets in the main building's bedchambers, dressing room and guest rooms. Some were made of mahogany, as fashion dictated, and a couple of them featured intricate veneer inlays in coloured birch, jacaranda, brazilwood, citron wood and tinted maple.[75] The piece of furniture with its cupboards and drawers had a raised apron around the table top to prevent water spillage and could be complemented with washing vessels, hygiene articles and mirrors. One of the washstands at Näs is stated as having a built-in mirror and folding leaves on each side of a recessed wash basin.[76] As the bedside cabinets' Swedish name *kommod* suggests, from the French *commode* ('comfortable', but also 'chest of drawers'),

room, and dressing table chairs stood in each of the two library rooms, 'Inwentarium öfwer all befintelig Lös Egendom på STOLA … upprättadt den 10 Junii År 1796 i Högwölborne Herr Grefwen C. I. Ekeblads närwaro', Karlsson, William, *Ett svenskt herremanshem på 1700-talet. Clas Julius Ekeblads inventarium över Stola 1796*, Lund 1940, pp. 67ff.

73 Selling, Gösta, *Svenska herrgårdshem under 1700-talet*, Stockholm (1937) 1991, p. 128. The dressing room's significance for female 'self-fashioning' is discussed in Ruth Kenny, ''Apartments that are not too large': Pastel Portraits and the Spaces of Femininity in the English Country House', *Placing Faces. The Portrait and the English Country House in the Long Eighteenth Century*, Manchester 2013, pp. 143–6.

74 Riksarkivet, Näs Silverstolpeska arkivet, Personarkiven, vol. 60, Carl Eric Wadenstierna (1723–1787).

75 Sylvén, Torsten, *Mästarnas möbler. Stockholmsarbeten 1700–1850*, Stockholm 1996, p. 173.

76 Näsström, Gustaf, *Forna dagars Sverige*, III, *Kulturhistorisk bilderbok om frihetstid och gustaviansk tid*, Stockholm 1962, p. 150.

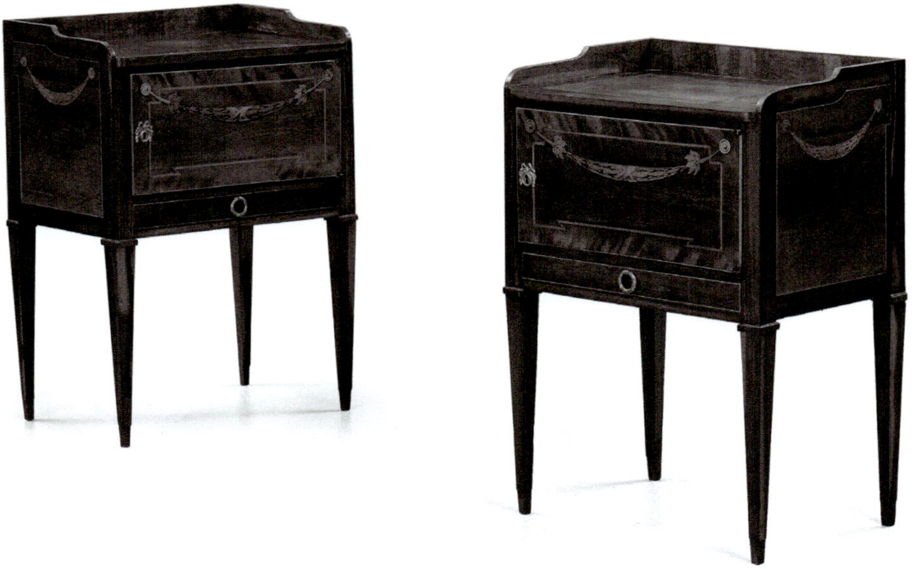

68. Georg Haupt, Wadenstierna's bedside cabinets, *c.* 1775. Veneered with jacaranda, citron wood, birch and maple, L 54 cm, W 38 cm, H 78 cm. Private ownership. Photo: Bukowskis.

this item of furniture was regarded as a concrete expression of the new culture of comfort in the latter part of the eighteenth century. The later prosaic word *pottskåp* (chamber pot cupboard) admittedly indicated another of its functions, but this piece of furniture should not be confused with the many and simple commode chairs called *nattstolar* in Swedish (literally, 'night chairs'), which were hidden away in box rooms and closets. The bedside cabinets at Näs were instead exclusive pieces of furniture, on which the shiny veneer and ornately inlaid laurel festoons diverted your thoughts to other subjects.[77] The mild, pleasant scents of the various types of wood were also thought to counteract other, less welcome odours.[78] With its different functions as a dressing table and bedside table, this item of furniture thereby met the demands that the era's fastidious upper-class consumers could place on both comfort and elegance.

The bedside cabinets appear to have taken over many of the dressing tables' functions. Their significance in Wadenstierna's newly furnished home is also seen in their exclusivity – two of the cabinets with intarsia decoration at Näs have

77 Compare Sofia Albertina's washstand in her contemporary bedchamber at Gripsholm Castle, *Möbelhistoria på Gripsholm*. Bo Vahlne (ed.), Stockholm 1986, pp. 76–7.

78 DeJean, Joan, *The Age of Comfort. When Paris Discovered Casual – And the Modern Home Begun*, New York 2009, p. 136.

been ascribed to Georg Haupt.[79] In all probability, they are part of the furniture that Wadenstierna ordered before moving into the main building in 1775. There, they were placed in the large bedchamber on each side of the Imperial bed with its showpiece bed cover made of silk. The room was the highlight of the home's suite of reception rooms and was clearly furnished to also serve as a room for socialising.[80] It contained a sofa, six armchairs and two tea tables – one made by Haupt and one with a faience tray from the Marieberg factory in Stockholm, which nicely complemented the room's tiled stove and large potpourri urn, which were also made by Marieberg. The stand for the faience tray was also made by Haupt, and with its veneered fleurons and laurel festoons, it was linked to the bedside cabinets and a woman's 'bureau' (chest of drawers) with inlays that also stood in the room.[81] These pieces of furniture with their decorative intarsia inlays by Haupt commanded a considerable value, and together with the room's lavish large mirror with its gilt frame and a pendulum clock with a gilt case, the overall impression must have been resplendent.[82]

By the time Georg Haupt's furniture arrived at Näs in 1775, he had already established himself as one of Sweden's foremost cabinetmakers with royal patronage and royal commissions.[83] Through the prestigious commission from Haupt's studio, Wadenstierna thereby manifested himself as wealthy, someone with taste and an appreciation of quality, and someone who supported the beneficial Swedish production of luxury goods. The bedside cabinets were not only elegant dressing tables but also key markers in the social life at Näs. Here, they were multifunctional pieces of furniture that to the initiated viewer offered several different functions and meanings.[84] The economic, social and cultural capital that they manifested – elite consumption, taste and cultivation – was formed in the interplay between the physical manor

79 Sylvén 1996, p. 173.

80 The status of the bedchamber as a reception room in accordance with French court culture stems from older traditions but was also highly topical within the contemporary French elite, Aurélie Chatenet-Calyste, 'A Feminine Luxury in Paris: Marie-Fortunée d'Este, Princesse de Conti (1731–1803)', *Luxury and Gender in European Towns*, 1700–1914, Deborah Simonton, Marjo Kaartinen and Anne Montenach, (ed.), New York 2015, p. 180.

81 Riksarkivet, Näs Silverstolpeska arkivet, Personarkiven, vol. 60, Carl Eric Wadenstierna (1723–1787).

82 Riksarkivet, Näs Silverstolpeska arkivet, Personarkiven, vol. 60, Carl Eric Wadenstierna (1723–1787); Asplund 1960, pp. 34–5.

83 By 1775 Haupt had established himself as a master with royal commissions and an extensive record of work from Amsterdam, Paris and London. The previous year, commissioned by King Gustaf III, he completed a minerals cabinet that was gifted to the Prince of Condé, Louis Joseph Bourbon. The washstands were accompanied by a piece of the French elite culture that Haupt's name was now associated with; Ljungström, Lars, *Georg Haupt. Gustav III:s hovschatullmakare*, Stockholm 2006, pp. 45–69.

84 Hellman, Mimi, 'Furniture, Sociability, and the Work of Leisure in Eighteenth-Century France', *Eighteenth-Century Studies*, vol. 32, no. 4, Baltimore 1999, pp. 415–45; *The Social Life of Things. Commodities in Cultural Perspective*, Arjun Appadurai (ed.), Cambridge 1986.

environment and the people who lived in it. Although the cabinets contained chamber pots and were used as bedside tables, they could also serve as elegant side tables together with the tea tables. In these environments, Haupt's bedside cabinets marked a melding of comfort, taste and representativeness. At Näs they were part of an intricate context, where furniture, clothes, body language and social hierarchies were united. The bedside cabinets and the modern comfort in these environments also required effective interplay in a hierarchically ordered social structure – that someone emptied the chamber pots, filled up the tea water and polished the mahogany.

The dressing room and Pehr Hilleström's paintings at Näs

The series of paintings that Wadenstierna commissioned from Pehr Hilleström in the early 1770s also came to be part of the new environment that was created at Näs. Hilleström's extensive and multifaceted oeuvre in the following decades captured several aspects of the Gustavian era, but with his genre scenes he above all became the era's foremost painter of interiors and home environments – from rustic kitchens and bourgeois cabinets to the drawing rooms of palaces and manors. The paintings that he created for Wadenstierna belong to this category and formed his first major commission. Without depicting the specific rooms at Näs, in various ways they nonetheless seem adapted to this particular environment. The paintings thereby appear to offer paths to deeper understanding of the life in the family's new home. Everyday tasks in the dressing room and during the morning toilette constitute a particularly important theme in the paintings. One starting point for Hilleström's interior scenes consisted of Boucher's and Chardin's oeuvres, which he first encountered during a study trip to Paris in the 1750s. Impressions from famous paintings such as *La marchande de modes* and *La toilette* also emerge in Hilleström's pictorial world, and several of his Boucher-inspired pictures include scenes with fashionable dressing tables. The motifs he created for Näs are also closely connected with this French pictorial world, yet they have a somewhat different focus.

Several of the paintings that Wadenstierna commissioned from Hilleström depict tasks and functions that probably could have been linked to the dressing room at Näs. It was primarily a room for handling clothes, storage and dressing, and the paintings correspondingly show clothes being prepared during the mornings in bedchambers and dressing rooms: one girl receives help to lace her corset, another ties a garter. A third painting depicts a moment's amusement amidst the tasks, with a girl telling someone's fortune using cards, while the pile of clothes waits on the adjacent chair. But they differ from Hilleström's other paintings on the theme because no dressing table is included. Instead, the washstand or bedside cabinet has taken its place – just like in real life at Näs. In one of the paintings, a mirror of

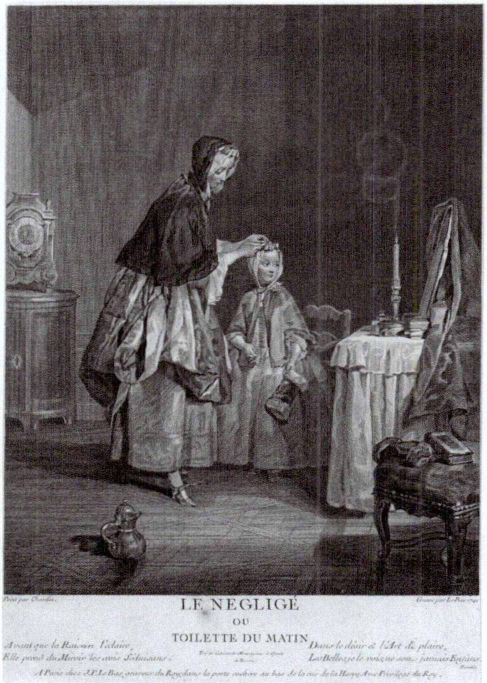

69. Jacques-Philippe Le Bas after Jean-Baptiste Siméon Chardin, *Le negligé ou toilette du matin*, 1741. Engraving, 37.2 × 25.7 cm. The Metropolitan Museum of Art, New York (53.600.528).

the type named in the estate inventory as a 'bedside mirror' has been placed on the cabinet. These elements in the motifs can evidently be perceived as an adaptation to the Wadenstierna family's interiors at Näs, where the paintings were to be displayed. The intention was probably to create recognition and identification with the depicted scenes. The paintings appear to be comments on the family's own everyday life with the two teenage daughters, aged thirteen and seventeen when the paintings were created. As mentioned, the suite of everyday scenes also included a painting in which Wadenstierna's daughters doing needlework were the models, and a few items in the pictures have also been identified as objects that Wadenstierna actually owned.[85] Hilleström clearly seems to have known that the rurally located Näs Manor was furnished with bedside cabinets rather than dressing tables.

However, the furniture rendered in the paintings lacks the classicising Gustavian shapes that characterised Haupt's new furniture.[86] The paintings' cabinets and

85 Regarding the painting *2ne Fröknar Wadenstiernas portraiter – i Conversation*, see Chapter 2. Realistic elements in Hilleström's paintings at Näs are discussed in Sven Drakenberg, 'Pehr Hilleström och det gustavianska hemmet', *Rig*, Stockholm 1929, pp. 76–8.

86 Hilleström was possibly unaware of Wadenstierna's commission of furniture for Näs when the suite of pictures was created. Wadenstierna's Stockholm residence, where the furnishings were installed earlier, was perhaps a more probable source of inspiration instead.

console tables indicate an older design idiom. Armchairs with curved legs stand next to simpler ladderback chairs, and the corset lies waiting on a tabouret with an upholstered seat, while the girl with her garter rests her foot on a homemade wooden stool (Image 71). Hilleström's lingering in Rococo idiom can be seen as a conscious reference to Chardin's and Boucher's pictorial worlds, a way of alerting the viewer to the shared points of reference that the famous artists' motifs constituted and the ideals that they were associated with. The combination of simple, everyday utilitarian goods and more upper-class furnishings simultaneously gave the interiors credibility, without being authentic depictions of Wadenstierna's home. Even though the scenes with the morning activities referred to an established tradition with accepted pictorial conventions, Wadenstierna and his family would have been able to nod in recognition at the rooms' untidy piles of clothes and rolled-up sleeves.

In Hilleström's paintings, the clothes and fabrics often catch the eye, and in comparison with them, the furniture plays somewhat more of a background role. Long curtains have been pushed aside to let daylight in from the windows. The light falls over the fabrics' folds and creases and it accentuates their colours and qualities. The coarser ticking and linen fabrics of the unmade bed are illuminated, as a contrast to the gauzy linen of blouses and caps. The skirts' shining silk, smooth or pattern-woven, with soft fullness and weight, is juxtaposed with rigid corsets and stays or thicker qualities in lined coats, hats and shoes. Details such as stockings, garters and bows are rendered through insightful observation. In the pictures, Hilleström provides a detailed description of the textile goods that surrounded an upper-class woman in everyday life. This was also an important aim of the dressing room and bedchamber interiors – to present the rooms in which many of the home's expensive textile items were gathered.

As stated, Hilleström was a trained weaver and thereby had special knowledge of textiles, which is clearly shown in his paintings. He made extensive use of the effects offered by the fabrics' folds, shadows and accents of colour in the compositions. But the paintings also show his awareness of prevailing fashion and its significance for his clientele. The pale-red coat that recurs in the foregrounds of the paintings, on the top of the pile of clothes draped over the chairs' backrests, was one of many references to current fashion. This was also a garment associated with various morning activities. A pelisse, a fur-lined sleeveless coat, wide enough to cover the top part of the era's voluminous skirts, could be worn both outdoors and indoors, and in the era's French fashion images, it is part of the elegant woman's informal yet presentable morning attire, or '*négligé du matin*'.

Engravings and newspapers conveyed current fashions. For example, *Galerie des modes et costumes français* published the latest styles of 'pelisse de satin doublée de poil' (Image 70). But Hilleström could also rely on a model that he

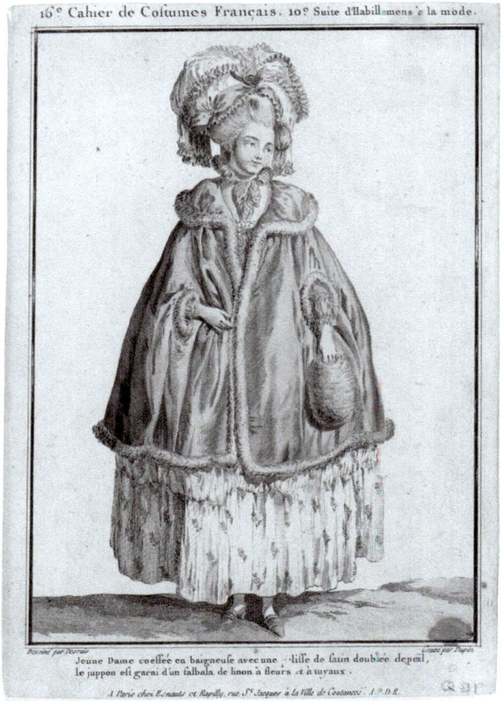

70. Nicolas Dupin after Claude-Louis Desrais, *Jeune dame coeffée en baigneuse, avec une pilisse de satin*. Engraving, 25.9 × 18.1 cm. From *Galerie des modes et costumes français*, 1778, 16e. Rijksmuseum, Amsterdam (RP-P-2009-2105).

knew in detail. In François Boucher's *La toilette* from 1742, a pale-red pelisse lined with dark fur hangs over the backrest of the chair in the far right of the pictorial space (Image 72). The fur-lined garment on the chair emphasises that the room is warm enough for the woman to take it off – a concrete marker of privileged comfort. Hilleström directly transferred the Parisian arrangement to the scenes in Wadenstierna's Näs Manor. He probably correspondingly used a French artwork as a model when he created the painting of a woman lacing a girl's corset for Näs (Plate 15). Chardin's painting *Le negligé ou toilette du matin* from 1741 depicts a woman arranging a young girl's head covering while the girl looks contentedly in the mirror on the dressing table (Image 69).[87] Hilleström modified the scene by removing the dressing table and replacing it with a chair cluttered with clothes. The chemises, corsets, peignoirs, dressing gowns and pelisses that indicated the theme of Hilleström's dressing room pictures were

87 The painting had reached Sweden through Carl Gustaf Tessin's acquisition, and the motif was distributed through Jacques-Philippe Le Bas' engraving from the same year. Charles Étienne Pesselier's epigram for Le Bas' engraving states how the woman, irrespective of age and sense, seeks the beauty that seduces and pleases: 'Avant que la Raison l'éclaire, Elle prend du Miroir les avis séduisans; Dans le désir & l'art de plaire, Les Belles, je le vois, ne sont jamais Enfans.' Charles Étienne Pesselier's verse was published in *Mercure de France* in December 1741, pp. 2697–9.

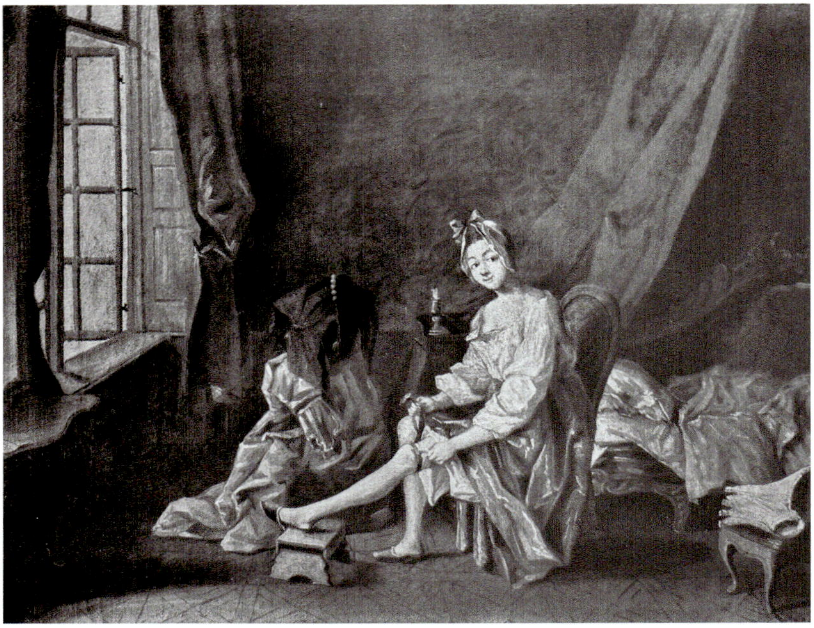

71. Pehr Hilleström's *Ett fruent: som knyter sitt strumpeband* (A woman tying her garter) belonged to Wadenstierna's Näs Manor in the mid-eighteenth century. Oil on canvas, 32 × 41 cm. Private ownership.

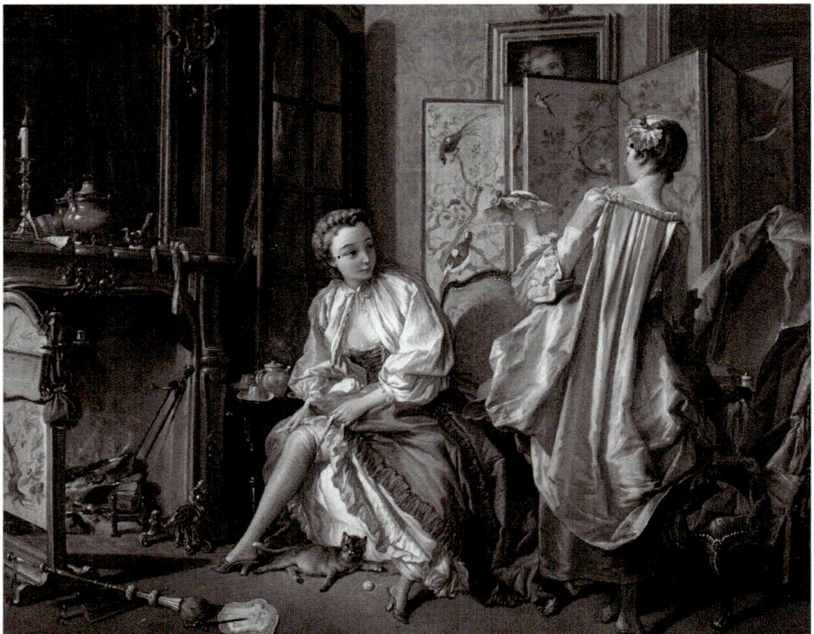

72. François Boucher, *La toilette*, 1742. Oil on canvas, 52.5 × 66.5 cm. Museo Thyssen-Bornemisza, Madrid, inv. no. 58 (1967.4). Credit/Provider Musée du Louvre, https://creativecommons.org/publicdomain/mark/1.0/.

therefore key markers.[88] The lack of dressing tables at Näs, in both Hilleström's suite of paintings and in the manor itself, meant that the focus has here been moved from this high-status piece of furniture. The elegant bedside cabinets could be glimpsed in the pictures, but here the focus has above all been placed on the expensive textiles. As described, clothes and fabrics played a central part in morning toilette rituals and were equally strong status markers. The depiction of the informal, yet exclusive, morning attire conveyed both modern comfort and social class.

The Wadenstierna family's estate inventories show that these clothes and fabrics were not only part of the artist's pictorial world and what he borrowed from the worlds of other artists. The real significance of the textile goods for the client and his family may have also contributed to them gaining a prominent place in the paintings. The stock of linens, just as the quality of everyday clothes and bed linen, is meticulously noted in the inventories, and the value of the clothes was often remarkably high. One of Jacobina Psilanderhielm's twelve silk dresses mentioned in the estate inventory from 1769 commanded a value equal to the bedchamber's large Imperial bed and bedclothes. The value is also stated in the manor's accounts for the Crown, where a special tax on silk fabric was applicable to these items.[89] The highly valued pink silk coat lined with squirrel fur that is also listed in the estate inventory may well be connected with the pelisse fashion that Hilleström referred to in his paintings.[90] Jacobina Psilanderhielm's five chemises and two peignoirs may have also been similar to the one depicted in Hilleström's painting *Ett Fruent: som snör en flicka*, intended for Näs (Plate 15). She is also wearing one of these gauzy peignoirs in Lafrensen's posthumous portrait miniature (Plate 1).

The value ascribed to these garments is a reminder that they also fulfilled an important representative function, far from the attitude in more recent times that negligee-type clothes belong to a separate, private sphere. Although the Wadenstierna family did not receive visitors in their dressing room at Näs, Hilleström's paintings served a somewhat similar purpose. They offered, not only family members but all guests who entered chambers and cabinets at Näs, an idea of the family's morning activities. The dressing gowns that are included in the estate inventories were also explicit expressions of the social dimensions and appurtenant material status of the culture of comfort. Wadenstierna's silk dressing gown, a valuable garment later inherited by his daughter Carolina, can be compared to his court

88 The status that a pelisse encompassed is also seen in the following comment in *Sedolärande Mercurius*, vol. 3, No. 6, 22 June 1731: '[It] was not enough to be rich, she also wanted to wear a velvet fur and sit at the front during the party.'

89 Näs Silverstolpeska arkivet, Personarkiven, Vol. 2, Gårdsarkivet. Old cash books.

90 The same applies to a similar one in black velvet with ermine edging, Riksarkivet, Näs Silverstolpeska arkivet, Personarkiven, vol. 60, Carl Eric Wadenstierna (1723–1787).

dress in terms of economic value.[91] It is beyond all doubt that both his and his wife's dressing gowns were part of the elegant and upper-class clothing *en déshabillé*. In a painting depicting a morning visit at the Müller family from the 1780s, Hilleström further confirms this fact. The host couple receive guests at the tea table: Müller, a senior official from the board of trade, is wearing a dressing gown, cap and slippers made of silk, and his wife is wearing a peignoir and modern night cap *à la dormeuse*.[92] A corresponding scene could have taken place at the home of Wadenstierna, the senior government official.

Toilette in a time of change

This chapter has highlighted the dressing table as a hub for many issues and shifting themes. The table was a symbol of French luxury consumption, but also a space onto which to project the era's moral, social, economic and political issues. The fact that Swedish portraits generally avoided the dressing table mirror and that Wadenstierna's dressing room at Näs lacked dressing tables, was probably a consequence of such deliberations. Depictions and interior decoration were the result of several deliberations that were less about personal preferences or economic possibilities and more about the norms and conventions that accompanied social standing. Nevertheless, through his choices, Wadenstierna could signal both social ambitions and political standpoint. The choice of Hilleström's motifs perhaps ultimately also reflected the father's care for his young daughters, who would soon be married off and into a circle in their social class in which they should not appear ignorant of what awaited them and was demanded of them.

But Hilleström's paintings were not the only objects that reflected everyday life at Näs. In the manor's library, the Wadenstierna sisters were also able to gain insight into what was expected of them and the role that the morning tasks and the dressing table culture played in privileged upper-class life. The list of books at Näs includes a number of titles directly linked to this subject. There were examples of both edifying literature for young people and fictional texts that described milliners and the luxurious, comfortable and intensive social life led in the *'cabinet de toilette'* of the French elite.[93] For instance, a volume from 1777, with the fictitious correspondence between Countess Rivière and Baroness Neufpont, states how the countess, *en déshabillé,* receives the milliners at her toilette and how they offer

91 Riksarkivet, Näs Silverstolpeska arkivet, Personarkiven, vol. 60, Carl Eric Wadenstierna (1723–1787).

92 *Förmiddagsbesök hos kommerserådet Jörgen Kristoffer Müller*, 1780s, Cederblom 1927, Image 42.

93 In Stéphanie Félicité de Genlis, *Théâtre À L'Usage Des Jeunes Personnes*, IV, Paris 1780, p. 111, the Wadenstierna sisters at Näs could read the comedy '*La marchande des modes*'.

exquisite fabrics, lace, jewellery and diamond-encrusted mouche boxes.[94] In other books in the library, they could further deepen their knowledge of the various accoutrements that belonged to the privileged toilette – peignoirs, slippers and canapé sofas – but also read about erotically charged scenes where blushing young men on social calls were drawn in among scantily dressed women at the dressing tables.[95] The library also included the manor's own volumes of Mercier's *Tableau de Paris* with the informative descriptions of '*la seconde toilette*'. The fact that the Wadenstierna sisters were familiar with the era's ideas of the French-influenced dressing table culture is also evident from their own notes. In her poetry book, Sophia Wadenstierna has noted a few lines from a French song about precisely this – about all the tempting fashion accessories, but also about how these trinkets proved to be superfluous to the beautiful country girl Jeannetton.[96]

Despite the winds of change in the late eighteenth century, Pehr Hilleström did not abandon the dressing room motifs. In his 1798 painting *Morgontoilette*, only the corner of the dressing table mirror rim is visible, discreetly, at the edge of the picture (Image 73). On the cluttered table, one single powder box is a reminder of the toilette, but there is no lavish silverware or expensive lace. The eye-catching details are instead the table's piles of books and a strategically placed crucifix. Perhaps this hinted at the moral conflict that often recurred in public debate on women's aptitude for superficial pastimes, fashion and consumption in contrast with more edifying and educational tasks.[97]

This was also related to changed attitudes to the era's major issues in the last few years of the eighteenth century. The levelling of social classes had become increasingly noticeable, and old social structures and forms of expression were changing. Fashion had also changed, and the former significance of make-up in the manifestation of upper-class identity had gradually declined by a considerable extent. Late-eighteenth-century classicising currents, combined with new bourgeois attitudes to nature and culture advocated other ideals. The cluttered and overheated

94 Mlle Poulain de Nogent, *Lettres de Mme la comtesse de La Rivière à Mme la baronne de Neufpont, son amie*, Paris 1777, I, pp. 278–83.

95 Descriptive details such as '*caraco élégant*', '*jolie mule*', '*vaste canapé*' drew the reader's attention to the accessories that belonged to the privileged dressing room, Pierre-Jean-Baptiste Nougaret, *Aventures Diverses, &C. Avec quelques Pièces curieuses & fort rares: Le tout fidèlement recueilli par M. Nougaret*, Paris 1781, p. 8. Read about how the canapé was associated with a form of comfort with virtually erotic overtones in DeJean 2009, pp. 113–15.

96 The verses possibly allude to Marie Justine Benoîte Favart's popular vaudeville *Les encorcelés, ou Jeannot et Jeannette, parodie des Surprises de l'amour* from 1757, which contained songs that were widely distributed. Fashion images such as 'Bonnet à la Jeannot' and 'Coëffure à la Jeannette' were also inspired by the comedyç; *Suite des Coeffures à la Mode en 1783*, Esnauts et Rapilly, Paris, 1783.

97 Jean Jacques Rousseau's attitude to women and their role contributed in particular to the debate; J.J. Rousseau, *Emile*, II, 1762, p. 161.

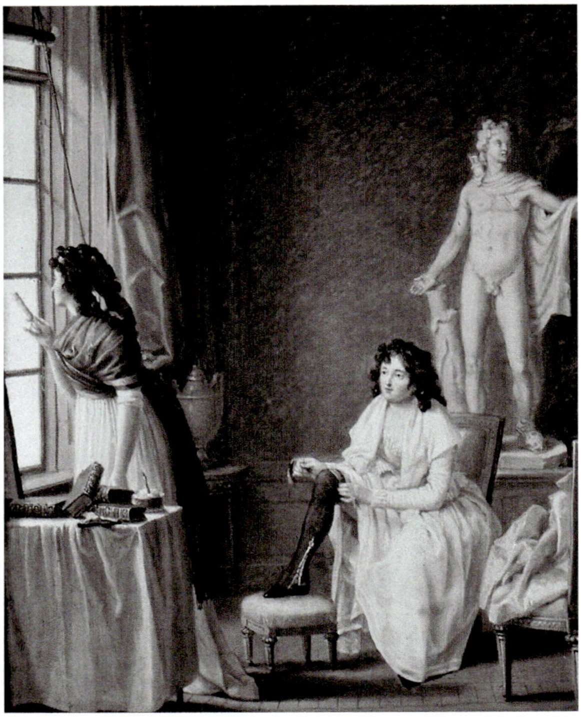

73. Pehr Hilleström, *Morgontoilette*, 1798. Oil on canvas. Östergötlands museum (B 625).

atmosphere in Boucher's *La toilette* had cooled down fifty years later in Hilleström's enlightened morning toilette. The aristocratic '*seconde toilette*' as described by Mercier just a few years earlier, now seemed antiquated and artificial. In Anna Maria Lenngren's poem 'Toiletten' from 1797, the ageing countess symbolises the artificiality and hierarchical role-play of bygone days.[98] Her French phrases, just as her white lead and carmine red make-up, evoke nothing but ridicule. Instead, the women in Hilleström's painting the following year, dressed in white and free of conspicious make-up, represent the new era.

98 Anna Maria Lenngren, 'Toiletten', *Stockholms Posten* 1797.

5. At the games tables

Abstract
The chapter is based on one of the paintings by Pehr Hilleström at Näs Manor, *Ett Fruent: spår i kort* (A woman fortune-telling with cards). A woman puts out a handful of cards on a small folding surface of a bureau. The temporary arrangement shows how different games became a constantly recurring activity in everyday and social life, in Europe as in Sweden. The upper-class home was adapted, in terms of layout and furnishings, in relation to an expanding gaming culture. The gaming tables at Näs were intended for different and particular games and were also associated with different forms of status, which in turn assigned men and women different roles and spheres.

Keywords: billiards and card games, polite society, eighteenth-century painting, conversation piece, manners and morality

The eighteenth century's popular games often focused on the impact of chance or fate on people's lives. In the games of chance, a card was turned, a die was cast or a lot was drawn, and the outcome of chance determined wealth, love or happiness. In Hilleström's painting at Näs – *Ett Fruent: spår i kort* (A woman fortune-telling with cards) – a woman is seated at the pull-out leaf of a chest of drawers, on which she is laying out rows of playing cards (Image 74).[1] She pauses, mid-gesture, with a card in each hand. The scene is like a moment captured in time, where the woman's clothing, with an unbuttoned dressing jacket and lace bonnet, shows that it is still morning. The curtain has been pushed to one side and left hanging over one edge of the chest of drawers, and garments lying on the adjacent ladderback chair have partly fallen onto the floor. A bed can be glimpsed in the chiaroscuro of the background next to a bedside cabinet with a dressing table mirror standing on it. Games and amusements were clearly also part of life in the mornings.

The title of the painting in the artist's list tells us about the eighteenth century's amusements and pastimes, possibly also with a more serious undertone about

1 Cederblom, Gerda, *Pehr Hilleström som kulturskildrare*, I, Stockholm 1927, Image 15.

Brown, C., *Comfortable Everyday Life at the Swedish Eighteenth-Century Näs Manor.*
Taylor & Francis Group, 2024
DOI 10.5117/9789048562374_CH05

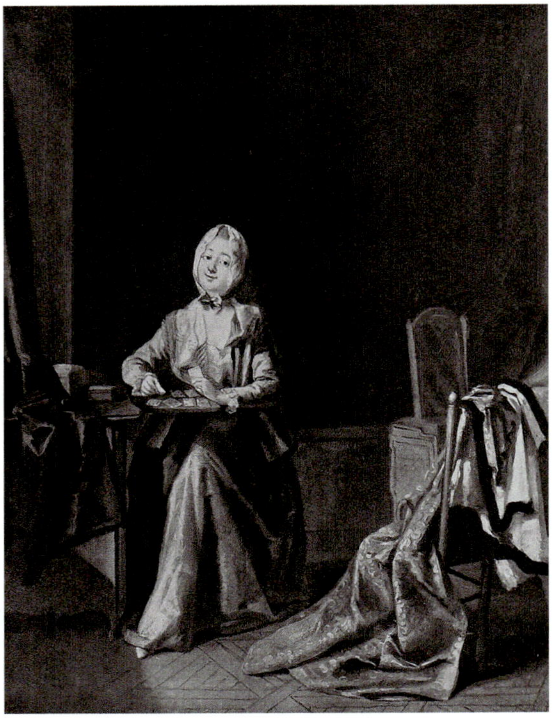

74. Pehr Hilleström, *Ett Fruent: spår i kort* (A woman fortune-telling with cards) was part of Wadenstierna's collection at Näs in the 1770s. Oil on canvas, 39 × 30 cm. Private ownership.

the futility and transience of life, but also about the comfortable and carefree everyday life in which morning tasks are tranquilly framed by piles of clothes and unmade beds. The viewer of the painting's apparently private sphere is met by the woman's gaze. She tilts her head to one side while arranging the cards, and her smiling face is directed at the viewer. The motif demanded its fellow player in the 'conversation' that was part of the genre. The card game could be compared to an engaged conversation, and the intimate corner was consequently transformed into a social stage. Just as Chardin, Hilleström wanted to illustrate the era's fashionable everyday life, but perhaps also tell us something about life at Näs. The various games tables listed in the Wadenstierna family's estate inventories also relate to the pictures of everyday life that once adorned the walls at Näs.

Around the games tables and billiard table at Näs

Carl Eric Wadenstierna's estate inventory mentions: 'In the dining room, two games tables inlaid with green baize.'[2] Cards were played in all social groups, but furniture

2 Riksarkivet, Näs Silverstolpeska arkivet, Personarkiven, vol. 60, Carl Eric Wadenstierna (1723–1787).

specially designated for that purpose was a distinguishing feature of upper-class environments. The two games tables in the large dining room at Näs were among the furniture you would expect to find in the most important room of the main building, as well as drop-leaf tables and sideboards. A guest entering the dining room from the entrance hall, where the mottos in the overdoor decorations spoke of the good life, could see at a glance that the Wadenstierna family practised what they preached. The games tables not only manifested economic prosperity but also participation in the established social life of upper-class culture. Here, the game could serve as an amusement that simultaneously created a sense of affinity and deepened contacts and conversation. Alliances and business deals, or everyday events, were aptly discussed during a good round at the games tables.

After a meal, it was customary for the group to move to the games tables or the adjacent drawing room's coffee tables. The games tables were also designed for optimal *commodité* (comfort). The green baize on the table top prevented the playing cards from sliding and muffled the distracting clink of coins and jetons. The table apron often included small inbuilt drawers for storage of playing cards and accessories. The edges of the table could also feature small dish-shaped recesses for gaming counters (counter wells), and in the rounded corners of the table top, recesses for candlesticks enabled the use of comfortable lighting. Perhaps the tables at Näs also had curved legs (*en cabriole*), which left space for long skirts or coats, and rounded edges to avoid wear and tear on delicate lace cuffs. If the tables were also fitted with castors, they were easy to roll to be placed near the warmth of the fireplace or a cooling breeze by an open window. After the game, the tables could be conveniently folded and the support legs folded inwards so that the tables took up as little space in the room as possible.

The placing of the games tables in the heart of the home's suite of formal rooms was therefore a sign that games belonged to the area that was also the hub for socialising. From the dining room, the tables were also easy to move to both the gentleman's suite and the lady's suite when necessary. Equivalent positioning of the games tables in other upper-class homes was a long-established tradition. Some royal environments also had a room specially designated for games, a *cabinet de jeux* according to French models, in connection with a centrally located room, where guests gathered before or after dinner.[3] The drawing room that generally followed on from the dining room was otherwise often the room in which the games tables were found. From the inventory of Count Claes Julius Ekeblad's Stola Manor in the 1790s, we can gain a picture of social life in the white drawing room

3 The Marquise de Pompadour's pleasure palace Bellevue by Jean Cailleteau (around 1750) at Versailles had, as its first reception room to the right of the centrally located large dining room, a *cabinet de jeux* for card games (Gordon 2008, p. 47).

next to the large dining room. The room was dominated by the games tables: '1 large inlaid games table' and '1 smaller ditto, lacquered' together with '8 diverse games'.[4] The room also contained a sofa, chairs, armchairs and tabourets as well as a tea table and the Saxony porcelain service ready to be used for serving the tea. Sewing tables, a lace making pillow and a dressing table were found in the drawing room beyond, but also a board game table and a coffee service.[5] Large groups could spread out in the various reception rooms based on what they wanted to do after dinner. Depending on the season, games could also be played in the garden or park buildings. The orangery at Stola, furnished with green-painted sofas and eleven chairs placed among the plants and sculptures, had both board games with counters and dice and '*Fortuna Bord*', a bagatelle table, with balls and cues.[6]

Ekeblad, who divided his time between serving at the Gustavian court in Stockholm and his life as a country gentleman at Stola, knew – as did Wadenstierna – how to arrange socialising to meet social and class requirements. The fact that the games culture was also a key part of court life is seen when Ekeblad writes from Stockholm to his wife, Brita Horn, at Stola in May 1778: 'Goodness gracious, games are played so much here,' he sighs, and in the same breath hints at a royal debt of '4,000 ducats'.[7] The previous year, the king himself had regulated court life in detail through a formalised agenda for the time when the court stayed at Drottningholm Palace and the adjacent Kina Slott (Chinese Pavilion). Games were on the daily schedule. After the meal, the court circle gathered at the pavilion, either in its white drawing room for '*lécture*', where the ladies also found their sewing tables, or at the games tables that awaited in '*la salle octogone*' as well as in the green drawing room of the right-hand wing. Those who wished to play billiards were urged to find the guard to obtain the key for the billiard wing.[8] Members of the court took such routines with them to their own country estates.

At Näs, the billiard table also stood in one of the wing buildings, the southern wing, which had been furnished for the amusements and comfort of the guests and the host family. The billiard table was a showpiece that in the estate inventory

4 Karlson, William, *Ett svenskt herremanshem på 1700-talet. Clas Julius Ekeblads inventarium över Stola 1796*, Lund 1940, pp. 76–7.

5 Karlson 1940, pp. 49, 76–7.

6 Karlsson 1940, p. 121.

7 *Claes Julius Ekeblads bref till sin hustru*, I, May 1778, p. 706, Kungliga biblioteket, Stockholm, Handskriftsavdelningen. Ep. E. &: 1: Letter from Claes Julius Ekeblad to Brita Ekeblad b. Horn, 1773–82.

8 'Pendant le cours de l'Après diner il y aura Lécture dans le Salon Blanc et Or, òu les Dames trouveront des petites tables pour travailler; Des tables de Jeu dans la Salle octogone du milieu, ainsi que dans le Pavillion droit, peint en verd et or, du Bátiment Principal. Ceux qui voudront jouer au Billard S'adresseront au Concierge pour en avoir la clef' ('Sejour de Drottningholm', 1777). See also *Kina slott*, Göran Alm (ed.), Stockholm 2002, p. 337.

from 1787 had a higher value than any other piece of furniture at the manor.[9] The Wadenstierna family probably stood out in the rural Roslagen region with this grand item of furniture. In terms of chattels, the only items comparable to the expensive billiard table as an expression of male consumption were the manor's carriages, of which Wadenstierna's sporty phaeton also commanded a considerable value.[10] When the author Jonas Carl Linnerhielm visited Näs in 1816, and in his romantic description characterised the place based on its surrounding nature and the beautifully varied landscape, he could not resist highlighting the billiard room and the book collection as Näs Manor's distinguishing special features. This evidently conveyed something important about Näs and the man who commissioned its construction, as well as how it was managed by its owner at that time, Baron Lars August Mannerheim, 'the former's enlightened son-in-law'.[11] The billiard table stood in the large room of the wing building, which also served as a library room. In addition to books, it contained collections of pictures and maps, as well as a writing table, eight armchairs and a long green sofa. The room was decorated with framed engravings: '52 engravings, varnished – all with gilt frames', which gave the room characteristics of a print room that was typical of the era. The manor's six cast iron cannons also stood there, which were fired on special occasions and were reminders that library rooms were linked to armouries and weapon collections in the past. The other four rooms in this wing building were furnished to be guest rooms, all with beds that had checked or striped bed hangings and tables equipped with bedside mirrors. One chamber was complemented with a tea table and another with a walnut board game table.[12]

The southern wing building at Näs with its steep mansard roof was thus well appointed for guests and amusements (Image 75). The interior decoration demonstrated well-ordered comfort and the Wadenstierna family's taste and cultivation. The billiard table, books and artworks were in harmony here, and guests who spent time with the host family around the billiard table could hardly avoid glancing at the books' titles or the engravings' motifs and forming a picture of the family's interests and pretensions. The novelty value of the newly published books and the imported engravings indicated the informed consumer, well-acquainted with the market's range of products and its abundance of choice. The quality of the books and pictures as physical objects, beautifully bound or framed and gilded, and their quantity in the form of collections vouched for aesthetic discernment and knowledgeable and conscious choices and constituted an unmistakable status marker. These displays

9 Riksarkivet, Näs Silverstolpeska arkivet, Personarkiven, vol. 60, Carl Eric Wadenstierna (1723–1787).

10 Ibid.

11 Jonas Carl Linnerhielm, *Bref under senare resor i Sverige*, Stockholm 1816, p. 148.

12 Riksarkivet, Näs Silverstolpeska arkivet, Personarkiven, vol. 60, Carl Eric Wadenstierna (1723–1787).

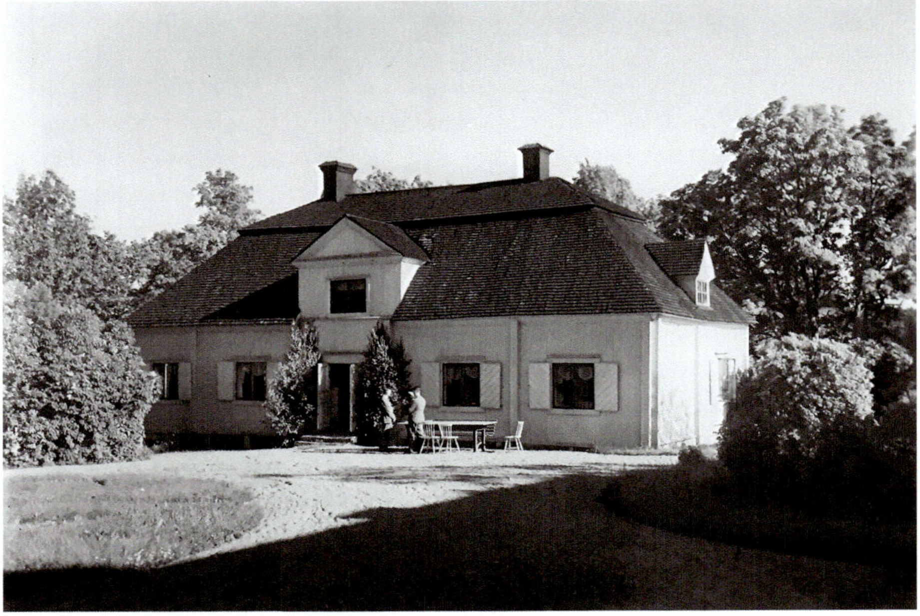

75. The southern wing at Näs, built in the first half of the eighteenth century. Photo: N.E. Åzelius, 1931, Archives of the Nordic Museum, Stockholm.

of upper-class status were especially distinguished alongside the exclusive billiard table. Few families in eighteenth-century Sweden owned a billiard table.[13] The mottos of the main building's overdoor decorations that embellished the entrance hall clearly proclaimed that the good life was to be found in good company: '[being] among books and among good friends ... enables you to feel the force of life and right sweetness'. The book collection and billiard table were there to be shared with others but also to be admired by others.

The significance of billiards during the eighteenth century

In the early eighteenth century when the wings were built at Näs, the aim would have hardly been to house a billiard table, but rather to accommodate visitors. But the elite's country estates gradually gained these designated billiard wings, some built solely with this particular function in mind. The billiard table was a piece of furniture, but its considerable dimensions and the space needed to play the game required a separate room – or a separate building. These demands are what gave

13 Runefelt, Leif, *Att hasta mot undergången: anspråk, flyktighet, förställning i debatten om konsumtion i Sverige 1730–1830*, Lund 2015, p. 157.

the game of billiards its status: it was expensive and large, it required its own room and its social context. Billiards, or its predecessor *carambole*, was played at the French court as early as in the sixteenth century and spread through Europe in the seventeenth century.[14] The establishment of the game within the social elite was related to this privileged background and the fact that it was associated with significant expenditure. It was not until public gambling halls started to become common in the eighteenth century that the game also became available to people outside aristocratic circles. In turn, this contributed to the popularity of the game, and during the eighteenth century billiards became a coveted amusement and reached somewhat wider circles.

Billiard tables were clearly accompanied by social prestige. Floor plans of the French nobility's modern private residences in Paris, known as *hôtels particuliers*, show how the billiard rooms were included in the suite of reception rooms during the first half of the eighteenth century. The position of the billiard room, generally next to the dining room, illustrates its function in social life. As the rooms were situated on the ground floor, the billiard room preferably opened onto the garden, accessible through the French windows. The importance of both *commodité* and *société* in these new upper-class residences shows how highly the informal gatherings were valued alongside the formal receptions. In function and design, the rooms were to meet needs for comfort and relaxation and facilitate unaffected socialising. A key part of the comfort was the physical proximity of different functions. A few steps away from the dining table you reached the games table, and from there it was easy to step out into the verdant garden. A drawing for a *trianon* by French architect Jacques-François Blondel in 1738 shows how these principles were above all suitable for upper-class country homes (Image 76). The drawing depicts what can best be described as a pleasure palace, but the idea could be transferred to the smallest wing building or garden summer house. Blondel's concept was an architectural expression of the eighteenth century's longing for informal country life – here combined with all the new trends in diversions, luxury and amusements.

Here, a carriage could drive the guests up to the first step of the entrance, and the reception rooms were just a stride away from the vestibule. The floor plan shows that the centrally located room was not intended to be used as a dining room but as a magnificent drawing room for socialising, and on either side of this room, fashionable games rooms were established: one a *salle à jouer* for card and board games, and the other a *billard*. Blondel also indicated suitable positions for practical cupboards for storing gaming counters and playing cards, and that fragile mirrors, paintings and ornaments had no place in the billiard room, where

14 Adriaen Moetjens, *Divertissemens innocens contenant les règles du jeu des échets, du billard, de la paume, du palle-mail et du trictrac*, The Hague 1696.

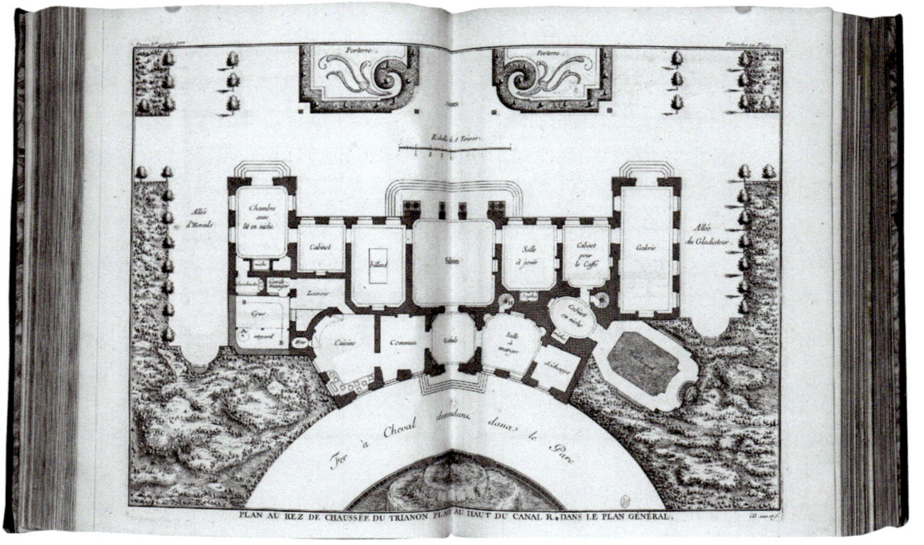

76. Charles-Nicolas Cochin after Jacques-François Blondel, 'Trianon'. From Blondel, *De la distribution des maisons de plaisance et de la décoration des edifices en general*, 2 vols, Paris, 1737, vol. 1. Bibliothèque de l'Institut National d'Histoire de l'Art, Paris.

they risked being subjected to fast-flying billiard balls or prodding cues.[15] These games rooms were in turn each flanked by a cabinet room, where one was specially designated for the fashionable activity of drinking coffee: *cabinet pour le caffe*. The rooms also featured niches and alcoves, which met the era's requirements for comfort and informality. A *lit en niche* was elegantly integrated with the interior decoration, unlike the free-standing beds that were pompous in comparison. Both of the games rooms were fitted with alcoves for comfortable seat furniture, from which the games could be observed from a draught-free place. A rounded alcove in the room for card games, where a space for a *sopha* is stated, is particularly notable. The plan also illustrates how additional rooms were equipped with daybeds *en alcove* to signal the access to privileged comfort.

Blondel inserted several *dégagements* in the form of hidden passages and staircases so that servants did not need to disturb the games and gatherings, but they also offered easy escape routes for guests or hosts who no longer wished to participate. The building included a laundry room, kitchen and dining room to meet additional needs. However, the distinctive element is how the building's suite of prominent rooms was intended to be used for games and amusements. They all face the garden, where the idea of the refreshing greenery and opportunity for privacy

15 Jacques-François Blondel, *De la Distribution des Maisons de Plaisance et de la Décoration des Edifices en general*, I, Paris 1737, pp. 87–9.

in the outdoor space complemented the interiors. The description underlines the significance of the environment for relaxation ('délassement de l'esprit') but also the freedom of devoting oneself to vivacity and playfulness ('peut prendre l'essor & s'abandonner à la vivacité de ses caprices') in contrast to the strict etiquette that belonged to more formal reception rooms.[16] In this respect, Blondel's exemplary drawing clearly reflects the new social life of the upper-class culture, in which various forms of games and games tables also occupy a central position.

The Wadenstierna family's billiard wing at Näs may not be comparable with Blondel's *trianon*, but it shares the same desire for recreation and a comfortable social life. The wing at Näs housed the billiard table, a library and pictures and was surrounded by comfortable guest rooms. The surrounding garden with its upland views over the local landscape was just a short step away. Näs also had the smaller property's proximity to '*commodités*' that was often lost in more large-scale environments, where both food and enthusiasm for games had cooled down before you reached the appropriate rooms. Comfort, 'lost in a palace, and found in a cottage', as Englishman Peter Beckford wrote in a letter from his travels in the late eighteenth century, was something that Blondel had already understood.[17] A small *trianon* was often preferable to a large Versailles, and Ange-Jacques Gabriel's Petit Trianon or Richard Mique's Hameau became treasured royal havens on the Versailles estate in the eighteenth century – both equipped for billiards. The eighteenth century's aristocratic dream house was small, but large enough to accommodate a billiard table.[18]

In Jean-François Bastide's story *La petite maison* from 1758, in which Trémicour seduces Mélite by tempting her through the rooms in his house, the ideal is literally a pleasure palace. The comforts present themselves as each new door is opened: boudoirs with fashionable sofas and beds – 'Les ottomanes, les duchesses, les sultanes' – a bathroom or a music room. Appropriately, there is also a *cabinet de jeu* that opens onto a lush airy outdoor space.[19] The games room, with walls and furniture decorated with Chinese lacquer, cushions made of embroidered Indian fabric, and embellished with Saxony and Japanese porcelain, creates an atmosphere of excess in terms of time and money. From the cabinet, a door opens to a room for coffee drinking and another to a dining room where served dishes await. The story could have taken place in a building by Blondel.[20] In amazement, Mélite asks where the servants are as someone must help to provide this comfort. Trémicour's reply

16 Blondel 1737, p. 87.

17 Beckford 1805, p. 54.

18 Castan, Nicole, 'The Public and the Private', *A History of Private Life*, III, Roger Chartier (ed.), Massachusetts and London 1989, pp. 433–5.

19 Jean-François Bastide, *La Petite Maison* (1763) Paris 1879, pp. 30–5, 43.

20 In Blondel's 'trianon' the 'cabinet pour le caffe' is decorated with exotic details: 'Indiennes & Chinoises', as well as wall consoles with various curiosities, Blondel 1737, p. 88.

hints that the servants are not allowed to be seen or heard: the laid table had been hoisted up through the floor from the kitchen below. This calls to mind Kina Slott, on the outskirts of the royal family's Drottningholm Palace, built in the 1760s, and the surrounding pavilions that complete the environment. One of them housed the billiard room and another a dining room *en confidence*, where tables and serving cabinets were hoisted up through trapdoors in the floor. Wadenstierna's admittedly more modest Näs Manor here appears to be the country gentleman's equivalent dream of the comfortable, country pleasure palace, where the wing buildings that flanked the single-storey main building met the same needs: one with a kitchen and food, the other with billiards and books.

The rules of the game

Billiards was originally an outdoor game with clubs and balls, and when it found its format as an indoor game, the table's green baize was seen as a reminder of the lawns that the game was once played on. In contemporary sources, the game was sometimes presented as an activity that was also associated with physical health: 'Not unsuitable for exercise.'[21] In an advertisement in *Stockholms Posten* in August 1797 for a book on beneficial physical exercise, billiards was highlighted as a healthy exercise of the same type as dancing, hunting, swimming and fencing.[22] Billiards was regarded as a way of cultivating a social choreography that belonged to both an elegant urban pastime and socialising in the country.

But the passion for games in the era's social life was not just for billiards. The Wadenstierna family's city residence did not include a billiard table, but instead six smaller games tables of varying shapes, designs and values:

1 Inlaid square games table
2 Triangular mahogany games tables, with baize
1 Square ditto ... with board game top
1 Inlaid ditto with green baize
1 Ditto smaller, with green baize[23]

The number of tables was in proportion to the number of rooms and their respective functions, but it also informs us of the self-evident place occupied by the games

21 Johan Adolph Hoffmann, *Tvänne böcker om förnöjsamheten efter förnuftets och trones grundsatser, på tyska språket tolf gånger uplagde, och nu efter mångas åstundan på swenska öfwersatte*, Stockholm and Uppsala, 1752.

22 *Stockholms Posten*, 22 August 1797.

23 Riksarkivet, Näs Silverstolpeska arkivet, Personarkiven, vol. 60, Carl Eric Wadenstierna (1723–1787).

culture in the family and social life and of the many different games that were prevalent in the latter half of the eighteenth century. Board games such as chess and draughts, and certain dice games and card games remain recognisable, but many of the games' names – 'ombre', 'piquet' or 'faro' – link them to fashionable associations that have been generally forgotten over time.[24] While 'cambio' was a fashionable card game in 1758, the games 'Karniffel' and 'Pittela-pump', mentioned in Georg Stiernhielm's epic poem *Hercules* from 1658, had definitively lost their novelty appeal and thereby status, or possibly been updated with new names and new associations. Many of the games in the eighteenth century had a long history but were made topical through a new format and new names, or by being associated with famous people or prestigious social environments and contexts. The games and their accessories, with everything from games furniture to fashionably designed gaming counters, cards, boxes, cases and bags, became an important part of the era's growing culture of consumption, where the market rapidly launched novelties in relation to current trends.

In Gustavian Stockholm, the forms of the court's social life and the aristocracy's private socialising were similar to some degree. The court and aristocracy constituted a fairly homogeneous circle, whose lifestyles followed much the same social patterns. For many members of the nobility, serving at court involved maintaining the representative everyday life around the royal family, and letters and diaries include recurring descriptions of the court's carefully regulated routines.[25] Baron Gustaf Johan Ehrensvärd was a chamberlain of Gustaf III when he wrote an account in 1776 of what a day in May at Drottningholm Palace could look like:

> 30 May, Thursday 1776. As this day was exactly like so many other days at the court, when nothing happens, I must describe how such a day was used. … At two o'clock it is time for food. … After the meal, coffee is drunk in the king's drawing room; then groups for games are formed or rather groups for dozing; everyone remains in this room and the reading room beyond. … During this time, until the games groups are formed, or until five o'clock, the king either holds a cabinet meeting or speaks to a person who has urgently applied for a conversation. Then the ladies sit, in full symmetry, along the walls, each at her work table, with work that is never finished, and with ever wandering thoughts. Those of the gentlemen who find happiness in ogling at a distance of twenty paces, sit in a corner and await slow reading aloud. … From nine o'clock until supper, there is a general game of

24 Carl-Herman Tillhagen, 'Spel och dobbel', *Det glada Sverige. Våra fester och högtider genom tiderna*, Gösta Berg, Birger Beckman, Bengt Idestam-Almquist and Gustaf Munthe (ed.), Stockholm 1947, pp. 1309–10.
25 Ehrensvärd 1877, pp. 236, 260, 361; *Lewenhauptska arkivet på Sjöholm. Bref och Handlingar utgifna af Adam Lewenhaupt*, Stockholm 1919, pp. 10–11, 39.

> biribi, vingt-un, lotterie, cavagnole; then supper from eleven until one or two. ... Often games are played after supper, unless one has previously kept watch for a sufficiently long time, and then everyone retires to their own rooms, satisfied that the day has been spent so well, and that one has thus amused oneself.[26]

This description calls to mind Pehr Hilleström's painting *Conversation på Drottningholm* (Plate 7) and a reminder of the king's instructions for a 'Sejour de Drottningholm' from 1777. An inventory of Gripsholm Castle, drawn up at the end of the Gustavian era, further confirms the picture of an intensive games culture at court. The castle's large reception room, the round drawing room, was furnished with fifteen games tables and two board game tables, sixty chairs and a number of benches.[27]

Admittedly, the routines that Ehrensvärd describes could have felt restrictive when spring started to head into summer and evoked a longing for the outdoors, but despite his acerbic closing comments, the games could serve as a vent in an otherwise confined and entrapped social life. The rules of the game within eighteenth-century European upper-class culture confirmed the morals and decorum that were expected of this class – playing fairly and in all situations showing self-restraint and control – but also offered plenty of opportunities to challenge these virtues. Gambling debts were a recurring reason for overheated emotions and sometimes drastic actions. Although playing for money was the rule rather than the exception, it was deemed unworthy to play for the sake of the winnings. According to the rules, a game that ended in some form of settlement was about honour, not money.[28]

But above all, the rounds of games created opportunities for various kinds of encounters. Ehrensvärd describes how the 'games groups are formed', and who played with whom constituted a strategic game in itself.[29] Here, private or political alliances could be confirmed or dissolved, and an invitation to the royal games tables was an evident acknowledgement of status and position. What played out at these tables reflected events on the larger playing field of court life and upper-class life. According to contemporary witness accounts, the specific game between the sexes also developed around the games tables. In his diary, Ehrensvärd complained about how all attempts at emotions withered in the court environment, where all movements and facial expressions were observed and interpreted.[30] But the concentrated closeness around the cramped games tables, which demanded awareness

26 Ehrensvärd, Gustaf Johan, *Dagboksanteckningar förda vid Gustaf III:s hof, utgifna af D:r E. V. Montan*, I, Stockholm 1877, pp. 15–17.

27 *Möbelhistoria på Gripsholm*, Bo Vahlne (ed.), Stockholm 1986, p. 86.

28 *Paris. Life & Luxury in the Eighteenth Century*, Charissa Bremer-David (ed.), Los Angeles 2011, p. 102.

29 Svante Norrhem, *Kvinnor vid maktens sida, 1632–1772*, Lund 2007, p. 56.

30 Ehrensvärd 1877–8, pp. 15–16.

of how legs were positioned and hands were moved and what facial expressions revealed, also offered opportunities for contact and wordless conversation. Author Carl Gustaf Leopold expressed these feelings in the concluding lines of his poem 'Till Fru B. C. O * * *', addressed to a woman after a games evening in 1787:

> And while you turn the cards,
> Carefully spread them out one at a time,
> Of your allurements as on a counter for sale;
> Arch a pair of swansdown-soft hands
> To take a trick, sent by the God of fortune;
> Smilingly lament your luck recurring,
> And between lips of coral,
> A double row of alabaster teeth;
> Furtively cast a consulting glance at your opponent in the game,
> Tenderly letting him know what game he could play;
> In your thoughts drop a card next to your foot,
> That signals to his hand your permission to touch it;
> And opportunely bare, too forced and too warm,
> The contour of a snow-white bosom,
> Which could seduce Socrates.[31]

The games groups also included the spectators, who followed the various games and the players' expressions without taking part themselves. Ehrensvärd mentions '*lorgnera*', a Swedish word loaned from French meaning 'to furtively look at something', as one of the pastimes at court. This could be performed with or without a lorgnette, the designated spectacles that were above all used for studying actors and guests at the era's theatre and opera performances. In Jean Michel Moreau the Younger's engraving *La partie de Wisch* from 1783, a man can be seen in the right of the picture scrutinising the players with some sort of eyeglass (Image 77). The picture was included in the volume of prints titled *Monument du costume physique et moral de la fin du dix-huitième siècle, ou tableaux de la vie*, a project that was launched in the early 1770s and finished in 1789, with the aim of presenting modern contemporary life in words and pictures.[32] The work's third volume describes how the fashionable man – *le petit maître* – spends his time, from morning to evening. The afternoon round of games and the players are described

31 The original 'Skalde–Bref til Fru**' was sent by Carl Gustaf Leopold to Brita Christina Odel in February 1787. It was not until 1798 that the poem was published in the magazine *Läsning i blandade ämnen*, with the title 'Till Fru B. C. O***'.

32 *Monument du costume* 1783, in the Gallica database: gallica.bnf.fr.

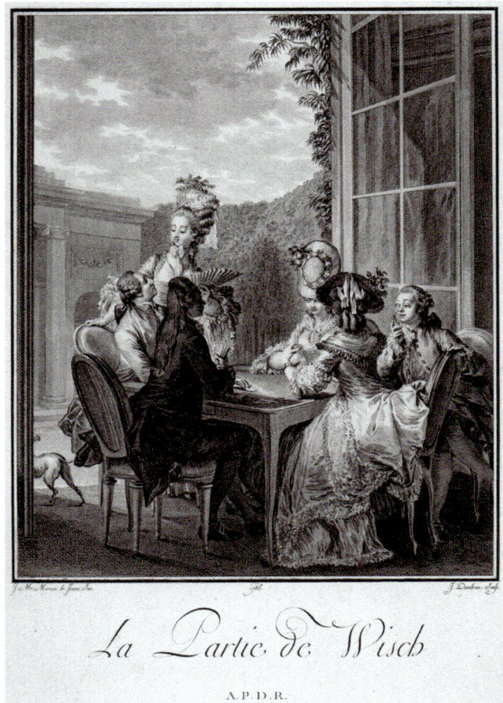

77. Jean Dambrun after Jean Michel Moreau the Younger, *La partie de Wisch*, 1783. Engraving, 55.4 × 41.2 cm. From Nicolas-Edme Rétif de La Bretonne, *Monument du costume physique et moral de la fin du dix-huitième siècle, ou tableaux de la vie*, Paris, 1783. Paris Musées/ Musée Carnavalet.

ironically in the caption by Rétif de La Bretonne: one player who is concentrating on guarding his cards, the second who is distracted by the beautiful woman leaning forwards over his chair, and the third who is furtively ogling at the glances and gestures of others. Bretonne states that this is how six friends entertain themselves in the late eighteenth century – they have nothing to say to each other, so they play. The game frees them of everything: 'd'esprit, de raisonnement, de lumières, & d'amour. Vive le jeu!'[33] The group observe each other but are also there to be observed by us. Clothes, hairstyles, furniture and playing cards are all parts of the silent communication that identifies the actors and their stage. A contemporary observer of the picture in *Monument du costume* could perhaps read the tension in the silent group, but also the anglomania that was typical of the era and that they express in their choice of clothing, in straw hats and comfortable redingotes, and the fact that they, with the doors open onto the verdant park, have chosen to play whist.

Specialised chairs could be placed next to the elite's games tables, with the sole purpose of making the viewing of the game comfortable. A *voyeuse*, as the name

33 Nicolas-Edme Rétif de La Bretonne, *Monument du Costume Physique et Moral de la fin du dix-huitième siècle, ou Tableaux de la Vie*, II, London 1790, p. 72.

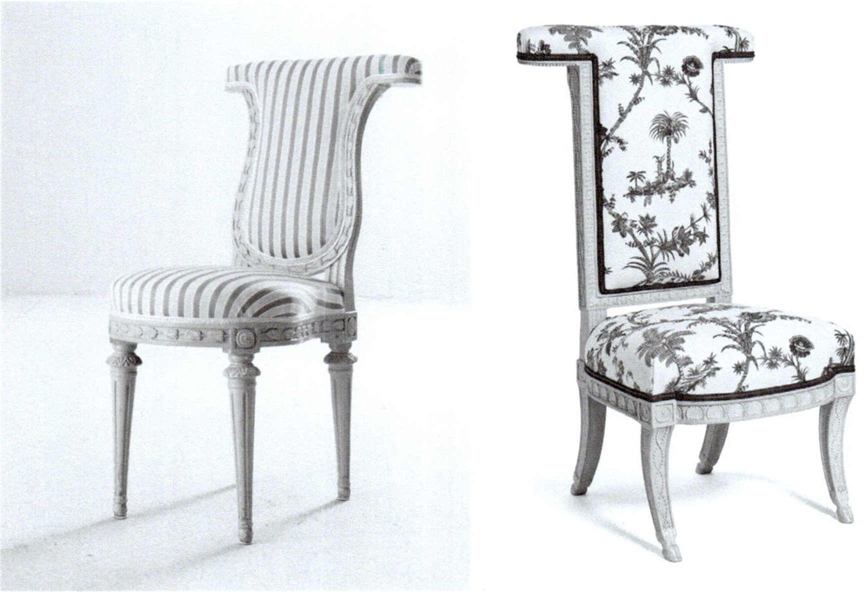

78. *Voyeuse* made by Melchior Lundberg in Stockholm during the latter half of the eighteenth century. Later painting and upholstery. Private ownership. Photo: Stockholms Auktionsverk and *Voyelle* or *voyeuse à genoux* by Jean-Baptiste-Claude Sené, 1789. Sothebys.

suggests, was intended for a male voyeur. By straddling the chair and leaning against the padded top edge of the backrest, a spectator could effortlessly follow the game. The female version was called a *voyelle* or *voyeuse à genoux*, indicating that the woman instead knelt on the chair, which was therefore designed with shorter legs and a longer backrest (Image 78). Accordingly, there were games tables adapted to the different types of games that were in fashion, but also chairs adapted to the game's different players – and spectators. These specialised pieces of furniture, designed to suit the era's new forms of socialising and to comply with gender-specific codes, as well as new ideals linked to functionality and comfort, were only aimed at the knowledgeable upper-class consumer. A *voyeuse* called for specialised use and lost its meaning and comfort if used incorrectly. Just as the game had its rules, the furniture and objects that belonged to the game demanded to be used in a manner that followed new rules, new ways of moving and conducting oneself.[34]

34 Mimi Hellman clarifies the purpose of a *voyeuse*: 'Spectatorship was thus rendered spectacle; acts of looking and being looked at were formalized and aesteticized through the intervention of a physical device. The existence of specialized furniture that so precisely engineered what may seem to be the most casual and natural of supporting social roles – the mere bystander at a game – suggests not only that leisured sociability could not exist without objects, but also that it could not exist without viewers.', 'Furniture,

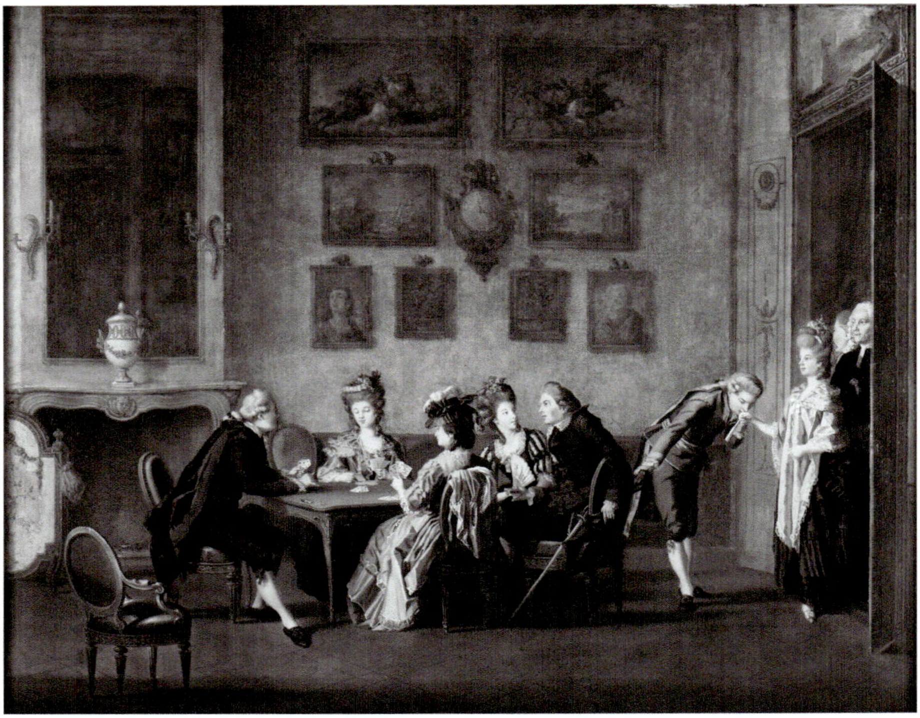

79. Pehr Hilleström, *Spelparti hos Statssekreterare Elis Schröderheim*, 1779. Oil on canvas, 111 × 138 cm. Nationalmuseum, Stockholm (NM 5296).

Jean Michel Moreau's engraving was a fashion image through and through, which aimed to document the era's fashionable lifestyle in all its characteristic details, where the comfortably appointed game was a particularly distinctive element. Pehr Hilleström's painting of a group playing cards in Stockholm from the late 1770s can be regarded in a similar way (Image 79). The scene depicts a lavish interior. The ceiling height is impressive, and the room is adorned by an eye-catching mirror that crowns a fireplace and the walls of densely hung pictures around a gilt pendulum clock. Double doors and parquet flooring accentuate the upper-class style of the room. A group of women and men sit around a games table; three are engaged in a card game, while two are deep in conversation. Perhaps 'ombre' is being played here, which was a fashionable card game for three people. Another group is just arriving and being welcomed at the door. The men and a couple of the women are wearing the national costume that the king introduced in 1778 – the year before Hilleström's painting – and the scene seems to be both a demonstration of

Sociability, and the Work of Leisure in Eighteenth-Century France', *Eighteenth-Century Studies*, vol. 32, no. 4, Baltimore 1999, p. 430.

this particular costume and a staging of well-mannered modern social life. This is how courtiers were to look and occupy themselves when they wore the new costume. This is surely what the king wanted. The details – a snuff box being held out, a fan being closed, a hand being kissed, well-arranged curls and pointed toes of shoes – chime in with this purpose. Here, we are viewers of Hilleström's own *Monument du costume.*

The painting shows a games group at the home of State Secretary Schröderheim in Stockholm.[35] Of those depicted, the following have been named: Princess Sofia Albertina by the door, followed by Archbishop Lindholm; at the table sit Ulla von Höpken, Lovisa Meyerfelt and Augusta Löwenhielm flanked by Gustaf Mauritz Armfelt and Lars August Mannerheim, who later became Wadenstierna's son-in-law when he married Wadenstierna's eldest daughter, Sophia.[36] The women's visiting coats and the hats in the men's hands clarify how the visiting culture and the games culture were combined in the era's social life. Elis Schröderheim described how the games evenings at his home on Nybrogatan Street were organised:

> Members of high society see each other twice a week. ... Meet at six o'clock, play cards, talk and drink tea until half past nine, when we part. The doors are open during these hours, and everyone is welcome. They greet the host and hostess and then play their game. They are not obliged to be attentive. Instead, each person does as he pleases, etc. No one stands up for the other, and if they so wish, they perform music in a separate room. We burn tallow candles and lamps and amuse ourselves or at least others without any significant cost.[37]

Schröderheim describes informal and undemanding socialising imbued with comfort. However, Hilleström's painting conveys a different picture. The scene simultaneously demonstrates how Gustavian high society is portrayed in accordance with French fashion images. The elegant body language of the 'actors', their well-fitting new clothes and the ease with which they choose their cards show how well they play their parts in the era's upper-class role-play. Participating in such games evenings was a performative action that ultimately aimed to create social distinction and build identity within the participants' own group, where everyone involved understood the rules of the game – be it at court, at the Schröderheims' home or at Näs Manor.

35 Compare Pehr Hilleström, *Gustaviansk interiör med kortspelande sällskap*, 1779, oil on canvas, 60.5 × 145.5 cm, Nationalmuseum, Stockholm, NM 2403. Overdoor decoration from Fredrikshofs Slott around 1779; Cederblom 1927, I, Image 41 and Hilleström's list No. 397.

36 Cederblom 1927, I, Image 41.

37 Gösta Selling, Gotthard Johansson and Göran Axel-Nilsson, *Si Ulla dansar. Bilder från Bellmans Stockholm*, Stockholm 1945, p. 136.

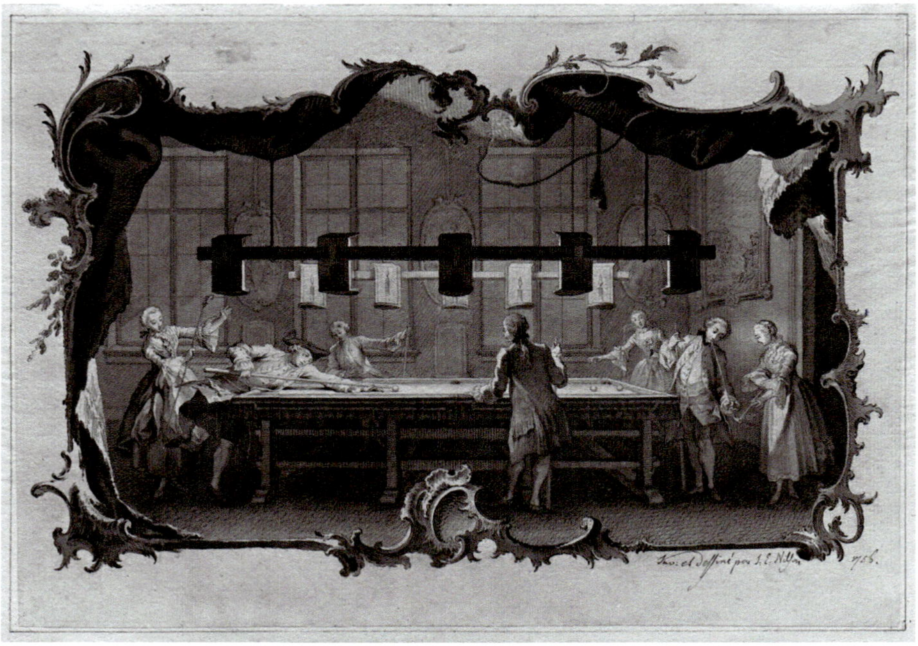

80. Johann Esaias Nilson, 1756. Pen-and-wash drawing, 17.6 × 25.1 cm. National Gallery of Art, Washington, DC.

Private billiards and public gambling clubs

Johann Esaias Nilson's drawing from 1756 depicts a group playing billiards (Image 80). Gestures and poses indicate that the game is in full progress: a man balances on tiptoe when he aims at the ball, and a woman raises her arm in enthusiasm. The elaborate Rococo ornament that frames the scene connects the game with the era's sophisticated fashion. The picture also shows how the game demanded a considerable room, with large windows for daylight and with a device that required ten wax candles for evening lighting. In addition to the expensive billiard table, everything from the space to the lighting was associated with significant costs.

At the same time, Stockholm's privileged elite gathered around the billiard table at the Svindersvik country residence just outside the city. With the help of the architect Carl Hårleman, the affluent businessman Claes Grill had built a *maison de plaisance* equipped with all the comforts of the era. Next to the ground floor's centrally located large room lay a *cabinet d'assemblée* for socialising, decorated with Chinese wallpaper that the business manager Grill had brought home via the Swedish East India Company, of which he was a part-owner. Above the dining room on the upper floor, the billiard room stood well-lit by three windows and an additional one that opened towards the inner stairwell. Eight Chinese paintings also decorated the walls here – the billiard table and the exotic paintings seemed to summarise Grill's taste and assets and expressed a luxury of less common dimensions. Grill's ironworks manor Österby in Uppland Province also included a billiard room on the upper floor of the main building, surrounded by guest suites.[38]

When Carl Gustaf Tessin was granted use of Svindersvik in the summer of 1759, he enthusiastically gathered his selected circle of friends around the billiard table during the recurring Saturday parties that he organised.[39] That same year, he celebrated Midsummer at Skånellaholm Castle in Uppland and took the opportunity to also visit the ironmaster and marshal of the court, Charles De Geer, at the nearby Wäsby Manor. In his diary, Tessin repeatedly notes De Geer's clearly considerable economic resources. The newly built Wäsby Manor outshone his own Åkerö, which he was struggling with at the time. De Geer also owned the large Leufsta ironworks and an upper-class residence in Stockholm. Wäsby, the exemplary construction by architect Jean Eric Rehn in the spirit of Blondel, housed (as at Svindersvik) a large reception room to the left of the large central ground-floor room – a *grand piece de compagnie* – and on the upper floor above that room, a splendid *salle de billard*. Tessin notes that the manor had tempted His Majesty the King to visit several times who had enjoyed its amusements.[40] At Skånelaholm Castle, which belonged to business magnate John Jennings, there was also a billiard room, just as at his ironworks manor Forsmark in northern Uppland. The economic assets, such as the billiard tables, primarily appeared to be amassed at the homes of these successful businessmen, ironmasters and merchants – or government officials such as Wadenstierna. Yet, billiard tables were notable by their absence on many estates owned by the old noble elite.

The private billiard room was thus a key manifestation of personal economic success and status. Public billiards could also to some degree be associated with this privilege, even though life in the public gambling venues was often described in different terms. The games culture at the city's various licensed premises was often connected with rowdy behaviour and mischief. During the eighteenth century's recurrent gambling bans, billiards was generally exempt from the restrictions as 'billiards has throughout the ages been classed as one of the nobler games', as stated in the Swedish parliament, the Riksdag, in conjunction with a proposed bill in 1731.[41] Everyone who applied for and was granted royal privilege therefore enjoyed the

38 Selling, Gösta, *Svenska herrgårdshem under 1700-talet*, Stockholm (1937) 1991, p. 252.

39 Gunnar W Lundberg, 'Ett rokokoporträtt och dess tillkomst', *Fataburen*, Nordiska museets och Skansens årsbok, Stockholm 1960, p. 135 and Sigrid Leijonhufvud, *Carl Gustaf Tessin och hans Åkerökrets*, Stockholm 1931, pp. 114, 131.

40 Selling 1991, pp. 164–8.

41 *Sveriges ridderskaps- och adels riksdags-protokoll*, Part 6, Stockholm 1731, p. 318, and Runefelt 2015, p. 157.

right to play billiards, both in private and in public. This right could apparently also be rented, as shown in the following notice in the newspaper *Dagligt Allehanda*: 'I have discovered that someone who owns a billiard table rents it out for 166 riksdaler per year; what interest will such furniture yield for the landlord?[42] The quotation shows how owners of billiard tables could earn a sizeable sum by renting it out to various businesses, often for use at public coffee houses and inns.

Other venues for amusements and recreation, including the popular spas, also attracted visitors with fashionable facilities such as billiard tables:

> The first assembly at the spa Kongl. Djurgårds-Brunnen will commence today, on Wednesday, 1 July, and will subsequently continue each week during the spa season. Entry tickets can be obtained from the apothecary Brunns-Apotequet for 6 daler copper coins. Entertainment available in the form of music, billiards and dancing, with tea and lemonade as refreshments at no extra charge. The assembly commences at 5 o'clock in the afternoon and ends at 9 o'clock in the evening.[43]

Advertisements in *Dagligt Allehanda* and *Stockholms Posten* give an idea of the many 'billiard clubs' that were open to the public in the Gustavian era. Certain names recur as more permanent establishments, such as 'Hr. Hedmans Biljard wid Riddarhus-Torget i Bergstrahlska huset', whereas others appear temporarily in the city's range of amusements.[44] Visitors to public billiard clubs or halls were charged fees, and those who managed popular venues that attracted many visitors possibly developed lucrative businesses. Money could also be earned by those who had empty premises to rent out, as shown in an advertisement in *Dagligt Allehanda* in April 1785. There, an apartment by Norrmalmstorg Square in Stockholm is offered, where 'the dining room is so large that it can comfortably be used for billiards'.[45]

In June 1769, Count Johan Gabriel Oxenstierna conveyed a lively picture of what a games session could be like at a venue in Stockholm that he called 'the club'. In the dense tobacco smoke he glimpsed the tables at which the groups 'play and swear', and he noted that the players also included 'the people who govern our nation'. Someone stood on a table and shouted, bribes were accepted, politics and parliamentary quarrels were mixed with gossip, rumours and slander and, to his alarm, Oxenstierna escaped a duel. He described the scenes that took place:

42 *Dagligt Allehanda*, 18 December 1779.

43 *Dagligt Allehanda*, 1 July 1772.

44 In Stockholm there were, for example, De Broens Billard, Hambergs Billard, Ahlgrens Billard, Getz Billard, Robinots Billard, Monsieur Delangs Billard, Fru Boegles Billard, Lois Antoine de Lands Billard and Benedictii Billard, to name but a few.

45 *Dagligt Allehanda*, 29 April 1785.

> Streams of drink from knocked-over bottles run between shards of broken tobacco pipes. Glasses are smashed against the walls, the floor is littered with shredded cards, innocent victims of an angry player. … Folly and drunkenness embrace, and a nobleman drowns the little sense he has in floods of arrack punch.[46]

The description is in stark contrast to the elegant groups who, surrounded by beautiful rooms or views of well-kept gardens, silently examine their playing cards in the flora of contemporary pictures. Wadenstierna could also gather his selected guests around the billiard table in the wing at Näs in much more peaceful circumstances. The newspapers confirm this special freedom that Wadenstierna and other billiard table owners enjoyed in their country homes. Recurring notices reported on quarrels and disorder in the city's inns and billiard venues, and on problems with stolen billiard balls, gold watches gambled away, unsettled gambling debts, inferior hats swapped for better ones – all under the heated impact of the game of billiards. The particularly common notices were those about unpaid fees for playing a game, which dishonest people often seemed to evade by saying that they needed to go to the '*apartementet*' (a euphemism for the toilet). But instead they sneaked out of a back door or 'tricked the *marqueur* [marker] to follow him all the way to the top of the Södermalm district in order to obtain payment from his lodgings', but then slyly disappeared behind the nearest street corner.[47] The playing of games not only entailed a rowdy city life for the general public, but was increasingly highlighted as an addiction that drove the individual to ruin and destruction, and in the long run contributed to disintegration of the social order. According to opinion pieces and articles, gambling addiction was widespread in all social groups and was often stated as being the factor that unleashed a series of other misfortunes – an attitude that recurs throughout the eighteenth century.[48]

Playing cards could be bought in many places in Stockholm, and the regular newspaper advertisements show that the decks of cards seemed to be just as common as snuff and tobacco.[49] A tax on the use of playing cards was imposed in the early eighteenth century to regulate gambling and to generate income for the state.[50]

46 Johan Gabriel Oxenstierna, *Dagboks-anteckningar af Johan Gabriel Oxenstierna. Åren 1769–1771*, Uppsala 1881, p. 34.

47 *Dagligt Allehanda*, 12 May 1792. About stolen billiard balls: *Dagligt Allehanda*, 9 June 1773; a watch lost through gambling: *Hwad Nytt*, 2 March 1784; gambling debts: *Dagligt Allehanda*, 11 August 1785 and 23 September 1797; swapped hats: *Dagligt Allehanda*, 5 December 1791; evading gambling bills: *Dagligt Allehanda*, 26 March 1798 and 14 August 1794.

48 *Sedolärande Mercurius*, 16 June and 11 August 1730, and 6 July 1731.

49 *Dagligt Allehanda*, 26 October 1785, where ombre cards with smooth and gilt edges were advertised.

50 *His Royal Majesty's placard and ban regarding all manner of illicit gambling at restaurants and coffee houses, as well as at home. Issued in Stockholm on 12 November 1719* and *His Royal Majesty's additional declaration and ban regarding gambling in restaurants and coffee houses. Dated Stockholm*

Each deck of cards was stamped by the *hallrätten*, the supervisory authority for manufactories, in order to be classed as legal, and vendors of unstamped cards risked considerable fines. The idea was that the income from the card and billiard taxes would benefit the poor and sick, and the gambling bans were also intended to rein in the plague that 'has tempted unwise and unoccupied youth into all manner of debauchery and disruptions'.[51] The criticism that fuelled the debate was due to the various trends that swept through the eighteenth century's urban culture of consumption and that were often associated with non-Swedish luxury and lifestyles, for instance, regarding new fashions, types of coffee or games of chance. In the light of the proximity of the public billiard halls and gambling venues to cramped, rowdy coffee houses and inns, the privately owned billiard tables for select groups seem particularly exclusive. Wadenstierna, with his lavish billiard table at Näs, and the guests he invited, thereby belonged to an extremely privileged circle.

Women who played games

Women, who were tempted by fashion and consumption, were thought to be particularly at risk of the dangerous 'gambling sickness'.[52] But to the same degree that gambling and games were associated with vulgarities in restaurants and coffee houses, card games were clearly part of the upper-class culture's *politesse* and social rituals. In various contexts, the pleasant and moderate forms of playing games were juxtaposed with the destructive forms, for example, in a fictitious correspondence published in Stockholm in 1773:

> Indeed, when one observes all the misfortunes that games cause, it is easy to think that their inventor is the devil, in order to add countless time wasters to the nation, and among them, many money thieves. Nonetheless, I admit that playing games for a moment of tranquillity, in honourable company, is both proper and nearly unavoidable, but I criticise the misuse of it, causing uproar

5 December 1719. Additional ordinances and bans were introduced in the eighteenth century: 'His Royal Majesty's ordinance regarding a certain fee that will be imposed on all decks of cards', Stockholm, 1730; 'Proclamation, regarding the fee for cards made in Sweden that will henceforth be payable', Stockholm, 1756; and 'Proclamation and ban on illicit gambling in restaurants, coffee houses and other business establishments, and on the organising of risky gambling at home', the Office of the Governor of Stockholm, Stockholm, 1785. The final gambling ban of the eighteenth century was announced in 1792.

51 *Gustavianskt 1771–1810. En bokfilm av Ingvar Andersson, Agne Beijer, Bertil Kjellberg, Bo Lindorm*, Stockholm 1945. p. 298.

52 *Om medlen att förhöja qwinliga skönheten, Handbok för damer. Öfwersättning af O. Fr. Lindén*, Lund 1806, pp. 17–18.

> to both sense and conscience, and that it is associated with the ruin of your fellow man.[53]

Knowledge of current games was not only 'proper and nearly unavoidable' as claimed in the quotation but also served an identity-building purpose. The game could be compared to an international language, and knowledge of the game's *when, where* and *how* was shared by a broad and heterogeneous upper-class group. Just as the coffee culture, it was the special framework in the form of rituals and designated rooms, furniture and objects that marked it as being an upper-class activity that was refined and thereby separate from the boundary-crossing games of the general public.

Games as expressions of politeness thus required their social stage and their context.[54] This could consist of the court's social life in specially designated games rooms, or assemblies and visits where coffee and games were part of polite conversation. However, contemporary literature also expressed concern about playing games excessively at home, where a gambling addiction was assigned especially female overtones.[55] Women's natural weakness was thought to make them easy victims of addictive games, which could have a destructive impact on both body and soul. Hours of sedentary pastimes at tables without doing important tasks also challenged the established order and allocation of roles between the sexes. Where diligence and good housekeeping should be performed, the hands were instead wasted on futilities, irrespective of the time of day or year. The book *Qwinno-könets wän* (Friend of the female sex) from 1763 is full of indignation at this form of wasted female industriousness and its rapid route to women's moral and physical ruin.[56] Today's reports warning of a sedentary generation using digital games and media clearly had their predecessors in the eighteenth century's appeals. In the moralising texts aimed at women, special emphasis was placed on how idleness spoiled health and entailed beauty risks:

> Among all sedentary tasks, playing games undeniably contributes quite considerably to the sickness of the body, the circulation of fluids to the most sensitive parts is increased, and the body thereby daily becomes ever weaker. … Through

53 *Brefwäxling Emellan Adelaide och några Wittre Snillen I Omwäxlande Ämnen*, N.o 22, Stockholm 1773, pp. 86f.

54 Vickery, Amanda, *The Gentleman's Daughter. Women's Lives in Georgian England*, New Haven 1998, pp. 208ff.; Noël Riley, *The Accomplished Lady. A History of Genteel Pursuits c. 1660–1860*, Plymouth 2017, pp. 71–8.

55 Bellman, Carl Michael, Tankar *om flickors ostadighet*, Stockholm 1758; *Verlden är sig altid lik, översatt från franskan av J Selin*, Stockholm 1781.

56 *Qwinno-könets wän* (translated from French into Swedish), [Anon.], Västerås 1763, p. 26.

> this excessive irritability of the nerves, the beautiful vivacious colour disappears, the entire body's plump, beautiful curved form, the strength of this work of art; the complexion becomes grey, while thinness, in addition to the general nerve illnesses, of which the symptoms no physician has yet calculated, and of which the fits have not yet been possible to cure, will eventually materialise.[57]

In his book on women's education, *Plan for the Conduct of Female Education in Boarding Schools* (1797), Erasmus Darwin stated that chess was less unsuitable 'from its bearing so great analogy to common life'.[58] Via chess, young women could learn strategic thinking that was useful in everyday life, while frivolous card games should only be kept within the family – and never involve money. Women were often associated with games of chance, *jeux de hasard*, while men were linked to games that demanded practice, *jeux de commerce*, rather than the impact of chance.[59] When women's educational literature did emphasis the benefits of chess, it referred to the intellectual training in positioning and calculation of consequences that the game involved – which was deemed useful in the social power game that upper-class culture consisted of.[60] This division into 'male' and 'female' games and codes of conduct was also shown in eighteenth-century genre scenes. It is the man who concentrates on aiming for the billiard ball in Johann Esaias Nilson's drawing, while the women observe or wait on other people (Image 80). They play a more active part in depictions of the era's popular games of chance instead.

Jacques-Philippe Le Bas' engravings after Charles Eisen's paintings from the mid-eighteenth century displayed elegant couples engaged in games in a double sense. The engravings' epigrams allude to the parallels between the capricious outcome of the fashionable games of chance *La cométe* or *Le tric-trac*, in which a card is turned or a die is cast, and the amorous hints between the players.[61] Shapely male legs are stretched out under the games table, and the woman's bare forearms draw attention to her hands' expressive gestures (Image 81). The youth and physical beauty of the players associate the pleasures of the game with those of love. It is the woman who is leading the game in *Le tric-trac*; her active, exhorting

57 *Om medlen att förhöja qwinliga skönheten*, 1806, pp. 17–18.

58 Darwin, Erasmus, *Plan for the Conduct of Female Education in Boarding Schools*, London 1797, p. 86.

59 *Dangerous Liaisons. Fashion and Furniture in the Eighteenth Century*, Harold Koda and Andrew Bolton (ed.), Metropolitan Museum of Art and Yale University Press, 2004, p. 99f.

60 Laine, Merit and Brown, Carolina, *Gustaf Lundberg 1695–1786. En porträttmålare och hans tid*, Stockholm 2006, p. 134.

61 'Vous combinés, Philis, d'un dez le sort frivole, chacque coup, à ce jeu, vous fait craindre une école hesitez vous ainsi, lorsqu'un amant heureux se paye de l'hommage offert à vos beaux yeux? dans les jeux de l'amour, conduit à la tendresse un jeune coeur balance à montrere son yvresse mais ou premier hazard, le coup de l'Ecolier devient un coup de maitre, et donne le laurier.'

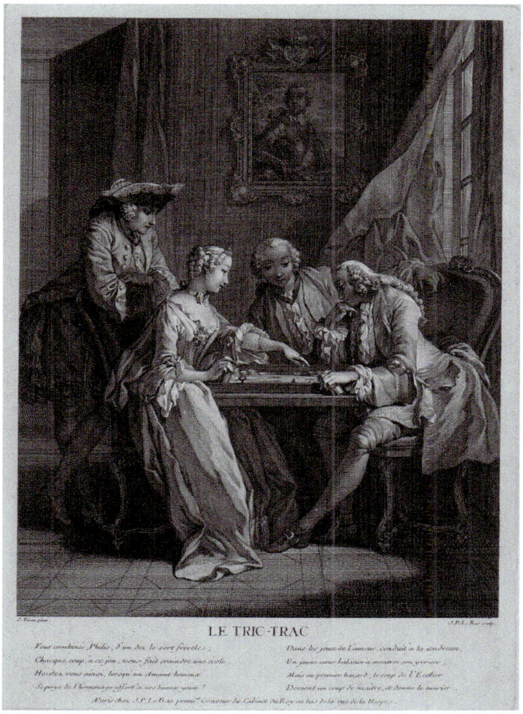

81. Jacques-Philippe Le Bas after Charles Eisen, *Le tric-trac*. Engraving, 38 × 27.3 cm. National Gallery of Art, Washington, DC (1942.9.2166).

gesture is met by the man's smile and contemplative pose. The two male spectators attentively follow the game, looking at the woman's hand. In pictures such as this, the woman is often portrayed as enterprising in games of chance. Chance was here in interplay with what was deemed to be women's capricious nature, governed by emotions and impulses, rather than sense and logic.[62] In the pictures, she smiles at fate that has gifted her a playing card with the ace of hearts or a winning cast of the dice. Bonnart's engravings in Paris in the 1670s had already presented a similar situation, where the most beautiful woman draws the best cards and attracts the most glances.[63] In Dutch seventeenth-century art, the game as an erotic metaphor had reappeared as a motif in moralising genre scenes and thereby contributed to the motif's popularity in the subsequent eighteenth century.[64]

In the pictorial world of the late eighteenth century, women's relationship to the games of chance is also portrayed as a union with the powers of fate. It is only

62 *Dangerous Liaisons. Fashion and Furniture in the Eighteenth Century*, Harold Koda and Andrew Bolton (ed.), Metropolitan Museum of Art and Yale University Press 2004, p. 99f.

63 Bonnart, *Dame de qualité* or *Campagnie jouant au jeu de l'ombre, Receueil des modes de la cour de France*, Paris, 1678–93.

64 See Judith Leyster's *A Game of Tric-Trac*, 1630, Worcester Art Museum, Worcester, Massachusetts, or Jan Steen's *Tric-Trac Players*, 1667, the Hermitage Museum, Moscow.

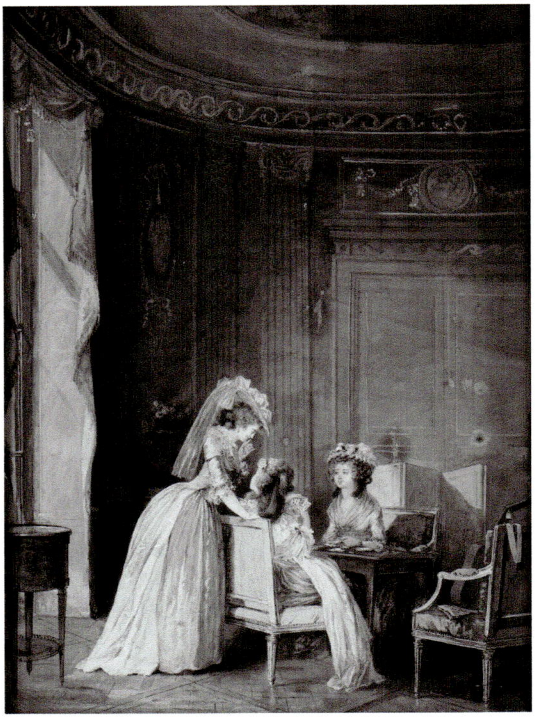

82. Niclas Lafrensen the Younger, *Damer som spelar kort*, 1780s. Gouache, 29 × 21 cm. Nationalmuseum, Stockholm (NMB 13). Photo: Anna Danielsson/Nationalmuseum.

women who have gathered around the playing cards in Niclas Lafrensen's gouache from the early 1780s (image 82). They are preoccupied with each other and the game, unaware of the picture's viewer, who is given a glimpse of the cards in one woman's hand. The intimate circle around the games table turns the backs of their chairs on the surrounding world, and behind the folding screens they share glances and confidences. Perhaps on the subject of the game in progress or a completely different type of game. The women in their pale clothes, illuminated in the dark pictorial space, sit here in private in their own world, uninterested in turning to face the viewer, which was otherwise part of the genre. The surrounding world disturbs in a way that is reminiscent of Pehr Nordquist's later painting *Caffe-Beslaget*, in which the officials surprise the women who have drunk the forbidden coffee and where the playing cards fall off the games table that is hastily cleared away (Image 89).

Lafrensen describes the game as especially feminine, yet also closely connected with fashion and fashionable lifestyle. The viewer is excluded from the group but is in return treated to meticulous descriptions of all the fashionable details. The scene presents a lavish room, where classicising furnishings, patterned oak parquet and gilt armchairs indicate taste and economic resources. The women's clothes, hairstyles and head coverings harmonise with the wall decorations' festoons and friezes of roses and bows. Like the mythological three Graces, the women are reminders of the joys of life and are as decorative to the viewer as the French fashion plates that were sold in Stockholm's bookshops. In that respect, the scene was both normative and identity-building.

The market rapidly adapted its range of products to the female consumer of games. Games of chance such as lotto, biribi or cavagnole and various board games were designed to be tempting consumer goods that alluded to current fashion. The pictures on the games were often directly copied from contemporary fashion plates. One of the many examples was the board game *Le nouveau jeu du costume et des coeffures des dames dédié au beau sexe* from the 1770s, where the players are led through the fashion-conscious upper-class woman's day via named hairstyles and hats. The winner is the player who first reaches *La Belle Poulle*, the name of one of the French ships that fought against the English in 1778.[65] Fashion as a comment on current trends and political events probably gave the game extra appeal. The wide distribution of engraved pictures and prints helped to market the growing games culture, and attractively packaged games were seen in newspaper advertisements:

> The bookshop Holmbergs Boklåda sells: The Queen's almanac in silk binding with additional pictures of Ladies a 24 ß. Triple Calendars, 1 R:d. Lotto game, complete 2 Rd. 24 ß. Playing cards for children, engraved in copper, 12 ß in a case. Conversation cards, 24 ß. New parlour games from Norrköping, 16 ß. Moral mottos, 40 in number, a 12 ß., all in cases.[66]

At Näs in the late eighteenth century, there was a modern copperplate engraving puzzle, of the type advertised in *Dagligt Allehanda* in April 1793 (Image 83). Bookbinder Samuel Martin here launched the engravings by his brothers Elias and Johan Fredrik for edification and entertainment: 'suitable both to decorate a cabinet and to educate young people'. Alongside the plates, the advertisement presented 'the now common cut copperplates in their boxes, or puzzle games in various sizes'.[67] This novelty was for sale at the Martin brothers' shop on Regeringsgatan Street as well as in the 'Mechaniska Factorie-boden' shop at Riddarhustorget Square. Sophia Wadenstierna, who by this time had taken over Näs and started a family with Lars August Mannerheim, perhaps spent some of her free time with her daughters on puzzles, conversation games or pick-up sticks, which are also among the effects from Näs.

65 *Le nouveau jeu du costume et des coeffures des dames dédié au beau sexe*, 1778. Victoria and Albert Museum, London (E.1515-1959).

66 *Dagligt Allehanda*, 17 December 1798.

67 *Dagligt Allehanda*, 9 April 1793.

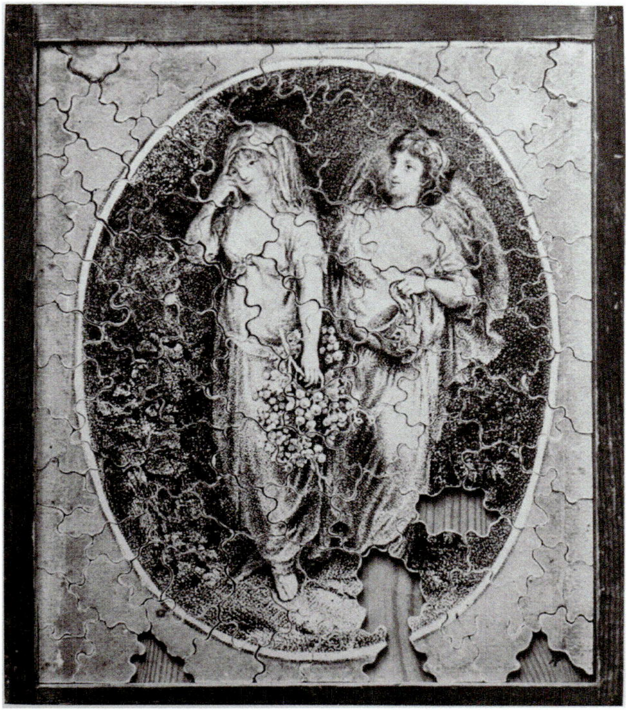

83. Puzzle from the late eighteenth century at Näs. Engraving by the Martin brothers. From Gustaf Näsström, *Forna dagars Sverige*, 3 vols, Stockholm, 1962, vol. 3. Photo: Hans Hammarskiöld.

In Gustaf Johan Ehrensvärd's description of a day at the Gustavian court, the hours spent on the games of chance – biribi, vingt-un, lotterie, cavagnole – are what reinforced his feeling of having a meaningless pastime. The associations made between games of chance and female traits were further strengthened when gender constructions changed in the latter part of the eighteenth century. Fashion whims, consumption and comfortable pastimes were increasingly clearly connected with French taste that had feminine overtones. In his notes, Ehrensvärd, and his brother, Carl August, held women responsible for the dissatisfaction that he felt about the era's social and cultural phenomena.[68]

The culture of comfort went hand in hand with the games culture, where the meaningless games of chance crushed all ambitions of useful activities, cultivation and taste. As a sign of the times, the Ehrensvärd brothers thought it was a result of women's bad influence. Here, 'masculinity in ways of thinking' was required, but also laws and ordinances that counteracted the dissemination of a culture of

68 Gustaf Johan Ehrensvärd's brother, Carl August, formulated the same feeling in one of his letters: '[I] f you care to look, our comfort is perhaps the reason for the many sins we commit against taste. It is not really the fault of the men, but it is our socialising with women that has made us feel forced to facilitate this habit in all ways possible', Carl August Ehrensvärd, *C. A. Ehrensvärds brev. Utgivna av Gunhild Bergh*, I, Stockholm 1916, p. 62.

consumption and comfort with female overtones.[69] The recurring gambling bans did not solve the problem, however, and popular lottery games such as *La belle* spread like the plague in Stockholm in the 1780s. The game did give rise to a proclamation from the government, but that was counteracted by the king's own intervention: anyone who paid a monthly sum to the police received dispensation to open his games venue for the specific game of *La belle*.[70] Councillor of the realm and governor Carl Sparre, who issued the proclamation in 1785, had exempted billiards from the ban, as it enjoyed royal privilege and belonged to the world of male cliques in lavish billiard wings or in the capital city's clubs. An advertisement in *Dagligt Allehanda* in 1789 hints at this special games culture and women's place in it: 'If a girl who is young and beautiful, wishes to serve as an attendant at billiards, she can apply at house no. 89 on Swartmangatan Street.'[71]

Back to Näs

The difference between Wadenstierna's high-status billiards in the wing building at Näs and Hilleström's painting of the woman fortune telling with cards on the pull-out leaf of a chest of drawers is reminiscent of the role distribution that assigned women and men separate spheres (Image 74). Even if the Wadenstierna sisters possibly played billiards just as much as their father, or if he sometimes used playing cards to predict the future, this gender-normative order recurs in the eighteenth century's various texts and pictures. According to this attitude, it was self-evident that the person holding the playing cards next to the dressing table mirror and piles of clothes in Hilleström's painting was a woman. When Carl Eric Wadenstierna wrote his verse about wastefulness regarding the household's expensive candle-ends that are used for all sorts of nonsensical things, he consequently adds: 'and one for cards telling Lena's fortune' (see Chapter 2).[72]

Although this Lena could have been the model for the woman in Hilleström's painting, it was probably not intended to be a portrait of an identifiable woman from

69 Here, Ehrensvärd alludes to women's weakness for fashion consumption, which he claimed forced the king to establish the national costume, Gustaf Johan Ehrensvärd, *Dagboksanteckningar förda vid Gustaf III:s hof, utgifna af D:r E. V. Montan*, II, Stockholm 1878, p. 347.

70 *Utdrag Utur alle ifrån den 7 dec. 1718 utkomne Publique Handlingar, Placater, Förordningar, Resolutioner ock Publicationer, Som Riksens Styrsel samt inwärtes Hushållning och Författningar i gemen, jämwäl ock Stockholms Stad i synnerhet, angå*, 1–15, Stockholm, 1742–1829. XIII, p. 197; *Gustavianskt 1771–1810. En bokfilm av Ingvar Andersson, Agne Beijer, Bertil Kjellberg, Bo Lindorm*, Stockholm 1945, p. 298.

71 *Dagligt Allehanda*, 13 August 1789.

72 Näsström, Gustaf, *Forna dagars Sverige*, III, *Kulturhistorisk bilderbok om frihetstid och gustaviansk tid*, Stockholm 1962, p. 158.

the Wadenstierna household. Her general identity was instead an exhortation for all viewers to relate to. Perhaps this painting hung next to the suite of images that depicted women washing, ironing, carding and spinning, which Pehr Hilleström created for the family at Näs. Highly visible to Wadenstierna's wife and daughters as well as the various maids, it was a reminder of where women were expected to be and what tasks they should fill every day with. In the same way as was formulated in the lines of verse in the 'moral mirror' *Unga Fruentimbers Hushålls Spegel*, published in 1754, the picture conveyed the importance of making good use of your time and avoiding the pastimes that easily became bad habits:

> Read beautiful books now and then,
> Write useful things to remember,
> Never hastily snap at anyone,
> Pursue virtuous pastimes.
> Dice, cards and such games,
> Deepen the roots of laziness,
> Those who do so, are sure to err,
> The habit rarely withers away.[73]

The game in visual art was often a metaphor for the real-life social game, between different groups and between men and women, and for the changeableness and transience of life. When Hilleström paints the young woman fortune telling with the playing cards, he depicts her next to a dressing table mirror. Both the game and the mirror were symbols of vanity and superficialities.

The painting's depiction of everyday early and mid-morning messiness and the woman's untidy clothing and carefree facial expression unquestionably contained a reminder that duties awaited. But Hilleström's painting also showed a life that included moments of freedom from obligations and compulsory conventions. In this case, the woman's apparently spontaneous game did not require any visiting coats or demands on politeness, and no special room or specific furniture. The painting appears to highlight the contrast to the urban life's elegant drawing room amusements or its rowdy games at smoke-filled coffee houses and restaurants. The peaceful, informal socialising in country life was instead an expression of a comfortable and harmonious lifestyle, without grand mannerisms. The innocence (or simplicity) contained the ideals that were formulated in the entrance hall's overdoor decorations. In that context, the painting expresses a different and more informal aspect of the new culture of comfort. The comfort could be accentuated through loosely fitting clothes, furniture with soft cushions and practical pull-out leaves, but

73 *Unga Fruentimbers Hushålls Spegel*, Stockholm (1754) 1788.

it is also seen through the unaffected, unpretentious amusements. For visitors to Näs, Hilleström's painting of the woman with the playing cards emphasised the tranquil diversions of country life – just as the overdoor decorations in the entrance hall.

This chapter has been about the eighteenth century's extensive games culture and about how important it was for members of the upper class to show that they were knowledgeable about current games, to observe moderation and to furnish their homes and social lives in accordance with the era's fashion. The ownership of a billiard table or the knowledge of how to play cavagnole correctly formed part of upper-class culture. However, allusions to this games culture are often noticeable by their absence in eighteenth-century portraiture. The genre scenes and fashion images conveyed the rules of the game, but these ephemeral pastimes seemed to have be removed from an image category that intended to have a longer lifespan than the person depicted. The portrait was not only a statement to the world on role and position, it was also to fulfil key functions in a longer, future perspective. Niclas Lafrensen's painting of the card-playing women displayed an ideal that the social elite probably aspired to, but when he was commissioned to paint portraits of the same elite, he opted to omit the playing cards. Despite all the games tables in the Wadenstierna home, neither Lafrensen nor Hilleström placed the family close to them, in accordance with the pattern already highlighted. Jacobina Psilanderhielm and her daughters were depicted at sewing tables, and Fredrica Carleson at a writing table, but the games tables had no given place in the contemporary Swedish portraits of women.[74]

Pehr Hilleström's painting of a group playing cards at State Secretary Schröderheim's home has been described as a 'portrait', even though it also displays similarities with the fashionable genre pictures that were spread throughout Europe (Image 79). Just as his painting *Conversation på Drottningholm* incorporated portraits of members of the royal family and the court, these pictures can be regarded as expressions of the era's conversation pieces within visual art. Hilleström was careful to point out this affinity with an internationally topical genre of pictures by referring back to the conversation in the titles of his works: *Conversation på Drottningholm* or *2ne Fröknar Wadenstiernas portraiter – i Conversation.* In this respect, the group playing games at the Schröderheims can be compared to John Zoffany's portrait of the Dutton family in their drawing room in Sherborne Park, Gloucestershire, in the 1770s, in the country where this type of picture celebrated its foremost triumphs (Image 84). The family members are less absorbed in the game and more in a conversation with each other. Although the scene is a manifestation

74 References to games did appear, however, in the special disguised portraits, *portrait déguisé* or *portrait historié*, which, among other things, alluded to historicising or mythologising representations. The exceptions include Gustaf Lundberg's portrait of *Adolf Ludvig Gustaf Albert Couschi* (known as Badin) playing chess, 1775. Pastel, 74 × 57 cm, Nationalmuseum; Laine 2006, pp. 129–35.

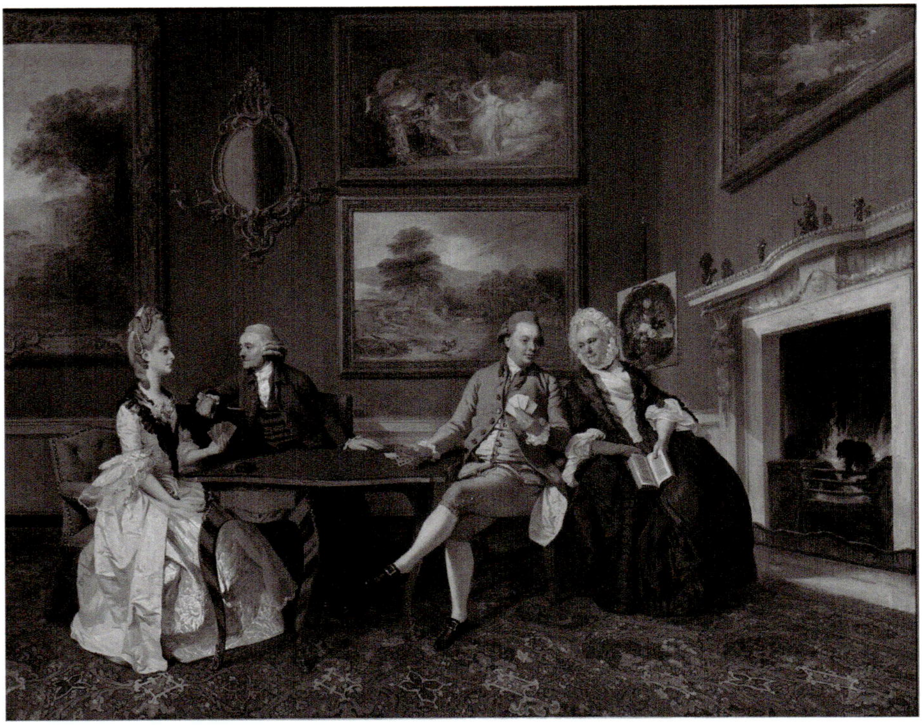

84. Johann Zoffany, *The Dutton Family in the Drawing Room of Sherborne Park, Gloucestershire, c.* 1772. Oil on canvas, 101.5 × 127 cm. Leonard C. Hanna Jr. Fund (2023.122), the Cleveland Museum of Art.

of material prosperity and the refinements and social ambitions of the drawing room culture, the closeness between the figures portrayed is the main message of the painting. Here, the game was an aspect of the conversation and the aim an expression of togetherness.

Jacobina Psilanderhielm's estate inventory from 1769 noted eight different games tables.[75] Games had obviously been part of family life and social life. Nevertheless, she was depicted at the sewing table in the portrait by Niclas Lafrensen. We do not know at which table she was happiest or spent most time, or what was actually hidden in her workbag. Among spools of thread, notes and sweets, perhaps also playing cards.[76] However, it is well documented that the embroidery thread found in a workbox and sewing drawers at Näs in the mid-twentieth century was neatly wound around the playing cards used by previous generations.[77]

75 Jacobina Sophia Psilanderhielms bouppteckning, 4 December 1769, *Riksarkivet*, Näs Silverstolpeska arkivet, Personarkiven, vol. 60, Carl Eric Wadenstierna (1723–1787).

76 On the workbag as a fashion accessory, see Chapter 2.

77 Söderberg, Bengt G., 'Näs', *Slott och herresäten i Sverige*, Malmö 1967, p. 12.

6. At the coffee table

Abstract
The concluding chapter discusses the importance of coffee and porcelain as established symbols of elite luxury consumption in relation to the new culture of comfort in Europe, and how it was integrated in the everyday life at Näs. The question of how, when and by whom coffee (or tea) was drunk was circumvented by a series of social and cultural codes, especially at a time when both the beverage and its vessels became increasingly widespread commodities. The European pattern is however here modified by the specific Swedish debate and legislation connected to coffee.

Keywords: portraiture and print culture, coffee, tea, fashion, private and public spheres, sociability

An elegant small table from Paris in the 1770s has been designed with a well-decorated apron, on which a cup, pot and sugar bowl have been depicted in the various types of wood of the veneer (Image 85). The delicate accoutrements used when drinking coffee or tea could be brought out from under the divisible table top, and more storage was available in the drawers hidden behind the sliding tambour door. The coffee or tea service was laid out on the round trays, and the table was conveniently rolled to wherever it was needed at the time, by the sofa, the armchair or the fire place. The table took up little space in a corner but was nonetheless extremely conspicuous. Signed by the *ébéniste* Léonard Boudin, one of the leading *marchands-merciers* in Paris, it was a coveted piece of furniture that evoked associations with all parts of the eighteenth century's exclusive coffee culture.[1] During the century, similar tables appeared in upper-class homes all over Europe, including in Sweden, and engravings after Niclas Lafrensen's genre paintings show how they could be used in the era's wealthy environments (Image 48).

1 Christie's, Paris, sale 14636, 7 March 2017. Two tables by Boudin were part of King Adolf Fredrik and Queen Lovisa Ulrika's furniture, including a *bonheur du jour* with veneer inlays representing a tea service. Bukowskis, Classic Auction, no. 566, Spring 2010, catalogue no. 901; Bukowskis, Auction 425, Spring 1984, catalogue no. 658.

Brown, C., *Comfortable Everyday Life at the Swedish Eighteenth-Century Näs Manor.*
Taylor & Francis Group, 2024
DOI 10.5117/9789048562374_CH06

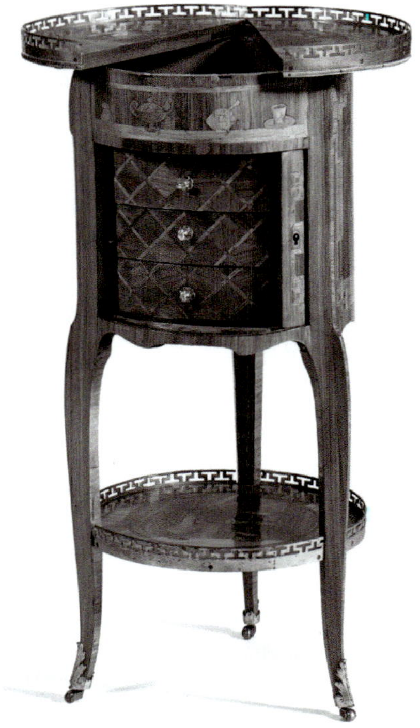

85. Léonard Boudin, *Table tambour*, 1770s. Private ownership. Photo: Christie's.

Chocolate, tea and coffee had in turn reached Europe as a result of expanded travelling and trade in the sixteenth and seventeenth centuries.[2] The new beverages were accompanied by the development of markets for cocoa beans, tea leaves and coffee beans, but also for the special cups, pots, strainers, grinders and tables that the beverages required. The round teapot differed from the narrow, tall coffee pot, and the tea table with its faience top from the veneered coffee table. Visual art provides indications of how these various fashionable pieces of furniture and utensils were intended to be used and tell us that coffee and tea were also drunk at both games tables and dressing tables. These hot drinks, and everything required for them, clearly occupied a central place in eighteenth-century upper-class culture – which also applied at Wadenstierna's well-equipped Näs Manor.

The exquisite tea table that was housed at Näs, with its frame made by Georg Haupt and faience tray by the Marieberg factory in Stockholm, was probably used for tea, coffee and chocolate. In many ways, the social contexts and rituals that developed surrounding the new beverages were also closely interwoven with

2 Yao-Fen You, 'From Novelty to Necessity: The Europeanization of Coffee, Tea, and Chocolate', *Coffee, Tea, and Chocolate. Consuming the World*, Yao-Fen You (ed.), Yale University Press 2016, pp. 11–29.

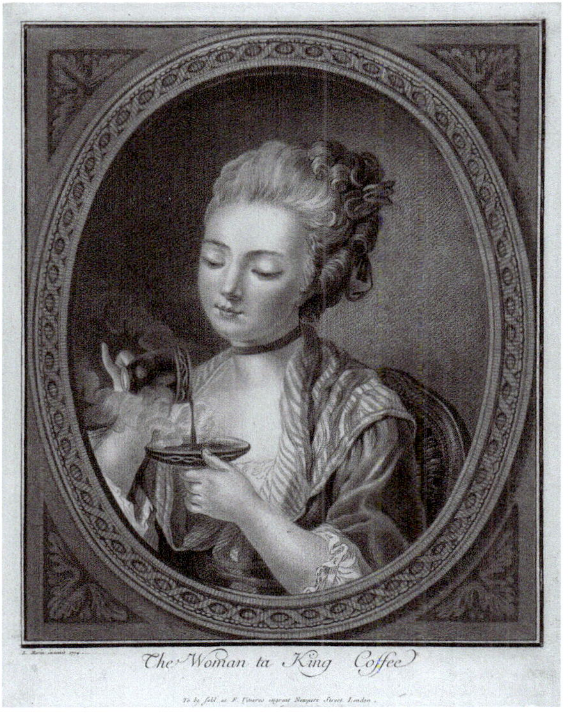

86. Louis-Marin Bonnet, *The Woman ta King Coffee*, 1774. Engraving, 29.6 × 23 cm. The Metropolitan Museum of Art, New York (65.692.6). (Regarding the title in English rather than in French, see Chapter 6, note 4.)

each other during the century.[3] This chapter will mainly focus on coffee drinking, although the closeness to and connection with tea culture is constantly evident. Carl Eric Wadenstierna's engagement in politics and the debate on sumptuary laws and coffee bans gives the subject special relevance in this context.

At the same time that Lafrensen painted the portraits of Wadenstierna's wives in the early 1770s, the Parisian engraver Louis-Marin Bonnet launched an engraving of a woman drinking coffee, surrounded by a gilt frame (Image 86).[4] The motif belonged to a suite of pictures that decoratively illustrated a fashionable woman's pleasant mornings (Image 66). Bonnet's engravings can be regarded as a visual guide to modern and comfortable life – how to live it and what belonged to it.

3 Michael North, 'The New Stimulants and Sociability', *Material Delight and the Joy of Living. Cultural Consumption in the Age of Enlightenment in Germany*, Ashgate 2008, pp. 153–67; Hanna Hodacs, *Silk and Tea in the North. Scandinavian Trade and the Market for Asian Goods in Eighteenth-Century Europe*, London 2016.

4 Bonnet experimented early on with gilt frames for the engravings – a risky project as gold leaf was regulated by law, and only a few limited craft guilds in Paris were permitted to use it. To avoid penalties, he signed the engraving with a different name, used an English title and stated an incorrect printing location (London), *Colorful Impressions. The Printmaking Revolution in Eighteenth-Century France*, Margaret Morgan Grasselli (ed.), Washington 2003, pp. 82–4.

Clothes, accessories, furniture and objects are depicted in detail.[5] The woman with her splayed little finger, pleasurably pouring her morning coffee was an image that conveyed a trend that increasing numbers of people could identify with in the 1770s. The dissemination of the engravings effectively reproduced the identity-building ideals, notably not least in how they were repeated in portraiture. But although coffee tables, services and coffee-drinking women recur in Niclas Lafrensen's pictorial world (Plate 18 and Image 98), no coffee cups are visible in his portraits of the Wadenstierna family (Plates 1–3). Why did the artist avoid these fashionable attributes in these specific portraits, when they played such a large part in the real life of the people he depicted?

Coffee, which was introduced in the seventeenth century as a luxury beverage with health benefits among the elite, became a stimulant within increasingly broad social strata in the eighteenth century. In around 1780, there were nearly 2,800 *limonadiers* in Paris. In the late seventeenth century, they would have been exclusive establishments for the enjoyment of expensive imported goods – besides tea and coffee, also exotic fruit and nuts and all conceivable liqueurs and sweets that could be made from them with the help of sugar.[6] When France started to import coffee from its own colonies, coffee drinking increased, and the *limonadiers* became the predecessors of the subsequent cafés.[7] In 1788, there were forty-five coffee houses in Stockholm, but the number fluctuated in the latter half of the eighteenth century due to the coffee bans. In addition to these premises, there were ambulant coffee vendors on streets, markets and squares.[8] There were both differences and similarities between Stockholm and Paris. In both cities, drinking coffee in public was associated with alcohol, but in Stockholm this was less about the consumption of exotic liqueurs and perhaps more about rowdiness and disorder.[9] Drinking coffee or tea was hardly no longer an activity that characterised the elite. Craftsmen, maids and farmhands could also have the equipment required to make

5 Another picture in the suite shows a woman opening a basket of gifts that she has received as wedding presents: a pocket watch, a fan, jewellery and a portrait miniature of her husband. Louis-Marin Bonnet, *The Marriage Presents*, mid-1770s, 29.1 × 23.3 cm, the National Gallery of Art, Washington D.C.

6 Pierre Masson, *Le parfait limonadier, ou La maniere de preparer le thé, le caffé, le chocolat & autres liqueurs chaudes & froides*, Paris 1705; Woodruff D. Smith, *Consumption and the Making of Respectability 1600–1800*, New York 2002, pp. 90–2.

7 Carolyn Purnell, *The Sensational Past. How the Enlightenment Changed the Way We Use Our Senses*, New York 2017, pp. 48–51.

8 Anita Du Rietz, *Kvinnors entreprenörskap under 400 år*, Stockholm 2013.

9 The 'Royal Council' issued a letter regarding the disturbances in the city's 'Coffee huus' dated 24 October 1705, which is available in the database: https://stockholmskallan.stockholm.se/post/30150. During the years of the coffee bans, sales of aquavit provided compensation for the coffee houses, Karin Sennefelt, *Politikens hjärta, Medborgarskap, manlighet och plats i frihetstidens Stockholm*, Stockholm 2011, p. 155.

tea or coffee, and this situation was largely the same throughout Europe.[10] But the differences lay in the framing of the hot drinks, precisely as illustrated in Lafrensen's or Bonnet's gold-rimmed engravings – namely, the access to porcelain cups, silver spoons and sugar tongs, tea tables and armchairs, and not least a privileged use of time.[11] The crude public coffee houses here contrasted a more refined way of drinking tea and coffee in private upper-class homes – during the mornings or in connection with social life and visits. It was in these contexts that the beverages were integrated into a new culture of comfort and new ways of socialising. And here, the social aspirations were marked through new rituals and through an increasingly pretentious material culture.

In the portraits of Wadenstierna's wives, an East Indian coffee cup could have stood decoratively next to a workbag or sheet of writing paper. The family's inventory lists reveal an abundance of everything required for taking coffee: silver coffee pots, rows of red, blue and colourfully decorated cups with or without handles, cups made of Saxony porcelain and pots from the Marieberg factory in Stockholm.[12] There was also East Indian tableware embellished with the Wadenstierna family's coat of arms and the Royal Order of the Polar Star, painted in gold and enamel (Plate 19). The home also included a multitude of all the accessories required, not only for making the coffee in the kitchen, such as a coffee roaster, coffee grinder, coffee funnel and a number of large pots and pans made of copper, but also for serving the coffee and tea in polite style in dining and drawing rooms. There were tea urns for heating, tea trays, tea caddies and sugar bowls, sugar tongs, cream jugs and milk jugs, bowls for coffee grounds and tea leaves, dozens of spoons and saucers, and monogrammed napkins.[13]

However, neither tea nor coffee cups are shown in the Wadenstierna family's portraits. This may be explained by the specialisation of the culture of comfort during the eighteenth century, in which every need and function had its specific tools. But perhaps a coffee cup would have also marred the image of the women's

10 *Dagligt Allehanda*, 28 September 1773: a 'poor servant' from a travelling carriage was robbed of his possessions in a sack. Among coarse crispbread and towels there was also a large teapot. For a review of the ownership of tea and coffee utensils in eighteenth-century Stockholm: Anders Eklöv, "…och all den Egendom som efter mig finnes är genom flit och arbetsamhet förvärfvat.' – Om konsumtion och ägande bland stockholmarna under 1700-talet.', unpublished Bachelor's thesis, the Department of Economic History and International Relations, Stockholm University, 1997, pp. 29–32. Regarding the social distribution of coffee and tea consumption in Sweden: Christer Ahlberger, *Konsumtionsrevolutionen, I, Om det moderna konsumtionssamhällets framväxt 1750–1900*, Gothenburg 1996. On coffee drinking in Europe: Jon Stobart, *Sugar & Spice. Grocers and Groceries in Provincial England, 1650–1830*, Oxford 2013, p. 218; E.C. Spary, *Eating the Enlightenment. Food and the Sciences in Paris, 1670–1760*, Chicago 2012, Chapter 3 'The Place of Coffee'.

11 You 2016.

12 Riksarkivet, Näs Silverstolpeska arkivet, Personarkiven, vol. 60, Carl Eric Wadenstierna (1723–1787).

13 Ibid.

diligence and skills and created associations with not only repose and comfort but maybe also idleness and frivolity. During the eighteenth century, certain notions regarding women's coffee consumption developed that were not readily compatible with the identity and self-image that a portrait was supposed to express. To understand the *absence* of the symbol-laden cup, the way in which coffee culture was presented in other pictures and texts must be discussed before we return to the tea and coffee tables at Näs and the portraits of the Wadenstierna family.

Coffee drinking and coffee criticism

Coffee was drunk in the eighteenth century by men, women and children, but there were clear and gender-coded differences regarding when, how and where it was consumed. Male coffee drinking was often associated with the coffee houses and the outspoken culture that developed there, while female coffee consumption mainly belonged to the home sphere. The political significance of the coffee houses as hubs of news within the growing urban bourgeoisie has often been highlighted, as well as the impact of the coffee houses on the formation of a male-dominated public sphere.[14] But women also took part in the public coffee culture, and in the Gustavian era in Stockholm, several coffee houses were run by women.[15] Mademoiselle Maja Lisas Caffehus by Riddarhustorget Square was among the better known ones, and other establishments such as Fru Holmings Kaffeservering next to Barbara Suzanne Pauli's renowned large fashion shop Temple du Goût at Mynttorget Square were surely also visited by women.[16] During the spring and summer seasons, coffee was also served in the Kungsträdgården park and at other fashionable excursion destinations. In *Stockholms Posten* on 18 May 1779 it was announced that: 'As usual, in Kungsträdgården park by St Jacobi Church, the serving of coffee has now started, in both the mornings and the afternoons.'

However, in the era's satirical texts and pictures, the presence of women in the coffee houses was often linked to gambling and stronger beverages and to

14 Jürgen Habermas *The Structural Transformation of the Public Sphere. An Inquiry into a Category of Bourgeois Society*, (1962), Cambridge, Massachusetts 1989, Habermas claims that this structural division is based on the eighteenth century's Enlightenment ideal. Although Habermas' theories have been questioned, they have validity in relation to the eighteenth century's idealised pictorial world. On coffee houses and the development of the political culture in the eighteenth century see Marie-Christine Skuncke and Henrika Tandefelt, *Riksdag, kaffehus och predikstol: frihetstidens politiska kultur 1766–1772*, Stockholm 2003.

15 Smith 2002, pp. 156f.

16 Regarding Maria Elisabeth Borgman's coffee house and 'Fru Holmings Konditori' next to Pauli's large fashion shop Temple du Goût, see Du Rietz, Anita, *Kvinnors entreprenörskap under 400 år*, Stockholm 2013 and Elers, Johan, *Stockholm*, I, Stockholm 1800, p. 97.

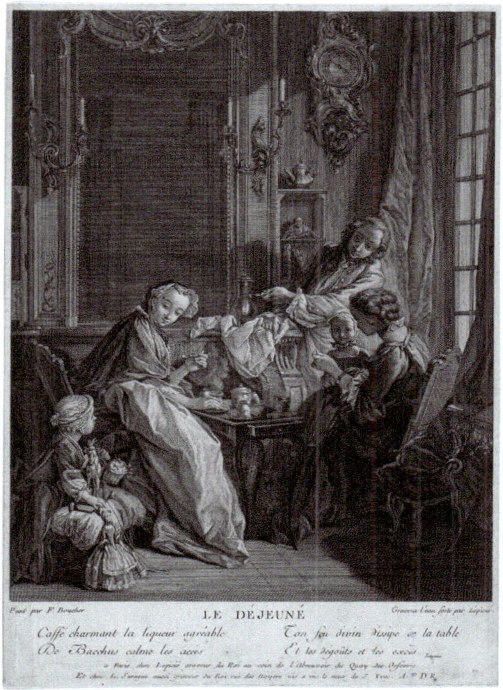

87. François-Bernard Lépicié after François Boucher, *Le déjeuné*, 1744. Engraving, 37.3 × 26.6 cm. The Metropolitan Museum of Art, New York (50.567.34).

other unsuitable conduct. The subtitle of William Hogarth's engraving *The Rake's Rendez-vous* from the latter half of the 1730s clarifies that the scene, showing how fashionable dandies have arranged to meet scantily dressed women, takes place at 'Tom King's Coffee House in Covent Garden' in London.[17] Wadenstierna's library at Näs included the popular play *Le caffé, ou l'ecossaise* from 1760, written by Voltaire under the pseudonym 'Mr Hume' (referring to the cousin of philosopher David Hume, who was a clergyman in Edinburgh).[18] Here, the coffee house is also the scene for love plots involving a young man and a scantily dressed girl. *Dagligt Allehanda* advertised performances of the play at 'Swenska Theatren' in Stockholm on several occasions in 1784.[19] In this play, the coffee house was a place that challenged the boundaries of the prevailing order yet also strengthened the expected images of

17 *The Rake's Rendez-Vous; or the Midnight revels wherein are delineated the various humours of Tom King's Coffee House in Covent Garden*, 1735–40, engraving, 21.1 × 34.6 cm, British Museum, London (1860, 0623.35). Covent Garden was London's hub of entertainment and amusements, and the coffee houses were often meeting places for prostitution; *Harris's List of Covent Garden Ladies*, Hallie Rubenhold (ed.), London 2012.

18 Voltaire, *Le caffe, ou l'ecossaise, comedie. Par Mr. Hume prêtre écossais, traduit en français*, London 1760.

19 *Dagligt Allehanda*, Stockholm 13 and 29 September and 23 December 1784.

male and female coffee drinkers. The real-life situation in Sweden was probably more nuanced, but Wadenstierna's wife and daughters perhaps nonetheless realised that it was safest to drink coffee at home.[20]

In contrast to the chaotic coffee house, the coffee drinking in François-Bernard Lépicié's contemporary engraving *Le déjeuné* is surrounded by delicate cups, elegant tables and refined gestures (Image 87). The motif is from a painting by François Boucher dated 1739.[21] The elegant women in the picture serve the well-behaved children morning coffee, '*caffé charmant*', with sugar and milk.[22] The teapot and Chinese figurine in the cupboard under the clock are reminders that everything has its place and follows an order in the well-appointed home. The special utensils and accoutrements for taking coffee are presented in harmony with the modern interior decoration. Women's coffee drinking clearly differed from men's, and in Sweden just as in other countries women were expected to drink their coffee in more cultivated ways.[23] When Carl Michael Bellman made ironic remarks about young women's whims and fashions in *Tankar om flickors ostadighet* (Thoughts on the fickleness of girls) in 1758, one of the breaches of etiquette consisted of women's excessively uninhibited and loud yelling at the coffee table.[24]

The poet Bellman's satire about coffee drinking and social norms also reflected a deep criticism of the coffee culture that gradually grew in the eighteenth century. Jean-François de Troy's painting from 1723 shows a woman in morning attire drinking her breakfast coffee (Image 88).[25] The epigram accompanying the print of the picture gives an interpretation of the lightly dressed and smiling woman's intentions with the hot morning drink: to make blood boil and feelings run high.[26] In the contemporary world of ideas, strong coffee was often ascribed healthy and even aphrodisiac qualities.[27] But even though men also drank coffee, women were often the focus of the eighteenth century's countless satires and popular

20 In the 1730s, Carl Eric Wadenstierna's father-in-law, Edvard Carleson, had warned about the lifestyle taught by the coffee house clientele – the elegant fashionable dandy who lives on credit and whose only merits are tying a cravat and playing billiards. *Sedolärande Mercurius*, III, No. 10, Stockholm 20 July 1731.

21 François Boucher, *Le déjeuner*, 1739, oil on canvas, 81.5 × 61.5 cm, the Louvre (RF 926), Paris.

22 The epigram by Lépicié: 'Caffé charmant ta liqueur agréable / Ton feu divin dissipe de la table / De Bacchus calme les acces / Et les dégoûts et les excès.' Also see Johanna Ilmakunnas, 'Måltidsupplevelser i 1700-talets Sverige och det tidiga 1800-talets Finland', *Historisk Tidskrift för Finland*, the 100, 2015:4, Helsinki 2015.

23 Smith 2002, pp. 156f.

24 The women are described as crowing cockerels at their over-full coffee tables, Bellman, Carl Michael, Tankar *om flickors ostadighet*, Stockholm 1758; Burman, Carina, *Bellman. Biografin*, Stockholm 2019, p. 69.

25 Jean-François de Troy, *Le petit-déjeuner*, 1723, oil on canvas, 34 × 25 cm, Gemäldegalerie, Berlin.

26 'A quel dessein aimable enfant / Vous servés vous de ce breuvage / Si c'est pour emouvoir le sang que le caffé est en usage / A t'on jamais veu à vôtre âge / Fille manquer de mouvement', Jacques Chéreau after Jean-François de Troy, *Jeune fille prenant un café*, 1730–50, Rennes, Musée des Beaux-Arts.

27 Qualities that were also ascribed to chocolate beverages, You 2016, p. 15.

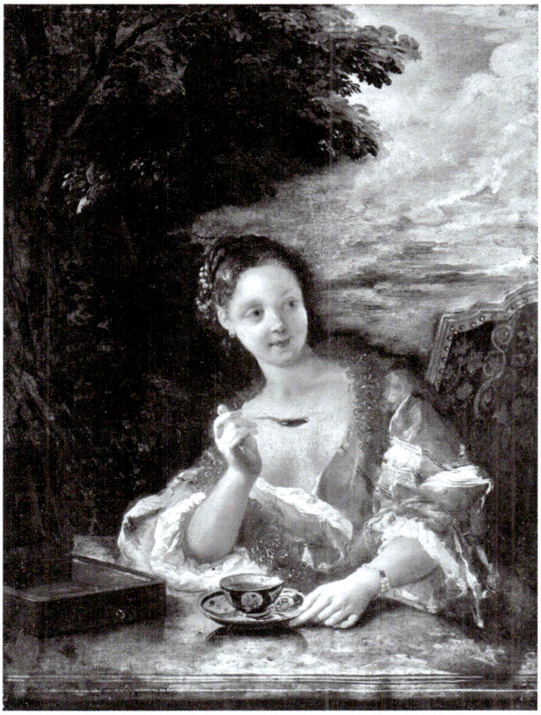

88. Jean-François de Troy, *The Breakfast*, 1723. Oil on canvas, 34 × 25 cm. State Museums of Berlin, Picture Gallery/Jörg P. Anders (Kat. Nr. KFMV.297).

genre images on the theme of drinking coffee.[28] The libretto for Johann Sebastian Bach's short comic opera *Coffee Cantata* from 1732 is about Lieschen's addiction to coffee.[29] When her desperate father threatens to prevent her from marrying unless she stops drinking coffee, his daughter's defiant answer – Who needs kisses when there is hot coffee? – illustrates the bad influence of the fashionable beverage on the woman's duties and calling.

Coffee's origins in distant foreign countries also connected it with various tales of the mysteriousness and heated emotions of the Orient. The long journey taken by coffee, from Ethiopia to Yemen and to Europe via Venice, spiced it with exoticism.

28 Criticism of women's coffee drinking already existed in the seventeenth century: *The Women's Petition against Coffee*. Representing to Publick Consideration the Grand Inconveniencies Accruing to their Sex From the Excessive Use of that Drying, Enfeebling Liquor, London 1674. Equivalent satires existed regarding women's tea drinking. *The Tea Table*, an engraving from London in the 1710s shows a group of women who have gathered around a tea table: '[A]t each Sip a Lady's Honour Dies', The Lewis Walpole Library, Yale University. In Anna Maria Malmstedt's *Thé-Conseillen* from 1775 the expected female confidences of tea drinking are combined with notions of the male cabinet meetings. *Thé-Conseillen* was preceded by *La matinée de Clarisse*, published in *Hvad Nytt* in December 1774, which makes ironic comments about the fashionable young woman's morning toilette, during which even her lapdog was fed with sugared coffee.
29 The libretto for the *Coffee Cantata* was written by 'Picander', the pseudonym for the author Christian Friedrich Henrici (1700–1764).

When the Turkish ambassador Süleyman Aga brought coffee to Louis XIV in 1669, it became known as the 'Turkish drink', and coffee remained strongly associated with fanciful notions of life in the Levant for a long time.[30] In the eighteenth century's orientalism and interest in Turkey, the image of luxury, lust and frivolity flourished, personified by a coffee-drinking sultan in his harem.[31] Sophia Wadenstierna wrote Bellman's verses about 'the Turk's audience' from memory in her poetry book.

> ... windows fling open,
> pour coffee and liqueurs
> give hugs give bribes
> Adonis leads Astrild away
> from barbarism.[32]

The satires about drinking coffee were accompanied by more serious criticism and over time also regulations and bans. Although coffee had previously been ascribed healthy properties, these began to be questioned, and opinions on the health risks of the beverage were presented in various contexts.[33] The idea of the irresponsible coffee-drinking woman, addicted to ostentation, amusements and idleness, fuelled the criticism, which also questioned expensive imports and warned of the lax morals that seemed to be spreading. In these notions, the coffee-dependent woman was regarded as an addict, damaging herself and those around her.[34] In *Fahlu Weckoblad*, a weekly newspaper published in Falun, Dalarna Province, an article in the summer of 1787 did not mince its words in describing the damaging effect of coffee:

> Nerve illnesses, tremors, pale complexion, difficult childbirth, miscarriage and infertility, dries out the bodily fluids and expels the natural warmth of the

30 You 2016, pp. 22, 25.

31 You 2016, pp. 22–5. Tea drinking was also initially associated with exoticism, as part of the era's fashion for chinoiserie.

32 Riksarkivet, Näs Silverstolpeska arkivet, Personarkiven, vol. 61, Sophia Wadenstierna (1758–1830), Carolina Wadenstierna (1762–1848). The lines refer to Carl Michael Bellman's 'Vid turkens audience 1773', *Fredmans sånger*, No. 30, which was first published in 1791. Sophia Wadenstierna's transcriptions of several of Bellman's songs and epistles show that these were part of an oral tradition much earlier on; see Chapter III.

33 Nicolas de Blégny, *Le bon usage du thé, du caffé, et du chocolat pour la preservation & pour la guerison des maladies*, Paris 1787. In *De la santé. Ouvrage utile à tout le monde*, Paris 1771, pp. 218–20, Armand Pierre (Abbé) Jacquin stated how coffee with sugar and milk generally constituted the breakfast of women and children, but that this heavy drink could have dangerous consequences: the coffee may activate body and soul, but soon 'coagulates' them to coldness and inactivity.

34 Runefelt, Leif, *Att hasta mot undergången: anspråk, flyktighet, förställning i debatten om konsumtion i Sverige 1730–1830*, Lund 2015, pp. 86–8, 218–27.

> elderly, emaciates the nutritious sap of the young, agitates the senses, prevents their growth and manliness, and makes them delicate and weak.[35]

The damage did not just affect the individual's body but also society, through the economic loss entailed by the consumption. The woman who wished to save herself and her beauty, was over time recommended to choose hot chocolate instead.[36]

Coffee consumption also became a target in the increasingly heated debate on luxury and excess. Imports of the expensive coffee beans increased markedly after the mid-eighteenth century.[37] Carl Linnaeus warned about the development in his dissertation *Potus Coffeae*, published in 1761. It was not only the imports of coffee that were a strain on households' economy in matters large and small, but also everything associated with it: roasting pans, grinders, boiling pans, cups and pots made of imported porcelain, silverware for serving, lacquered trays and tables. 'To say nothing of the rest, which are deemed absolutely necessary, although they can barely be purchased for a price of a thousand riksdaler', writes Linnaeus.[38] Coffee drinking was surrounded by costs and complicated procedures and rituals. Swedes would have been happier and healthier without it.[39] In addition, when coffee drinking had spread to even larger groups of society, warnings were issued that the consumption could have serious consequences.[40] 'Coffee is a drink that has recently become consumed among us to such an extent that no one, who wishes to be more than a peasant, believes that they are able to and should manage without it,' wrote Elias Granroth in his dissertation on coffee in 1755.[41]

Drastic attempts to prevent the development were made through the recurring coffee bans in the latter half of the eighteenth century: 1756, 1766, 1794 and 1799.

35 *Fahlu Weckoblad*, 24 August 1787, p. 2. Abraham Bäck, royal physician at the Gustavian court, advised Queen Sofia Magdalena against taking unsettling beverages such as coffee and tea during her pregnancy in 1778; Lena Rangström, *Kanonsalut och vaggor Kungliga födslar och dop*, The Royal Armoury, Stockholm 2012, p. 56.

36 *Om medlen att förhöja qwinliga skönheten. Handbok för damer*, Lund 1806, p. 18.

37 Alf Larsson, 'Kaffe, Alkohol m.m.', *Svensk Kemisk Tidskrift*, 1914, p. 33; Ahlberger, Christer, *Konsumtionsrevolutionen 1. Om det moderna konsumtionssamhällets framväxt 1750–1900*, Faculty of Humanities, Gothenburg University, Gothenburg 1996.

38 *Potus Coffeae* Academic dissertation during Linné's presidium, Uppsala 1761, translated from Latin by Ejnar Haglund, the Swedish Linnaeus Society, Ekenäs 1966, p. 12.

39 *Potus Coffeae*, p. 3.

40 'A craftsman goes to the coffee house in the morning, the inn in the afternoon, and lives entirely according to his comfort; his wife and children are ostentatious in damask and silk and look like noblewomen,' *Sedolärande Mercurius*, 20 July 1731.

41 Elias Granroth, *Enfaldige tanckar om caffé och de inhemska wäxter som pläga brukas i des ställe*, Turku 1755, [diss], p. 1. In March 1798, Märta Helena Reenstierna refers in her diary to the custom of offering visitors a sandwich and aquavit as 'peasant mannerisms', Reenstierna, Märta Helena, *Årstadagboken*, I, Stockholm 1985, p. 165.

The first ban had been pushed through by the peasant estate and the political party the Caps (Mössorna) in response to the ban by the Hat party (Hattarna) on home distilling.[42] The coffee ban that accompanied the strict sumptuary law of 1766 was also preceded by party political disputes. Carl Eric Wadenstierna went on a counter attack when Françoise Marguerite Janiçon, married to literary scholar Carl Gustaf Warmholtz, intensified the image of Swedes' (and specifically merchants') unbridled consumption of luxury in her 1767 pamphlet.[43] In response, Wadenstierna claimed that the description, not least of the laden dinner and dessert tables, was exaggerated fabrication and the result of envy, and that it was a misunderstanding that merchants were the ones who plundered the Crown's assets and snatched bread from the hands of the poor.[44] But the problem with coffee, unlike coffee services or tea tables, was that there were no satisfactory Swedish alternatives, despite enthusiastic endeavours.[45] The second-hand market for reused tea and coffee, as well as the widespread fraud of selling tea and coffee that not always contained what was claimed, became a consequence and an extensive problem.[46]

The drive for bans on coffee consumption was depicted satirically in a rich flora of texts and pictures.[47] Per Nordquist's painting *Caffe-Beslaget* (The confiscation of coffee) was widely disseminated through an engraved version of the motif by Martin Rudolf Heland in 1799 (Image 89). Coffee drinking appeared to be continued despite all the bans.[48] In her diary entries from the 1790s, Märta Helena Reenstierna paraphrases coffee using terms such as 'tasty dark-brown beverage' or replaces it

42 The final coffee ban was introduced in 1822; Ahlberger 1996, pp. 58–64.

43 Françoise Marguerite Janiçon Warmholtz, *Tankar i anledning af sista öfwerflöds-förordningen och dess wärkställighet*, Stockholm 1767.

44 Carl Eric Wadenstierna, *Bref Til Auctoren Af Tanckar I Anledning Af sista Öfwerflöds Förordningen Och Dess wärckställighet*, Stockholm 1767.

45 There were Swedish plants and herbs that could be used as replacements for the sought-after tea leaves; *Kongl. Collegii medici kundgiörelse om thet missbruk och öfwerflöd, som thé och caffé drickande är underkastat, samt anwisning på swenska örter at bruka i ställe för thé*, Stockholm 1746. A coffee substitute could be made from peas. Märta Helena Reenstierna tastes 'pea coffee' in conjunction with the coffee ban in 1799, *Årstadagboken*, I, 1985, p. 197.

46 In a letter dated 7 June 1790, Carl August Ehrensvärd complains about the wretched tea he was served at an inn during his travels: '[...] My tea from the inn tastes deuced, you can imagine it consists of a stale potpourri of lemon rind mixed with cobwebs – and I think that my sugar has been in someone's mouth before,' Ehrensvärd, Carl August, *Brev till Kickan*, i urval av Holger Frykenstedt, Stockholm 1971, p. 39. Accounts of how members of the upper class had been tricked into drinking substandard products were popular tall stories. They were often about French women or a 'lofty group from Stockholm' who were fooled into drinking tea made of hay or coffee mixed with burnt toast, Granroth 1755, pp. 14, 16; Hodacs 2016.

47 Anders Eklöv, "Denna klara Caffe-Ström' – En studie av det svenska 1700-talets syn på kaffet speglad genom pamflett- och broschyr litteraturen', unpublished thesis, the Department of Economic History and International Relations, Stockholm University, 1995.

48 In the debate on the sumptuary laws' coffee bans, Carl Eric Wadenstierna stated the impossibility of a ban that would constantly be contravened and thereby undermine the strength of the law; Eklöv 1995, p. 13.

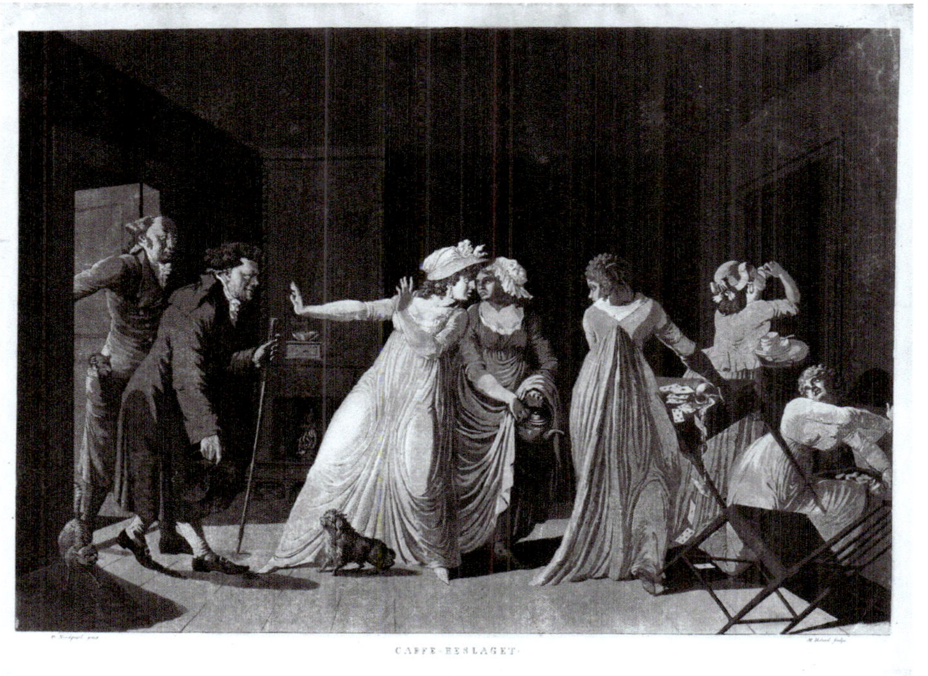

89. Martin Rudolf Heland after Per Nordquist, *Caffe-Beslaget*, c. 1799. Engraving, 36.3 × 52.4 cm. Stadsmuseet, Stockholm (SSM 108190).

with 'C:' followed by a few telling points.[49] Satirical dirges lamenting the death of coffee proclaimed the futility of the endeavours to stem the use of this indispensable luxury item.

Farewell!
You lavish suit of velvet!
Farewell!
To Lace! Plumes! Silk!
Now we've finally got rid of you and all your companions
Just the coffee drink
We will mourn.[50]

Coffee remained popular in wider circles despite the political and social charge that was reflected in satires, bans and regulations throughout the eighteenth century.

49 *Årstadagboken*, I, 1993, pp. 100, 111.
50 *Caffeets sista stunder* 1767.

In the idealised genre scenes in visual art, housemaids or footmen continued to bring the coffee trays. But the question is whether it was equally uncomplicated for an upper-class person in the era of coffee bans and coffee satire in Sweden to be depicted in a portrait with a coffee cup in their hand. Perhaps the unwillingness to be associated with luxury consumption, irresponsibility and idleness contributed to the drink occasionally being banished from the domains of portraiture.

Intimate conversations: Coffee drinking and manorial culture

Elias Martin's mezzotint engraving *The Confidants*, created during his years in London in the 1770s, conveyed a more positive image of women exchanging confidences over cups of tea and coffee, in contrast with men's outspokenness at the coffee houses (Image 90).[51] One of the women fiddles with the portrait miniature that she wears on a ribbon around her neck while she listens to the other woman close beside her, who is reading a letter. The women's informal morning attire, the letter, and the portrait that the woman is pressing to her heart, hint at intimacy and heartfelt conversations about love. The commercially astute artist Martin also knew to design the motif as a scene from modern life, where each detail was consciously selected to illustrate the fashionable, urban woman's comfortably appointed life.[52]

The intimate conversation between two women next to a coffee pot was also the theme of one of the paintings by Pehr Hilleström that was purchased for Näs Manor (Plate 16). After the coffee has been drunk, the tablecloth has been folded to one side, and in the patterns of the coffee grounds the older woman is now reading the fortunes and adventures that might follow on from the letter that the younger woman is holding in her hand. Their engrossment in the cup is revealed by the clearly disregarded yarn winder in the foreground, and that they have not noticed how the pug has sunk its teeth into the expensive fur muff at their feet. The young woman's body language, with her arm around the fortune teller's shoulders

51 The arranged gender constructions of visual art should, however, be regarded in the light of a significantly more multifaceted social reality. Noblemen Johan Gabriel Oxenstierna, Gustaf Philip Creutz, Gustaf von Carlson and Carl August Ehrensvärd formed a circle called 'The Tea-Making Brothers' who met during the Gustavian era for broad-minded evening conversations over a cup of tea, Holger Frykenstedt, *Poetens historia. Carl August Ehrensvärd och Johan Gabriel Oxenstierna, konstellation i Vänskapens och Poesins tecken*, Stockholm 1969, p. 37.

52 Amanda Vickery nuances this distinction in *The Gentlemans Daughter, Women's Lives in Georgian England*, New Haven 1998, where the differences between an urban and a rural upper-class culture could be expressed in various ways in relation to different fashion phenomena and consumption, p. 169ff. Tea parties as expressions of female sociality are discussed as well on pp. 206–9. Regarding Elias Martin's business career in London, see Ahlund, Mikael, *Landskapets röster. Studier i Elias Martins bildvärld*, Stockholm 2011.

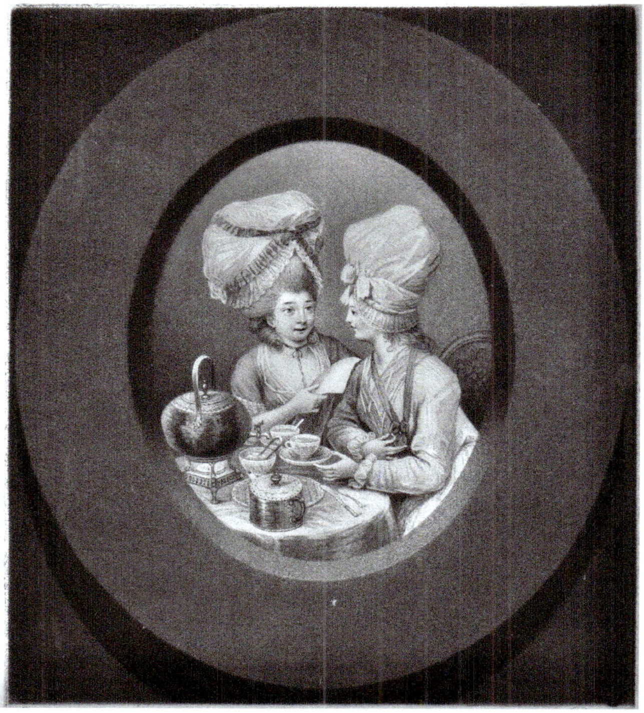

90. James Watson after Elias Martin, *The Confidants*, 1780. Mezzotint engraving, 25.8 × 19.7 cm. From Karl Asplund, *Två gustavianska mästare. Niklas Lafrensen d.y. och Elias Martin i samtida gravyrer*, Stockholm, 1925.

and leaning forwards with her legs apart, indicates her eagerness to find out more, irrespective of the duties and responsibilities that she is thereby neglecting. The kettle, shining silver coffee pot, sugar bowl and East Indian porcelain cups form an eye-catching still life that symbolises ideas associated with both women's conversation and their inclination for idleness and gossip.

Hilleström's genre-style motifs here render a scene from modern life that the family at Näs could relate to.[53] The bedchamber included a tea table that was deceptively similar to the one depicted in the painting (Image 94). The yarn winder, kettle and coffee service were part of their everyday life, and the pink pelisse lined with squirrel fur was part of their wardrobe. But alongside the coffee utensils and fashion accessories, the painting also illustrates one of the era's popular amusements.[54] Men's gambling in coffee houses could be compared to women's interest in fortune telling at coffee tables. The largest painting by Hilleström at Näs,

53 The motif was common in eighteenth-century genre scenes and often reproduced in international engravings. A very similar scene is reproduced in the English engraving *The Fortune Teller* by Robert Laurie 1772, after an original by Philippe Mercier, the British Museum (2010,7081.1824).

54 Anna Ulrica Arfvidsson (1734–1801) was a successful fortune teller in Gustavian Stockholm. Her speciality was reading coffee grounds. She was well known among the upper circles of society, and her services were used by the royal family and the court.

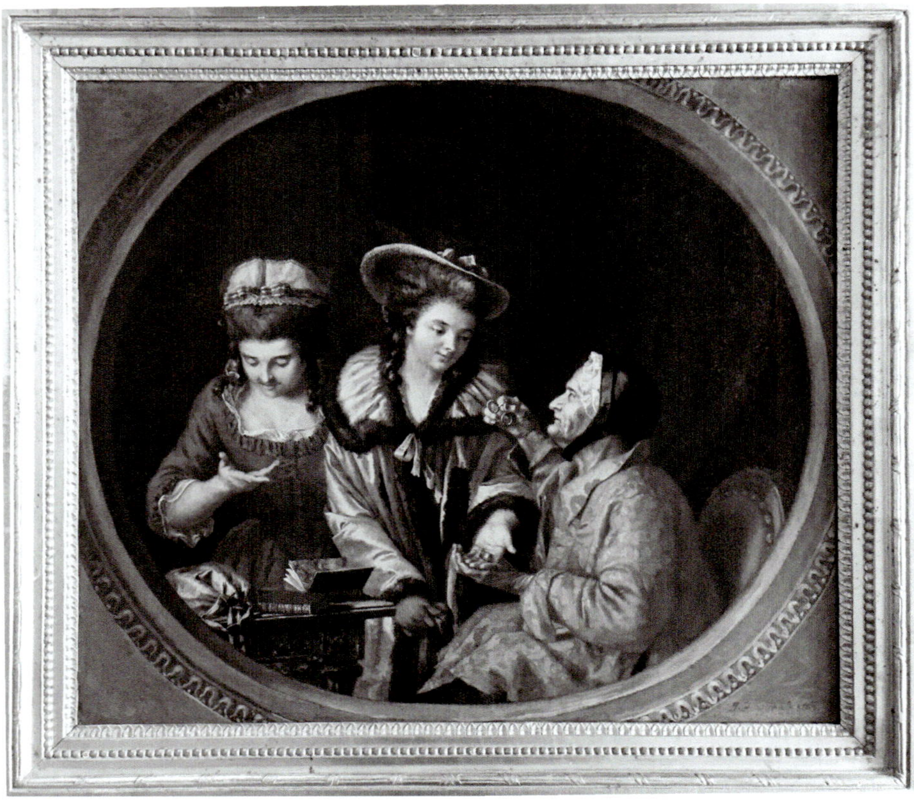

91. Wadenstierna's final commission from Pehr Hilleström was the painting *En gumma som spår i handen på ett fruent. och ett annat som hör derpå* (An old woman reading the palm of a woman, and another listening), 1784. Oil on canvas, 52.5 × 63 cm. Private ownership.

signed 1784, shows a visit to a fortune teller (Image 91).[55] Perhaps Wadenstierna's two daughters, aged twenty-two and twenty-six at the time, could recognise themselves in the motif and in the inquisitiveness or anxiety that they felt about the future – in the painting two women of the same age have their palms read and fortunes told. These aspects of coffee culture were represented in the genre paintings that Hilleström created for Näs, but the portraits of the Wadenstierna family lacked cups and coffee pots. The paintings that showed women busy reading coffee grounds were perhaps displayed here as moralising examples, next to the depictions of female diligence and productivity when carding wool and using spinning wheels. Maybe there was a more serious message here that time should not be wasted. Coffee and amusements should not distract women from duties and virtues.

55 Cederblom, Gerda, *Pehr Hilleström som kulturskildrare*, I, Stockholm 1927, Image 45.

But even though coffee could be linked to idleness and gossip, there was still a degree of difference between the pronounced satires and other representations of female coffee drinking that were distributed in Swedish upper-class homes in various ways. Although elements in the pictures could allude to notions that were recognisable from the criticism of coffee, these scenes were above all about lifestyle and fashion – about women conversing at dainty tables with cups and pots, drinking their coffee or tea, elegantly arranged in comfortable chairs. Here, the consumption of these beverages is part of an identity-building pictorial world that reflected the eighteenth century's modern culture of comfort. The motifs also had a tangible presence at Swedish manors, where they reflected the everyday amusements that shaped life in these environments. Pehr Hilleström's genre paintings at Näs are just one example.

In these pictures, coffee and tea drinking was framed by an elegant material culture that in all its details was evidence of highly fashion-conscious consumption. This is also clear in another painting by Hilleström from 1775, which the artist described in his own list as 'A woman sits reading, the lady's maid brings tea' (Plate 17).[56] Here, the informed viewer could pick out all the products and '*kommoditeter*' (comforts) that undoubtedly also existed in the environments where this type of painting was on display – an East Indian teapot and cups, a sugar bowl and cream jug made of silver, the tea urn on its bed of charcoal next to the laid table. The painting also includes an expensive potpourri urn, which in design was a good match with the East Indian porcelain on the table. Similar faience urns from the Marieberg factory were available for purchase at Storkyrkobrinken in the capital, and there were also several of them at Näs.[57] According to the estate inventory, potpourri urns from Marieberg stood in both the lady's drawing room and the large bedchamber, and in Fredrica's own cabinet there were two smaller ones of the same type.[58] This recognition evoked by the idealised pictures, in everything from urns to cups, is likely to have strengthened the feeling of social affinity.

Pictures with similar motifs were spread in various ways. The fashion engravings presented related scenes, in which the latest outfits and accessories complemented the fashionable compositions. As described, Hilleström's motifs included a connection with French artists such as Boucher and Chardin. Through their original paintings in the royal collections, but above all through engravings after these paintings, this pictorial world also became highly significant in Sweden. Hilleström's

56 Cederblom, I, 1927, Image 21; the artist's own list No. 250.

57 Sofia Murhem and Göran Ulväng, 'To Buy a Plate: Retail and Shopping for Porcelain and Faience in Stockholm during the Eighteenth Century', *A Taste for Luxury in Early Modern Europe. Display, Acquisition and Boundaries*, Johanna Ilmakunnas and Jon Stobart (ed.), London 2017, p. 205.

58 Carl Eric Wadenstierna's estate inventory 1787. Riksarkivet, Näs Silverstolpeska arkivet, Personarkiven, vol. 60, Carl Eric Wadenstierna (1723–1787).

paintings on these themes contain recurring echoes of their representations of the comfortable, good life in French upper-class homes. Here we find constant reminders of Chardin's *Les amusements de la vie privée* or Boucher's *La toilette*, both created in the 1740s (Images 32 and 72).[59] Impressions from Chardin's and Boucher's pictures also appear elsewhere in Swedish upper-class culture in the eighteenth century. In the library at Näs, Wadenstierna's daughters could read about and perhaps identify with the young girls Émilie and Laure in the novel *Les dangers d'un premier choix. Ou lettres de Laure a Émilie.*[60] Laure, who during a visit to the studio of the famous Boucher, finds her own facial features in one of his pastoral, amorous paintings, reproaches the artist at the same time that one of her secret dreams comes true. The references to the French artists that recurred in the collections of books and pictures at Swedish manor houses consequently played a significant part in the era's identity-building processes.

When Fredrik Wilhelm Hoppe, a student of the architect Carl Hårleman, was commissioned by the Rosenhane family in 1766 to design the new main manor building at Tista Slott in Södermanland Province, he also created various pictures of life at manors in the area. For example, he depicted Countess Rosenhane, Eva Sofia Stenbock, reclining comfortably in her armchair in a composition that was directly borrowed from Chardin's *Les amusements de la vie privée* (Image 92).[61] The Falkenberg family's nearby manor, Lagmansö, also included echoes of contemporary French genre painting. In 1762, the walls in one of the wings had been adorned with decorative painting that referred to familiar pictures by Chardin, Boucher and their contemporaries (Image 93). Lépicié's engraving after Boucher's *Le déjeuner* from 1744 was used here as a model by the unknown Swedish artist who copied the scene

59 Hilleström's *A Woman Sits Reading, the Lady's Maid Brings Tea* includes clear references to Chardin and Boucher. The woman wearing her morning lace bonnet, sitting with crossed feet and having a rest from her needlework with a book, is a paraphrase of the woman in Chardin's *Les amusements de la vie privée.* François Boucher's *La toilette* from 1742 presented both the model for the servant and a few key details in Hilleström's pictorial space: the tea service and the blue workbag, both with symbolic significance in the narratives of the respective pictures. The physical similarities of the women in the paintings, from made-up faces to small feet, reproduced an ideal that the artists knew characterised the audience of the era, just as the depictions of exemplary versus disorderly morning life *en privée.* Also see Pehr Hilleström (ascribed), *Morgontoilette – boudoirinteriör*, oil on canvas, 53 × 63 cm, after François Boucher's painting *La toilette.* Stockholms Auktionsverk 2011; Cederblom, II, 1929, plate 19.

60 Bricaire de La Dixmerie 1777, pp. 102–7.

61 Brown, Carolina, 'Bilder, sällskapsliv och herrgårdskultur. Maskeradporträtt, silhuetter och andra bilder från 1700-talets Tista', *Historisk Tidskrift för Finland*, årg. 98, 2013:2, Helsinki 2013, pp. 209–15. Also compare Lorentz Sparrgren's watercoloured drawing of the couple Claes Julius Ekeblad and Brita Horn, with an open book, called *Amusements de la vie privée de Stola.* Nationalmuseum, Stockholm, (NMB 1402). In contemporary Russia, references to Chardin's *Les amusements de la vie privée* also appear, for example in the form of a piece of beadwork (State Historical Museum, Moscow), depicted in Priscilla Roosevelt, *Life on the Russian Country Estate. A Social and Cultural History*, New Haven and London 1995, p. 184.

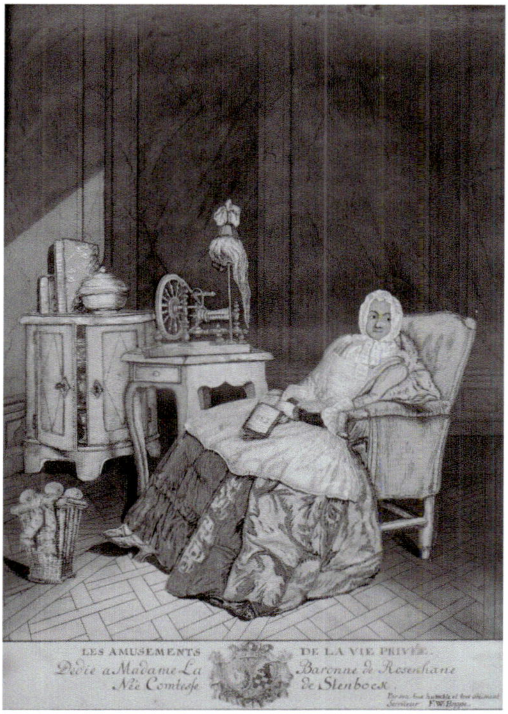

92. Fredrik Wilhelm Hoppe after Jean-Baptiste Siméon Chardin, *Les amusements de la vie privée. Dedie a Madame la Baronne de Rosenhane née Comtesse de Stenbock*. Découpure and drawing. Private ownership. Photo: Hans Thorwid.

of the well-known coffee-drinking women and children. This was created next to a painting of a woman in morning attire with a baby next to an unmade alcove bed, with a waiting teapot on the adjacent mantelpiece. This motif was also copied from a contemporary French engraving.[62] The presence of such pictures at Swedish manor houses during the eighteenth century is evidence of the lifestyle that the residents wanted to identify themselves with. The motif taken from Boucher with the representative French women gathered around the coffee table was not solely a decorative scene to look at; it reproduced a culture which residents of Swedish country houses also felt that they participated in and had co-created.

The fashionable coffee and tea drinking were therefore the hub around which a cultural context of comfort and cultivation took shape. In visual art, the home is its stage and the exemplary women its actors.[63] The coffee is surrounded by symbol-laden objects that all tell us about their world; a comfortably appointed

62 The model was probably a contemporary engraving by Jean-Joseph Baléchou after an original by Michel François Dandré-Bardon (*La naissance*, 1743, Musée Granet in Aix-en-Provence).

63 The ideals also resonate in the literary descriptions of the exemplary wife and mother, who through her tasks creates harmony in the home: 'At a dainty tea table, surrounded by polite children, as love gods at the belt of Cythera, they prattle with each other – we see her fulfil her obligations as a hostess, and the whole house is regulated in a tidy exemplary way; there is no lack of beauty or order, thrift or excess

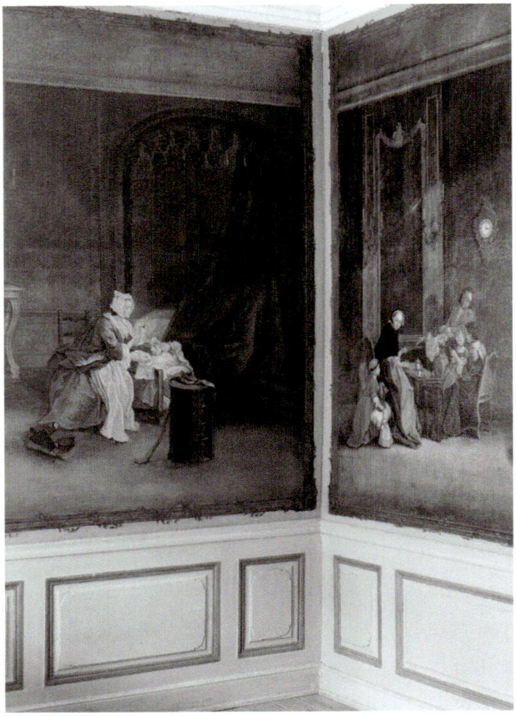

93. Unknown artist after François Boucher's *Le déjeuner* and Michel François Dandré-Bardon's *La Naissance*, 1762. Oil on canvas. Lagmansö. Photo: Christer Vallstrand.

material culture designed for the eighteenth century's fastidious connoisseurs and consumers. In the pictures, the objects, just as the women themselves, are aesthetically appealing eye-catchers. Sleek and delicate objects are in interplay with dainty and elegant women, who fully master the choreography of drinking coffee. Informal clothing and relaxed poses were also indications of an intimacy and familiarity that belonged to the woman's sphere in the home. Niclas Lafrensen's gouache of a tea-drinking woman embellished with roses and bows from around 1780 illustrates the ideal (Plate 18). From the minimal table that can easily and conveniently be moved close to her, with her dainty fingers she has lifted a cup so small that it can only be handled with utmost care using her fingertips. Here, the social dimension of coffee and tea culture re-emerges, along with the refined gestures required at these tables, where cups, spoons, saucers and rolling tables were supposed to be in harmony with trained body language.[64] As shown in the pictures,

here – the smallest corner presents a joyful view; each place resembles a doll's house and the entirety runs like clockwork.' Carl Johan von Holthusen, *Svenska fruntimrets fyra åldrar*, Stockholm 1785, p. 21.

64 Alicia M. Annas, 'The Elegant Art of Movement' in *An Elegant Art. Fashion & Fantasy in the Eighteenth Century*, Edward Maeder (ed.), New York 1983, pp. 35ff. The fact that the woman in the introductory engraving by Louis-Marin Bonnet (Image 86) is pouring her hot coffee onto the saucer possibly indicates an informal morning rather than an elegant visit; Hellman, Mimi, 'Furniture, Sociability, and the Work

it was the woman's task to ensure compliance with the demands of cultivation when socialising in the home through elegant conduct and conversation around the coffee table.

But the eighteenth century's source material also bears witness to the fact that this social role-play could be a thankless task.[65] Märta Helena Reenstierna's pride in displaying her home and offering guests tea and coffee in new tableware was occasionally crushed by an antisocial man, a hung-over son or a noisy servant who disturbed the well-mannered ambition that she aimed for.[66] Nonetheless, it was the woman's 'natural' obligation to seem pleasant to those around her and exercise a civilising influence on the man, which was constantly emphasised in literature at that time.[67] In one of Sergel's many drawings from Carl August Ehrensvärd's manor, Dömestorp, it is therefore the lady of the house who serves the tea from a slender samovar placed on a dainty tea table to the stout, weathered gentlemen in their heavy boots.[68] Märta Helena Reenstierna regarded it as her duty to entertain her group of visitors with 'miscellaneous small anecdotes and beautiful words', even though she had felt nauseous all day.[69]

The significance of conversation for the coffee and tea culture was linked to the visits that were part of social life and their conventions. Women in the elite could hold a tea party on a set day of the week for a select circle of invitees, and these gatherings combined social life at the tea table with the intellectual ambitions of the literary salon – contexts in which women had held a prominent position since the early seventeenth century.[70] A consumption behaviour that was effectively

of Leisure in Eighteenth-Century France', *Eighteenth-Century Studies*, vol. 32, no. 4, Baltimore 1999, pp. 415–45.

65 Vickery 1998, pp. 212ff.

66 *Årstadagboken* 1993, p. 137.

67 Johan Gottlieb Burkhardt, *Philosophie öfwer Naturen. Til bättre kännedom af Skaparen och de skapade tingen, men i synnerhet af Människans wärde och bestämmelse*, Lund 1797, p. 82: 'Socialising with women refines the manners, dispels serious sorrows, and lightens the work among the men [...] their charming manners mitigate our natural rawness.'

68 Sergel's drawing is depicted in *Carl August Ehrensvärd 1745–1800. Tecknaren och arkitekten*, Stockholm, Nationalmuseum 1997, p. 159.

69 *Årstadagboken*, I, 1985, p. 194.

70 My Hellsing, *Hedvig Elisabeth Charlotte: hertiginna vid det gustavianska hovet*, Stockholm 2015, p. 84. What Märta Helena Reenstierna called 'the tea hour' or 'tea water's visit' (*Årstadagboken* 1993, p. 136 and Årstadagboken, II, 1985, p. 250) can be compared to Malla Silfverstolpe's memories from the tea evenings of her youth in Stockholm in the 1790s. Her own Friday evenings in Uppsala in the early nineteenth century, where the academic world gathered around the East Indian porcelain table with its simmering tea urn, showed how she had been shaped by the drawing room culture, in which female sociality was expressed through the rituals of drinking tea and coffee and a literary salon culture, *Malla* Montgomery-Silfverstolpes *memoarer*, utgifna af Malla Grandinson, I, Stockholm 1908, p. 215; Ingrid Holmquist, *Salongens värld. Om text och kön i romantikens salongskultur*, Stockholm 2000, p. 119.

fuelled by the era's growing market also belonged to the visiting culture. Newspaper advertisements tended to be directly aimed at the female consumer. The same place where you could buy a straw hat for summer also sold comfortable rugs suitable under tea and coffee tables.[71] The gatherings over tea and coffee were an opportunity to display an upper-class environment, with elegant tableware and tasteful furniture, but also, with refined gestures and an elegant posture, to lead the conversations around the coffee table in accordance with the era's decorum.[72]

Conversation and social skills were fundamental elements of Swedish manor house culture. This is particularly clear in one of the paintings that Carl Eric Wadenstierna commissioned from Hilleström for Näs. In the painting, which the artist called *Portraits of Two Young Wadenstierna Ladies – in Conversation*, his wife and daughters have gathered together with their needlework in polite conversation with each other and with the painting's viewer – gestures, gazes and the positioning of the group of women draw the viewer into the conversation (Plate 5).[73] Correspondingly, Niclas Lafrensen's portraits of Wadenstierna's two wives, one depicted with her needlework and the other with her letter writing, can be said to be engaged in conversation with the viewer of the portraits. The pictures present the women in the Wadenstierna family skilfully carrying out their upper-class social roles. But no tea or coffee cups are visible in these paintings. Instead, needlework and letter writing occupy the actors in the pictures.

A coffee table could have been a natural element in the portraits, but there was no such item of furniture here. This is possibly related to Carl Eric Wadenstierna's position in public life at the time. With the debate concerning the coffee bans and with a patriotic economising approach in mind, allusions to drinking coffee were

71 *Dagligt Allehanda*, 19 June 1786 and 3 June 1799, in which a boutique advertised the sale of silk thread and nightcaps as well as 'Swedish coffee'.

72 As early as in the 1730s, a writer in the *Sedolärande Mercurius* made fun of the women's visits: 'More to have the opportunity to see a new piece of furniture that she has bought for her house or a new dress, rather than in friendship and intimacy profit from her company', and where boasts, envy and slander bring 'all socialising and conversation between both of these pretty close-knit sisters to an end' (*Sedolärande Mercurius*, 31 August 1731).

73 The family pictures or group portraits that were named conversation pieces, originating in Dutch painting traditions, became popular from around 1720 onwards in English visual art, where a group was often depicted around the tea or coffee table. Conversation pieces became a portrait category, which through the well-mannered rules of the tea and coffee culture, displayed a family's social standing and material comfort, and which normatively reflected the ideal of good housekeeping in which everyone took on their given role. The significance of conversation in this context is demonstrated by the relationships between the people depicted, but also by how in the composition they turn to face the viewers of the picture in order to invite them to the table. The English artists associated with this category of motifs include William Hogarth, Arthur Devis, Charles Philips and Thomas Gainsborough. Flemish artist Joseph van Aken, who worked in London during the 1720s and until his death in 1749, strongly contributed to the development of this type of portrait.

perhaps deemed less suitable here. A few years before the painting was created, in the heated party political wrangling, Wadenstierna had taken part in the public debate on these issues, at the same time that satires and critical voices directed their gibes at the era's coffee-drinking women. Perhaps the subject was far too highly charged. Cultivated conversation could be effectively staged even without the ambivalent allusions of the coffee table. Just as the portraits that depicted women at their dressing tables, the motif at coffee tables did not become widespread in Swedish portraiture.[74] Instead, coffee drinking could be presented more directly in fashion images and genre pictures.

Coffee at home with the Wadenstierna family

Despite this, coffee was drunk in the Wadenstierna family. A number of preserved receipts in the archive include a notable purchase of two pounds of coffee beans among other essentials such as prunes, washing blue, anchovies, powder and Venetian soap.[75] Everyday life at Näs, just as the social calls, festivities and spa visits, were accompanied by regular coffee drinking. Wadenstierna's recurring stays at Medevi spa, for example, were social occasions, but also opportunities where representatives of the political party the Hats could continue their conversations in less formal settings, and where taking the spring water was alternated with frequent coffee drinking.[76] The estate inventory after Carl Eric Wadenstierna's death in 1787 also indicates that a more extensive social life in the city increased the need for large coffee and tea services. In the city residence there were a total of forty-three coffee cups and forty-three tea cups, compared to the twenty-six coffee cups and sixteen tea cups at the rural Näs Manor.[77] There were probably fewer visits there, but the fact that some pieces of Wadenstierna's armorial tableware were also kept at Näs testifies that the tea and coffee culture also had social significance in the countryside.

The 'tea table with inlaid base and blue and white porcelain top' that was among the family's possessions was also a clear expression of the representative aspects that enveloped tea and coffee drinking. The base of the tea table was part

74 With the exception of, for example, the portrait of the coffee-drinking Stenbock family at Rånäs, around 1740, Skokolster, (3053).

75 Riksarkivet, Näs Silverstolpeska arkivet, Gårdsarkivet, Äldre kassaböcker (Old cash books).

76 Gustaf Näsström, *Det gamla Medevi. Kulturhistoriska anteckningar*, Stockholm 1928, pp. 177, 194. *Inrikes Tidningar* advertised which guests had arrived at Medevi on 1 July, and State Secretary Wadenstierna's name recurs during the period 1763–83: *Inrikes Tidningar*, Stockholm 21 July 1763; 28 June 1764; 22 July 1779; 11 July 1782, 14 July 1783.

77 Riksarkivet, Näs Silverstolpeska arkivet, Personarkiven, vol. 60, Carl Eric Wadenstierna (1723–1787).

of Wadenstierna's major commission of work by Georg Haupt in preparation for the move to Näs Manor. With its veneer made of jacaranda, amaranth (purpleheart wood), citron wood, birch and maple, it was an especially beautiful piece, and the sides of the table were embellished with inlays in the form of laurel garlands and rosettes (Plate 20).[78] The faience tray that crowned the table was made in the Marieberg factory in Stockholm in 1775 and constituted a decorative eye-catching element in an era that had a passion for porcelain and faience. But it also had a practical function in keeping splashes of hot tea and coffee in their place, thereby protecting delicate clothing and upholstery fabrics. Haupt was also a master of designing tea tables' elegant details for comfort. The table's rounded corners created space for more people to gather round it, and the angled and narrowing table legs enabled you to sit close to the table without knocking against sharp edges. The small brass castors also made the table easy to move as required. Haupt had also designed round versions of these tables with porcelain platters in the table tops, and the decorated apron used spring mechanisms to conceal fold-out drawers in which to store all the accoutrements required for the rituals surrounding tea and coffee. A similar table belonged to Wadenstierna's friend Carl August Ehrensvärd.[79]

The tea table at Näs was a showpiece designed to meet all the requirements of comfort and of manifesting upper-class status. It stood in the bedchamber at Näs, one of the most lavishly decorated rooms in the reception suite. Together with blue and white textile items, blue-painted wall panels and a tiled stove adorned with a pattern of blue flowers, the tea table with its decorative faience tray fitted in well with the style of the room. The aesthetically cohesive whole was perfected by Haupt's bedside cabinets with their laurel festoon decoration that tied in with the tea table. Coffee in bed was most comfortably drunk at these conveniently close bedside cabinets, whereas the tea table could be moved between the sofa and chairs at breakfast or when visitors were invited into the room.

The bedchamber was also home to a round mahogany tea table, a folding table that was stored against the wall and could also be rolled into place on its brass castors when required (Image 94).[80] The design of the table with its classicising frame and claw and ball feet finishing off the curved legs, is reminiscent of Thomas Chippendale's furniture.[81] Perhaps it had been made in Carl Diedric Fick's workshop,

78 Bukowskis, Stockholm 5 December 2017.

79 Lagerquist, Marshall, *Georg Haupt. Ebeniste du Roi*, Nordiska museets handlingar 92, Stockholm 1979, p. 212f.

80 Riksarkivet, Näs Silverstolpeska arkivet, Personarkiven, vol. 60, Carl Eric Wadenstierna (1723–1787).

81 Chippendale's furniture designs were disseminated in Europe through engraved exemplary drawings in the 1754 book *The Gentleman and Cabinet-Maker's Director: Being a Large Collection of the Most Elegant and Useful Designs of Household Furniture, in the Most Fashionable Taste*. It was published in new editions during the latter half of the eighteenth century.

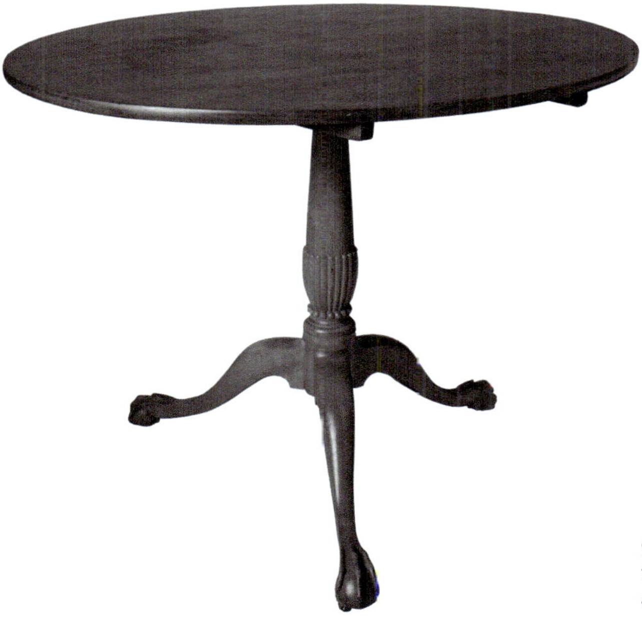

94. A round mahogany tea table stood in the bedchamber at Näs. Private ownership.

where very similar mahogany folding tables were created during the Gustavian era, or by another contemporary master working in Stockholm.[82] It was no coincidence that the tea tables were placed in the lady's suite of rooms. This connected with ideas of the woman's role in the home and the attitude that the tea and coffee culture was a female area of responsibility. The silver tea urn on a stand with a burner or charcoal, which Wadenstierna had given to his wife as a Christmas present in 1783, was also an expression of the era's gender-coded consumption.[83] The tea urn was a modern accessory that was expected to be found in the suite of rooms of a fashionable woman, and Pehr Hilleström therefore placed a similar tea urn in the foreground of one of his paintings (Plate 17). Tea tables on castors and tea urns that kept the water hot for hours reduced the need for servants and therefore created new opportunities for the development of the home's private dimensions. The new comfort not only meant an increasing physical well-being but also a distance from elements that disturbed everyday life.

The dining room at Näs could seat large numbers of dinner guests, and two games tables also offered the guests entertainment after the meal. But coffee after dinner was often taken in adjacent rooms in the lady's suite. In the upper-class

82 Sylvén, Torsten, *Mästarnas möbler. Stockholmsarbeten 1700–1850*, Stockholm 1996, pp. 119–21.

83 Carl Eric Wadenstierna's estate inventory from 1787. Riksarkivet, Näs Silverstolpeska arkivet, Personarkiven, vol. 60, Carl Eric Wadenstierna (1723–1787).

home's traditional division into a gentleman's and a lady's suite, the dining room often appeared to be characterised as a male sphere, while drawing rooms and the bedchamber were characterised as female.[84] After the meal, when the men remained in the dining room around aquavit and games tables, the women withdrew to drink coffee in the drawing room or bedchamber.[85] Women organising the coffee after dinner was a fashion with French overtones that gained ground in the eighteenth century: 'C'est une mode presque générale à Paris, que de prendre une tasse de Café après le diné,' states a travel guide as early as in 1727.[86]

Tea and coffee were also served on other occasions and for guests and visitors from a wide social spectrum, where social status and decorum determined *where* the coffee was served and also what coffee service was deemed suitable for different groups and contexts.[87] Wadenstierna's Saxony or English porcelain were distinctive luxuries and signalled different messages compared to Swedish faience. Similarly, Count Clas Julius Ekeblad at Stola Manor displayed his Saxony tea service in the white drawing room next to the dining room, ready to use but also as an eye-catching aesthetic complement to the room's lavish interior decoration with a silk-taffeta-upholstered sofa and armchairs and large mirrors.[88] When Märta Helena Reenstierna intended to celebrate her husband's name day and the installation of a new cabinet with the 'Berlin red and white cups with accessories' specially selected for the occasion, she consequently had to abandon her plans when, among others, the butcher and saddler arrived unexpectedly and lingered.[89] She evidently had different guests in mind for the cups from Berlin. The status associated with the expensive porcelain is also seen in a later diary entry where she describes how the cups bearing her coat of arms and names are arranged 'as now is customary (*en parade*) on the table in both drawing rooms'.[90] A few weeks later, possibly inspired by a visit to Princess Sophia Albertina's royal residence, where she admired the

84 Wall, Cynthia, 'Gendering Rooms. Domestic Architecture and Literary Acts', *Eighteenth-Century Fiction*, 5, nr. 4, Toronto 1993, pp. 349–72.

85 Compare how the drawing room in English-language culture becomes a room that is ascribed female overtones and is placed in the lady's suite of rooms; Wall 1993, p. 353.

86 'It is practically a general fashion in Paris to have a cup of coffee after the meal', J.C. Nemeitz, *Séjour de Paris, c'est à dire, Instructions fidéles, pour les Voiageurs de condition, Comment ils se doivent conduire, s'ils veulent faire un bon usage de leur tems & argent, durant leur Séjour à Paris*, Leiden 1727, p. 110.

87 Vickery 1998, p. 206 and p. 208; *Årstadagboken* 1993, pp. 157, 164, 212.

88 Karlson, William, *Ett svenskt herremanshem på 1700-talet. Clas Julius Ekeblads inventarium över Stola 1796*, Lund 1940, p. 77. The Saxony porcelain enjoyed a high status, which is confirmed by it being on display in the drawing room. In the royal Christmas Eve lottery at Haga Palace in 1790, one of the prizes was a coffee service made of Saxony porcelain; Christopher O'Regan, *En bädd av dun. Livet vid Gustaf III:s hov*, Stockholm 2012, p. 181.

89 *Årstadagboken*, I, 1993, p. 212.

90 *Årsta Dagboken* 1985, p. 212.

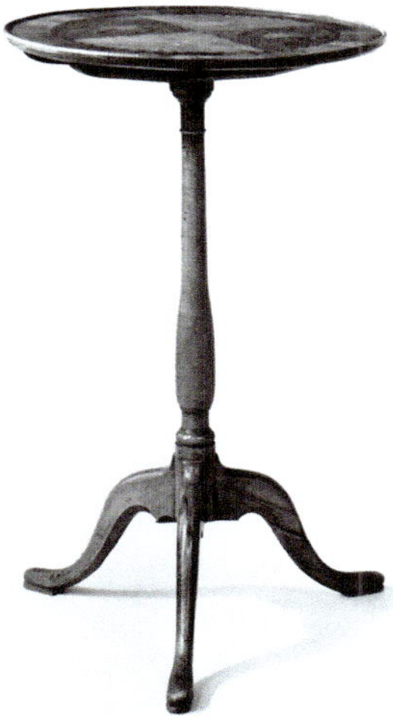

95. Small folding table from Näs, in birch, oak and pine. Table top veneered with ash. H 72.5 and table top diameter 43.8 cm. Photo: Märta Claréus, 1958, Archives of the Nordic Museum, Stockholm.

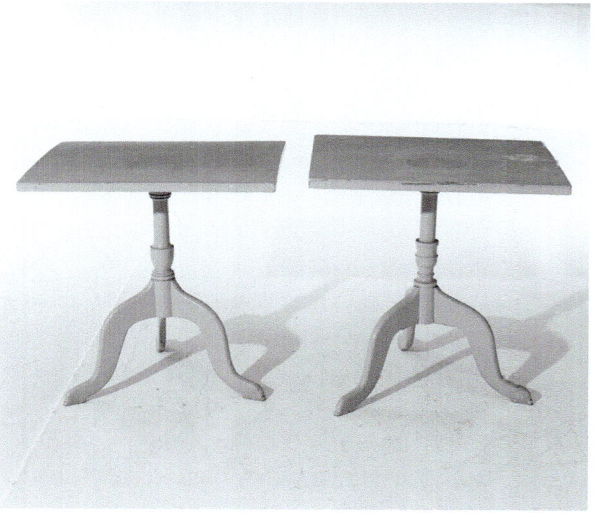

96. Lantern tables from Näs. W 50 cm, H 66 cm. Photo: Stockholms Auktionsverk.

multitude of small tables and ornaments, she brought out 'beautiful tea cups, eighteen pairs, and placed them on the gilt table in the drawing room according to current customs, as I have seen.'[91]

The eighteenth century's multitude of light, elegant tables were designed to assist in the many and varied contexts in which coffee and tea were served.[92] At Näs, there were a number of small folding tables, including the one depicted here made of birch, oak and pine and with a table top veneered with ash (Image 95). It was easy to lift into place when needed and to put away equally quickly. With a folding table top, it took up no space when stored, yet constituted a decorative eye-catcher with the top's inlaid veneer decoration. In the library wing's guest rooms there were also simple grey-painted tea tables at which the guests could eat their breakfast without being inconvenienced by demands on social politeness during the mornings.[93] These simple, functional tables may have resembled the lantern tables that stood

91 *Årsta Dagboken* 1985, p. 219.

92 The tea tables could naturally also be used for other purposes. In her diary on 6 December 1796, Märta Helena Reenstierna writes about a hastily arranged dinner at the tea table, consisting of a pie baked in the tiled stove in the large main room, *Årstadagboken* 1993, p. 131.

93 Here, a comparison can be made with court visits at Gripsholm Castle during the Gustavian era. The mornings and afternoons were often spent in the guest rooms, where each person ate breakfast, took care of their morning toilette, read, and wrote letters. See examples of small tables that were in the guest rooms of the Cavalier Wing in *Möbelhistoria på Gripsholm,* Bo Vahlne (ed.), Stockholm 1986, pp. 126–7.

in the entrance hall of the main building (Image 96). The flexibility and movability of the tables harmonised with the comfortable and social aspects of the coffee and tea culture. Temporary groupings around sofas and bedsides created a feeling of informality and intimacy. In words and pictures, contemporary sources show how these movable tables met the needs of the moment. For example, when teenage Malla Silfverstolpe caught sight of handsome Gustaf Fredrik Åkerhjelm at a tea party one afternoon in 1795, she utilised the opportunities offered by the context:

> Malla had never seen such an attractive person, and she placed the tea table so that in the mirror she could see the man who she otherwise would not have dared to look at, as much as she wanted to.[94]

In an interior by Niclas Lafrensen, a lady's maid discretely removes a coffee table that a woman and her male companion have just abandoned. As easily as a laid tray, the messy remains of the coffee break are banished from sight behind a folding screen.[95] Pehr Hilleström's many interior scenes also display how the folding tables were quickly lifted into place for various everyday purposes, and how coffee and tea cups jostle for space with letters, open books and needlework next to unmade beds or crackling tiled stove fires, during social calls or during sudden impulses to read coffee grounds, as shown in the picture at Näs. The world that Hilleström's paintings demonstrate thereby concerns both relaxed everyday life and the aspects of the new culture of comfort that were class markers. They also convey the highly demanding expectations that accompanied the upbringing of women and the social skills associated with the tea and coffee culture – which Wadenstierna's daughters were also expected to master. One intention behind the commission of the paintings for Näs was probably that they would contribute to this knowledge.

The Marieberg tray in the tea table at Näs features a picture of an idyllic small village, framed with a border of flowers and leaves. The view with its bridges, arches and towers, embedded in greenery and surrounded by birds soaring in the sky, is reminiscent of a pastoral golden age or a picturesque '*hameau*' from François Boucher's suggestive landscape paintings. The foreground's rural mill with dilapidated steps and nesting doves is also a free copy after Boucher's painting *Moulin à Charenton* and again shows how the French pictorial world reappears in Swedish manor houses.[96] In harmony with Korn's idyllic landscape paintings at

94 Malla Montgomery-Silfverstolpe, I, 1908, p. 172.

95 The painting is shown on the website of the French auction firm Drouot: https://www.drouot.com/lot/publicShow/1472365?controller=lot&&action=publicShow&id=1472365&lang=en2019-03-05.

96 François Boucher, *Le moulin à Charenton*, 1750s, oil on canvas, 72 × 91 cm, Musée de Beaux-Arts d'Orléans (73). Boucher returned to the motif, which was also engraved.

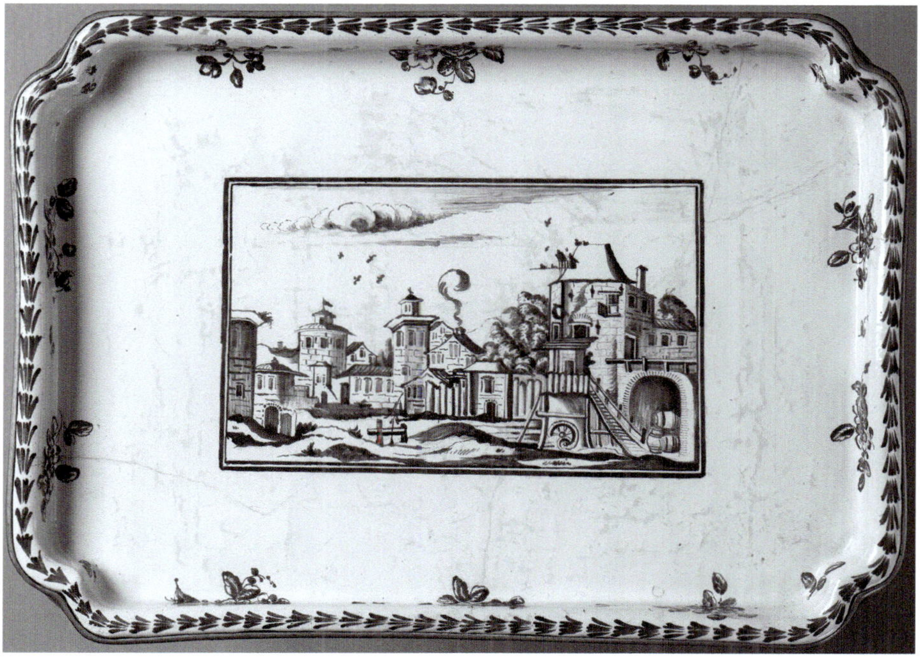

97. Faience tray from the Marieberg factory in Stockholm for Wadenstierna's tea table by Georg Haupt, 1775. Private ownership. Photo: Bukowskis.

Näs, the tea tray's scene conveys an ideal that also recurred in the entrance hall's overdoor decorations. There, the phrases are about the simple life that Wadenstierna wished for himself, his family and his friends here – to live 'free of the noise of the wider world'. When the tea or coffee was served on the faience tray, the image became a reminder of the good life that the visits to Näs were to offer.

From the table, the group with their cups could look through the windows over the garden, meadows and adjacent lake landscape and – season and weather permitting – continue to spend time together by taking a walk to follies and bowers for a second cup of tea or coffee in the great outdoors. The image on the faience tray was a pastoral fantasy, but it resonated in the reality surrounding Näs, at least for the enlightened viewer who could visualise references to a pastoral pictorial world beyond time and space. Coffee drinking was incorporated in a web of symbols and emotionally charged atmospheres.[97]

97 In July 1797, Märta Helena Reenstierna describes an equivalent context: '[I]n the morning we drank coffee in the Solitude [retreat, folly] and I read for a while from a polite French book, called *Bibliotheque de Campagne*.' The choice of reading to accompany the coffee in the garden perfected the image of the pleasantness of country life. The French novella, the coffee and the cultivated garden space civilised and idealised nature and enhanced the experience, *Årstadagboken*, I, 1993, p. 151. Näs was also home to

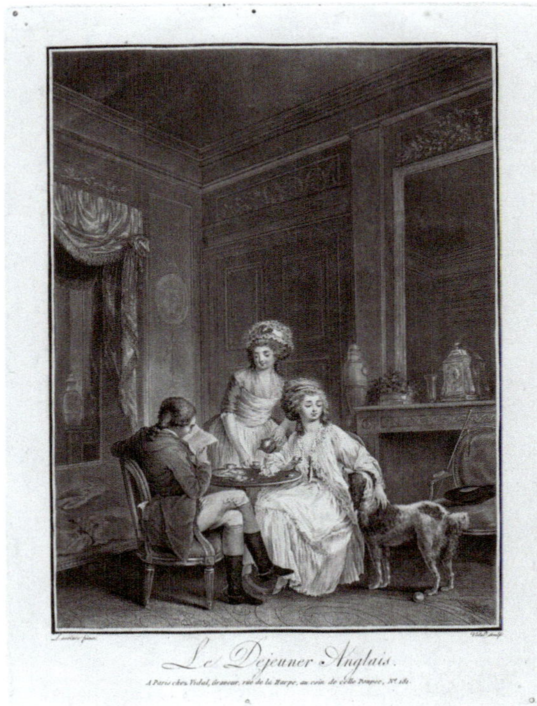

98. Gérard Vidal after Niclas Lafrensen the Younger, *Le dejeuner anglais*, 1785. Engraving, 34.5 × 25.2 cm. Widener Collection, National Gallery of Art, Washington, DC (1942.9.2101).

It is easy to imagine Carl Eric Wadenstierna and Fredrica Carleson sitting in their dressing gowns in their respective corners of the bedchamber's sofa with Haupt's tea table placed conveniently between them. A spicy scent from the room's potpourri urns mingles with the aroma of coffee and the soft ticking of the wall's pendulum clock. Perhaps they are browsing *Lettres d'un voyageur anglois*, fetched from the library, while they eat their breakfast, their *petit déjeuner anglais*. Géraud Vidal's aquatint engraving *Le dejeuner anglais* from 1785 after Niclas Lafrensen's gouache presents breakfast in the bedchamber as a fashionable *sujet galante* (Image 98).[98] The English breakfast was the name of an informal meal in private, and the title of the engraving highlights the influence of English fashion in the last few decades of the eighteenth century. *À l'anglais* was the trend associated with the freedoms of country life: horseback instead of carriages, boots instead of buckled shoes, a coat made of broadcloth instead of silk, the garden's winding nature paths instead of the poker-straight rows of the formal park. But in the

Bibliothéque de campagne ou amusemens de l'esprit et du coeur, as well as coffee, follies and a summer dining room in the greenery by the manor's bosquets, a framework that turned the image on the tea tray into an ideal within reach.

98 Martin Sherlock, *Nouvelles lettres d'un voyageur anglois*, London 1780.

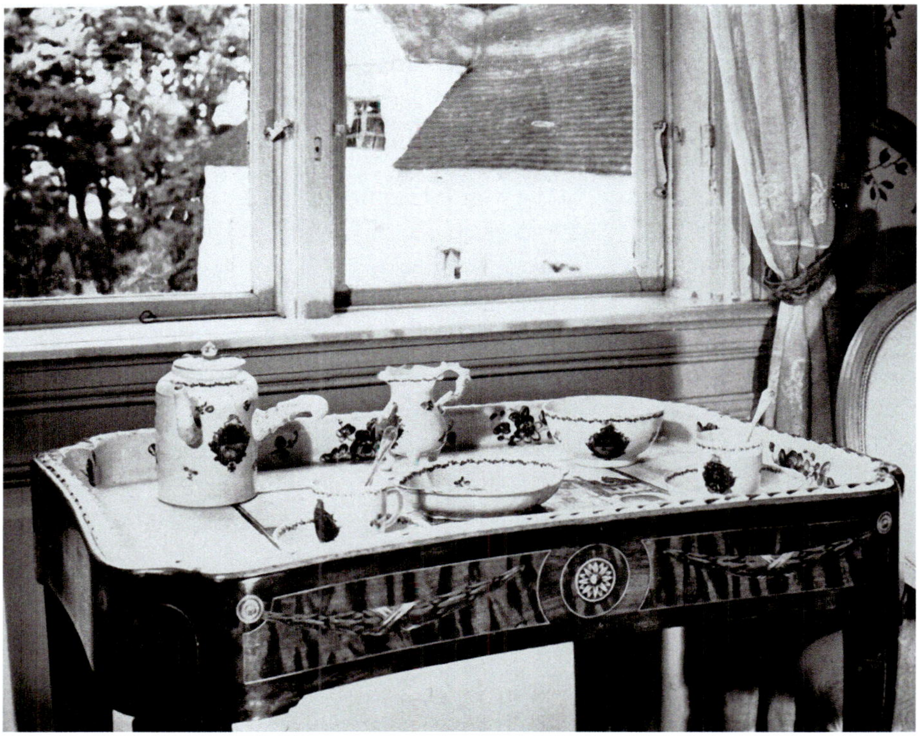

99. Wadenstierna's armorial tableware set on the tea table by Georg Haupt, 1775. The south wing of Näs is glimpsed through the window. Private ownership. From Gustaf Näsström, *Forna dagars Sverige*, 3 vols, Stockholm, 1962, vol. 3. Photo: Hans Hammarskiöld.

background there was also an interest in a new attitude to the development of society as a whole.[99]

The picturesque view that embellished the tea table at Näs conveyed a central ideal from that time – a longing for a simpler and more comfortable life. In this sense, the entire environment at Näs represented the 'new luxury', the functional

99 The man's presence in Lafrensen's *Dejeuner anglais*, dressed in boots with spurs and holding a newspaper containing the latest daily news, is no coincidence. This English style was above all thought to appeal to men, while women were attracted to French fashion; Michael North, 'Fashion and Luxury in Eighteenth-Century Germany', *A Taste for Luxury in Early Modern Europe. Display, Acquisition and Boundaries*, Johanna Ilmakunnas and Jon Stobart (ed.), London, New York 2017, p. 102. This was accompanied by a gender-normative description of fashion, but also a change in the specific rules and spheres that were ascribed to the sexes, Jones, Jennifer Michelle, *Sexing la Mode. Gender, Fashion and Commercial Culture in Old Regime France*, Oxford and New York 2004, pp. 1–6. In contrast with François Boucher's coffee-drinking women and children in Paris in the 1740s, a man and a woman share the breakfast table '*à l'anglais*' in the equivalent environment in the 1780s.

comfortable everyday life – not the differentiating, status-filled formal entertaining and representation. The shapes and functions of the rooms and furniture invited new lifestyles.[100] And the pictorial world, be it in the form of the tea table's faience landscape or Hilleström's, Lafrensen's and Korn's paintings, together contributed to shaping this new social and cultural identity.

Pehr Hilleström's painting of the women reading coffee grounds was perhaps within view from where Wadenstierna and his wife sat at the tea table in the bedchamber at Näs. Perhaps Fredrica Carleson also glanced at the pattern in her own drained breakfast cup. If she could have seen into the future, she might not have been surprised that over time Sweden would become one of the world's top coffee-drinking nations. However, she may have been surprised that the aristocratic culture of comfort designed by her era fundamentally remains an ideal for lifestyle and consumption 250 years later – for a significantly broader stratum of the population.

100 Hellman 1999, pp. 414–45.

Concluding words

Abstract
The culture of comfort in eighteenth-century Europe was shaped by a constant interaction between individuals, countries and social contexts. It was a dynamic and innovative period, when it came to the approach to everyday and family life. But the various expressions of a new culture of comfort also developed national features. It could concern the proportions and materials of the buildings or the layout and actual use of the rooms. It could prove to be the choice of tiled stoves, faience ware or printed cotton cloth, instead of open fireplaces, porcelain and silk. The aesthetic and economic ideas in Sweden had laid the foundations for approaches which were both about interacting with and marking a distance to continental ideals.

Keywords: portraiture; social roles; material culture; visualising comfort; consumer goods

Pictures and tables

The narrative about eighteenth-century comfort has taken place at various tables. New types of tables met new needs during the century. The tables facilitated new ways of socialising or new needs to withdraw from social contexts. They could be designed for specific purposes or shift their function as quickly and easily as they were lifted into place or were rolled away. The multitude of new types of table also became associated with a consumption culture that gained increasingly clear female overtones. The modern and convenient tables made comfortable everyday domestic life easier, and in the latter half of the eighteenth century the home also became the place that ideal femininity as a construction was referred to. In Carl Johan von Holthusen's *Svenska fruntimrets fyra åldrar* (The four ages of the Swedish woman) from 1785, the tasks at the tables also symbolise the woman's path through life. The young girl initially places her doll on the table, the same table at which she during 'corrections, moral warnings and exhortations' then learns reading, writing and

Brown, C., *Comfortable Everyday Life at the Swedish Eighteenth-Century Näs Manor.*
Taylor & Francis Group, 2024
DOI 10.5117/9789048562374_CON

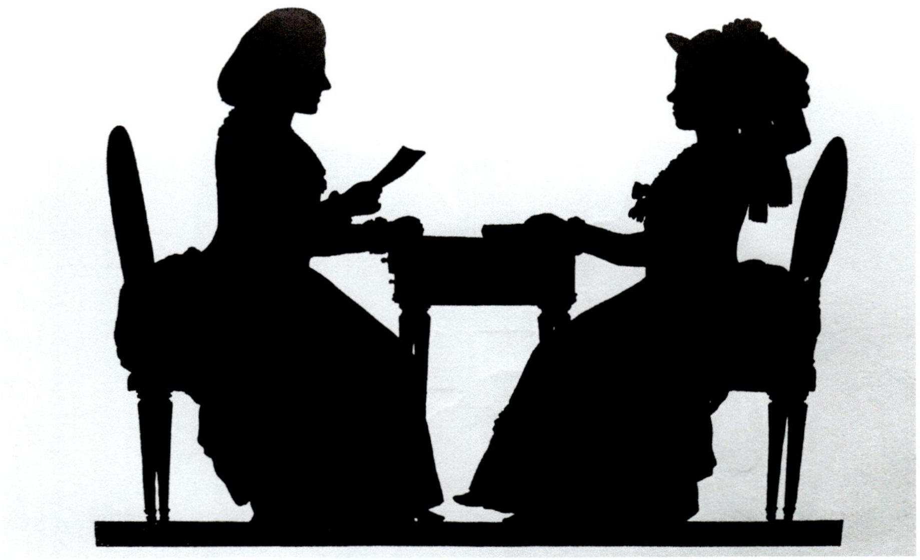

100. *Emilie von Werthern & Sophie von Schardt*, 1780. Silhouette, ink on paper, 17.3 × 21.8 cm. From Anne Gabrisch, *Schattenbilder der Goethezeit*, Leipzig, 1966.

arithmetic.[1] She is shaped into a role model, a young woman without artificiality and dissemblance. Her bedside table is not littered with any make-up or false love letters. 'Brazen seducers of innocence, gaudy exhibitionists and impudent fools do not encircle her table; nor do sanctimonious sisters, who taint the morning with thoughtless prayers and the afternoon with loquacious news, disturb her working time.' As a wife, she gathers her angelic children around the elegant tea table in her beautiful, ordered home. Everything is neat and tidy at all the tables; the perfect woman 'utilises her comforts with decorum, in moderation – she is satisfied and feels no desire for more'.[2]

The image of the half-dozing woman in her soft armchair possibly corresponds more clearly to today's ideas of comfortable everyday life, through the relaxed informality and feeling for the private life that it expresses (Image 1). But the many and different depictions of women at tables seen throughout the book offer additional interpretations. The study has shown that the perceptions of comfort not only concerned seclusion and private life but also extensively concerned various social aspects. It was in the interplay with the surrounding world that the principal parts of comfort were formed. As in Von Holthusen's notions of ideal femininity, it

1 Carl Johan von Holthusen, *Svenska fruntimrets fyra åldrar*, Stockholm 1785, pp. 7–9.
2 von Holthusen 1785, pp. 21, 23.

could concern norms, decorum and social constructions; or it could concern the messages formulated in the mottos that Carl Eric Wadenstierna commissioned for the entrance hall at his newly built Näs Manor – it was in the unaffected company of his family and friends that comfortable life manifested itself. The furnishing of the family's country residence showed how the home aimed to meet all these needs. Around the dining table, tea tables, games tables, sewing tables and writing tables, a social interaction could occur that created the feeling of informal and emotional closeness that was the raison d'être of comfort and the home – in sharing confidences over a cup of coffee or in maintaining friendship ties through correspondence.

The visual art that the Wadenstierna family commissioned for their new home also confirmed the purpose of modern comfort. Wadenstierna's wives and daughters were portrayed at sewing tables and writing tables with all the new accoutrements that facilitated their everyday tasks, and they were depicted in conversation or participating in the social contexts that they co-created. Other paintings displayed other tables, at which the household's work with linens and yarn was performed – well-stocked linen cupboards and a wealth of textile items were prerequisites for comfortable life as well as key markers of social status. Such pictures of the servants' tasks therefore also conveyed the complex signification of comfort.

Social roles

In the study, the women at different tables have been busy with a variety of activities. They have paused their sewing, letter writing or morning toilette to invite the viewer into their world. Comfort was about spending time together, conversations and relaxed socialising. It was also about creating contexts that involved as little irritation and disturbance as possible from, for example, bulky pieces of furniture or the presence of noisy servants. The tables' coffee services, candlesticks, tea urns or workbags were all cogs in the social machinery of comfort. They were *commodités* that met the requirements of comfort, but they were also expressions of modern consumers' informed taste and lifestyle in relation to their surroundings. The silhouette from Goethe's Weimar at the beginning of this chapter summarises comfort as a sign of the times (Image 100). The contour of the women in conversation at a table illustrates how comfort and well-being arose in the interplay between people and the material world around them. Details associated with comfort can be glimpsed in the picture – the correct clothing for the context, the dainty and practical table and the softly upholstered chairs. But their activity is also linked to the theme – the letter that their conversation seems to focus on can symbolise the significance of correspondence in the eighteenth century's comfortable everyday life. Writing or reading letters is a constantly recurring motif in the era's pictures, and the correspondence connected both the social networks and the shared ideas about the good life.

Swedish?

In this respect, was there a difference between Goethe's Weimar and Wadenstierna's Näs? Comfort as an idea hardly had a national domicile of its own. It developed in various locations in Europe and in various social contexts, but it was also formed through constant interaction between individuals, countries and places – whether it be in France, England, Germany or Sweden. In Europe, the late eighteenth century was in many ways a dynamic and groundbreaking time regarding attitudes to everyday life and family life. But the culture of comfort that developed from these revolutionary decades could have more or less distinctive national characteristics.[3] The Wadenstierna family's life at Näs has here served as the example of the Gustavian culture of comfort within the Swedish upper class. But how did Näs actually relate to the international ideals?

During the period when Wadenstierna created his new home in the Roslagen region north-east of Stockholm, European upper-class culture was permeated by both French and British influences regarding aesthetics, material culture, the art of socialising and social ideas. Various ideals were interwoven on the Swedish stage. Georg Haupt and Pehr Hilleström were influenced by French role models during their study trips, and when Niclas Lafrensen moved back to Sweden following his years in Paris, he painted 'French' portraits that were also tinged with the fashionable anglomania that became appreciated by the Swedish elite. The English influence was also seen in landscape art and through contact with the British engravings market. Marieberg's ceramics factory in Stockholm was founded by Johan Ehrenreich, summoned from Germany, and was at times run under French management, for instance, by Pierre Berthevin.[4] But despite all the foreign influences, Swedish construction projects such as Näs differed from corresponding French and English examples. They differed in aspects such as the proportions and materials of the houses or the disposition and actual use of the rooms. This could be seen in the choice of tiled stoves, faience or calico, instead of fireplaces, porcelain and silk.[5]

3 Prytz, Cristina and Stobart, Jon, 'Comfort in English and Swedish country houses, c. 1760–1820', *Social History*, 43, nr 2, London 2018.

4 Johan Ehrenreich founded Marieberg's ceramics factory in Stockholm in 1759, and Frenchman Pierre Berthevin took over the business in 1766.

5 Prytz and Stobart 2018 and Stobart, Jon, *Comfort in the Eighteenth-Century Country House*, Routledge, New York 2022.

The aesthetic and economic ideas formulated in the Age of Liberty had laid the foundation for different approaches that concerned both integrating with and distancing oneself from the Continental ideals. In a spirit of patriotism, the Swedish identity was not perceived as inferior to European culture, and it was instead emphasised as setting a good example in matters large and small, in the political and private spheres. This patriotic starting point affected choices and actions connected with taste, consumption and comfort. The balance between identifying oneself as an informed participant in an international upper-class culture and as a patriot recurs in the entire study, reflected through Wadenstierna as an example. The Wadenstierna family chose 'Swedish' when Näs was decorated with furniture by Haupt, faience from the Marieberg factory and paintings by Hilleström and Korn, but the idiom and visual language effectively and interactively crossed national and cultural boundaries.

Being a good citizen and acting in the best interests of one's home country by supporting its domestic production was regarded as an upper-class virtue, not least in times when the burning political issue of luxury consumption and its consequences for the nation's economy and identity was debated most intensively. The material culture, what people bought and owned, was the crucial point. Although the new luxury in the form of a new culture of comfort with Swedish overtones concerned notions of a pleasantly well-ordered everyday life in the company of good friends, it was equally shaped by an increasingly widespread European culture of consumption in a growing international market. Näs thereby appears to be the result of a combination – that was typical of the period – of international impulses and Swedish elements in interior decoration, room functions and in the choice of artists and craftsmen. Through Wadenstierna's manor house project in rural Roslagen, Sweden, was united with the surrounding world. The book collection contained volumes written in French and English, and the maps on the library walls illustrated the countries and continents of the world. The cups in the dining room's tableware pantry came from China and Germany, and the tea and coffee that filled them were long-distance imports. The game of billiards, which was the focal point of socialising in the southern wing building, gained its modern form in England, and the popularity of the game had a clear link to the eighteenth century's rising interest in the British way of life. But were there also signs here that the Continental taste and lifestyle could be perceived as problematic in this context?

The picture of comfort

Portraiture, so closely connected with self-image and identity, may hint at an answer. The study has shown how elements in different international types of portrait did not make a major impact in Sweden. They evidently did not fit in with the

Swedish contexts and the national ideals that had taken shape during the century. Women depicted at dressing tables, one of the clearest symbols of French luxury consumption, are infrequently represented in Swedish portraiture. Nevertheless, the French pictorial world was extensively reused and reshaped to suit the Swedish context. Throughout the study, works by French artists – mainly François Boucher and Jean Siméon Chardin – have been recurring points of reference. Pehr Hilleström filled his Gustavian interiors with references to their pictures, knowing that his audience saw and appreciated these visual quotations. This gesture show how aesthetic and cultural expressions were clearly shared among upper-class people all over Europe. For Wadenstierna, the pictures must have created a link between his life in Stockholm and at Näs, but also with a larger context branching off far and wide around the world.

The affinity among the upper class conveyed by this visual culture was an important contributory factor to the development and dissemination of the eighteenth century's culture of comfort. The pictures conveyed *what* comfort was and *how* it should be applied and manifested. Niclas Lafrensen's French interiors showed how comfortably appointed drawing rooms and cabinets were furnished and used, who were in the rooms and what emotions they expressed. Here, Lafrensen contributed to creating a visual idea of the modern, comfortable life. Correspondingly, Chardin's pictures presented the well-ordered home, the well-functioning everyday life, and women's role in and significance for the comfort that was formulated here. These artworks served as models for new pictures while also disseminating and nuancing attitudes and ideals.

In this pictorial world, women were often the protagonists, and they have also been given the prominent position in this study. In the pictures, the home as the hub of family life, social relationships and emotions was the obvious stage for the new culture of comfort – and the stage on which the women interacted with new consumer goods and habits. This comfort associated with women could in contemporary sources occasionally be presented as a vice that is difficult to master in a vain and sensuous woman who is susceptible to idleness and consumption. However, when handled correctly, comfort above all appeared to be a virtue and a key aspect of the normative role of woman. Wadenstierna soon remarried after the death of his first wife – the comfortably appointed everyday life required a woman in the home. The paintings that Wadenstierna commissioned, just as the library's books, intended to contribute to the education of his daughters according to the same ideals. The multifaceted pictorial world also illustrated how everyday tasks – sewing, writing letters and drinking coffee – were filled with new connotations during the eighteenth century. The conception of good everyday home life gained a fashionable touch, associated with a privileged, modern lifestyle and an expanding culture of consumption.

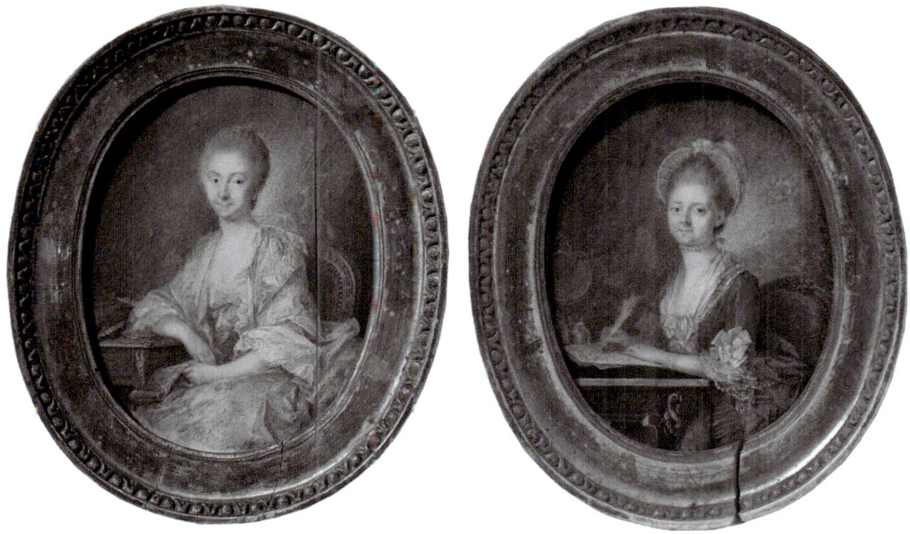

101. Niclas Lafrensen the Younger, *Jacobina Sophia Psilanderhielm von Seulenberg* (1733–1768) and *Fredrica Carleson* (1743–1794). Watercolour and gouache on ivory, 8.5 × 6 cm. Nationalmuseum, Stockholm (NMGrh 4324).

Alongside the material culture at Näs, the visual art has been the main research material for this study. This includes the paintings by Hilleström and Lafrensen, and those by Boucher and Chardin. But the visual culture also includes the clothes that people wore and the furniture in the home. The contextualisation of these visual expressions has given the elusive term 'comfort' a clearer shape, specific to the Wadenstierna family at Näs, yet necessarily linked to a larger context and to an international upper-class culture. Views of the Continent's social and cultural contexts, shared through an international pictorial world and material culture that communicated shared ideals, have therefore been central to the study. The formation of a home, the commissioning of a portrait or the purchase of a coffee service or dressing gown were all expressions of a will to display an identity-building affinity with the social stratum that people belonged to. And perhaps comfort was above all about this: feeling at home in your context.

Niclas Lafrensen's portraits of Jacobina Sophia Psilanderhielm and Fredrica Carleson have continually reappeared in various parts of the study. The portraits have been studied as bearers of social and cultural signs that tell us about the Wadenstierna family and the time and situation they lived in. Their clothes, furniture, objects and gestures have conveyed messages about their everyday life and social contexts. But the women's facial features and expressions have played a lesser role in the narrative. Yet it was perhaps these features that created the most important 'comfort' in a contemporary context, for the commissioner and viewers of the portraits. The portraits' function to represent the individual and create closeness between the family members reconnects with the emotional dimensions of comfort. The home, with its practical tables and soft sofas, could not be appreciated as comfortable without this emotional presence.[6] The portraits, just as the entrance hall's mottos, wanted to remind us of the significance of this fundamental need, so essential for comfort. It may therefore be appropriate to also conclude the study with these portraits. They serve as reminders of how emotional ties today still create the conditions for comfortable everyday life.

6 Prytz and Stobart 2018, pp. 250–7; Stobart 2022, chs 5 and 6.

Bibliography and sources

Archives

Kungliga biblioteket [Royal Library], Stockholm

Handskriftsavdelningen [Manuscripts Department]. Ep. E. 6: 1–2: Brev [Letters] från Claes Julius Ekeblad till Brita Ekeblad, f. Horn, 1773–82.

Nordiska museets arkiv [Archives of the Nordic Museum], Stockholm

Förteckning över arkivalier på Näs herrgård, 18–22/9 1967.
Inventering av huvudbyggn [Inventories], 10–21/7 1967.
KU 3542, Uppland, Sjuhundra hd, Röö sn, Näs.

Riksarkivet [The National Archive], Stockholm

Börstorpssamlingen. E. 3099. Brev [Letters] från Charlotta Fredrika Hamilton af Hageby till Brita Stina Sparre.

Bouppteckning [Estate records] efter Ottiliana Vilhelmina Transchiöld, gift Liljecrantz (1741–1788), upprättat 1789, SE/RA/420422/01/E IX b/131.

Celsingska familjearkivet [Celsing Family Archive]. Gustaf och Ulric Celsing, SE/D123/AS_1124-2.

Näs Silverstolpeska arkivet, Gårdsarkivet. Äldre kassaböcker.

Näs Silverstolpeska arkivet, Personarkiven [Personal archives], vol. 60, Carl Eric Wadenstierna (1723–1787), Jacobina Sophia Psilanderhielm (1733–1768).

Näs Silverstolpeska arkivet, Personarkiven [Personal archives], vol. 61, Sophia Wadenstierna (1758–1830), Carolina Wadenstierna (1762–1848).

Svea hovrätt [Swedish Court of Appeal]. Adliga bouppteckningar [Noble estate records], 1788–97. Bouppteckning [Entail document] efter Carl och Ebba Margareta Bonde, upprättat 1796. E. IX B: 129–52.

Testamentariska Fideicomiss-Förordnanden af Framl. Envoyén och Commendören af Kongl. Nordst. Orden, herr Ulric Celsing Gustafson; af d. 1 mars och 3 Dec. 1804 samt d. 5 och 22 Nov. 1805, 1806 [Entail documents].

Stadsarkivet [The City Archive], Stockholm

Handlingar rörande tomten Fyrfoten större 41,5 vid hörnet Klara västra kyrkogata och Stora Vattugränden: planritning och elevation till nybyggnation, 1759; brandförsäkring,

1760; registerkort, 1770; köpebrev, 1761; uppbudsprotokoll 1761: 279; 1762: 5.19; 1787: 104, 119, 144 [Documents relating to properties].

Printed sources

Ackroyd, Paul, Roy, Ashok, and Wine, Humphrey, 'Nicolas Lancret's "The Four Times of Day"', *National Gallery Technical Bulletin*, vol. 25, 2004, pp. 48–61.

Adams, Christine, *A Taste for Comfort and Status: A Bourgeois Family in Eighteenth-Century France*, University Park, 2000.

Adelcrantz, Carl Fredric, *Tal om de fria konsters värde och nytta*, Stockholm, 1757.

Ahlberger, Christer, *Konsumtionsrevolutionen 1. Om det moderna konsumtionssamhällets framväxt 1750–1900*, Gothenburg, 1996.

Ahlund, Mikael, 'Konsten att försörja sig som konstnär. Pehr Hilleström och konstmarknaden i 1700-talets Stockholm', in Klas Nyberg (ed.), *Ekonomisk kulturhistoria. Bildkonst, konsthantverk och scenkonst 1720–1850*, Stockholm, 2017, pp. 55–71.

Ahlund, Mikael, *Landskapets röster. Studier i Elias Martins bildvärld*, dissertation, Stockholm, 2011.

Ahlund, Mikael, *Pehr Hilleström. Att se vardagen*, Konstmuseet Sinebrychoff, Helsinki, 2014.

Alenius, Marianne, 'Brevet – en genre för kvinnor. Traditioner och förebilder för kvinnors brev', in Elisabeth Møller Jensen (ed.), *Nordisk kvinnolitteraturhistoria*, Höganäs, 1993, vol. 1, pp. 364–70.

Allzén, Britta, and Tunander, Ingemar, *Yppighets nytta. Liten encyklopedi över människor, idéer och dyrbarheter i svensk rokoko*, Malmö, 1979.

Alm, Göran (ed.), *Kina Slott*, Stockholm, 2002.

Alm, Mikael (ed.), *Performing Herself: Everyday Practices and the Making of Gender in Early Modern Sweden*, Uppsala, 2017.

Almanac de Gotha, Gotha, 1776–92.

Almanach de Gotha pour l'année MDCCXCI, Gotha, 1791.

Ananoff, Alexandre, *François Boucher*, 2 vols, Paris, 1976.

Andersson, Gudrun, *Stadens dignitärer. Den lokala elitens status- & maktmanifestation i Arboga 1650–1770*, Stockholm, 2009.

Andersson, Gudrun, and Nyberg, Klas (eds), *Kommers. Historiska handelsformer i Norden under 1700- och 1800-talen*, Gävle, 2010.

Anfält, Tomas, 'Offentlighet och privatliv. Om livet på Leufsta herrgård på 1700-talet', in Erik Kjellberg (ed.), *Herrgårdskultur och salongsmiljö. Rapport från en nordisk konferens på Leufsta bruk 12–14 maj 1995*, Uppsala, 1997, pp. 3–14.

Annas, Alicia M., 'The Elegant Art of Movement', in Edward Maeder (ed.), *An Elegant Art: Fashion & Fantasy in the Eighteenth Century*, New York, 1983, pp. 35–60.

Appadurai, Arjun (ed.), *The Social Life of Things: Commodities in Cultural Perspective*, Cambridge, 1986.

Argenson, René Louis de Voyer [Marquis de Paulmy], *Mélanges tirés d'une grand bibliothèque. Manuel des châteaux, ou, Lettres contenant des conseils pour former une bibliothèque romanesque, pour diriger une comédie de société & pour diversifier les plaisirs d'un salon*, Paris, 1779.

Ariès, Phillipe, and Duby, Georges (eds), *A History of Private Life*, Cambridge and London, 1989.

Asplund, Karl, 'En gammal mans dröm om Paris', in *Gustavianskt. Studier kring den gustavianska tidens kulturhistoria tillägnade Sigurd Wallin på hans femtioårsdag*, Stockholm, 1932.

Asplund, Karl, 'Näs i Rö', in *Fataburen*, Nordiska museet, Stockholm, 1960, pp. 7–40.

Asplund, Karl, *Två gustavianska mästare. Niklas Lafrensen d.y. och Elias Martin i samtida gravyrer*, Stockholm, 1925.

Auslander, Leora, *Taste and Power: Furnishing Modern France*, London, 1996.

Bäärnhielm, Göran, 'En karthandlare i Storkyrkobrinken', *Biblis*, no. 23, 2003, pp. 33–8.

Bailey, Colin B., *Jean-Baptiste Greuze:* The Laundress, Los Angeles, 2000.

Bastide, Jean-François, *La petite maison* (1758), Paris, 1879.

Bastide, Jean-François, *The Little House: An Architectural Seduction*, trans. Rodolphe El-Khoury, New York, 1996. Translation of *La petite maison*, 1758.

Beckford, Peter, 'Letter V', in *Familiar Letters from Italy to a Friend in England*, 2 vols, London 1805, vol. 1, pp. 45–58.

Bellman, Carl Michael, Tankar *om flickors ostadighet*, Stockholm, 1758.

Bellman, Carl Michael, 'Vid turkens audience 1773', *Fredmans sånger*, no. 30, 1791.

Benoist, Françoise-Albine Puzin de la Martinière, *Sophronie ou lecon prétendue d'une mère à sa fille*, Paris, 1768.

Berg, Gösta, and Svensson, Sigfrid, *Svensk bondekultur*, Stockholm, 1969.

Berg, Maxine, *Luxury and Pleasure in Eighteenth-Century Britain*, Oxford, 2005.

Berg, Maxine, and Eger, Elizabeth, 'The Rise and Fall of the Luxury Debates', in Maxine Berg and Elizabeth Eger (eds), *Luxury in the Eighteenth Century: Debates, Desires and Delectable Goods*, London, 2003, pp. 7–27.

Bernez, Marie-Odile, 'Comfort, the Acceptable Face of Luxury: An Eighteenth-Century Etymology', *Journal for Early Modern Cultural Studies*, vol. 14, no. 2, 2014, pp. 3–21.

Berry, Helen, 'Prudent Luxury: The Metropolitan Tastes of Judith Baker, Durham Gentlewoman', in Rosemary Sweet and Penelope Lane (eds), *Women and Urban Life in Eighteenth-Century England*, Farnham, 2003, pp. 131–56.

Berzén, Yngve, *Sveriges bebyggelse, Stockholms län*, Uddevalla, 1952.

Bibliothéque de campagne ou amusemens de l'esprit et du coeur, 12 vols, Amsterdam 1742–9.

Biographiskt lexicon öfver namnkunnige svenska män, 23 vols, Uppsala, 1835–57.

Biurman, Johan, *En kort doch tydelig bref-ställare, at med godt sammanhang concipera och författa allehanda slags bref, skrifter, suppliquer och contracter med mera, samt rätt distinguera dem, med de wanlige skiljeteknen, punct, colon, semicolon, comma &c*, Stockholm, 1729.

Bjurman, Eva Lis, *Catrines intressanta blekhet. Unga kvinnors möten med de nya kärleks-kraven 1750–1830*, dissertation, Eslöv, 1998.

Blégny, Nicolas de, *Le bon usage du thé, du caffé, et du chocolat pour la preservation & pour la guerison des maladies*, Paris, 1787.

Blondel, François, *Cours d'architecture*, 3 vols, Paris, 1675–83.

Blondel, Jacques-François, *De la distribution des maisons de plaisance et de la décoration des edifices en general*, 2 vols, Paris, 1737.

Blondel, Jacques-François, *Cours d'architecture ou traité de la décoration, distribution et constructions des bâtiments contenant les leçons données en 1750, et les années suivantes*, 6 vols, Paris, 1771–7.

Bonnart, Nicolas, *Recueil des modes de la cour de France*, Paris, 1678–93.

Boudier de Villemert, Pierre Joseph, *Qwinno-könets wän. Öfwersatt ifrån fransyskan*, Västerås, 1763.

Boyd, Diane E., and Kvande, Marta, 'Introduction: Reading Women, Reading Public and Private', in Diane E. Boyd and Marta Kvande, Marta (eds), *Everyday Revolutions: Eighteenth-Century Women Transforming Public and Private*, Newark, 2008, pp. 17–29.

'Bref ifrån en Landsort om Tjenstefolk', *Hushållnings Journal*, September 1777, pp. 476–77.

Brefwäxling Emellan Adelaide och några Wittre Snillen I Omwäxlande Ämnen, Stockholm, 1773.

Bremer-David, Charissa (ed.), *Paris: Life & Luxury in the Eighteenth Century*, Los Angeles, 2011.

Brewer, John, and Porter, Roy, *Consumption and the World of Goods*, New York, 2003.

Bricaire de La Dixmerie, Nicolas, *Les dangers d'un premier choix. Ou lettres de Laure a Émilie*, Haag, 1777.

Bringéus, Nils-Arvid, *Skånska kistebrev*, Stockholm, 1995.

Brown, Carolina, 'Bilder, sällskapsliv och herrgårdskultur. Maskeradporträtt, silhuetter och andra bilder från 1700-talets Tista', *Historisk Tidskrift för Finland*, 98, 2013, pp. 185–216.

Brown, Carolina, 'Den vita lyxen. Spetsar i 1700-talets visuella och materiella kultur', in Paula von Wachenfeldt and Klas Nyberg (eds), *Det svenska begäret. Sekler av lyxkonsumtion*, Stockholm, 2015, pp. 74–105.

Brown, Carolina, *Liksom en herdinna. Litterära teman i svenska kvinnoporträtt under 1700-talet*, dissertation, Stockholm, 2012.

Brown, Carolina, *Skönhetens mask. Historia om kropp och själ, ideal och verklighet*, Stockholm, 2011.

Bunth, Christopher Daniel, *An Essay on English Lecture, Selected for the Most Part from Late Authors*, Lund, 1792.

Burkhardt, Johan Gottlieb, *Philosophie öfwer Naturen. Til bättre kännedom af Skaparen och de skapade tingen, men i synnerhet af Människans wärde och bestämmelse. I sammandrag af Doct. Joh. Gottl. Burkhardt*, Lund, 1797.

Burman, Carina, *Bellman. Biografin*, Stockholm, 2019.

Cabinet des modes, ou les modes nouvelles, décrites d'une manière claire et précise, et représentées par des planches en taille-douce, enluminées, Paris, 1785–6.

Caffeets sista Stunder Då Den Mäktiga Frun Fru Öfwerflöd, herskarinna öfwer Yppighet, Nipper och all fåfäng Granlåt. Utblåste sin yppiga anda i Swerige [Coffee's final moments, when the powerful lady, Lady Excess, mistress of luxury, trinkets and all vain finery, exhaled her last luxurious breath in Sweden], Stockholm, 1767.

Candid [pseud.], *Nyheter för toiletten*, Stockholm, 1782.

Carleson, Edvard, *Möjeligheten At i Swerige inrätta Fabriquer och Manufacturer*, Sockholm, 1731.

Carleson, Edvard, and Höpken, Carl Fredrik von, *Relation, om herrar envoyéernes och cancellierådens, herr baron v. Höpkens och herr Carlesons hafde audience wid Ottomanniske porten 8/19 julii 1740*, Stockholm, 1740.

Castan, Nicole, 'The Public and the Private', in Roger Chartier (ed.), *A History of Private Life, Vol. 3: Passions of the Renaissance*, Cambridge and London, 1989, pp. 403–45.

Cederblom, Gerda, *Pehr Hilleström som kulturskildrare*, 2 vols, Stockholm, 1927–9.

Cederlöf, Ulf, *Carl August Ehrensvärd 1745–1800. Tecknaren och arkitekten*, Stockholm, Nationalmuseum, 1997.

Chatenet-Calyste, Aurélie, 'A Feminine Luxury in Paris: Marie-Fortunée d'Este, Princesse de Conti (1731–1803)', in Deborah Simonton, Marjo Kaartinen, and Anne Montenach (eds), *Luxury and Gender in European Towns, 1700–1914*, New York, 2015, pp. 171–89.

Cheng, Diana, *The History of the Boudoir in the Eighteenth Century*, dissertation, Montreal and Quebec, 2011.

Cheyne, George, *The English Malady; or, A Treatise of Nervous Diseases of All Kinds, as Spleen, Vapours, Lowness of Spirits, Hypochondriacal and Hysterical Distempers*, Dublin, 1733.

Chippendale, Thomas, *The Gentleman and Cabinet-Maker's Director: Being a Large Collection of the Most Elegant and Useful Designs of Household Furniture, in the Most Fashionable Taste*, London, 1754.

Chomel, Antoine-Angelique, *Aménités littéraires, et recueil d'anecdotes*, 2 vols, Amsterdam, 1773.

Chrisman-Campell, Kimberly, 'Dressing to Impress: The Morning Toilette and the Fabrication of Femininity', in Charissa Bremer-David (ed.), *Paris: Life & Luxury in the Eighteenth Century*, Los Angeles, 2011, pp. 53–74.

Contant d'Orville, André-Guillaume, *Le mariage du siècle, ou lettres de Mme la Comtesse de Castelli à Mme la Baronne de Fréville*, Lille, 1767.

Corbin, Alain, 'Domestic Atmospheres', in Chiara Briganti and Kathy Mezei (eds), *The Domestic Space Reader*, Toronto, 2012, pp. 105–8.

Correspondence litteraire, Paris, 1761.

Corson, Richard, *Fashions in Hair*, London, 1965.

Corson, Richard, *Fashions in Makeup: From Ancient to Modern Times*, London, 1989.

Crébillon, Claude-Prosper Jolyot de, *Le sopha, conte moral, par Mr. Crebillon, fils.*, Paris, 1742.

Crowley, John, *The Invention of Comfort: Sensibilities and Design in Early Modern Britain and Early America*, Baltimore, 2003.

Dagligt Allehanda, Stockholm, 1772–98.

D'Alembert, Jean le Rond, and Diderot, Denis, *Encyclopédie, ou dictionnaire raisonné des sciences, des arts et des métiers*, 28 vols, Paris, 1751–72.

Dalin, Olof von, *Framledne Hof-Cancellerens och Riddarens af Kongl. Maj:ts Nordstierne-Orden Herr Olof von Dalins Witterhets-Arbeten, I bunden och obunden Skrif- Art*, vol. 6, Stockholm, 1767.

Dalin, Olof von, *Poetiska arbeten*, Stockholm, 1783.

Dalin, Olof von, *Then Swänska Argus*, no. 29, Stockholm, 1733.

Dancourt, Florent Carton, *Then a la Modiske Cavallieren. Comoedie uti Fem Öpningar*, trans. Carl Eric Wadenstierna, Stockholm, 1747.

Darwin, Erasmus, *Plan for the Conduct of Female Education in Boarding Schools*, London, 1797.

DeJean, Joan, *The Age of Comfort: When Paris Discovered Casual – and the Modern Home Began*, New York, 2009.

De Maistre, Xavier, *Voyage autour de ma chambre*, Lausanne, 1794. Translated into Swedish in 1798.

De Maistre, Xavier, *Voyage Around my Room*, New York, 1994.

Det Götheborgska wetenskaps och witterhets samhällets handlingar. Wetenskaps afdelningen, Gothenburg, 1778–1808.

De Vries, Jan, *The Industrious Revolution: Consumer Behavior and the Household Economy, 1600 to the Present*, Cambridge, 2008.

Diderot, Denis, *Regrets sur ma vieille robe de chambre ou avis à ceux qui ont plus de goût que de fortune*, Paris, 1772.

Drakenberg, Sven, 'Pehr Hilleström och det gustavianska hemmet', *Rig: Föreningen för Svensk kulturhistoria*, no. 1–2, 1929, pp. 73–82.

Du Rietz, Anita, *Kvinnors entreprenörskap under 400 år*, Stockholm, 2013.

Ehnmark, Elof, *Ur den gamla Stockholms Posten. En samling artiklar*, Stockholm, 1931.

Ehrensvärd, Carl August, *Brev till Kickan*, i urval av Holger Frykenstedt, Stockholm, 1971.

Ehrensvärd, Carl August, *C.A. Ehrensvärds brev. Utgivna av Gunhild Bergh*, 2 vols, Stockholm, 1916.

Ehrensvärd, Gustaf Johan, *Dagboksanteckningar förda vid Gustaf III:s hof, utgifna af D:r E.V. Montan*, 2 vols, Stockholm, 1877–8.

Eklöv, Anders, '"Denna klara Caffe-Ström" – En studie av det svenska 1700-talets syn på kaffet speglad genom pamflett- och broschyr litteraturen', thesis, Department of Economics and History, Stockholm University, 1995.

Eklöv, Anders, '"... och all den Egendom som efter mig finnes är genom flit och arbetsamhetförvärfvat." – Om konsumtion och ägande bland stockholmarna under 1700-talet', BA thesis, Department of Economics and History, Stockholm University, 1997.

Elek, Paul, Elek, Elizabeth, and Johnston, Moira (eds), *The Age of the Grand Tour*, New York, 1967.

Elers, Johan, *Stockholm*, 4 vols, Stockholm, 1800.

En fullkomlig Ägta Hustrus Bild, Tecknad Efter den målning, som finnes i Ord-språks-Bokens sidsta Capitel, trans. Eric Forssén, Gothenburg, 1787.

Erdmann, Nils, *Ur rokokons liv. Typer och seder*, Stockholm, 1925.

Eriksdotter, Gunhild, 'När slottet blev beboeligt. Inneklimatets betydelse på Skoklosters slott under Wrangels tid', *Bebyggelsehistorisk tidskrift*, no. 66, 2013, pp. 8–29.

Fahlbeck, Erik, *Lars August Mannerheim. Politiker. Justitieombudsman. Bruksägare. Jordbrukare*, Lund, 1969.

Fahlu Weckoblad, Falun, 1787.

Farrell, Michèle Longino, *Performing Motherhood: The Sévigné Correspondence*, Hanover, 1991.

Favart, Marie Justine Benoîte, *Les encorcelés, ou Jeannot et Jeannette, parodie des Surprises de l'amour*, Paris, 1757.

Festa, Lynn, 'Cosmetic Differences: The Changing Faces of Britain and France', *Studies in Eighteenth Century Culture*, vol. 34, no. 1, 2005, pp. 25–54.

Fischerström, Johan, *En gustaviansk dagbok. Johan Fisherströms anteckningar för året 1773*, ed. Gustaf Näsström, Stockholm, 1951.

Fogelström, Per Anders, 'Stockholms oordentligheter', in Björn Hallerdt, *Yppighet och armod i 1700-talets Stockholm, Sankt Eriks årsbok*, Stockholm, 1994.

Forselius, Tilda Maria, 'Min nådiga pappas Uprigtiga Vän och fiolliga flicka. Julie Ekerman/Björckegrens brev till Carl Sparre lästa utifrån frågor om makt och identitet', MA thesis, Stockholm University, 2002.

Forsskål, Peter, *Tankar om borgerliga friheten*, Stockholm, (1759) 2009.

Frängsmyr, Carl, *Klimat och karaktär. Naturen och människan i sent svenskt 1700-tal*, dissertation, Stockholm, 2000.

Frykenstedt, Holger, *Poetens historia. Carl August Ehrensvärd och Johan Gabriel Oxenstierna, konstellation i Vänskapens och Poesins tecken*, Stockholm, 1969.

Fryxell, Anders, *Berättelser ur svenska historien. Fyrationdeandra delen. Frihets-tidens sista år och revolutionen 1772*, Stockholm, 1873.

Gabrisch, Anne, *Schattenbilder der Goethezeit*, Leipzig, 1966.

Galerie des modes et costumes français, Paris, 1778–87.

Genlis, Stéphanie Félicité, comtesse de, *De l'esprit de étiquettes de l'ancienne cour et des usages du monde de ce temps*, Paris, 1996.

Genlis, Stéphanie Félicité, comtesse de, *Memoirs of the Countess de Genlis*, 8 vols, London, 1825.

Genlis, Stéphanie Félicité, comtesse de, *Théâtre à l'usage des jeunes personnes*, 4 vols, Paris, 1780.

Gersault, François-Alexandre de, *L'art de la lingerie*, Paris, 1771.

Gisborne, Thomas, *An Enquiry into the Duties of the Female Sex*, London, 1797.

Gjörwell, Carl Christopher, *Carl Chr. Gjörwells brev till Fredrik Sparre 1768–1795*, Stockholm, 1938.

[Gjörwell, Carl Christopher], *Fruntimmers-Tidningar*, Stockholm, 1772.

Goffman, Ervin, *Jaget och maskerna. En studie i vardagslivets dramatik*, Stockholm, 2004. Translation of *The Presentation of Self in Everyday Life* (1956).

Goggin, Maureen Daly, and Tobin, Beth Fowkes (eds), *Material Women, 1750–1950: Consuming Desires and Collecting Practices*, New York, 2009a.

Goggin, Maureen Daly, and Tobin, Beth Fowkes (eds), *Women and the Material Culture of Needlework and Textiles, 1750–1950*, New York, 2009b.

Goggin, Maureen Daly, and Tobin, Beth Fowkes (eds), *Women and Things, 1750–1950: Gendered Material Strategies*, New York, 2009c.

Goodman, Dena, *Becoming a Woman in the Age of Letters*, Ithaca, 2009.

Gordon, Alden R., 'The Art Patronage of the Marquise de Pompadour and of the Marquis de Marigny', in Philippe Le Leyzour and Penelope Hunter-Stiebel (eds), *La volupté du goût: French Painting in the Age of Madame de Pompadour*, Paris, 2008, pp. 39–57.

Gordon, Daniel, *Citizens without Sovereignty: Equality and Sociability in French Thought, 1670–1789*, Princeton, 1994.

Gowrley, Freya, 'The Sister Arts: Textile Crafts between Paint, Print, and Practice', *Journal of Eighteenth-Century Studies*, vol. 53, no. 2, 2020, pp. 139–59.

Granroth, Elias, *Enfaldige tanckar om caffé och de inhemska wäxter som pläga brukas i des ställe*, dissertation, Turku, 1755.

Grasselli, Margaret Morgan (ed.), *Colorful Impressions: The Printmaking Revolution in Eighteenth-Century France*, Washington, DC, 2003.

Grate, Pontus, *French Paintings, Vol. 2: Eighteenth Century*, Nationalmuseum, Stockholm, 1994.

Greig, Hanna, 'Eighteenth-Century English Interiors in Image and Text', in Jeremy Aynsley and Charlotte Grant (eds), *Imagined Interiors: Representing the Domestic Interior Since the Renaissance*, London, 2006, pp. 102–12.

Grundy, Isobel, 'Women and Letters', in Tiffany Potter (ed.), *Women, Popular Culture, and the Eighteenth Century*, Toronto, 2012, pp. 103–49.

Gustavianskt 1771–1810. En bokfilm av Ingvar Andersson, Agne Beijer, Bertil Kjellberg, Bo Lindorm, Stockholm, 1945.

Habermas, Jürgen, *The Structural Transformation of the Public Sphere: An Inquiry into a Category of Bourgeois Society* (1962), Cambridge, 1989.

Hallesvik, Stig, 'Partimotsättningarna vid 1771–72 års riksdag som bakgrund till Gustav III:s statskupp', *Statsvetenskaplig tidskrift för politik – statistik – ekonomi*, Lund, 1962, pp. 383–405.

Hamilton, Carl Axel Hugo, 'Utdrag ur Carl Axel Hugo Hamiltons Dagbok år 1744', *Personhistorisk tidskrift*, Svenska autografsällskapet, Stockholm, 1900, pp. 57–77.

Hammar, Britta, 'Modebubblor – kvinnlig fägring under två sekel', in Britta Hammar and Pernilla Rasmussen, *Kvinnligt mode under två sekel*, Lund, 2001, pp. 9–38.

Hedge, Elaine, 'The Needle or the Pen: The Literary Recovery of Women's Textile Work', in Florence Howe (ed.), *Tradition and the Talents of Women*, Urbana, 1991, pp. 338–64.

Hellman, Mimi, 'Furniture, Sociability, and the Work of Leisure in Eighteenth-Century France', *Eighteenth-Century Studies*, vol. 32, no. 4, 1999, pp. 415–45.

Hellsing, My, *Hedvig Elisabeth Charlotte: hertiginna vid det gustavianska hovet*, Stockholm, 2015.

Helmius, Agneta, 'Äktenskap som mål och mening. Könskonstituering i 1700-talets Sverige', *Kjønn, makt, samfunn i Norden i et historisk perspektiv*, Konferensrapport fra det 5. nordiske kvinnehistorikermøte, Dragvoll, 1997, pp. 247–70.

Hemliga handlingar hörande till Sveriges historia efter Konung Gustaf III:s anträde till regeringen, 3 vols, Stockholm, 1822.

Hesse, Carla, *The Other Enlightenment: How French Women Became Modern*, Princeton, 2001.

Hilleström, Gustaf, 'Pehr Hilleström', *Svenskt biografiskt lexikon*, Stockholm, 1971.

Hisinger, Mikael, *Resedagbok från Europa 1783–1784*, presented by Jouni Kuurne and Märtha Norrback, Borgå, 2015.

Hochschild, Rutger Fredrik, *Rutger Fredrik Hochschilds Memoarer*, edited by Henrik Schück, 3 vols, Stockholm, 1908.

Hodacs, Hanna, *Silk and Tea in the North: Scandinavian Trade and the Market for Asian Goods in Eighteenth-Century Europe*, London, 2016.

Hoffmann, Johan Adolph, *Tvänne böcker om förnöjsamheten efter förnuftets och trones grundsatser, på tyska språket tolf gånger uplagde, och nu efter mångas åstundan på swenska öfwersatte*, Stockholm and Uppsala, 1752.

Holmquist, Ingrid, *Salongens värld. Om text och kön i romantikens salongskultur*, Stockholm, 2000.

Holmström, Israel, *Samlade dikter.* 1, *Kärleksdikter, förnöjsamhetsvisor, sällskapspoesi, dansvisor, burleska dikter, fabler, gåtor, spådomar, epigram*, ed. Bengt Olsson, Barbro Nilsson, and Paula Henriksson, Svenska Vitterhetssamfundet, Stockholm, 1999.

Höpken, Anders von, *Tal, om yppighets nytta. Hållit för kongl. swenska wetenskaps academien, år 1740*, Stockholm, 1741.

Hushållnings Journal, Stockholm, 1777.

Hvad Nytt, Stockholm, 1774.

Hyde, Melissa, *Making up the Rococo: François Boucher and His Critics*, Los Angeles, 2006.

Ilmakunnas, Johanna, 'Adelns arbete och vardag på 1700-talets svenska herrgårdar. Johan Gabriel Oxenstiernas och Jacobina Charlotta Munsterhjelms dagböcker', *Historisk Tidskrift för Finland*, 98, 2013, pp. 156–84.

Ilmakunnas, Johanna, *Ett ståndsmässigt liv. Familjen von Fersens livsstil på 1700-talet*, Stockholm, 2012.

Ilmakunnas, Johanna, 'Konsten att avbilda arbete. Kvinnors sysselsättningar och vardag på Pehr Hilleströms genremålningar från 1770-talet till 1810-talet', *Historisk Tidskrift för Finland*, 103, 2018, pp. 1–45.

Ilmakunnas, Johanna, 'The Luxury Shopping Experience of the Swedish Aristocracy in Eighteenth-Century Paris', in Deborah Simonton, Marjo Kaartinen, and Anne Montenach (eds), *Luxury and Gender in European Towns, 1700–1914*, New York, 2015a, pp. 115–31.

Ilmakunnas, Johanna, 'Måltidsupplevelser i 1700-talets Sverige och det tidiga 1800-talets Finland', *Historisk Tidskrift för Finland*, 100, 2015b, pp. 453–84.

Ilmakunnas, Johanna, and Stobart, Jon, 'Display, Acquisition and Boundaries of Luxury and Taste', in Johanna Ilmakunnas and Jon Stobart (eds), *A Taste for Luxury in Early Modern Europe: Display, Acquisition and Boundaries*, London and New York, 2017a, pp. 1–17.

Ilmakunnas, Johanna, and Stobart, Jon (eds), *A Taste for Luxury in Early Modern Europe: Display, Acquisition and Boundaries*, London and New York, 2017b.

Inrikes Tidningar, Stockholm, 1763–4, 1779, 1782–3, 1787–8.

'Inventaire après décès d'Alexandre Roslin, Paris, A.N., M.C.XXXI, 271, 17 juillet 1793', *Art Bulletin of Nationalmuseum Stockholm*, no. 7, 2000, pp. 71–83.

Jacquin, Armand Pierre (Abbé), *De la santé. Ouvrage utile à tout le monde*, Paris, 1771.

Jarrick, Arne, *Kärlekens makt och tårar. En evig historia*, Stockholm, 1997.

Johannesson, Lena, 'Att studera konsthistoria och visuell kultur. Begrepp, metod och historiografi', in Lena Johannesson (ed.), *Konst och visuell kultur i Sverige. Före 1809*, Stockholm, 2007, pp. 12–21.

Jones, Jennifer Michelle, *Sexing la Mode: Gender, Fashion and Commercial Culture in Old Regime France*, Oxford, 2004.

Jönköpings Allehanda, Jönköping, 1803.

Jonsson, Leif, 'Silhuetter ur det gustavianska musiklivet', ed. Peter Söderbäck, *Svenskt musikhistoriskt arkiv*, Bulletin no. 29, June 1995, pp. 3–38.

Josephson, Ragnar, *Tidskrift för konstvetenskap*, Stockholm, 1922.

Journal des Luxus und der Moden, Weimar, 1788.

Journal för allmänna upplysningen och sederne, Stockholm, 1797.

Karlson, William, *Ett svenskt herremanshem på 1700-talet. Clas Julius Ekeblads inventarium över Stola 1796*, Lund, 1940.

Kenny, Ruth, '"Apartments That Are Not Too Large": Pastel Portraits and the Spaces of Femininity in the English Country House', in Gill Perry et al. (eds), *Placing Faces: The Portrait and the English Country House in the Long Eighteenth Century*, Manchester, 2013.

Knapas, Rainer, *Monrepos, Ludwig Heinrich Nicolay och hans värld i 1700-talets ryska Finland*, Stockholm, 2003.

Koda, Harold, and Bolton, Andrew (eds), *Dangerous Liaisons: Fashion and Furniture in the Eighteenth Century*, Metropolitan Museum of Art and Yale University Press, 2004.

Kolmodin, Olof, *Biblisk Qwinno=Spegel. Det är: Alla i den Heliga Skrift för något särdeles Bekanta och Märkwärdiga Qwinnors Exempel; Det Ädla och Dygdälskande Swenska*

Qwinnokönet Til wälment tienst Såsom en Odygds Warning Samt Sann Gudsfruktans och Dygds upmuntring, I enfaldiga och otwungna Swenska Rim föreständ, Stockholm, 1750.

Kongl. Collegii medici kundgiörelse om thet missbruk och öfwerflöd, som thé och caffé drickande är underkastat, samt anwisning på swenska örter at bruka i ställe för thé, Stockholm, 1746.

Kongl. maj:ts nådige Förordning Angående En wisz afgift som kommer at läggas på alla Kortlekar, Stockholm, 1730.

Kongl. maj:ts Placat Och Förbud, Angående Hwarjehanda otilbörligt Spel och Dobbel på Källare och Caffee Hus, så wäl som hemma i husen, Stockholm, 1719.

Krutmejer, David, *Fransk parleur, eller vald samling af fransyska och svenska samtal, innehållande en praktisk vägledning för begynnare att tala franska språket*, Stockholm, 1811.

Kundgiörelse, Angående afgiften, som för Inrikes tilwärkade Kort hädanefter kommer at erläggas, Stockholm, 1756.

La Fayette, Madame de [Marie-Madeleine Pioche de La Vergne], *La princesse de Clèves*, Paris, 1678.

Lagerquist, Marshall, 'Blomstermålning i trä', *Fataburen, Nordiska museets och Skansens årsbok*, Stockholm, 1962, pp. 51–62.

Lagerquist, Marshall, *Georg Haupt. Ebeniste du Roi*, Nordiska museets handlingar 92, Stockholm, 1979.

Laine, Merit, 'Skönhetsgalleriet på Drottningholm', in Merit Laine and Carolina Brown, *Gustaf Lundberg 1695–1786. En porträttmålare och hans tid*, Stockholm, 2006, pp. 182–93.

Laine, Merit, and Brown, Carolina, *Gustaf Lundberg 1695–1786. En porträttmålare och hans tid*, Stockholm, 2006.

Lambert, Anne Thérèse de Marguenat de Courcelles, *Reflexions nouvelles sur les femmes, par une dame de la cour de France*, London, 1730.

Lamm, Martin, *Upplysningstidens romantik. Den mystiskt sentimentala strömningen i svensk litteratur* (1920), 2 vols, Lund, 1963.

Lange, Ulrich, *Ladugården. Om lantbrukets bebyggelse och arkitektur 1600–2000*, Nordiska museet, Stockholm, 2011.

La Place, Pierre-Antoine de, *Lettres à Myladi***, et autres œuvres melées*, Bruxelles, 1773.

Larsson, Alf, 'Kaffe, Alkohol m.m.', *Svensk Kemisk Tidskrift*, Stockholm, 1914, pp. 33–42.

Läsning i blandade ämnen, Stockholm, 1798.

Legrand d'Aussy, Pierre Jean-Baptiste, *Histoire de la vie privée des français depuis l'origine de la nation jusqu'à nos jours*, 3 vols, Paris, 1783.

Leijonhufvud, Sigrid, *Carl Gustaf Tessin och hans Åkerökrets*, Stockholm, 1931.

Le manuel des toilette dédié aux dames, Paris, 1777.

Lenngren, Anna Maria, 'Förlorade saker [Lost things]', *Stockholms Posten*, 1795.

Lenngren, Anna Maria, 'Toiletten', *Stockholms Posten*, 1797.

L'esprit des journaux, françois et étrangers. Par une société de gens-lettres, Liège, 1784–93.

Levertin, Oscar, *Niclas Lafrensen d.y. och förbindelserna mellan svensk och fransk målarkonst på 1700-talet*, Stockholm, 1899.

Levy, Allison (ed.), *Widowhood and Visual Culture in Early Modern Europe*, Farnham, 2003.

Lewenhauptska arkivet på Sjöholm. Bref och Handlingar utgifna af Adam Lewenhaupt, Stockholm, 1919.

Lindberg, Anna Lena, *En mamsell i akademien. Ulrica Fredrica Pasch och 1700-talets konstvärld*, Lund, 2010.

Lindgärde, Valborg, and Mansén, Elisabeth (eds), *Ljuva möten och ömma samtal. Om kärlek och vänskap på 1700-talet*, Stockholm, 1999.

Linné, Carl von, *Potus Coffeae*, Akademisk avhandling under Linnés presidium, Uppsala, 1761, trans. Ejnar Haglund, Svenska Linné sällskapet, Ekenäs, 1966.

Linnerhielm, Jonas Carl, *Bref under senare resor i Sverige*, Stockholm, 1816.

Ljungström, Lars, *Georg Haupt. Gustav III:s hovschatullmakare*, Stockholm, 2006.

Löwendahl, Marie, *Min allrabästa och ömmaste vän! Kvinnors brevskrivning under svenskt 1700-tal*, dissertation, Gothenburg, 2007.

Lundberg, Gunnar W., 'Ett rokokoporträtt och dess tillkomst', *Fataburen*, Nordiska museet, Stockholm, 1960, pp. 135–44.

Lundberg, Gunnar W., 'La charmante rose. Carl Gustaf Tessins nièce', *Vision och gestalt. Studier tillägnade Ragnar Josephsson*, Stockholm, 1958, pp. 150–73.

Lundberg, Gunnar W., *Svenskt och franskt 1700-tal i Institut Tessins samlingar*, Malmö, 1972.

Lycko-hjul, eller en ny och lustig kast-bok, hwaruti man uppå 50 lustiga frågor, Örebro, 1793.

Mackie, Erin, *Market à la Mode: Fashion, Commodity and Gender in* The Tatler *and* The Spectator, Baltimore, 1997.

Maeder, Edward (ed.), *An Elegant Art: Fashion and Fantasy in the Eighteenth Century*, Los Angeles, 1983.

Magasin des modes nouvelles, françaises et anglaises, Paris, 1786–9.

Malmborg, Boo von, *Svensk porträttkonst genom fem århundraden*, Malmö, 1978.

Mandeville, Bernard, *The Fable of the Bees: or, Private Vices, Publick Benefits*, London, 1714.

Marmontel, Jean-François, *Lucile, opera-comique i en act, öfversatt från fransyskan och upförd på kongl. svenska theatren, i deras majestäters och det kongl. Husets närvaro, första gången den 19 junii 1776*, Stockholm, 1776.

Martin, Johan Fredrik, 'Fru Hedvig Charlotta Nordenflycht', in *Svenska Galeriet, eller portraiter af märkvärdige svenske herrar och fruntimer*, Stockholm 1782, pp. 1–19.

Martin, Morag, *Selling Beauty: Cosmetics, Commerce, and French Society, 1750–1830*, Baltimore, 2009.

Masson, Pierre, *Le parfait limonadier, ou la maniere de preparer le thé, le caffé, le chocolat & autres liqueurs chaudes & froides*, Paris, 1705.

Mercier, Louis-Sébastien, *Tableau de Paris*, Amsterdam, 1783.

Mercure de France, Paris, 1734, 1739, 1755, 1789.

Moetjens, Adriaen, *Divertissemens innocens contenant les règles du jeu des échets, du billard, de la paume, du palle-mail et du trictrac*, Haag, 1696.

Molière, Jean Baptiste, *Qwinno-Skolan, Eller: Den Enfaldige Agnes, i Fem Acter, Föreställd på den Swenska Theatren i Stockholm Anno 1738*, trans. Gustaf Palmfelt, Stockholm, 1739.

Montesquieu, Charles-Louis de Secondat, *De l'esprit des loix*, Geneva, 1748.

Montgomery-Silfverstolpe, Malla, *Malla Montgomery-Silfverstolpes memoarer*, ed. Malla Grandinson, 4 vols, Stockholm, 1908–20.

Monument du costume physique et moral de la fin du dix-huitième siècle, ou tableaux de la vie, Paris, 1783.

Munsterhjelm, Jacobina Charlotta, *Jacobina Charlotta Munsterhjelms Dagböcker, 1799–1801*, ed. Bo Lönnqvist, Svenska Litteratursällskapet i Finland, Helsinki, 1970.

Murhem, Sofia, and Ulväng, Göran, 'To Buy a Plate: Retail and Shopping for Porcelain and Faience in Stockholm during the Eighteenth Century', in Johanna Ilmakunnas and Jon Stobart (eds), *A Taste for Luxury in Early Modern Europe: Display, Acquisition and Boundaries*, London, 2017, pp. 197–218.

Näsström, Gustaf, *Det gamla Medevi. Kulturhistoriska anteckningar*, Stockholm, 1928.

Näsström, Gustaf, *Forna dagars Sverige*, 3 vols, *Kulturhistorisk bilderbok om frihetstid och gustaviansk tid*, Stockholm, 1962.

Nemeitz, J.C., *Séjour de Paris, c'est à dire, Instructions fidéles, pour les Voiageurs de condition, Comment ils se doivent conduire, s'ils veulent faire un bon usage de leur tems & argent, durant leur Séjour à Paris*, Leiden, 1727.

Neufforge, Jean-François de, *Recueil élémentaire d'architecture*, 6 vols, Paris, 1757–68.

The New Lover's Instructor; or, Whole Art of Courtship. Being the Lover's Complete Library and Guide; and Containing ... Love Letters, ... Cards of Compliment, ... Love Epistles in Verse, Written in an Elegant Style; [etc.] London, 1780.

Nixon, Cheryl, and Penner, Louise, 'Materials of the "Everyday" Woman Writer: Letter-Writing in Eighteenth-Century England and America', in Maureen Daly Goggin and Beth Fowkes Tobin (eds), *Women and Things, 1750–1950: Gendered Material Strategies*, New York, 2009, pp. 157–87.

Nordenflycht, Hedvig Charlotta, *Fru Hedvig Charlotta Nordenflychts Utvalda arbeten*, edited by Johan Fischerström, Stockholm, 1774.

Nordenflycht, Hedvig Charlotta, *Qwinligt Tankespel för Åhr 1744*, Stockholm, 1744.

Nordin, Carl Gustaf, *Historiska handlingar. Till trycket befordrade av Kong. Samfundet för utgifvande af handskrifter rörande Skandinafviens historia, vol. 6, Dagboksanteckningar för åren 1786–1792*, Stockholm, 1868.

Norrhem, Svante, *Kvinnor vid maktens sida, 1632–1772*, Lund, 2007.

Norrtälje Municipality, *Kulturmiljöutredning, no 18, Näs*, Norrtälje, 2016.

North, Michael, 'Fashion and Luxury in Eighteenth-Century Germany', in Johanna Ilmakunnas and Jon Stobart (eds), *A Taste for Luxury in Early Modern Europe: Display, Acquisition and Boundaries*, London and New York, 2017, pp. 99–118.

North, Michael, *'Material Delight and the Joy of Living': Cultural Consumption in the Age of Enlightenment in Germany*, Farnham, 2008.

Nougaret, Pierre-Jean-Baptiste, *Aventures diverses, &c. avec quelques pièces curieuses & fort rares. Le tout fidèlement recueilli par M. Nougaret*, Paris, 1781.

Odlinder Haubo, Stina, 'Georg Haupt. Sekretär', in *Från Makalös till Haupt*, Åmells konsthandel, Stockholm, 2006, no. 28.

Öfwer-Ståthållare-Embetets Kungörelse och Förbud, emot otilbörligt spel och dobbel på Källare, Cafée-hus, och andre Näringsställen, samt emot äfwentyrliga spels anställande hemma i husen, Stockholm, 1785.

Öhrberg, Ann, 'Françoise Marguerite Janiçon: en kvinnlig aktör på frihetstiden politiska arena', in Marie-Christine Skuncke and Henrika Tandefelt (eds), *Riksdag, kaffehus och predikstol. Frihetstidens politiska kultur 1766–1772*, Stockholm, 2003, pp. 191–208.

Olausson, Magnus, 'Återfunna konstnärer, återvunna identiteter', *Athena och Ares*, Statens Försvarhistoriska Museer, document no. 3, Stockholm, 1999, pp. 239–48.

Om medlen att förhöja qwinliga skönheten. Handbok för damer. Öfwersättning af O. Fr. Lindén, Lund, 1806.

O'Regan, Christopher, *En bädd av dun. Livet vid Gustaf III:s hov*, Stockholm, 2012.

Oxenstierna, Johan Gabriel, *Dagboks-anteckningar. Åren 1769–1771*, Uppsala, 1881.

Oxenstierna, Johan Gabriel, *Journal*, Stockholm, 1964.

Oxenstierna, Johan Gabriel, *Ljuva ungdomstid. Dagbok 1766–1768*, Uppsala, 1965.

Paillasson, Charles, *L'art d'écrire réduit à des démonstrations vraies et faciles, avec des explications claires pour Le dictionnaire des arts, par Paillasson expert écrivain juré*, Paris, 1763.

Petersson, Sonya, *Konst i omlopp. Mening, medier och marknad i Stockholm under 1700-talets senare hälft*, dissertation, Stockholm, 2014.

Pettersson, Ronny (ed.), *Bekvämlighetsrevolutionen. Stockholmshushållen och miljön under 150 år och i framtiden*, Stockholm, 2008.

Piron, Alexis, *Oeuvres complettes d'Alexis Piron*, 7 vols, Paris, 1776.

Planck, Brita, *Förnuft eller känsla. Adel, kärlek & äktenskap*, Stockholm, 2018.

Popiel, Jennifer J., *Rousseau's Daughters: Domesticity, Education, and Autonomy in Modern France*, Durham, 2008.

Poulain de Nogent, *Lettres de Mme la comtesse de La Rivière à Mme la baronne de Neufpont, son amie*, 3 vols, Paris, 1777.

Pristash, Heather, Schaechterle, Inez, and Carter Wood, Sue, 'The Needle as the Pen: Intentionality, Needlework, and the Production of Alternate Discourses of Power', in Maureen Daly Goggin and Beth Fowkes Tobin (eds), *Women and the Material Culture of Needlework and Textiles, 1750–1950*, New York, 1999, pp. 13–30.

Purnell, Carolyn, *The Sensational Past: How the Enlightenment Changed the Way We Use Our Senses*, New York, 2017.

Radisich, Paula, *Pastiche, Fashion and Galanterie in Chardin's Genre Subjects: Looking Smart*, Plymouth, 2014.

Rand, Richard, *Intimate Encounters: Love and Domesticity in Eighteenth-Century France*, Princeton, 1997.

Rangström, Lena, *Kanonsalut och vaggor. Kungliga födslar och dop*, Stockholm, 2012.

Rasmussen, Pernilla, *Skräddaren, sömmerskan och modet. Arbetsmetoder och arbetsdelning i tillverkningen av kvinnlig dräkt 1770–1830*, Nordiska museets handlingar 136, dissertation, Stockholm, 2010.

Reenstierna, Märta Helena, *Årstadagboken*, 3 vols, Stockholm, 1993.

Regnér, Gustaf, *Svenska Parnassen*, Stockholm, 1784.

Rétif de La Bretonne, Nicolas-Edme, *Monument du costume physique et moral de la fin du dix-huitième siècle, ou tableaux de la vie*, 2 vols, London, 1790.

Richardson, Samuel, *Pamela, or Virtue Rewarded*, 4 vols, Manchester, 1811.

Riley, Noël, *The Accomplished Lady: A History of Genteel Pursuits c. 1660–1860*, Plymouth, 2017.

Ripa, Cesare, *Iconologia* (1603), Milano, 1992.

Roosevelt, Priscilla, *Life on the Russian Country Estate: A Social and Cultural History*, New Haven and London, 1995.

Roosval, Albin (ed.), *Svenska slott och herresäten vid 1900-talets början, Västmanland*, Stockholm, 1910.

Roubo, André Jacob, *L'art du Menuisier*, Paris, 1769.

Rousseau, Jean-Jacques, *Julie, ou la nouvelle Héloïse*, Amsterdam, 1761.

Ruano, Elise Urbain, 'The Négligé in Eighteenth-Century French Portraiture', *The Journal of Dress History*, vol. 1, no. 1, 2017, pp. 92–99.

Rubenhold, Hallie (ed.), *Harris's List of Covent Garden Ladies*, London, 2012.

Runefelt, Leif, *Att hasta mot undergången: anspråk, flyktighet, förställning i debatten om konsumtion i Sverige 1730–1830*, Lund, 2015.

Runefelt, Leif, 'Från yppighets nytta till dygdens försvar – den frihetstida debatten om lyx', *Historisk Tidskrift*, vol. 124, no. 2, 2004, pp. 203–23.

Rybczynski, Witold, *Home: A Short History of an Idea*, New York, 1986.

Sander, Fredrik, *Nationalmuseum. Bidrag till taflegalleriets historia* (1872), Stockholm, 1878.

Saumarez Smith, Charles, *Eighteenth-Century Decoration: Design and the Domestic Interior in England*, London, 1993.

Scott, Katie, *The Rococo Interior: Decoration and Social Spaces in Early Eighteenth-Century Paris*, New Haven and London, 1996.

Scott, Katie, and Cherry, Deborah (eds), *Between Luxury and the Everyday: Decorative Arts in Eighteenth-Century France*, Oxford, 2006.

Sedolärande Mercurius, Stockholm, 1730–1.

Sennefelt, Karin, *Politikens hjärta, Medborgarskap, manlighet och plats i frihetstidens Stockholm*, Stockholm, 2011.

Selling, Gösta, *Svenska herrgårdshem under 1700-talet* (1937), Stockholm, 1991.

Selling, Gösta, Johansson, Gotthard, and Axel-Nilsson, Göran, *Si Ulla dansar. Bilder från Bellmans Stockholm*, Stockholm, 1945.

Sherlock, Martin, *Nouvelles lettres d'un voyageur anglois*, London, 1780.

Showalter, Elaine, *Inventing Herself: Claiming a Feminist Intellectual Heritage*, New York, 2001.

Showalter, Elaine, *A Literature of Their Own: British Women Novelists from Brontë to Lessing*, Princeton, 1977.

Silfverstolpe, Gunnar Mascoll, 'Näs i Roslagen. En gustaviansk herrgård', *Svenska hem i ord och bilder*, no. 28, 1940, pp. 1–8.

Sirén, Osvald, *Pehr Hilleström d.ä., Väfvaren och målaren, hans lif och hans värk*, Stockholm, 1900.

Sjöberg, Lars, *Svenska trähus*, Stockholm, 2002.

Sjögren, Arthur, 'Silhuetter, 1700-talets fotografier', *Hela världen*, 1917, pp. 1598–1611.

Skuncke, Marie-Christine, and Tandefelt, Henrika (eds), *Riksdag, kaffehus och predikstol. Frihetstidens politiska kultur 1766–1772*, Stockholm, 2003.

Smith, Woodruff D., *Consumption and the Making of Respectability, 1600–1800*, New York, 2002.

Smollett, Tobias, *Fransoserne Äro ej Hvad De Utropas För, Eller Utdrag af några strödda Bref. Författade Under en resa genom Frankriket*, Stockholm, 1784.

Smollett, Tobias, *Travels through France and Italy*, London, 1766.

Söderberg, Bengt G., 'Näs', *Slott och herresäten i Sverige*, 1967, pp. 12–21.

Spary, E.C., *Eating the Enlightenment: Food and the Sciences in Paris, 1670–1760*, Chicago, 2012.

Spronk, Barbara, 'A House Is Not a Home: Witold Rybczynski Explores the History of Domestic Comfort' [Interview], *Aurora Online*, 1990, https://aurora.icaap.org/index.php/aurora/article/download/65/77.

Steorn, Patrik, 'Modebilder i det svenska 1700-talets trycksakskultur: migrerande motiv och produktiva instabiliteter', *Biblis*, 69, Kungliga biblioteket, Stockholm, 2015, pp. 10–18.

Stiernman, Anders Ant von, *Matrikel öfwer Swea Rikes Ridderskap och Adel, Uppå Des begäran wid 1751. Års Riks-Dag, Utgifwen med Historiska och Genealogiska Anmärkningar af Anders Ant von Stiernman*, 2 vols, Stockholm 1754–5.

Stobart, Jon, *Comfort in the Eighteenth-Century Country House*, Routledge, New York, 2022.

Stobart, Jon, *Sugar & Spice: Grocers and Groceries in Provincial England, 1650–1830*, Oxford, 2013.

Stobart, Jon, and Hann, Andrew (eds), *The Country House: Material Culture and Consumption*, Swindon, 2015.

Stobart, Jon, and Prytz, Cristina, 'Comfort in English and Swedish Country Houses, *c.* 1760–1820', *Social History*, vol. 43, no. 2, 2018, pp. 234–58.

Stobart, Jon, and Rothery, Mark, *Consumption and the Country House*, Oxford, 2016.

Stockholms Posten, Stockholm, 1779–97.

Strandberg, Runar, 'Berndes, Anton Ulrik', in *Svenskt konstnärslexikon*, Malmö, 1952, pp. 164–5.

Strödda handlingar, i synnerhet till publicitetens historia i Sverige under de sistförflutna femtio åren, Första Häftet, Stockholm, 1822.

Strokirk, Oscar Fredrik, *Kultur- och personhistoriska anteckningar*, 3 vols, Örebro, 1915–20.

Styles, John, and Vickery, Amanda, 'Introduction, in John Styles and Amanda Vickery (eds), *Gender, Taste and Material Culture in Britain and North America, 1700–1830*, New Haven and London, 2006b, pp. 1–34.

Sveriges ridderskaps- och adels riksdags-protokoll, Stockholm, 1731, 1765–6.

Swift, Jonathan, *Verses Wrote in a Lady's Ivory Table-Book*, London, 1698.

Sylvén, Torsten, *Mästarnas möbler. Stockholmsarbeten 1700–1850*, Stockholm, 1996.

Tal vid Förste Expeditions-Secreteraren m.m. Friherre Lars Aug. Mannerheims Kära Makas, Friherrinnan Sophia Mannerheims, född Wadenstjerna, Jordfästning, Den 17 Januarii 1830, Hållet af Johan Jacob Hedrén, Stockholm, 1830.

Tellerstedt, Diedrich, *Berättelse, om swenska meuble-handelens första inrättning, och de öden, meuble-handlaren Diedrich Tellerstedt uti 23 års tid, undergådt*, Stockholm, 1771.

Tessin, Nicodemus, the Younger, *Observationer Angående så wähl Publiqve som Priuate huus byggnaders Starkheet, beqwämligheet och skiönheet, in rättade, effter wår Swänska Climat och oeconomie* (1714), transcribed and with introduction by Bo Vahlne, Stockholm, 2002.

Thornton, Peter, *Authentic décor: The Domestic Interior 1620–1920*, London, 1985.

Tillhagen, Carl-Herman, 'Spel och dobbel', in Gösta Berg, Birger Beckman, Bengt Idestam-Almquist, and Gustaf Munthe (eds), *Det glada Sverige. Våra fester och högtider genom tiderna*, 3 vols, Stockholm, 1947, vol. 2, pp. 1265–317.

Toilette-lecture för fruntimmer och herrar, Stockholm, 1798.

Törnevall, Petrus, *Dygdz och Odygdz Spegel i hus-håld och Algemena Lefwernet*, Skara, 1730.

Ulväng, Göran, *Herrgårdarnas historia. Arbete, liv och bebyggelse på uppländska herrgårdar*, Uppsala, 2008.

Ulväng, Göran, *Hus och gård i förändring. Uppländska herrgårdar, boställen och bondgårdar under 1700- och 1800-talens agrara revolution*, dissertation, Hedemora, 2004.

Unga Fruentimbers Hushålls Spegel (1754), Stockholm, 1788.

Utdrag Utur alle ifrån den 7 dec. 1718 utkomne Publique Handlingar, Placater, Förordningar, Resolutioner ock Publicationer, Som Riksens Styrsel samt inwärtes Hushållning och Författningar i gemen, jämwäl ock Stockholms Stad i synnerhet, angå, 15 vols, Stockholm, 1742–1829.

Vahlne, Bo, *Frihetstidens inredningar på Stockholms slott. Om bekvämlighetens och skönhetens nivåer*, Stockholm, 2012.

Vahlne, Bo, 'Inredningskonst i teori och praktik', in Mårten Snickare (ed.), *Tessin: Nicodemus Tessin d.y. Kunglig arkitekt och visionär: en konstbok från Nationalmuseum*, Stockholm, 2002, pp. 127–49.

Vahlne, Bo (ed.), *Möbelhistoria på Gripsholm*, Stockholm, 1986.

Veblen, Thorstein, *The Theory of the Leisure Class: An Economic Study of Institutions*, London, 1899.

Verlden är sig altid lik, översatt från franskan av J Selin, Stockholm, 1781.

Vickery, Amanda, *Behind Closed Doors: At Home in Georgian England*, New Haven, 2009.

Vickery, Amanda, *The Gentleman's Daughter: Women's Lives in Georgian England*, New Haven, 1998.

Voltaire, *Le caffe, ou l'ecossaise, comedie. Par Mr. Hume prêtre écossais, traduit en français*, London, 1760.

Von Holthusen, Carl Johan, *Svenska fruntimrets fyra åldrar*, Stockholm, 1785.

Von Wachenfeldt, Paula, and Nyberg, Klas (eds), *Det svenska begäret. Sekler av lyxkonsumtion*, Stockholm, 2015.

Waddy, Patricia (ed.), *Nicodemus Tessin the Younger: Sources, Works, Collections: Traictè de la decoration interieure 1717*, Nationalmuseum & The Swedish Museum of Architecture, Stockholm, 2002.

Wadenstierna, Carl Eric, *Bref Ifrån En Opartisk Swensk*, Stockholm, 1769a.

Wadenstierna, Carl Eric, *Bref til auctoren af Tanckar i anledning af sista öfwerflöds förordningen och desz wärckställighet*. Stockholm, 1767a.

Wadenstierna, Carl Eric, *Bref til en wän innehållande swar på den af trycket utkomne skriften kallad Tankar i anledning af sidsta öfwerflöds-förordningen dedicerade til malcontenterne*, Stockholm, 1767b.

Wadenstierna, Carl Eric, *Fria Tankar*, Stockholm, 1769b.

Wadenstierna, Carl Eric, *Swar uppå et Betydeligt Bref ifrån En Wän i Stockholm*, Gothenburg, 1769c.

Wall, Cynthia, 'Gendering Rooms: Domestic Architecture and Literary Acts', *Eighteenth-Century Fiction*, vol. 5, no. 4, 1993, pp. 349–72.

Warmholtz, Françoise Marguerite Janiçon, *Tankar i anledning af sista öfwerflöds-förordningen och dess wärkställighet*, Stockholm, 1767.

Wigston Smith, Chloe, *Women, Work, and Clothes in the Eighteenth-Century Novel*, Cambridge, 2013.

Wijnblad, Carl, *Ritningar på Fyratio Wåningshus Af Sten, och Trettio af Träd, Samt åtskilliga Lusthus, m.m.*, Stockholm, 1755.

Wijnblad, Carl, *Ytterligare tillökning af Ritningar på wåningshus sextio af sten och tjugu af träd etc.*, Stockholm, 1756.

Wollstonecraft, Mary, *Letters Written during a Short Residence in Sweden, Norway and Denmark* (1796), Oxford, 2009.

The Women's Petition against Coffee: Representing to Publick Consideration the Grand Inconveniencies Accruing to Their Sex from the Excessive Use That Drying, Enfeebling Liquor, London, 1674.

You, Yao-Fen, 'From Novelty to Necessity: The Europeanization of Coffee, Tea, and Chocolate', in Yao-fen You, *Coffee, Tea, and Chocolate: Consuming the World*, New Haven, 2016, pp. 11–67.

Young, Paul J., *Seducing the Eighteenth-Century French Reader: Reading, Writing, and the Question of Pleasure*, Farnham, 2008.

Zätterström, Ann, 'Tenler, Johan Ludvig', *Svenskt konstnärslexikon*, Malmö, 1967, pp. 405–6.

Index

For Product Safety Concerns and Information please contact our EU representative GPSR@taylorandfrancis.com Taylor & Francis Verlag GmbH, Kaufingerstraße 24, 80331 München, Germany

Batch number: 10347035

Printed by Printforce, the Netherlands